Computer Law

Computer Law

Second Edition

Edited by

Chris Reed

Stephenson Harwood Senior Research Fellow
in Information Technology Law,
Centre for Commercial Studies,
Queen Mary and Westfield College, University of London

First published in Great Britain 1990 by Blackstone Press Limited,
9-15 Aldine Street, London W12 8AW. Telephone 081-740 1173

First edition, 1990
Second edition, 1993

ISBN: 1 85431 227 8

British Library Cataloguing in Publication Data
A CIP catalogue record for this book is available from the British Library

Typeset by Style Photosetting Ltd, Mayfield, East Sussex
Printed by Ashford Colour Press, Gosport, Hampshire

Contents

Preface

Although it is less than three years since the first edition of this book appeared, the changes in the law since then have been substantial. This, together with the gratifying number of favourable comments from practitioners and academics, has persuaded the authors to contribute to this second edition. The reason for the genesis of this book, that there were no adequate UK works on computer law, has since been ameliorated by the publication of the fourth edition of Colin Tapper's *Computer Law* and Stephen Saxby's *Encyclopedia of Information Technology Law*, but there is still a clear need for a conveniently sized and up-to-date guide to the subject.

The number of changes since the first edition is too great to highlight them all; some chapters have been completely rewritten and others substantially amended. The most obvious change is that the book now deals exclusively with computer law, as opposed to computers *and* law. The original plan was to have a section of the book dealing with computer applications to the legal field, but for various reasons the only survivor was my chapter on expert systems. This was clearly out of place[1] and has been replaced with a chapter on electronic data interchange, a subject which is rapidly growing in importance. The main omission from the first edition, telecommunications law, has not been remedied, as the subject is too large for a useful introduction to be provided in the space available. Electronic banking law is omitted for the same reason.[2]

As in the first edition, valuable insights and perceptions are the responsibility of the authors whilst, as editor, errors and omissions must be laid at my door. All corrections will be gratefully received.

---

1. Readers who would like a copy of that chapter, which will be revised erratically, should contact the Information Technology Law Unit at the Centre for Commercial Law Studies, Queen Mary and Westfield College (071-975 5321).
2. Detailed analysis of this subject can be found in Reed, *Electronic Finance Law* (Cambridge: Woodhead Faulkner, 1991) and Saxby, *Encyclopedia of Information Technology Law* (London: Sweet & Maxwell, 1990), ch. 5.

My thanks are due to a large number of people:

The authors, who in spite of the numerous calls on their time have responded quickly to my request for revised chapters.

The practising lawyers who have made helpful comments, particularly the members of the London Computer Law Group, organised by IBC Legal Studies and Services.

Stephenson Harwood, both for its generous sponsorship of my post at the Centre for Commercial Law Studies and for the opportunity as a consultant to the firm's IT Group to try out and, most importantly, modify my ideas in the light of their practical experience.

In particular I should like to record my gratitude to Lorraine Mulpeter, secretary to the Information Technology Law Unit at the Centre for Commercial Law Studies, and to my wife Jilly without whose help and encouragement this book would not have been possible.

Chris Reed, December 1992

Preface to the First Edition

The idea for this book came from teaching a course on the University of London LLM, and from conversations with practitioners working in the field of computer law. The problem seemed clear; the few books that existed on the subject were out of date, over simplistic, or covered the subject unevenly, and in some cases all three. What was needed was a book that provided a reasonably detailed coverage of all the important aspects of the subject, and it was needed soon. The solution also seemed simple; to gather together a team of authors, each of whom could offer specialist knowledge in some aspect of the field, and collectively produce a book which offered a broad coverage, but also went into the different areas in depth. My intention was that the book should interest and be useful to legal practitioners and those involved in the computer industry, as well as to students. How far this book succeeds in this aim is, of course, a matter that only the reader can judge.

I should like at the outset to point out that, although I relied on the individual authors to decide what topics should be dealt with in their own chapter, my task as editor was to coordinate the writing and to pull the book together into a harmonious whole. Bearing in mind particularly that they were generally writing in substantial ignorance of the precise contents of the other chapters, the responsibility for errors, particularly errors of omission, rests solely on my own shoulders. I should like to thank them all for the effort they put into this book, and in particular to thank Christopher Millard who made a number of valuable suggestions and helped at the planning stage as well as contributing his own chapter.

I should also like to thank my wife Jilly for her help in editing and proofreading, and for her patience during the months when I appeared more closely wedded to my word processor than to her. Thanks are also due to all at Blackstone Press, who listened sympathetically to many feeble excuses for the lateness of the manuscript and never nagged.

Chris Reed, November 1989

Contributors

THE EDITOR

Chris Reed is Stephenson Harwood Senior Research Fellow in Information Technology Law at the Centre for Commercial Law Studies, Queen Mary and Westfield College, University of London. He joined the Centre in 1987 and is responsible for the University of London LLM courses in Information Technology Law, Electronic Banking Law and Telecommunications Law. He has published widely on many aspects of computer law and is Managing Editor of the OUP *International Journal of Law and Information Technology*. Chris is the author of *Electronic Finance Law* (Woodhead Faulkner, 1991). He is a consultant to the City of London law firm Stephenson Harwood.

THE AUTHORS

Allison Coleman is a Lecturer in Law at the University College of Wales, Aberystwyth where she is Deputy Director of the Centre for Computers and Law and University Advisor on Intellectual Property and Industrial Contracts. She is the author of *The Legal Protection of Trade Secrets* (1992) and co-author of *Professional Issues in Software Engineering* (1990), and has contributed to many other books and journals. She is Book Reviews Editor for the *Journal of Business Law* and a member of the Editorial Boards of *Patent World* and *Law, Computers and Artificial Intelligence*. Allison acts as a consultant on intellectual property to a number of organisations, including a firm of solicitors, and is Director and Company Secretary to a number of University companies concerned with the exploitation of intellectual property and know-how.

Gerald Dworkin, LLB, Solicitor, is Herschel Smith Professor of Intellectual Property Law at the Centre for Commercial Studies, Queen Mary and Westfield College, University of London. He has written widely on intellectual property and other matters, and is particularly interested in patents for computer programs. He is a member of the editorial board of the *European Intellectual Property Review*, of the editorial committee of the *Modern Law Review*, a council member of the Common Law Institute of Intellectual Property and of the British Literary Artistic and Copyright Association. Recent books include *Blackstone's Guide to the Copyright, Designs and Patents Act 1988*. He is a consultant to Mishcon de Reya, solicitors.

Robert J. Hart, a Chartered Patent Agent and European Patent Attorney, is an independent consultant in intellectual property matters and Director of Intellectual Property International Limited. He was formerly Intellectual Property Development Executive for the Plessy Company Plc. He was inaugural chairman of the BCS Intellectual Property Committee, a member of the Chartered Institute of Patent Agents Software Protection Committee, and represents the BCS on the British Copyright Council. He represented IFIP at the WIPO Committee on the Legal Protection of Computer Software in Geneva, 1983, and the UK and the WIPO Working Group on Technical Questions Relating to the Legal Protection of Software in Canberra 1984. He has acted as a consultant to WIPO on the legal protection of semi-conductor products, representing UNICE at the WIPO experts meetings in 1986, 1987 and 1988. More recently he has acted as technical consultant to DG III of the Commission of the European Communities on the Directive on the legal protection of computer programmes and the directive on the legal protection of databases. He has published widely on many aspects of computer law, and is co-author of a book, *Legal Protection of Computer Programs in Europe – A Guide to the EC Directive* published by Butterworths in 1991.

Thomas Hoeren, Dr iur, Lic theol, is Lecturer in Computer Law, at the Faculty of Law, University of Münster (Germany). He is co-editor of the German journal *Computer und Recht* and member of the editorial board of 'Law, Computers and Artificial Intelligence'. Since 1992, he has been speaker of the Data Protection Committee within the German Society for Information Technology and Law (DGIR). He has published several books and articles on information technology law, antitrust law and legal informatics.

Ian Lloyd is Senior Lecturer in Law at the Law School, Strathclyde University, Glasgow, where he teaches classes in computer law on both undergraduate and postgraduate degree courses. He has published articles on a variety of topics in the computer law field and has recently completed a doctoral thesis on the topic of data protection. He is currently participating in an EC-funded Esprit project on software liability and certification.

Christopher Millard, LLB MA LLM, is a Partner in the London office of the international law firm, Clifford Chance. He is the author of a book entitled *Legal Protection of Computer Programs and Data*, and has published many articles and book chapters in the fields of computer and communications law. He is a Senior Visiting Fellow of QMW University of London where he teaches

LLM courses in Information Technology Law and Telecommunications Law. Mr Millard is Chairman of the International Special Interest Group of the Computer Law Association and is a member of the Council of the Society for Computers and Law. He is Chairman of the Confederation of British Industry's working group on Telecommunications Data Protection and is Co-Chairman of the Communications Technology joint sub-committee of the International Bar Association's committees on computer and communications law. He is a General Editor of the Oxford University Press International Journal of Law and Information Technology, is Legal Editor of *Electronics Europe* and is on the editorial boards of *The World Intellectual Property Report, The International Computer Law Advisor, Computer Law and Practice, The Computer Law and Security Report, Applied Computer and Communications Law, Telecommunications Policy,* and *Derecho de la Alta Technologia.*

Michael Silverleaf is a practising barrister specialising in intellectual property and computer disputes. He has always had an interest in technology and before entering this field he studied physics and computing. He is co-author with John Drysdale of *Passing Off Law and Practice* (Butterworths 1986).

Graham Smith is a partner of Clifford Chance, specialising in commercial law and particularly computer law. He has published articles on various aspects of computer law, including shrink-wrap licensing and the distribution of high-technology products in Europe. He has contributed the chapter on 'Computer Contracts' to *The Encyclopedia of Information Technology Law.* He is a member of the editorial board of *Computer Law Strategist* and a correspondent for *Computer Law and Security Report.*

Ian Walden has done research, consultancy and lectured in a wide variety of subjects relating to computer law. He has written numerous texts in the field and is editor of *EDI and the Law* (Blenheim Online 1989) and joint editor of *Information Technology & the Law* (2nd ed., Macmillan 1990). He is currently jointly editing *EDI: Audit and Control Issues* (NCC Blackwell, forthcoming and 1992). Ian is a member of the editorial team for the journal *Computer Law and Practice,* and of the UK EDI Association's Legal Advisory Group, and the ICC (UK) Computing, Telecommunications and Information Policy Committee. He is currently the Tarlo Lyons Research Fellow in Information Technology Law at the Centre for Commercial Law Studies, Queen Mary & Westfield College (London University) and is a consultant to London solicitors, Tarlo Lyons.

Table of Cases

Table of Statutes

Table of International Legislation

Table of Statutory Instruments and EEC Secondary Legislation

Introduction

Chris Reed

The law relating to computers presents a new and varied set of challenges to lawyers, whether they are practitioners or academics. The importance of this field of law has only recently been recognised. The first edition of Colin Tapper's *Computer Law* was published in 1978, but it is only in recent years that interest in the subject has grown to the extent that courses are now offered to students[1] and major law firms have set up information technology departments. Journals such as *Computer Law and Practice* and the *Computer Law and Security Report* deal exclusively with matters in this area, books on specific aspects of the field are becoming increasingly common[2] and there is now a UK *Encyclopedia of Information Technology Law*.[3]

This increasing interest in computer law derives from the rapid advances in the information technology industry. Computing has developed from an arcane art, practised in isolated and air-conditioned rooms by a few large companies, to an activity that has a direct effect and influence on the majority of the population. Lawyers make substantial use of computers, the largest firms investing millions of pounds in sophisticated information systems. Some

1. E.g., courses offered as part of the University of London LLM – Information Technology Law, Telecommunications Law and Electronic Banking Law – and undergraduate options at universities such as Southampton and Durham.
2. A random selection of UK books might include Arora, *Electronic Banking and the Law* (London: IBC Financial Books, 1988); Millard, *Legal Protection of Computer Programs and Data* (London: Sweet & Maxwell, 1985); Reed, *Electronic Finance Law* (Cambridge: Woodhead Faulkner, 1991); Robertson, *Legal Protection of Computer Software* (London: Longman, 1990); Walden (ed.), *EDI and the Law* (London: Blenheim OnLine, 1989). Added to this should be the substantial range of works from other European jurisdictions and from the US.
3. Saxby (ed.), *Encyclopedia of Information Technology Law* (London: Sweet & Maxwell, 1990).

courts have been designed specifically to take terminals which allow all participants access to the computer systems that are being developed to improve trials. It has been said that we are living in the 'information age', where the processing and dissemination of information made possible by computers represents the true possession of wealth.

0.1   WHAT IS COMPUTER LAW?

Computer law is that branch of the law which regulates information technology. Information technology primarily means computers,[4] but potentially encompasses also the means by which information is transmitted such as telecommunications and broadcasting.

The term 'information law' has been suggested as the proper field of study, but this is far too wide. It would, in addition to those areas considered in this book, also necessarily include such topics as (*inter alia*) defamation, much of negligence and contract, and some aspects of administrative law. The unifying aspect of computer law is that it examines the *technological* aspects of information – i.e., it is the law which governs information *processing*.

It could in theory be argued that there is no need for works which treat computer law as a separate topic, and that it is no more than the application of existing principles to novel sets of facts. However, the new facts encountered in the field of information technology are qualitatively different from novel sets of facts in other areas of technology. Traditionally, the law has divided the subject-matter of commerce into goods and services.[5] Manufacturing industry has been concerned with the processing of physical entities into other physical entities, which are then distributed under a well-defined legal framework. Services, such as advice or labour, were essentially ephemeral matters which had no permanent existence and could thus be regulated mainly as a question of whether the provider of the service provided it with proper care and in the proper manner. Information technology has enabled information, formerly something ephemeral, to be turned into something that has a quasi-physical existence and which can be traded as if it were a physical commodity. Thus database services sell pure information, whilst software houses sell applied information in the form of computer software. The traditional divisions of the law are more often than not inappropriate to regulate these activities, and the law is in a process of amendment to take account of them. Because of this, some of the suggestions made in the following chapters must necessarily be speculative. Nonetheless, those working with information technology or

---

4. Though it must be remembered that computers are not necessarily stand-alone machines with screens and keyboards. A specially designed semiconductor chip can be integrated into such commonplace appliances as motor cars and washing machines, performing substantial computing functions.
5. Clearly there are other things which can be traded, one of the most important of which is intellectual property. However, in traditional transactions involving commodities whose main value resides in their intellectual property content (such as books or sound recordings) the end user neither purchases nor is granted any kind of intellectual property right. As chapters 2 and 4 illustrate, this is not so with computer products.

advising others on the legal aspects of its use require guidance, and the authors have used their experience in their own particular specialisms to provide the best predictions that can be made at the moment. In some areas new legislation exists, though its precise application has still to be decided by the courts. Even where legislation is not forthcoming the problems will still arise, and will therefore have to be dealt with by judicial adaption of existing principles. This book attempts to identify those problems and suggest the solutions likely to be adopted by the courts.

0.2 COMMON THEMES

Throughout the law relating to computers run a number of common themes, which the reader should bear in mind.

0.2.1 Information or knowledge as a species of property

The law of intellectual property already recognises that certain types of knowledge should be treated to some extent as if they were private property and thus capable of 'ownership', for reasons such as the invention shown by their devisers, the effort put into their compilation or because they have been kept confidential. Other types of knowledge are incapable of ownership because of their nature as fundamental concepts or because they are mere ideas, and these are instead free to be used by all mankind. Thus the equation $e = mc^2$ cannot be the subject of a patent or of the law of copyright, nor can the basic concept of the internal combustion engine (though of course a specific implementation of that concept can). Because information technology concerns itself with applied information, however, it is difficult to classify it into either of these categories. Such information is normally very valuable, and in general most things which have a market value are dealt with by the law as a species of property. The law of intellectual property is in the process of developing techniques to decide which information technology products are to be treated as belonging only to one particular individual, and which are incapable of ownership and thus available to all.

The problems the law will face are not merely problems of classification. The ownership of information technology also raises moral issues. A good example of this is the work currently being undertaken by a private US biotechnology corporation in an attempt to map the human genome, that is, to produce a detailed description of the genetic structure of (one particular) human being. It has already been decided in the US that genetically altered bacteria are potentially patentable, and the corporation intends to patent the discoveries made in this project. How far should the law permit a private company to 'own' the basic information about humanity which every one of us carries about in our body cells? The structure of DNA is often described as a sequence of coded instructions, a description that could equally well be applied to computer programs, and programs have already been written which carry out medical diagnosis or give legal advice. Should the inventor of such programs be given what is effectively a monopoly on that area of medicine or the law?

0.2.2 Privacy versus the accumulation and dissemination of information

Continuing advances in data storage have made possible enormous economies of scale. A 100 megabyte hard disk for an IBM-compatible personal computer is capable of holding about 10 million English words and can be purchased for around £300.[6] Mainframe computers have proportionately larger capacities. This means that data which might formerly have had to be kept in a number of small collections for access to be feasible (e.g., a doctor's medical records) can now be brought together (e.g., the whole of an area health authority's medical records) in a form which makes access even easier and available to many more people. This accumulation of data, although it offers many benefits, also produces the potential for enormous invasions of privacy. For example, if databases such as those held on the Police National Computer, social security records, Inland Revenue records and medical records were linked together, the result would be an almost complete profile of every adult citizen. This giant database could be used for many purposes, some of which are incompatible with our notions of democracy and the individual's right to non-interference with his or her life.

The ability to communicate this information through telephone or dedicated lines and via satellite also raises problems. To whom should it be communicated, and how much information should be passed? Security from unauthorised access to the information is a further problem. Large databases must necessarily be accessible from remote terminals, and this opens the door to 'hackers' and other interlopers. Communications lines are not always as secure as they might be, and security procedures in general may not be particularly stringent. The law has a role to play, both in regulating databases and in dealing with those who access them without authority.

Finally, data stored and processed by computer raises psychological problems, as humans still have an unjustified belief in the infallibility of computers, whilst failing to recognise that the information comes from fallible humans. The effects this has on their behaviour when faced with a computer's output will be of particular relevance to the law of tort.

0.2.3 Information technology as a substitute for human endeavour

In many fields of human activity information technology is used to substitute for some or all of the functions previously undertaken by humans, or to perform functions that could not previously be performed at all. This has happened before – for example, the motor car has in part substituted for walking – but in each case the mechanism has remained largely under the control of the human user. The whole point of using information technology, however, is that the machine should control itself. This raises a number of problems that the law must eventually resolve:

(a)   Where does responsibility lie when someone who, in the absence of his using a computer to perform some task would be personally responsible for loss

---

6. In the first edition (1990) of this book the price was also £300, but the disk size available for that price was only 40 Mb.

caused to another, relies on the computer's proper operation rather than his own expertise, to avoid causing such injury?

(b) How are the courts to cope when the only evidence of a fact lies solely within the 'knowledge' of a machine? Legislation already attempts to provide for the situation where information collected by humans is stored on a computer, though the effectiveness of these provisions may be undermined by the fact that they are based on outdated industry practice. Increasingly, however, the process of collecting information is carried out by the machine directly, and cases such as *R* v *Pettigrew* (1980) 71 Cr App R 39 indicate the difficulties this may cause.

(c) The enhanced abilities of machines inevitably lead to increased expectations, and standards of performance that were acceptable before the introduction of computer technology may well now fall short of what ought to be achieved. Readers may remember the public outcry after the 'hurricane' of 1987, when many people complained that the Meteorological Office had failed to predict the violence and extent of the storm in spite of substantial investment in information technology. This raises questions of how far the law's allocation of responsibility (mainly in tort and contract) should reflect these increased expectations.

0.2.4 Trading in information products

Closely linked to the question of information as property is the legal classification of trade in information products. This is particularly relevant to the supply of computer software. Initially, when the only computers were mainframe systems and software was only available from the manufacturer, it was generally accepted that the relationship between software producer and user could be classified solely as a licence of intellectual property rights and thus as a supply of services for liability purposes. Today, however, the nature of the software market has changed radically. Software is produced by a large number of independent software houses, and particularly in the case of microcomputer software is mass-marketed in standard form through third-party retailers. In most cases there is little or no contact between the software house and the customer, either before or after the supply. It is now far harder to say exactly what is being traded: goods, services, or something entirely new which does not fit into any existing classification? The answers to these questions will largely determine the legal regime which governs the contract of supply.

The answers are also relevant to an assessment of the quality that the purchaser is entitled to expect from his information product. Unless this is defined in the contract of supply (and possibly, given the provisions of the Unfair Contract Terms Act 1977, irrespective of the terms of that contract) the approach to the problem of quality is initially determined by the legal nature of the product. Even when this has been decided, further investigation into the processes of software production will be needed to determine how far any particular level of quality is in fact achievable and can thus be demanded by the law.

0.2.5 Harmonisation of national laws

Because the information technology industry transcends national boundaries, there is a clear need for its products to be treated in substantially the same way in all jurisdictions if the market is to work effectively. By far the largest volume of technical innovation comes from the United States and Japan, and developments in the United States in particular have an important influence on other jurisdictions. There is a natural trend towards convergence of national laws – indeed, countries whose laws take a different direction to the trend may be forced by the requirements of the industry to enact amending legislation, as can be seen from the Australian amendment to its copyright laws following the High Court's decision that no copyright subsisted in object code.[7]

In addition to this natural trend, the European Community as part of its Single Market programme has produced legislation intended to harmonise many of the laws affecting the computer industry. These issues are examined in more detail in chapter 12.

0.3   SOFTWARE TECHNOLOGY

It is assumed that the reader has some familiarity with, and experience of using, computers, and that the difference between a keyboard, screen and printer will not need to be explained through a pictorial representation of a computer system. Those who require such an explanation (and anyone who wishes to work in the computer law field will need to be familiar with the hardware involved) will find it in any general book on computers.[8]

However, it is worth examining some aspects of software technology, and in particular outlining the process which leads to the production of software. An understanding of this process is particularly important when examining the intellectual property issues relating to software, and is also to some extent useful when dealing with the liability of software houses and programmers.

In essence, the software design process is a matter of defining the functions of the program at increasing levels of specificity. The highest level is an analysis of the problem which defines the general functions to be carried out and the order in which they are performed. Each of these functions can then be analysed in more detail until the program is sufficiently well specified to allow the various parts to be given to programmers for coding. These analyses will be *algorithms*, i.e., a complete analysis of a problem which if followed exactly produces a unique solution for each set of inputs, and which will reproduce the identical solution given the same set of inputs. These algorithms are often expressed in visible form in a *flowchart* (see figures 0.1 and 0.2).

The programmer's task is to write his section of the program in a computer language such as 'C'. In doing this he may well use standard pieces of code from a library (which might be developed in-house or bought in) to perform frequently used functions such as producing screen windows or menus. In some cases the prototype version or parts of the final code will be produced using a program generator or fourth-generation language (4GL) which takes a standardised, high-level description of the program and generates detailed code to perform the various functions. It is also worth mentioning that some

---

7. *Apple Computer Inc.* v *Computer Edge Pty Ltd* [1986] FSR 537.
8. See, e.g., R. Hinton, *Information Technology and How to Use It* (Cambridge 1988).

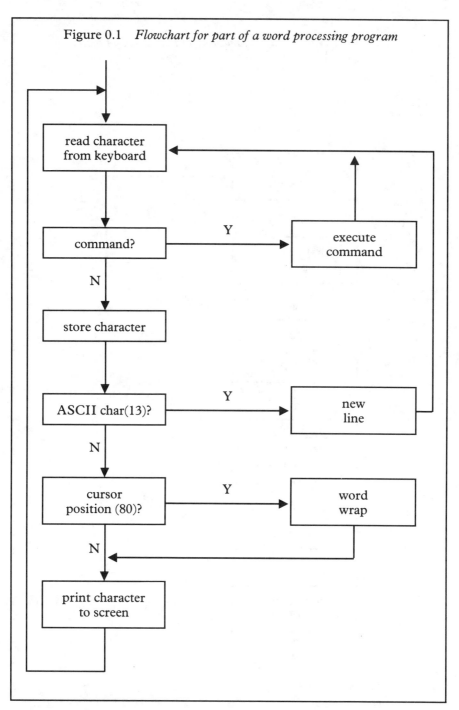

Figure 0.1   *Flowchart for part of a word processing program*

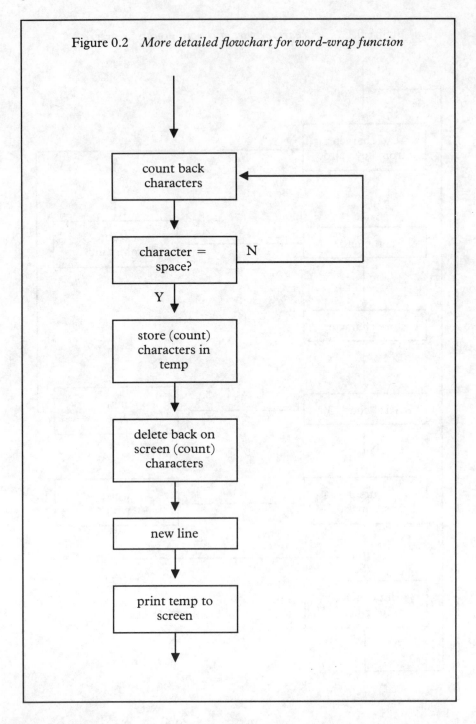

Figure 0.2   *More detailed flowchart for word-wrap function*

Figure 0.3
Source code and part of the executable object code of a Pascal program

```pascal
program diary;
uses dos, crt;
var
    year, month, day, y, m, d, dw: word;
    txt: string;
    f: text;

begin
    clrscr;
    assign(f, 'diary.dat');
    reset(f);
    getdate(y, m, d, dw);
    writeln('      DIARY for ', d, '/', m, '/', y);
    writeln;
    readln(f);
    while not eof(f) do
    begin
        readln(f, year, month, day, txt);
        if (year=y) and (month=m) and (day=d) then
        begin
            writeln(txt);
            writeln;
            end;
        end;
    close(f);

end.
```

```
9A 00 00 02 0C 9A 00 00 91 0B 89 E5 9A-0D 02 91 0B BF 0E 01 1E 57
BF 00 00 0E 57 9A D2-03 02 0C BF 0E 01 1E 57 9A 42 04 02 0C 9A 77
02-02 0C BF 06 00 1E 57 BF 08 00 1E 57 BF 0A 00 1E-57 BF 0C 00 1E
57 9A 15 00 F7 0B BF 2E 03 1E 57-BF 0A 00 0E 57 31 C0 50 9A 46 08
02 0C A1 0A 00-31 D2 52 50 31 C0 50 9A D1 08 02 0C B0 2F 50
31-C0 50 9A E8 07 02 0C A1 08 00 31 D2 52 50 31 C0-50 9A D1 08 02
0C B0 2F 50 31 C0 50 9A E8 07 02-0C A1 06 00 31 D2 52 50
```

routines may be written in *assembly code*, essentially a set of mnemonics for object code which another program translates directly into that code. This is normally done when the programmer needs to drive the hardware directly, or where speed is required, as it gives very precise control over the program's operation.

Once all the sections are complete, they are fitted together to produce a complete version in *source code*, i.e., in human-readable form. In order to run the program and so that it can be distributed in a form that gives the user as little information as possible about the details of the program (thus reducing the danger of copying), the source code is used as input for another program, the *compiler*. This compiles the program into *object code*, a machine-readable form which will have linked to it the standard pieces of code for the program to run as a stand-alone or executable file (see figure 0.3). This version will be run to test it, and any errors which are discovered will be fixed in the source code and the whole recompiled.

The final process is to produce the documentation which the user will need to operate the program. The completed product is the package of object code version and documentation. A complex piece of software may well consist of a number of programs which are called by a master program as different functions are required. Some writers distinguish between programs (the specific executable code modules) and software (the complete set of programs plus documentation). In this book, 'software' is used interchangeably for both of these unless the context otherwise makes clear.

The reader might also find it useful to have a brief description of how a program operates the hardware. The core of any computer is its processor unit, which will be made up of one or more semiconductor chips.[9] These chips perform operations at a very basic level, such as fetching data from a specific memory location, combining it with another memory location in some way, and writing the result to a third location. These simple instructions are combined in various ways to make the chip perform more complex functions, which are stored on the chip as *microcode*.[10] These instructions are called by the *operating system*, the program[11] which is responsible for the overall management of the computer's resources. In theory the operating system's instructions are called by applications programs (databases, word processing etc.) except where the chip is to perform some calculation directly, but in practice, with microcomputer software at least, many applications packages bypass some of the operating system's commands and address the processor chips directly. Thus the theoretical chain of command is as follows:

(a) The applications program calls an operating system function (or address the chip directly).

---

9. In a microcomputer, these might be the main processor, a floating-point maths processor, a video processor and the BIOS (basic input-output system) chips.
10. Thus the difference between RISC (reduced instruction set chips) and CISC (complex instruction set chip). To obtain increased processing speed, a RISC only contains a small number of simple instructions in its microcode, which execute faster but require complex compilers which necessarily produce more detailed object code.
11. This program may be stored on disk, or stored on a ROM (read-only memory) chip on the main circuit board.

(b)   The operating system calls a number of chip instructions held in microcode.

(c)   The chip translates its instructions into the individual memory operations and performs them.

This loop repeats until execution of the program is complete.

Other technical matters should become clear as the text progresses. It should be stressed, however, that theoretical reading is no substitute for 'hands-on' experience, and it is surprising how clear a picture of the detailed operation of a computer system can be gained from simply using applications packages on it.

CHAPTER ONE

Hardware contracts

Chris Reed

1.1 INTRODUCTION

Until recently it was uncommon for a piece of computer hardware to change hands without there being some written contract purporting to record the terms of the transaction. For this reason writings on hardware contracts have tended to underestimate the importance of the statutory provisions relating to the sale or supply of goods, particularly as these are in most cases overridden by any express terms. However, it is increasingly common to find mail-order advertisements for computer equipment, and in such cases the contract is often concluded over the telephone with the result that the only terms of the contract are those implied by the law. Even where there is a written contract it is likely that reference to the legislation will be necessary, either to fill the gaps in the contract or because the effect of the express provisions is to exclude a liability that would otherwise have arisen by implication. For these reasons, this chapter will examine:

(a) the application of the general law on the sale and supply of goods to hardware transactions, so as to identify the obligations imposed and solutions already provided by the law; and

(b) how far it is possible to fill any gaps and provide better solutions by express contractual provision.

Hardware contracts fall into two categories – outright sales where ownership of the goods passes to the buyer, and leases of equipment where ownership is retained by the supplier. With the advent of the business personal computer it is increasingly common to find equipment sold outright, though for more substantial systems leasing is still common. Although leasing contracts will necessarily contain quite different terms from sales the common core of the two types of contract is that the possession of goods changes hands, and so many terms will be similar in both.

It is also necessary here to say a few words about the anomalous position of firmware in the legal classification of computer technology. The law divides the subjects of commerce into two types, goods and services, when examining the terms implied into contracts. Software, because of its intangible nature, is often considered to be services (though off-the-shelf software packages are probably goods – for a more detailed discussion see chapter 2) and is normally licensed for use rather than sold outright. The problem with firmware is that a tangible item of goods, normally a semiconductor chip, is sold outright to the buyer, whilst the software encoded on the chip, which is what gives the chip its value, may well only be licensed. Although the point remains to be decided it seems likely that if the chip is a standard commercial product it will be treated as goods, the software being merely one of the attributes of the product, so that if the software is defective the chip *as goods* will be defective. If, however, the chip is custom-produced, e.g., for development purposes, the contract will be one for work and materials where the goods and services elements are treated separately, so that the supplier's obligations under the sale of goods legislation will only be to supply materials (i.e., the chip) that are of sufficient quality, and the quality that the buyer is entitled to expect of the software component will be assessed in relation to the express terms of the contract.

In many cases there will have been a supply of a complete system, both hardware and software (often called a 'turnkey' contract). Here the contract will be for both the supply of goods and the supply of services, and the different elements of the contract will need to be treated separately.

1.2   THE USER REQUIREMENTS SPECIFICATION

In an ideal world the potential purchaser of a computer system would approach one supplier who would, after detailed discussion of the customer's needs, supply the component parts of the system (hardware, software, documentation and training) as a complete package and set it up fully so that all the customer had to do was begin work. In practice this does not happen. Even where seller and buyer enter into a turnkey contract, it is likely that the buyer will discover additional requirements after the system has been installed, or even in the interval between signing the contract and installation as his understanding of his requirements increases. In any event, as his needs change, the system is certain to require additions and modifications.

There are in essence three ways of deciding what system to buy. The first is to employ an independent consultant who, for a fee, will attempt to discover the buyer's needs and match them to the available hardware and software. This is an effective method provided the consultant is both expert and truly independent (some so-called consultants are really no more than sales representatives for one manufacturer's equipment; buyers should enquire what commission the consultant expects to receive from his suppliers). Its main drawback is the expense of the consultant's fee, though this may well be saved in the better choice of system.

The second method is to approach a manufacturer or supplier for advice. The dangers here are obvious, for he is likely to exaggerate the advantages of his equipment and understate any disadvantages (for an extreme example, see *Mackenzie Patten* v *British Olivetti* (1984) 1 CL&P 92, 95, discussed in 1.7.2). However, if the buyer is sure that the supplier in question is capable of supplying an adequate system, then so long as he carefully specifies his requirements in writing and obtains an undertaking that the system will fulfil those requirements, he should obtain a reasonable system. This may be the only method available to buyers who wish to extend their existing system if they are 'locked in' to a particular manufacturer's products because of incompatibility with competing hardware.

The third method, really only appropriate for microcomputer systems, is for the buyer to build up his own system from a number of sources. The main reason for doing so is the savings to be made, as prices from different suppliers can vary by 50 per cent or more. Here the buyer must be particularly careful in his specifications, explaining to each supplier what other hardware and software comprises the system and attempting to obtain assurances that the various parts will work together.

In all cases, the best advice must be to choose the software first, as this largely dictates the nature of the hardware. This also has the advantage, if the software needs are disclosed to the hardware supplier, of helping to define the quality of performance the buyer is entitled to expect (see 1.7.3).

There are four reasons for negotiating a detailed specification:

(a)   It defines what the supplier will provide.
(b)   It helps define the quality standards which must be achieved.
(c)   If changes have to be made, it helps decide who bears the cost.
(d)   It forces both sides to think seriously about what is really wanted, and what is achievable.

In all cases, the specification should state what software is to be run, and any other hardware with which the system will be used. If compatibility issues are not dealt with at this stage, they are likely to lead to a dispute which will not be solved by the other terms of the contract.

A specification must be as detailed as possible, including a complete description of all machinery to be supplied. This should include full model numbers – in 1990 a Hewlett Packard 7575A plotter cost six times as much as a 7440A, for example – and clear choices where there are options. There should also be a technical description of its performance, which might need further explanation. For example, if the power of the CPU is expressed in MIPS (millions of instructions per second) or MegaFLOPS (millions of floating-point operations per second) the basis of calculation has to be known to make these figures meaningful. Many of these terms have been defined by standards organisations such as the BSI and ANSI, which can be referred to in the contract.

Useful starting-points for drawing up a user requirements specification are the BSI *Guide to Specifying User Requirements for a Computer-Based System*[1] and the Institute of Purchasing and Supply Model Form of Conditions of Contract (1) for the Supply and Installation (Purchase) of Computer Equipment and (2) for the Hire and Servicing (Maintenance) of Computer Equipment. Within the EC, reference might also be made to the Confederation of European Computer User Associations Model Conditions of Contract for the Purchase of Computer Equipment.

1.3 NEGOTIATION

Although most hardware suppliers attempt to deal on a set of standard terms which they or their lawyers have devised, these terms are always negotiable to some degree. How far the seller is willing to deviate from his standard terms depends mainly on the buyer's bargaining power – probably the only negotiable term in a contract for a single microcomputer is the price, whereas a buyer who is paying several million pounds for a mainframe system will be able to negotiate most of the terms.

Mackenzie Patten v *British Olivetti* (1984) 1 CL&P 92, 95 clearly illustrates the dangers of a poor contract. There a firm of solicitors bought an Olivetti computer system to run their accounts. They discussed their needs with the sales representative, but did not negotiate a proper contract. Instead they signed Olivetti's standard terms, which dealt only with the system's technical performance. The system proved totally unsuitable for the firm's purposes; it was slow, difficult to use, and could not expand to cope with new business. None of these matters was dealt with in the contract. Luckily for the solicitors, they were able to persuade a judge that Olivetti were bound by the sales representative's claims that the system would be suitable for their needs; but they had to take the matter to court (which cost both time and money) and then of course had to find another system which would do what they wanted.

The case also shows how unsuitable standard forms can be. The problem is that standard forms are only suitable for standard transactions. No matter how comprehensive your standard contract, it always fails to cover some essential point. This means that negotiating is essential. There is a further reason for negotiating a detailed contract, at least where the purchase is more substantial than a handful of microcomputers – unlike many sale of goods contracts, the delivery of a computer system is only the beginning of the relationship, not its culmination. Further work will be necessary to install the system and get it working properly, and the buyer is likely to return to the same supplier for upgrades and extensions to the system. Thus whilst the aim of the negotiator is to get the best possible deal for his or her client, this should not mean gaining at the expense of the other side. The aim is to produce a mutually satisfactory contract which will provide a comprehensive basis for the continuing relationship between them.

---

1. BS6719 : 1986.

Initially, negotiations are likely to begin with the supplier's standard terms. The ultimate goal is to define four things in advance:

(a)   what is to be done,
(b)   by whom,
(c)   when,
(d)   and for what price.

The most important thing is to ensure that no essential terms are missing from the contract. Some of these are contained in the checklist below; others relevant to the particular circumstances should come out of the negotiations themselves.

The following terms should at least be considered in any negotiations for a hardware contract:

(a)   The system specification. This is the most critical element to be negotiated in any hardware contract. If there is no proper specification, most of the remaining terms will be open to dispute.

(b)   The warranty of quality.

(c)   Exclusion clauses.

(d)   The price.

(e)   The specification and price variation.

(f)   Delivery dates.

(g)   Acceptance testing.

(h)   Waiver and variation clauses, to protect both sides from informal agreements made by their employees.

(i)   Liquidated damages.

(j)   Retention of title clauses.

(k)   Intellectual property rights.

(l)   Confidentiality. During negotiations, both parties will have to disclose confidential information about the hardware or the business, and more will be disclosed as the system is developed.

(m)   'Integration' or 'entire contract' clauses.

(n)   Maintenance.

(o)   Training to operate the system.

1.4   SALES AND LEASES

When the first edition of Tapper's *Computer Law* appeared in 1978 it was unusual for a computer system to be purchased outright, mainly because of the high cost of computers at the time. Today a workable microcomputer system can be purchased for a few hundred pounds, though substantial mainframe installations can still cost several millions. As a result outright purchase is increasingly common, though even microcomputer systems are leased where there are cash flow and tax advantages.

The legal difference between a sale and a lease is simple: the purpose of a sale is to transfer ownership to the buyer (though the seller may temporarily retain ownership as security for payment – see 1.6.2) whereas in a lease the lessor remains the owner, and all the lessee is entitled to under the contract is possession of the goods for a period of time. Although it is common to find in a lease a provision that the lessee has an option to purchase the system, either at the end of the lease or at some time during its subsistence, this does not amount to a sale. Exercise of the option, however, does create a sale (and thus a fresh contract).

The distinction between a 'finance' lease and an 'operating' lease[2] is important in US law because it determines the extent to which the UCC implies terms into the contract.[3] This problem does not occur under UK law, as the Supply of Goods and Services Act 1982 (or the Supply of Goods (Implied Terms) Act 1973 if it is a hire-purchase contract[4]) imply terms into the contract which are broadly the same as those implied by the Sale of Goods Act 1979 into a sale contract (see 1.7). The main distinction between the two types of lease is commercial, and the reasons for adopting leasing rather than a sale fiscal.[5] However, some specific problems which are raised only by leasing are worth considering here.

1.4.1 Enforcing rights against the supplier

In a finance lease, the customer's only contractual nexus is with the finance company, which in most cases will have no computing expertise and will therefore seek to exclude all liabilities in respect of defects. In any event, the obvious party against whom to seek a remedy (particularly if repair or rectification is likely to be required) is the supplier. The *Encyclopedia of Information Technology Law* suggests three ways of achieving such a state of affairs:

(a)   assignment by the finance company,
(b)   novation,
(c)   direct collateral contract.

1.4.1.1   Assignment by the finance company   Here the finance company agrees to assign to the customer its rights under the contract of sale (or occasionally to enforce them for the customer's benefit). The problem with such a solution is that the customer's claim is limited to the damages the finance company could have recovered, which in many cases will be nothing.[6]

1.4.1.2   Novation   In this case the deal is structured as a sale between the supplier and the customer which is then novated in favour of the finance company. The suggestion is that only the obligations dealing with delivery,

---

2. See *Encyclopedia of Information Technology Law*, 6.102.
3. See Tapper, *Computer Law*, 4th ed. (London: Longman, 1989), pp. 178–80.
4. I.e., if it contains an option to purchase.
5. On the tax position see *Encyclopedia of Information Technology Law*, 6.104, 15.24 et seq.
6. If, e.g., the lease excludes all liability for defects and the rental is payable irrespective of such defects.

acceptance, payment etc. should be novated, leaving the supplier still liable to the customer in respect of warranties, implied terms etc. The problem with such an approach is that there is no authority to the effect that such partial novation is possible.

1.4.1.3 Direct collateral contract Here the deal is structured as three separate contracts: a standard sale between supplier and finance company; a standard lease between finance company and customer; and a collateral contract containing the various warranties between the supplier and the customer. Consideration for the warranties given by the supplier is found from the customer's conduct in entering into the leasing agreement. Of the three, this seems the most certain to be effective, provided the supplier's warranties and the customer's remedies are drafted in the light of the terms of the leasing agreement.

In relation to exclusion clauses in the leasing contract, it should be noted that it is possible to exclude liability in respect of the right to transfer ownership and in respect of the warranty of quiet possession to the extent that the exclusion clause satisfies the test of reasonableness.[7] In all other respects the position is the same as if the transaction were a sale – see 1.10.

1.4.2 Remedies against the lessee

If the customer is in breach of the lease, the lessor's obvious remedies will be to repossess the equipment, retain or recover all rental payments already due, and to claim damages. In respect of these remedies a number of points are worth noting:[8]

(a) The right to repossess may be enhanced by giving the lessor a contractual right to enter the lessee's premises to recover the equipment.

(b) Damages may be difficult to calculate, particularly as the lessor has a duty to mitigate by attempting to relet the equipment. For this reason a liquidated damages clause may be appropriate.

(c) One way of solving the damages problem is to provide for minimum payments under the lease, though there is a problem if these are set too high as they may then constitute an unenforceable penalty rather than liquidated damages. It is possible to draft a clause which provides that in the event of default by the lessee (e.g., in respect of timely payment) *all* future payments become immediately due, the lessee retaining the right to possession for the remainder of the term, and there is authority to the effect that such a clause is not a penalty and thus enforceable.[9] The reasoning is that in such a case there is no *breach* by the lessee, his conduct merely changing the payment terms, and thus the rule against penalties cannot apply. Such a clause would clearly be beneficial from the lessor's point of view, but should be viewed with circumspection when advising a lessee.

---

7. Unfair Contract Terms Act 1977, s. 7(4).
8. See further *Encyclopedia of Information Technology Law*, 6.115.
9. *Export Credits Guarantee Department* v *Universal Oil Products Co.* [1983] 1 WLR 399.

1.5 DELIVERY AND PAYMENT

These terms will almost always be dealt with by express provisions in the contract of sale. The contract will normally set out the date on which delivery is to be made, whether all the hardware is to be delivered at one time or whether it is to arrive in instalments, and whether the seller is to install it. Similarly, the contract will set out the price, when it is to be paid, and the terms of any credit given by the seller. What the contract may omit to deal with, however, is what is to happen if either party is in breach of these terms.

1.5.1 Non-delivery or late delivery

Failure to deliver at all is simply an extreme case of failure to deliver on time, and the courts have consistently held that the obligation to deliver on time is a condition, breach of which entitles the buyer to reject the goods.[10] Where a specific date is fixed by the contract it is easy to see whether it has been achieved, but in some cases no clear date is specified. This might occur if the hardware has to be manufactured or modified before delivery, or where the seller has to obtain supplies from the manufacturer. In such a case delivery must be made within a reasonable time. As this is a question of fact it is difficult to find any real guidance from the cases, but it does appear that one of the most important factors in deciding how long a period of time is reasonable is the use to which the goods would be expected to be put. If the delay means that such use is no longer achievable, a reasonable time has elapsed.[11] These uses may not be obvious to the supplier in a hardware contract, so it would be desirable for the buyer to acquaint the supplier with the details of any particular projects for which the equipment is required. Even better would be an express provision permitting the cancellation of the contract, with or without compensation, if the goods are not delivered by some cut-off date, though the supplier may be unwilling to agree to this if undertaking an unusual modification to the buyer's requirements. An alternative, suitable for substantial contracts, is a notice period after which the buyer can withdraw, with an appeal against the notice to a third party.[12]

What commonly happens if delivery is late is that the buyer, or one of the buyer's employees, waives the seller's obligation to achieve that date and thus loses the right to reject (see 1.8.2 below). The most common way in which this occurs is when the buyer continues to request delivery after the contractual date has passed. This means that there is now *no* contractual date for delivery, and at best the seller is obliged to deliver within a reasonable time. In order to regain the right to reject, the buyer must reimpose a date by giving the seller

---

10. *Bowes* v *Shand* (1877) 2 App Cas 455.
11. Thus in *McDougall* v *Aeromarine of Emsworth Ltd* [1958] 1 WLR 1226 the contract was to build a yacht for delivery on 1 May but this date was specifically stated to be a target only. The court held that delivery on 19 September was beyond a reasonable time as at that point only 20 per cent of the yachting season remained and the boat would be of little use to the buyer until the following year. The buyer was therefore entitled to reject and refuse to pay for the boat. Here the expected use of the goods was obvious, as were the dates of the yachting season.
12. E.g., an arbitrator, the engineer in construction contracts, etc.

reasonable notice that the buyer will refuse to accept the hardware after a particular date.[13] Such notice is normally express, but it may be given impliedly (e.g., by service of a writ[14]).

Because a waiver of the delivery date has such drastic effects on the buyer's remedies, some contracts attempt to prevent this happening by including a provision that no waiver is effective unless it is in writing and signed by a director. Whilst this term may not work as a contractual obligation (the first term to be waived by an oral waiver would be the anti-waiver term itself) it is probably effective as notice that only a director has any authority to modify the terms of the written contract, thus preventing a junior employee from waiving the delivery date by pressing for delivery after the breach. It would seem sensible to state this expressly in the contract, rather than relying on the court to interpret an anti-waiver clause to this effect.

1.5.2 Payment and change control

The term setting out the price of the hardware is invariably an express term of the contract. However, in most substantial hardware purchases the specification (and thus the price) is likely to change at some point. It is important to make clear in the contract which of these changes are at the seller's expense, and which the buyer is to pay for. A procedure for making formal alterations to the specification and amending the price accordingly is a useful term to include.

In addition to agreeing the total price, it is important to agree precisely when it is payable. This links in with delivery dates. A common practice in hardware contracts is to pay by instalments as the various parts of the system are delivered, retaining a proportion of the price until the complete system has been tested.

The consequences of failure to pay on time should also be dealt with expressly. If there is no express term and the buyer has been given credit, failure on the buyer's part to pay on time will merely entitle the seller to damages (generally the interest forgone). However, if payment is due on delivery then, because under the Sale of Goods Act 1979, s. 28, delivery and payment are concurrent conditions, the seller is not obliged to deliver unless the buyer makes payment. The reaction of most sellers to the buyer's failure to pay is to treat the buyer's conduct as repudiating the contract, but this is not in fact the position. The Sale of Goods Act 1979, s. 10(1) provides that, unless otherwise agreed, time of payment is not of the essence, so late payment will almost never entitle the seller to treat the contract as at an end.[15] Thus the seller's conduct will itself be a repudiation of the contract and the buyer will be entitled to damages! The seller should instead give notice of intention to exercise the seller's right of resale (see 1.9.2), and once the period of notice has expired the seller can resell without being in breach.

---

13. *Charles Rickards Ltd* v *Oppenhaim* [1950] 1 KB 616.
14. *Tool Metal Manufacturing Co. Ltd* v *Tungsten Electric Co. Ltd* [1955] 1 WLR 761.
15. Though note that the time of payment is an innominate term – *Decro-Wall International SA* v *Practitioners in Marketing Ltd* [1971] 1 WLR 361 – and it is possible to imagine circumstances where late payment would go to the root of the contract.

To avoid doubt, a hardware contract should make express provision for the consequences of late payment.

1.6 TRANSFER OF OWNERSHIP AND RISK

1.6.1 Risk and property

At some point in the transaction the risk of accidental damage or destruction passes from the seller to the buyer. Ideally the contract should provide when this is to happen so that the buyer can take out insurance, but in many instances this point is forgotten. If that is the case, under the Sale of Goods Act 1979, s. 20(1), risk passes at the same time as ownership, or 'property' as it is referred to in the Act. If the contract does not contain specific provisions for the passing of property[16] the provisions of ss. 16 to 19 must be examined to discover when property passes. These should be borne in mind to ensure that they do not produce unexpected and unwanted results.

The passing of property is also relevant to the seller's claim for payment, as the seller is not normally entitled to sue for the price unless property has passed (see 1.9.2). It is also relevant if the buyer becomes insolvent after the goods have been delivered – if property has not passed, the seller can repossess the goods instead of proving in the liquidation for the price.

1.6.2 Retention of title

Where the seller gives credit to the buyer, there is always some doubt whether the seller will be paid. If the buyer is a well-established organisation this doubt is extremely small, but newer or smaller organisations may present a greater risk. For this reason, it is common for hardware suppliers to retain title in the goods they supply as security for payment.

A retention of title clause is a provision in the contract that although the buyer is to be given possession of the goods, ownership is to remain with the seller until certain conditions (normally payment in full) are complied with. If the buyer fails to comply with the conditions, the seller is entitled to repossess the goods, and can then sell them to recoup his losses. Such clauses are permitted under s. 19 of the Sale of Goods Act 1979. It is important that the seller retains title, property or legal ownership (all these terms are equivalent) – any careless or over-clever drafting which amounts to a retention of equitable ownership will result in the creation of a charge which must be registered under the Companies Act 1985 or the Bills of Sale Act 1878.[17] In recent years retention of title clauses have become more complex as suppliers of raw materials have attempted to extend their security from the goods supplied to the manufactured products made with those goods or to their proceeds of sale,[18]

---

16. A point that is easily forgotten unless the seller is retaining title to the hardware as security for payment (see 1.6.2).
17. See *Re Bond Worth Ltd* [1980] Ch 228.
18. See P. S. Atiyah, *The Sale of Goods*, 8th ed. (London: Pitman, 1990) pp. 455–66. Recently the courts have disallowed such extensions – see *Tatung (UK) Ltd* v *Galex Telesure Ltd* (1988) 5 BCC 325; *Compaq Computer Ltd* v *Abercorn Group Ltd* [1991] BCC 484.

but as the buyer of hardware is likely to keep it unchanged[19] such complicated clauses are usually unnecessary.

As risk normally passes with property, a retention of title clause will provide that the goods are at the buyer's risk from the moment of delivery. It should also contain a clear statement of when the seller is entitled to repossess the goods, normally if payment is not made within the credit period, or if the buyer commits an act of insolvency or a receiver is appointed. It is common to include a provision that the seller has the right to enter the buyer's premises to repossess the goods.

1.7   THE SELLER'S OBLIGATIONS

1.7.1   The right to sell
Section 12 of the Sale of Goods Act 1979 implies a condition into all contracts of sale that the seller has the right to sell the goods. This does not mean 'right' in the sense that the seller's actions must not be unlawful. Instead, it means that the seller must have the *power* to transfer ownership to the buyer,[20] and in many cases this is independent of whether the seller is the owner. The seller might be an agent for the owner, or in certain unusual circumstances might even be a thief who can nevertheless transfer ownership under s. 22. If the seller fails to transfer ownership, then there is clearly a breach of the term implied by s. 12, and the buyer is entitled to reject the goods and recover the price (plus damages if they can be proved).[21]

In order to satisfy s. 12 the buyer must receive full and unfettered rights of ownership unless the contrary has been agreed under s. 12(3). This means that the seller will be in breach of the condition if the goods are subject to rights belonging to a third party. The most obvious rights which exist independent of ownership are intellectual property rights. In *Niblett Ltd* v *Confectioners' Materials Co. Ltd* [1921] 3 KB 387 the contract was for the sale of a number of cans of condensed milk which the seller was exporting to this country. When they arrived, UK customs impounded them because their labels infringed Nestlé's trade mark. The seller argued that it had passed ownership to the buyer, and that its only liability was in damages for the cost of replacing the labels. The court, however, held that it was in breach of the condition that it

---

19. This will almost always be true, even where the hardware is to be attached to or incorporated in other hardware, because most computers are designed on a modular basis. For example, circuit boards plug in and can be removed, as do many semiconductor chips, and other components are usually removable and replaceable. It was held in *Hendy Lennox (Industrial Engines) Ltd* v *Grahame Puttick Ltd* [1984] 1 WLR 485 that where components (in this case diesel engines for pumps) were removable without damaging themselves or the goods into which they had been incorporated, the retention of title clause was effective to keep them in the seller's ownership until they were sold, thus passing title to the buyer under the Sale of Goods Act 1979, s. 25.
20. *Niblett Ltd* v *Confectioners' Materials Co. Ltd* [1921] 3 KB 387.
21. This is not affected by any use of the goods by the buyer. The essence of a sale of goods contract is the transfer of ownership from seller to buyer, and a failure to effect this means that there is a total failure of consideration (*Rowland* v *Divall* [1923] 2 KB 500).

had the right to sell the cans because the buyer did not obtain ownership free from third-party rights, and thus did not have the power to deal with the goods in the same unfettered way as an owner would expect.

The most obvious way in which a hardware producer could run into difficulty under this section is if the product infringes someone else's patent or design right. A patent holder has the right to prevent the use of any infringing equipment, so an innocent buyer can be prevented from using the hardware he has purchased. This is a clear breach of s. 12 on the seller's part. Similarly, if a ROM contains software that infringes copyright, the copyright owner may be able to claim delivery up of the infringing copy (i.e., the ROM) under s. 99 of the Copyright, Designs and Patents Act 1988. Again, the seller will be in breach. A good example in the hardware field is the continuing set of actions by Quantel Ltd to enforce its patent rights in its Paintbox graphic art system.[22] Although these actions are all for infringement of the patents, the effect (in those which are successful) will be to prevent the defendant from marketing further systems and spares, and to give Quantel the right to prevent purchasers of infringing systems from using those systems. Even if Quantel does not exercise this latter right, the fact that it exists will mean that the seller of such a system will be in breach of the condition implied by s. 12.

The seller will be in breach of this condition if the third party's rights existed at the time of sale. However, some intellectual property rights only come into existence on registration, e.g., patents and trade marks, and it is possible that these rights might arise *after* the sale was made. In such a case the seller is not in breach of the condition in s. 12(1), but is in breach of the warranty in s. 12(2)(b) that the buyer will have quiet possession of the goods.[23] This is in effect a promise by the seller that no person will in the future acquire rights over the goods and enforce them against the buyer. The warranty is broken only when the third party enforces rights, at which point the buyer becomes entitled to claim damages from the seller but not to reject the goods. However, if the owner of the intellectual property right prevents the buyer from using the goods, the buyer's damages will be assessed as the cost of buying a replacement, in effect returning the price. If claiming damages the buyer must take steps to mitigate loss, so if the buyer can obtain a licence from the owner of the right, the buyer should do so and claim the cost of the licence from the seller.

This distinction is particularly important in relation to limitation of actions. The limitation period for breach of contract actions is six years from the date of breach, which for s. 12(1) is the date when property was to pass, whereas for s. 12(2) it is the date the buyer's use of the hardware is interfered with by the third party. This could, in theory, be tens of years after the contract was made, though it is unlikely that much hardware currently on the market will remain in use that long.

---

22. See *Quantel Ltd* v *Spaceward Microsystems Ltd* [1990] RPC 83, *Quantel Ltd* v *Electronic Graphics Ltd* [1990] RPC 272, and *Quantel Ltd* v *Shima Seiki Europe Ltd* [1990] RPC 436.
23. For a clear illustration of the distinction see *Microbeads AG* v *Vinhurst Road Markings Ltd* [1975] 1 WLR 218.

In practical terms, however, the parties are unlikely to be happy with the position under s. 12. Where a third party purports to exercise intellectual property rights the buyer will often wish the seller to take some curative action, particularly if the hardware is a critical part of the buyer's business and mere rejection and return of the purchase price will leave the buyer in a difficult position. Similarly, the seller may wish to dispute the existence or extent of the third party's claims, in order to preserve reputation and position in the market. A clause which incorporates the following points should assist in removing some of the potential complications of such a situation:

(a)   A right on the seller's part to take over and litigate in the buyer's name any such action by a third party, and to settle the action.

(b)   A right for the seller to modify the hardware so that it does not infringe the alleged right, provided that it still conforms with the specification.[24]

(c)   An indemnity given by the seller against the buyer's losses in the event of a successful third-party claim.

1.7.2   Description

In general the description of the hardware will be the user requirements specification attached to the contract. However, the question arises whether any claims made by the sales representative or contained in the manufacturer's publicity material amount also to a description for the purposes of the condition implied by Sale of Goods Act 1979, s. 13.

The test traditionally used to decide this question is to ask whether the words used are a term of the contract or a mere representation, and this is answered by examining whether the seller intended to promise, as part of the contract, that the words were true. In practice, however, it is impossible to ascertain the seller's real intention (indeed, the seller may have had none) and what the courts appear to be asking themselves is whether the buyer got that which he was led to believe he was buying. The test would thus be whether a reasonable person in the buyer's position would have been led to believe that the seller was promising the words were a true description of the goods.

Where the buyer has not seen the goods the position is quite simple. The courts seem to treat any words descriptive of the goods as part of their description, even if the description has no effect on the usefulness of the goods.[25] If the buyer has in fact seen the goods, he may be buying what he was told, what he saw, or both.[26] As a general rule, only if the buyer examines the machine thoroughly before he buys will the court decide that descriptive words which had no influence on his decision to buy are not part of the description of

---

24. It must be noted that a seller cannot exclude or restrict the condition in s. 12(1) – see 1.10. However, until the third party has established that the right has in fact been infringed, the seller is arguably not in breach of that condition. In any event, most buyers should be satisfied with effective cure.

25. *Arcos Ltd* v *E. A. Ronaasen & Son* [1933] AC 470.

26. This is a question of fact, depending largely on the extent to which the buyer relied on the seller's description or on his own skill and expertise – see *Beale* v *Taylor* [1967] 1 WLR 983; *Oscar Chess Ltd* v *Williams* [1957] 1 WLR 370.

the goods for the purposes of s. 13. Because of the difficulty of predicting in advance whether any statements made by a sales representative or contained in publicity material will be held to be part of the description of the hardware, it is good practice to include a clause in the contract of sale restricting the description to any written statements in or incorporated into the contract itself, and making it clear that any oral statements are not a description of the goods.[27] The question whether goods correspond with their description is not always an easy one to answer. Where the description is of an objective fact[28] (e.g., memory size) this can be measured quite easily, though some apparently objective matters (e.g., processor speed) depend to a large degree on the software used when assessing this measurement. In many cases, however, the description is much more vague, and appears to be more a description of the quality of the goods. A good example is the words 'IBM PC compatible'. How far could such a machine depart from complete compatibility before the description becomes false? The test here is whether another buyer, knowing of the problem that is complained about, would still have bought the machine as 'IBM PC compatible'.[29] It is irrelevant that he would not have paid so high a price for it – that is a matter of defective quality and cannot be dealt with under s. 13.

Even if the statement which falsely describes the goods is not a term of the contract, the buyer may have a remedy under the Misrepresentation Act 1967, or by treating the statement as a term of a collateral contract. A collateral contract is created 'by the side of' the main contract in one of two ways:

(a)   In addition to the main contract of sale, the seller also promises that the sales representative's statements are true. In return for this promise the buyer enters into the main contract. This is what happened in *Mackenzie Patten* v *British Olivetti* (1984) 1 CL&P 92. Here a visible records computer for accounting was sold to a firm of solicitors. The sales representative made various claims about its appropriateness for the firm's business and the possibilities of operating it with existing staff. These statements were incorrect (the technology was outdated and obsolete) and the system proved unusable by the firm. The main contract of sale contained a provision that no statements made by the sales representative were to be part of the contract unless made in writing, and so these were not terms of the sale contract. Nonetheless the court found that a collateral contract had been formed, and that British Olivetti were in breach and liable in damages.

(b)   The manufacturer makes a number of claims about his product, in reliance on which the buyer purchases the goods from a retailer. Again, the courts can construe these claims as a promise that they are true, and the consideration given in return for this promise is the purchase of the goods from

---

27. Even though descriptions in an advertisement will not normally be held to be part of the contractual description, they may give rise to a collateral contract. This possibility can be avoided by proper drafting of the sales contract.
28. As should always be the case with the user requirements specification.
29. *Christopher Hill Ltd* v *Ashington Piggeries Ltd* [1969] AC 441.

the retailer.[30] It is theoretically possible for statements of this type to be made in advertisements, but the court will need to be convinced that the advertiser intended to promise to potential buyers that the statement was true, and was not merely indulging in advertiser's hyperbole or 'puffing' his goods.[31]

1.7.3 Quality

Obligations of quality raise particular problems in relation to the sale of hardware. The obligations imposed by the Sale of Goods Act 1979, s. 14, are expressed in terms of reasonable fitness for purpose, and so far as most other goods are concerned this test appears to be adequate. In relation to hardware, however, it is often difficult to define the equipment's purpose or purposes with sufficient precision, let alone decide if it is reasonably fit. In this respect, the description[32] of the goods can be very important – in some cases, it is almost the sole determinant of the quality the buyer is entitled to expect. Thus in *Mackenzie Patten* v *British Olivetti* (1984) 1 CL&P 92, although the buyer's true complaint was that the machine was totally unsuitable for its purpose, the case was fought on the false representations made by the sales representative.

1.7.3.1 Merchantable quality Section 14(2) of the Sale of Goods Act 1979 provides that where the seller sells goods in the course of a business there is an implied condition that the goods supplied under the contract will be of merchantable quality. The condition does not extend, however, to defects that the seller specifically reveals, nor to those defects that should have been discovered by the inspection (if any) that was *actually made* by the buyer. It should also be noted that it is not only the goods sold that must be of merchantable quality – any goods *supplied* under the contract (e.g., manuals or magnetic media) must also be merchantable, even if they remain the seller's property and are to be returned to him.

The term 'merchantable quality' is defined in s. 14(6). Goods are merchantable if they are 'as fit for the purpose or purposes for which goods of that kind are commonly bought as is reasonable to expect' and in deciding this question the description, price and any other relevant circumstances should be considered. It used to be thought that goods were merchantable if they were suitable for only one of their common purposes, as this would not prevent their resale under the same description,[33] but it is now probably the case that this definition means that goods will be unmerchantable if they are not fit for *all* their common purposes, 'purposes' being interpreted quite widely. In *Rogers* v *Parish (Scarborough) Ltd* [1987] QB 933, the buyer bought a new Range Rover which developed a number of faults, mechanical and cosmetic, none of which was serious enough to prevent the car being used on the road. The court held that the purposes for which expensive cars of this type are bought include not only driving them, but also doing so in reasonable comfort and safety and

---

30. *Shanklin Pier Ltd* v *Detel Products Ltd* [1951] 2 KB 854.
31. See, e.g., *Carlill* v *Carbolic Smoke Ball Co.* [1893] 1 QB 256.
32. I.e., the user requirements specification, assuming one has been negotiated.
33. *Christopher Hill Ltd* v *Ashington Piggeries Ltd* [1972] AC 441.

the intangible purpose of 'pride in ownership'. Although the car was reasonably fit for its main purpose, it was not reasonably fit for these lesser purposes, and as a result the buyer was entitled to reject and recover his money.[34]

Computers are commonly said to be general-purpose machines, and certainly in the case of mainframe systems it is difficult to see that their common purposes can be much more than running programs under the specified operating system or systems and interfacing with peripherals as provided for in the system specification. Additionally, it is not unknown for a particular system operating under, say, UNIX to have a number of problems in doing so, some of which can be corrected whilst the others must be endured. The system is not required to be perfect, just reasonably fit, and one of the relevant circumstances will be the extent to which other users are prepared to tolerate deviations from the operating system standard. The description applied to the system will be crucially relevant here in defining to some extent the purposes for which that type of hardware is commonly used.

Microcomputers, however, are a different matter. They are bought by naïve as well as sophisticated users, and it is strongly arguable that the common purposes of such machines include running standard business software – word-processing packages, spreadsheets, databases etc. Although it is unlikely that such a machine would be unmerchantable if it did not run a particular package (although it might be argued that packages such as Lotus 1-2-3 are so universally used in business that running that particular package *is* one of the common purposes), it *would* be unmerchantable if it did not run at least *one* of the common pieces of software for each type of normal business use, unless this inability was specifically disclosed by the seller.

Special attention should also be paid to those cases where hardware is manufactured or adapted specifically to the buyer's requirements. It seems likely that in such a case the buyer will have no claim that the goods are unmerchantable if the defect lies in the specification. This view was suggested in the House of Lords decision of *Christopher Hill Ltd* v *Ashington Piggeries Ltd* [1972] AC 441, using as an analogy a doctor poisoning himself with a defective prescription made up for him by a pharmacist. This does not, however, mean that the buyer has no remedy. If the unmerchantability is caused by faulty materials or workmanship the seller will be in breach of s. 14(2), and in any event he might be liable under s. 14(3).

1.7.3.2 Fitness for the buyer's particular purpose If the seller sells in the course of a business and the buyer expressly or impliedly makes known a particular purpose or purposes for which he intends to use the hardware,

---

34. Note, however, that shortly before *Rogers* v *Parish (Scarborough) Ltd* was decided, a differently constituted Court of Appeal in *Aswan Engineering Establishment Co.* v *Lupdine Ltd* [1987] 1 WLR 1 held that under s. 14(6) goods would be merchantable if they were fit for one or more of their common purposes, not necessarily all, if the effect would be that a buyer, knowing of the unfitness for a particular purpose would nonetheless buy the goods at substantially the same price. This case was not cited in *Rogers* v *Parish (Scarborough) Ltd*, which in the author's opinion represents the better interpretation of s. 14(6).

s. 14(3) implies a condition that it will be reasonably fit for those purposes. This condition is imposed because the buyer relies on the seller to use his expertise to select goods suitable for the buyer's needs.

If the buyer produces the user requirements specification himself, this would normally suggest that he is not relying on the seller's skill and judgment to select appropriate hardware, and that therefore s. 14(3) has no relevance. However, the seller will still be liable under that subsection in respect of matters not covered by the specification. In *Cammell Laird & Co. Ltd* v *Manganese Bronze & Brass Co. Ltd* [1934] AC 402 the contract was for the supply of a ship's propellor to be manufactured to the buyer's specification and used on a named ship. The propellor proved unsuitable for the ship because its pitch was incorrect, a matter not provided for in the specification. The court held that as this had been left to the seller's discretion it clearly showed reliance on the buyer's part. The court also made it clear that if the defect had been in the buyer's specification the seller would not have been in breach of the condition. It is possible, however, to imagine circumstances where the buyer of hardware relies on the seller to check his specification, particularly where the specification has been arrived at in consultation between them, and here the buyer will have relied on the seller's skill and judgment.

The condition is also not implied where it was unreasonable for the buyer to rely on the seller's expertise. This might be the case where the seller makes it clear that he cannot say whether the hardware will be suitable (e.g., where it is purchased for research purposes) or where the buyer fails to give him the information he needs to exercise his judgment properly.[35]

1.7.3.3 Express warranties of quality and acceptance testing The 'fuzzy' nature of the obligations in the Sale of Goods Act 1979, s. 14, can be argued to be useful in consumer transactions, but so far as commercial transactions are concerned (particularly in relation to hardware contracts) this fuzziness creates undesirable uncertainty. From both seller's and buyer's point of view, it is well worth attempting to define in the contract, so far as is possible, the quality the buyer is entitled to expect.

In order to avoid the uncertain meaning of such terms as 'reasonableness', an express warranty of quality can only be drafted in terms of material conformity with the user requirements specification. If the specification has been drawn up properly, conformity with the specification should mean that the hardware is reasonably fit for the buyer's purposes. Drafting in these terms has the beneficial effect that breach is a (comparatively) objective matter, thus reducing the likelihood of a dispute that cannot be resolved between the parties. A warranty of this type has the further advantage that it can be linked to the process of acceptance testing, which should be expressly provided for in the contract, thus defining a clear and objective procedure for deciding when the supplier has satisfactorily completed performance.[36] Acceptance testing

---

35. See *Griffiths* v *Peter Conway Ltd* [1939] 1 All ER 685.
36. See further H. Pearson, *Computer Contracts* (London: Financial Training Publications Ltd, 1984), ch. 7.

can be linked to the payment schedule, giving the buyer a lever to ensure that the seller performs.

Of course, these advantages are lost if the implied terms as to merchantability and fitness for purpose are not excluded. The extent to which such exclusion is possible is examined in 1.10, and it should be stressed here that the effectiveness of any exclusion can only be assessed in conjunction with the degree of liability which the seller accepts under this warranty of quality.

1.8   THE BUYER'S REMEDIES

1.8.1   Conditions and warranties

Some of the terms of the contract of sale are defined by the Sale of Goods Act 1979 or by case law as *conditions*, terms whose breach is considered so serious that under s. 11(3) the buyer has the right to bring the contract to an end by rejecting the goods. The buyer is not, however, required to reject – s. 11(2) permits him to elect to continue with the contract and claim damages for the breach. Other terms are defined in the Act as warranties. Although the Act provides that breach of such terms gives rise to a claim for damages only, the position adopted by the courts is rather different. If one of these terms is broken, the buyer will still have the right to reject if the breach 'goes to the root of the contract', i.e., is so serious that further performance is rendered pointless.[37] If the breach is not sufficiently serious to permit rejection, the buyer's only claim is for damages. This type of obligation is often known as an 'innominate term'.

1.8.2   Rejection of the goods

Where the seller is in breach of a condition of the contract, or where the breach is of an innominate term and sufficiently serious to go to the root of the contract, the buyer will be entitled to reject the goods and recover the purchase price in full. The seller's main obligations under the Sale of Goods Act 1979 are all conditions, and so rejection can be considered as the buyer's primary remedy. It is not necessary for the buyer physically to return the goods to the seller – all he is required to do by s. 36 is to inform the seller that he is rejecting and to make the goods available for collection. Rejection is a powerful remedy where the price has not yet been paid, as it forces the seller to initiate proceedings if he disputes that he is in breach.

However, there are a number of reasons why the buyer of goods, and particularly the buyer of computer hardware, will find this remedy less useful than at first sight it might appear. In practical terms rejection may be undesirable because the process of specifying the system and negotiating terms has taken so long that finding an alternative supplier would result in too great a delay in the installation of replacement equipment. In such a case the buyer's only real option is to negotiate with the seller for the faults to be rectified and to claim damages. Indeed, the buyer may be 'locked in' to one particular supplier because the new hardware needs to be compatible with an existing

---

37. *Hongkong Fir Shipping Co. Ltd* v *Kawasaki Kisen Kaisha Ltd* [1962] QB 26.

system. Even if these practical considerations do not prevent rejection, the right to do so can easily be lost. This occurs when the buyer 'accepts' the goods, or through election or waiver.

1.8.2.1 'Acceptance' 'Acceptance' is placed in inverted commas because the Act, unfortunately, uses the term in two distinct senses. One is the ordinary meaning of the term, to take possession, but it is the other which concerns us here and which bears no relation to the first meaning. 'Acceptance' is a process by which the buyer loses the right to reject, and can be defined as some act which indicates that he intends to keep the goods. The relevant provision is s. 35(1) which provides:

> The buyer is deemed to have accepted the goods when he intimates to the seller that he has accepted them, or (except when section 34 above otherwise provides) when the goods have been delivered to him and he does any act in relation to them which is inconsistent with the ownership of the seller, or when after the lapse of a reasonable time he retains the goods without intimating to the seller that he has rejected them.

Section 34 provides that where the buyer has not previously examined the goods, he is not to be taken to have 'accepted' them until he has had a reasonable opportunity to do so.

There are thus three ways in which goods may be 'accepted'.

(a)   If the buyer intimates to the seller that he 'accepts' the goods by, for example, telling the seller that he is satisfied with them. Acceptance testing clauses often provide that 'acceptance' in this sense is deemed to have occurred on satisfactory completion of the tests. It seems likely also that a buyer could impliedly intimate his 'acceptance' by performing some act which leads the seller to believe the goods are satisfactory. An example of this might be where the buyer, after the hardware has been installed and tested, orders further hardware of the same type from the seller.

(b)   If the buyer, having received the goods, performs an act inconsistent with the seller's ownership. It was at one time thought that this meant any act which showed that the buyer was treating the goods as his own, for example, reselling the goods, and in *Hardy & Co.* v *Hillerns & Fowler* [1923] 2 KB 490 the Court of Appeal held that a resale amounted to 'acceptance' under s. 35. However, the judgment of Devlin J in *Kwei Tek Chao* v *British Traders & Shippers Ltd* [1954] 2 QB 459 suggests that a resale or other disposition of the goods (in that case a pledge of the goods as security for a loan) will only be inconsistent with the seller's ownership if it amounts to an outright disposal so as to prevent the buyer from returning them, and this appears to be the better view.[38]

---

38. It also brings the case of *Molling & Co.* v *Dean & Son Ltd* (1901) 18 TLR 217 back within the mainstream of precedent on this point.

In any event such an act will not amount to 'acceptance' unless the buyer has had a reasonable opportunity to examine the goods as provided in s. 34. It seems not unreasonable to suggest that if the buyer has had such an opportunity but has failed to use it his resale should be seen as an act of 'acceptance', as it is clear that he is not over-concerned whether the goods conform with the contract.

Another type of act that is potentially inconsistent with the seller's ownership is use of the goods. Clearly the use must be prolonged beyond that which is reasonable for testing, but there is no authority on how much further use is permitted. If the contract contains a provision as to the time allowed for testing the hardware, this is likely to be accepted by the courts, and such provisions are both common and useful in substantial hardware contracts. If the buyer's use is such that the hardware cannot be returned to the seller in its original state (fair wear and tear excepted), e.g., where it is physically modified for installation, this clearly shows the buyer is treating it as his own and will thus amount to 'acceptance'.

(c) If the buyer retains the goods beyond a reasonable time without rejecting. As always this is a question of fact, but any express provisions as to time-limits for rejection, provided they are not clearly intended as an exclusion of the seller's liability, are likely to be accepted by the courts as the parties' view of the time that would be reasonable for the buyer to retain the goods. The lapse of time becomes particularly relevant if, as is often the case, the hardware is under some form of guarantee by the manufacturer. It is common for the seller to persuade the buyer that he should attempt to have faults rectified under the guarantee, and the buyer should make certain that, if he agrees to this option, he reserves his right to reject if the manufacturer is unable to cure the problem.

A further problem arises where the goods are not delivered all at the same time. Under s. 11(4) once the buyer has accepted' part of the goods he is not entitled to reject the rest. Thus if the buyer has ordered a microcomputer system consisting of processor, monitor, keyboard, printer and modem but the modem is delivered six weeks after the rest of the system, it is likely that he will have already 'accepted' the other parts of his order. However, s. 11(4) also provides that if the contract is severable, i.e., it can be treated as a number of distinct sales, the fact that part has been 'accepted' does not prevent rejection of the rest. The distinction appears to be between severable and entire contracts, where failure by the seller to deliver part would amount to a failure to perform at all. In the example above, the contract would probably be treated as severable as it is the sale of a number of distinct items, though the position might be different if the system was a 'package' at a special price to reflect the fact that all the component parts were being bought simultaneously. The mere fact that the contract provides for delivery of different items at different times does not necessarily make the contract severable[39] though it is strong evidence to that effect. If, of course, the contract contains an express term that each delivery is to be treated as a separate contract, that should be conclusive.[40]

---

39. *Mersey Steel & Iron Co. Ltd* v *Naylor Benzon & Co.* (1884) 9 App Cas 434.
40. *Regent OHG Aisenstadt und Barig* v *Francesco of Jermyn Street Ltd* [1981] 3 All ER 327.

Allied to this problem is the case where the contract provides that the parts of the system are to be delivered at different times and separately paid for. If one or more of the deliveries so far is defective the buyer may wish to terminate the contract and refuse to accept further deliveries. Under s. 31(2) whether he may do so is determined by the seriousness of the breach or breaches, whether they go to the root of the contract so as to make further performance pointless. The test for this as set out in *Maple Flock Co. Ltd* v *Universal Furniture Products (Wembley) Ltd* [1934] 1 KB 148 is the ratio the breach bears to the rest of the contract and the likelihood of its repetition. Thus if the contract were for a mainframe installation and the CPU proved defective, this would clearly go to the root of the contract, whereas a defective disk unit or printer, so long as workable replacements could be supplied, would not.

All the uncertainties introduced by s. 35 can be resolved by including a proper acceptance testing procedure. This has strong links to the problem of quality – see 1.7.3.3 above.

1.8.2.2 Election and waiver Election and waiver differ somewhat from 'acceptance'. Both these concepts have a connection with promissory estoppel in that the right to reject will be lost if the buyer leads the seller to believe that he will not enforce that right, though election and waiver do not always seem to require reliance on the seller's part. An election is a choice between two remedies, and the Sale of Goods Act 1979, s. 11(2), gives the buyer the right to decide not to reject but to claim damages instead. If he leads the seller to believe that this is what he is doing, he has made an election and loses his right to reject. This typically occurs in the case of late delivery, where the buyer accepts delivery but reserves his right to damages. By doing so in the knowledge that the delivery is defective, i.e., late, he loses his right to reject and is relegated to a claim in damages.

Waiver on the other hand is a more complete renunciation of rights, and requires a representation that the buyer will not enforce a particular contractual right at all. The most common examples of waiver occur where the goods are not delivered on time and the buyer, instead of immediately rejecting, presses the seller to make delivery as soon as possible. This amounts to a representation by the buyer that he is not insisting on the original date, and not only does he lose his right to reject for that breach but also any claim to damages. This is not necessarily as final as it might seem, for if the seller has still to perform his obligation the buyer can reimpose the condition by giving reasonable notice.[41]

1.8.3 Damages
The buyer's claim for damages will fall into one of two categories, depending on the nature of the breach of contract. The first is damages for failure to deliver the goods, either on time or at all. This is governed by the Sale of Goods Act 1979, s. 51. The normal measure of damages is the first limb of the rule in *Hadley* v *Baxendale* (1854) 9 Exch 341: 'the estimated loss directly and

---

41. *Charles Rickards Ltd* v *Oppenhaim* [1950] 1 KB 616.

naturally resulting, in the ordinary course of events, from the seller's breach of contract' (s. 51(2)).

However, in most cases the buyer can be expected to purchase alternative goods when the seller fails to deliver, and in such cases the measure of damages is the increase in the price the buyer has to pay.[42] This assumes an 'available market', with enough buyers and sellers and a sufficient supply of goods so that replacements can truly be said to be available reasonably quickly and at not too great a distance. This is unlikely to be a problem if the hardware in question is commercially available from a range of sources, e.g., IBM compatible microcomputer equipment. However, where the seller is also the manufacturer, or where the hardware has been modified or specially designed for the buyer's purposes, there will be no available market for the goods and thus the measure of damages in s. 51(3) will be inapplicable.

In such a case we must return to the measure in s. 51(2) and decide what the normal expected losses would be. These will often be particularly hard to estimate given the general-purpose nature of computing equipment, though if particular potential losses have been made known to the seller they will be within the contemplation of the parties, and thus recoverable as special damages under s. 54. The best solution to this problem is a liquidated damages clause that is a genuine pre-estimate of the potential losses arising from late or non-delivery.

The second category of damages is for other breaches under s. 53(2), which is in substantially the same terms as s. 51(2). If the breach is of a 'warranty of quality', which will often include breaches of description as well as of quality in the strict sense, s. 53(3) sets out a precise measure:

In the case of breach of warranty of quality such loss is *prima facie* the difference between the value of the goods at the time of delivery to the buyer and the value they would have had if they had fulfilled the warranty.

The effect of this is to compensate the buyer for his loss of bargain if he had obtained a good price. Suppose the contract was for a printer at a special offer price of £500 (the normal retail price being £600) but defects in the printer will cost £50 to repair. Its value at the time of delivery is thus £550, and if the measure were the difference between the price paid and its value the buyer would receive nothing. Under s. 53(3) he will receive £50, sufficient to effect the repairs. Consequential losses may also be recoverable if the hardware is sold for use rather than resale, either under s. 53(2) as direct and natural losses or under s. 54 as losses in the contemplation of the parties. Nonetheless, it may prove hard to recover all such losses – whilst it will be comparatively easy to prove losses caused by disruption of the buyer's business if the hardware proves defective, losses of expected increases in profit through productivity gains may well be impossible to demonstrate, and even if this can be done will probably be held to be too remote.

Because of the difficulty of assessing consequential losses, it is common to find a liquidated damages clause in hardware contracts. Such a clause defines

---

42. Sale of Goods Act 1979, s. 51(3).

in advance the precise sum to be paid as compensation for certain breaches (e.g., late delivery at £X per day), and provided the sum is a genuine estimate of the likely losses and not a penalty to force the seller to perform, the clause will be enforceable, even if the buyer's loss is in fact less than the agreed sum. It is also common for the seller to provide that he is not liable for further consequential losses, or that his liability is limited to a fixed sum (often the price of the hardware). Such a clause will be a limitation of liability and subject to certain restrictions (see 1.10).

1.8.4 Specific performance

Section 52 of the Sale of Goods Act 1979 gives the court a discretion to award specific performance where the goods are specific or ascertained. If the subject-matter of the contract is merely goods of a particular description it is assumed that the buyer will be able to obtain replacement goods elsewhere. In certain unusual cases, however, the courts have forced the seller to fulfil his obligations even though the goods are purely generic. Such a case might be where a dealer has a long-term contract with a manufacturer for regular deliveries of hardware, and there is no alternative source of supply. In *Worldwide Dryers Ltd* v *Warner Howard Ltd* (1982) *The Times*, 9 December 1989 the plaintiff claimed to have an exclusive right to purchase, import into the UK and market the defendant's hot-air hand driers, and that in breach of this agreement the defendant company was refusing to supply it with driers. Although the contract was clearly not for the supply of specific goods, Foster J granted an interlocutory, mandatory injunction to ensure that the plaintiff's business could continue until the trial of the substantive issue.

1.9   THE SELLER'S REMEDIES

1.9.1   Remedies to obtain the price

The preferred remedy of any seller will be the price of the goods, as this is what he contracted for. The basic assumption of the Sale of Goods Act 1979 is that he is not obliged to deliver the goods to the buyer until he has been paid, and so he has a right of lien (i.e., a right to retain possession) if payment is not forthcoming. This right lasts so long as he retains possession of the goods.[43] It is unusual, however, for a sale of hardware to be other than on credit terms, and in such a case there is no right of lien. In most cases, therefore, the seller will be restricted to an action against the buyer for the price of the equipment.

Section 49(1) allows the seller to claim the price of the goods only if property in them has passed to the buyer (see 1.6.1). This is an absolute requirement, and the reason property fails to pass is irrelevant. In *Colley* v *Overseas Exporters* [1921] 3 KB 302 the seller was to load the goods on to a ship nominated by the buyer. Property would not pass until the goods were loaded. The buyer nominated a series of ships but none of them had space to take the goods, so

---

43. Even if the seller parts with possession to a carrier, he has the right to stop the goods in transit before they reach the buyer if it is discovered that the buyer has become insolvent, and once he regains possession the seller resumes his right of lien.

the seller lost patience and sued under s. 49(1). The court held that even though it was the buyer's fault that property had not passed, nevertheless the seller was not entitled to claim the price but had to resell the goods and claim damages instead.

The fact that the contract between the parties stipulates that delivery and payment are to be made on a particular date does not necessarily entitle the seller to the price if the buyer refuses to accept delivery. Most contracts stipulate that the seller of hardware retains property in the goods until payment as a form of security (though if he has delivered the goods it is thought that he can waive this retention and thus allow property to pass) with the result that if the buyer refuses to accept delivery the seller's only claim is for damages. It is, however, possible under s. 49(2) to make the price payable where property has not passed. The contract must specify that payment is to be made on a day certain, irrespective of delivery, and so long as payment and delivery are truly independent the price will be payable. If, though, on the true construction of the contract, the buyer would be entitled to refuse payment if the seller failed to deliver, payment and delivery will not be independent and s. 49(2) will not apply.

1.9.2 Damages

If the buyer wrongfully fails or refuses to accept delivery, the seller will have a claim for damages against him. First he must attempt to mitigate his loss by reselling the goods. Even if property has passed, thus entitling him to the price, he may prefer to resell. In such circumstances, however, he will be guilty of conversion as the goods belong to the buyer, so he must first give notice under s. 48 that he intends to resell. If the buyer then fails to pay within a reasonable time, the seller may resell and claim damages.

Damages are assessed under s. 50, which is in almost identical terms to s. 51, and the majority of what has already been said about that section will apply here. It should be recognised that both sections are couched in theoretical terms: the measure of damages is the difference between the contract price and the theoretical price for which such goods could be bought and sold. It seems clear that the mere fact that the seller has resold at a price higher than that obtaining in the market will not reduce the buyer's damages. If the buyer had accepted the goods the seller could have bought others in the market and used them to make a profit on his second transaction.[44] However, it may be the seller who is claiming that the market price rule in s. 50(3) is inapplicable, particularly where there are few buyers. If he can convince the court that he has lost a sale it will decide that there was no available market and award him his lost profit under s. 50(2).[45] This principle will apply wherever the seller has a ready supply of the hardware in question and few buyers. It will not be applicable where the goods are in short supply and the number of potential buyers exceeds the availability of the goods.[46] In any event, the principle does

---

44. *Campbell Mostyn (Provisions) Ltd* v *Barnett Trading Co.* [1954] 1 Lloyd's Rep 65.
45. *W. L. Thompson Ltd* v *Robinson (Gunmakers) Ltd* [1955] Ch 177.
46. *Charter* v *Sullivan* [1957] 2 QB 117. Throughout most of 1988 this was true of DRAM chips, the market for which was distorted by US import restrictions which caused the Japanese manufacturers to cut back their production.

not apply where the seller does not have a number of identical items to sell, and it has been held in *Lazenby Garages Ltd* v *Wright* [1976] 1 WLR 459 that second-hand goods are always unique items. The same would presumably apply to hardware configured to the buyer's specification, so that if the seller were able to resell the complete system he would be unable to claim that he was entitled to his lost profit under s. 50(2). It is, however, arguable that if he reconfigures the system for resale, or if he can sell the component parts separately, he should be entitled to his lost profit, though the point has not been decided.

1.10   EXCLUSION CLAUSES

It is common for hardware contracts to contain provisions excluding or limiting the seller's liability. The most common exclusions or limitations refer to a breach of description or quality, and in particular it is common to exclude all liability for loss consequential on a breakdown or malfunction of the equipment. Such provisions need to be carefully drafted if they are to be effective, and some exclusions are not permitted by law. There are two levels of legal control over exclusion clauses – the common law and the Unfair Contract Terms Act 1977.

1.10.1   Common law controls[47]
In order for an exclusion clause to protect the seller of hardware, it must be contractually binding on the buyer. This is most easily effected if it is contained in a written contract signed by the buyer. Many contracts for goods of low value, however, are made by exchange of letters, each referring to the other's standard terms, and it may be a difficult matter to decide whether the clause in question is part of the contract.[48] Even if it is incorporated, the clause will only protect the seller if, as a matter of construction, it covers the breach that has occurred. The rules of construction are complicated, but in general the more serious the breach of contract, the more clearly worded the clause must be if it is to exclude liability for that breach. However, it was held in *Photo Production Ltd* v *Securicor Transport Ltd* [1980] AC 827 that this is merely a rule of construction not substantive law, and even an extremely serious breach, e.g., wilful refusal to deliver the system, can be covered by the clause if it is worded sufficiently clearly. Since the Unfair Contract Terms Act 1977 now gives the courts more subtle means to control exclusion clauses, it is likely that they will be slower to find that a particular clause is deficient in its wording.

1.10.2   The Unfair Contract Terms Act 1977
Section 6 of the Unfair Contract Terms Act 1977 deals with attempts to exclude liability under the Sale of Goods Act 1979. Section 6(1) provides that it is not

---

47. See generally P. S. Atiyah, *The Sale of Goods*, 8th ed. (London: Pitman, 1990) ch. 14.
48. This point is too complicated for examination here, but the rules for construing such an agreement can be found in any standard work on the law of contract.

possible to exclude the condition that the seller has the right to sell the goods (see 1.7.1). However, s. 7(4) permits the exclusion of this term in a lease provided the exclusion satisfies the test of reasonableness. Section 6(2) provides that where the buyer deals as a consumer, it is not possible to exclude the seller's liability under s. 13 or s. 14 of the Sale of Goods Act (1.7.2 and 1.7.3). A buyer deals as a consumer under s. 12 of the Unfair Contract Terms Act 1977 if (a) he does not buy in the course of a business, (b) the seller sells in the course of a business, and (c) the goods are of a type normally supplied for private use or consumption. Until a few years ago, no contract for the sale of hardware would have been a consumer contract, as computer equipment was not normally bought for private use or consumption. Now it is a question of degree – is the equipment more sophisticated than that normally bought for private use? At present the line would probably be drawn at 8088/86 to 80386SX PCs, whilst more powerful PCs and workstations would be seen as purely business machines. This will no doubt change; as recently as 1984 it would have been extremely uncommon to find a PC in private hands.

If the sale is by one business to another, s. 6(3) of the Unfair Contract Terms Act 1977 permits the exclusion of liability under ss. 13 and 14 of the Sale of Goods Act 1979 provided the exclusion clause satisfies the test of reasonableness. If the contract is a lease as opposed to a sale, similar provisions are found in s. 7(3). The test of reasonableness is set out in s. 11 of and sch. 2 to the Unfair Contract Terms Act 1977. Section 11(1) provides that it must have been fair and reasonable to include the clause at the time the contract was made. The court will take account of the matters mentioned in sch. 2 – the strength of the bargaining position of the parties; whether the buyer received some benefit (e.g., a lower price) for agreeing to the clause; how far the buyer knew or ought to have known of the existence and extent of the clause; if the exclusion is contingent on compliance with some condition (e.g., regular maintenance) whether it was reasonable to expect the condition to be complied with; and whether the goods were specially made or adapted to the customer's order. The courts have also held that the question as to which of the parties can most readily insure against the loss is a relevant consideration, and that a limitation of liability is more likely to be reasonable than a complete exclusion.[49]

This last point emphasises the importance of the express warranty of quality (see 1.7.3.3 above). If liability under the Sale of Goods Act 1979, ss. 13 and 14, is to be excluded, the seller should give something in return. Once some liability is accepted, the question becomes whether the extent of such liability is a reasonable allocation of the risk of defects between the parties. The arguments in favour of limiting liability to conformity to the user requirements specification are compelling:

---

49. *George Mitchell (Chesterhall) Ltd* v *Finney Lock Seeds Ltd* [1983] 2 AC 803. This was a case under the slightly different provisions of the Supply of Goods (Implied Terms) Act 1973 as its facts occurred before the 1977 Act came into force, but it was nonetheless clearly decided with at least one eye on that Act.

(a)   The specification has been agreed by the buyer, who presumably is the best judge of his needs.[50]

(b)   Assessment of whether the implied terms have been breached is difficult, whereas assessing breach of the express warranty is an objective process.

(c)   The risk of breach of the express warranty is clearly within the seller's control; the implied terms only have meaning in the context of the buyer's intended use of the hardware, which is outside the seller's control.

If these arguments convince the court that it is reasonable to exclude the implied terms, the next question is how far such liability can be limited. It is common to place a financial cap on the seller's liability, both for any one breach and also as a global limit (e.g., £100,000 for any breach, £500,000 in total). It is likely that any figures of this nature will be subject to negotiation, and it is clear from the limited case law under the Unfair Contract Terms Act 1977 that where the parties have negotiated a limitation the court will be likely to find that limitation to be reasonable.[51] Some sellers limit liability to the contract price, though this seems to set the limits rather too low.

A further provision which is common is a limitation of liability to direct losses only, totally excluding liability for all consequential loss. This could be a reasonable limitation, particularly as it can be argued that the nature of computer products means that their uses (and thus the potential consequential losses) are not easily foreseeable at the time a hardware contract is made. However, the point made above in relation to negotiation should not be forgotten, and a unilateral imposition of such a limitation will be less likely to be held to be reasonable than one which is negotiated. Records of the negotiations in respect of exclusion clauses will clearly be of great utility in the event of a dispute, and should therefore be preserved.

The Unfair Contract Terms Act 1977 also affects clauses that attempt to exclude liability for breaches of terms other than those imposed by the Sale of Goods Act 1979. The most relevant section is s. 3, which provides that where the buyer deals as a consumer, or where he deals on the seller's written standard terms, the clause must satisfy the test of reasonableness to be effective. In most hardware contracts s. 3 will apply as well as s. 6, in which case the section that provides the best protection for the buyer will be applied.

The only obvious case in which the Unfair Contract Terms Act 1977 will be irrelevant is where the parties depart substantially from the seller's standard terms and the breach is not of one of the implied terms. The theory is perhaps that if the parties are of such equal bargaining power that they can negotiate a non-standard contract, any exclusion clause is seen by both sides as fair. The question remains whether the entire contract needs to be in standard form, or

---

50. Of course, this argument fails if the seller has been entirely responsible for assessing those needs and the adequacy of the hardware to meet those needs. This is a particular problem for 'solutions' suppliers, who should be careful not to allow their keenness to make a sale to override a proper assessment of the buyer's requirements.

51. *Phillips Products Ltd* v *Hyland* [1987] 1 WLR 659.

whether it is sufficient to bring the case within s. 3 if the exclusion clause alone is the seller's standard term.

1.11 MAINTENANCE AGREEMENTS

Almost all new hardware is supplied with a manufacturer's warranty, though in the case of microcomputers this may amount to little more than repair or replacement at the supplier's premises, a process which can take several days. It is quite common for the supplier or manufacturer, in addition to this warranty, to offer a maintenance contract which covers part or all of the expected lifetime of the hardware. The extent of the maintenance offered will vary depending on the charge made; from regular preventive maintenance, through repair on a time plus parts cost basis, to a full maintenance service with every fault attended to within a certain number of hours of its reporting. Some important points that should be covered by any maintenance agreement are:

(a) Response time. The maintainer should guarantee that problems will be attended to within a specified time. The shorter the response time required, the more expensive the contract. Whilst it is not possible to provide in advance how long each repair should take, the contract should contain a term that the work will be carried out within a reasonable time, and should provide for liquidated damages in the event of late response or delayed repair.

(b) Replacement equipment. The contract should make it clear what is to happen if part of the hardware needs to be removed for repair or replacement, and in particular whether the maintainer will provide temporary replacement equipment and within what period of time.

(c) Duration, increase of charges and renewal. As the hardware ages, maintenance charges will necessarily increase. The contract should set out the period of time for which the maintainer agrees to provide the service, and some way of assessing the charges that will be made in future years. A phrase such as 'the maintainer's current charges as amended from time to time' should not be acceptable, as there is no ceiling on what he might decide to charge. One way of defining the charges in a maintenance agreement which provided for full maintenance in return for an annual payment might be to set the payment at 10 per cent of the manufacturer's list price for year one, 15 per cent for year two and so on, with a provision for assessing the charge if the manufacturer ceases production of those items. The agreement should, from the buyer's point of view at least, contain a right of renewal and a method of assessing the new charges.

(d) Transfer of the agreement. If the buyer wishes to resell the hardware at some later date, he will clearly obtain a higher price if he can also transfer the benefit of the maintenance agreement. The contract should therefore contain a provision to this effect. The maintainer might also wish to transfer the burden of the contract to another organisation, but a provision permitting this should be resisted by the buyer – there is no guarantee that the new maintainer will have sufficient expertise or experience of the hardware in question.

1.12   CONCLUSION

The achievement of a working system which meets the user's needs is a difficult enough task, as anyone who has tried to set up a home computer will testify. It is even more difficult to achieve in a contractual vacuum. In summary, there are three main advantages to a properly negotiated, well-drafted contract:

(a)   identification of the issues,
(b)   a clear statement of the obligations of *both* sides,
(c)   agreement *in advance* on how disagreements are to be resolved.

The overall aim is a good working relationship, leading to successful performance of the contract and an effective system. Whilst it is tempting to produce standard-form contracts, particularly given the cost of negotiating individual agreements, this factor is far outweighed by the expense of sorting out the mess when things not covered by the contract go wrong.

CHAPTER TWO

Software contracts

Graham Smith

2.1 INTRODUCTION

2.1.1 Types of software

Computer software is a term used to describe the programs that cause the computer to operate in a particular way. Sometimes the other non-hardware parts of a computer system (such as manuals) are also regarded as software but in this chapter we will use the term as meaning the programs alone.

Commercially, an important distinction must be drawn between standard package software and bespoke software. The former is marketed as a standard product that should meet the requirements of a large number of users. The latter, on the other hand, as its name suggests, is specially written to meet the particular requirements of the user. Needless to say, as with a suit, there is a trade-off between 'off-the-peg' and 'bespoke' software: standard package software will be cheaper than bespoke, but may not reflect the way the user's business operates, while bespoke will be more expensive but should be exactly tailored to the user's requirements. A hybrid form of software also exists: the software producer may be willing to alter his standard package so that it fits the customer's needs more closely, a process generally known as 'customisation'. Industry statistics show that package software is becoming more, and bespoke software less, important: sales of the former are nearly twice those of the latter, and are growing more rapidly.[1]

---

1. P. C. Bradley, *The UK Software Industry* (London, 1988), table 1 at p. 15. It has been forecast that between 1988 and 1994 the compound average growth rate of package software revenue in the EC will be 21.2%, against 13.9% for custom software and consultancy: *Panorama of EC Industry 1991–2* (Luxembourg: EC Commission 1991).

A further distinction, of a technical nature, must also be drawn, between system software, which organises the way in which the hardware operates, and application software, which performs the functions required by the user of the computer system, such as running a payroll or keeping accounting records. System software is generally supplied by the manufacturer of the hardware, as a standard package, while application software might be supplied as a package or as bespoke software.

2.1.2 Selecting software

The selection of software is the most important part of the planning of a computer system, since it is the software that performs the functions for which the system is being acquired. Thus, the selection process for any software, save the most simple, must begin with the user defining in writing his needs and requirements. This document is known as the functional or requirements specification and is a crucial document. The user will be able to compare against this document the extent to which package software offered by different vendors meets his needs. This may highlight certain changes that the user will request the vendor to make to the package, so that it more closely fulfils his requirements. Or it may demonstrate that no package software will satisfy the user's particular requirements, in which case he may contract with a software house to write bespoke software that meets those requirements. In this case the functional specification will constitute the initial 'blueprint' for the software house's work, and the benchmark against which its work will be measured.

The importance of the user making his requirements clear is illustrated by the case of *Micron Computer Systems Ltd* v *Wang (UK) Ltd*, unreported 9 May 1990 (QBD), in which one of Micron's complaints was that the computer system they bought from Wang did not provide 'transaction logging'. The judge, Steyn J, made this pertinent observation:

> The acknowledged absence of a transaction logging facility is not in reality a fault in the system which was sold. Micron can only complain about its absence if Micron can establish a contractual term, express or implied, of an actionable representation, to the effect that the system included such a facility. In order to make good its case on transaction logging, Micron must therefore establish that they made known to Wang that they required such a facility.

In the event, the judge found on the evidence that Micron had not made its requirement for transaction logging clear to Wang, and accordingly that part of Micron's case failed.

2.1.3 Types of software contract

Package software for microcomputers is generally supplied by computer and other retailers, or by mail order, without a written contract. Here the technique of 'shrink-wrap' licensing will often be used, to try to establish a contract between the software producer (rather than the retailer) and the customer.

Package software for mini- and mainframe computers will be very much more expensive, and will almost always be supplied pursuant to a signed, written software licence. This may be with the software house or other company that actually produced the software, or it may be with an intermediary who has the right to distribute the software.

Contracts for bespoke software are almost invariably written, and are generally entered into with a software house – a specialist company that only writes software – or a systems house – a company that also supplies the hardware on which the software will run.

In the next part of this chapter we will consider the legal nature of software, and attempt to analyse each of these types of contract.

2.1.4   What is software?

The legal nature of software is one of the central mysteries of computer law. As we have seen, software comprises the instructions which cause the hardware to work in a particular way: for example, to process a company's payroll. Looked at in this way, software is intangible, and difficult to classify in legal terms. It appears to be pure information, enjoying no physical form except that of magnetic notation on a tape or disk. Since it seems that pure information is not property[2] one might conclude that neither is software.

Such an argument was raised by the defendants in *Eurodynamics Systems plc* v *General Automation Ltd* (6 September 1988 unreported) and, unfortunately, the issue was not decided by the judge because he was able to decide the case without doing so. The defendants there relied on the view put forward by Scott[3] that, although software can be the subject-matter of a sale, software itself is pure information, and the transfer of software is a service, not a sale of goods. In this way the implied terms as to merchantability and fitness for purpose would apply to the recording medium, but not to the software recorded thereon.

This approach, however, is in the writer's view seriously flawed, because it draws a false distinction between the software and the medium on which the software is supplied. An analogy would be to define a book as a collection of words, and to ignore the fact that a book has covers, pages and a spine. A book is clearly tangible property, and in legal terms constitutes 'goods' notwithstanding that the major value lies in the words printed on the pages, not in the pages themselves. If a customer bought a cassette which contained a gap in the music recorded on it, there would be no doubt that the cassette was unmerchantable or unfit for its purpose, notwithstanding that the error was in the magnetic notations, rather than in the cassette itself. In the writer's view software should be viewed in the same way.

Accordingly, in analysing the legal nature of software it is suggested that the software and its physical medium should be considered together. In almost all cases software is supplied in the form of a hard or floppy disk, or a magnetic tape. Very occasionally software is supplied down a telephone line or over a

---

2. *Oxford* v *Moss* (1978) 68 Cr App R 183, *R* v *Stewart* (1988) 50 DLR (4th) 1.
3. A. Scott, 'Software as "goods": *nullum simile est idem*' (1987) 3 CL&P 133.

satellite link, or even broadcast, but in commercial terms these methods of supply are still a rarity. What, then, is software? It is suggested that the answer is that at least where it is supplied on a physical medium it should be regarded as physical property, like a book or a record, even though the nature of the contract under which it is supplied will vary, depending on the circumstances.

For example, standard microcomputer software, such as Lotus 1-2-3, is supplied over the counter by a retailer with no signed written contract. The transaction would appear to an observer no different from the purchase of a book or record and, it is submitted, is no different. In such circumstances the contract is a simple contract of sale. The fact that a 'shrink-wrap licence' is supplied with the software makes no difference because that licence, if it is effective at all, only operates as between the purchaser and the software producer; it has no impact on the contract between the retailer and the purchaser, the essence of which is the transfer of possession of, and title to, a diskette containing certain magnetic notations, as well as associated documentation.

There may also be a sale of goods where both hardware and standard software are supplied together. For example, in *Toby Constructions Products Pty Ltd* v *Computa Bar (Sales) Pty Ltd* [1983] 2 NSWLR 48, an Australian case, the court held that the sale and installation of hardware and software, and the training of the purchaser's staff, constituted a sale of goods. The total price was A\$14,390, of which A\$12,230 was for the hardware and A\$2,160 for the software. The judge stated that the 'system, software included, whilst representing the fruits of much research and work, was in current jargon off the shelf, in a sense mass produced'. Similarly, in *Micron Computer Systems Ltd* v *Wang (UK) Ltd*, unreported 9 May 1990 (QBD), referred to above, the court appears to have treated the supply of a Wang computer system, comprising both hardware and software, as a sale of goods. Cases such as *Toby Constructions* and *Micron Computer Systems*, or the simple sale of a diskette containing microcomputer software, lie at the end of the spectrum closest to a traditional sale of goods. In such cases the allegedly 'intangible' nature of software is no more important than is the intangibility of the music recorded on a cassette.

However, much package software is not sold, but is 'licensed', as we will see later on. It is submitted that this does not alter the underlying nature of the contract for the supply of the software. As Steyn J stated in *Eurodynamics Systems plc* v *General Automation Ltd* (6th September 1988 unreported): 'Although the ideas and concepts involved in software remained [the defendant's] intellectual property, the reality of the transaction is that there has been a transfer of a product.' It is submitted with respect that this is correct, and that where software is licensed there are effectively two contracts between the licensor and the licensee: a contract for the supply of the physical manifestations of the software, and secondly the grant of a licence to use the software. The contract for the supply of the software will be a contract of sale if title to the physical media passes to the licensee, and a hiring if it does not. The consequences of this conclusion, as regards the implication of terms as to quality, will be examined later in this chapter.

In relation to a contract that involves the development of bespoke software, to meet particular specified requirements of the customer, it might be argued that the contract is not a sale but is one for services or for work and materials. The difference is important because in the latter two types of contract the only warranty that would be implied by law in relation to the software itself would be that it had been written with reasonable skill and care, and not that it was merchantable or fit for its purpose. In *Robinson* v *Graves* [1935] 1 KB 579 the test for determining the difference between a contract of sale and one for work and materials was stated as follows:[4]

> If you find, as they did in *Lee* v *Griffin* (1861) 1 B&S 272 that the substance of the contract was the production of something to be sold by the dentist to the dentist's customer, then that is a sale of goods. But if the substance of the contract, on the other hand, is that skill and labour have to be exercised for the production of the article, and that it is only ancillary to that that there will pass from the artist to his client or customer some materials in addition to the skill involved in the production of the portrait, that does not make any difference to the result, because the substance of the contract is the skill and experience of the artist in producing the picture.

Where bespoke software is written, the value of the labour expended under the contract will far exceed the cost of the recording medium. On the other hand the main purpose of the transaction is nevertheless the supply of the completed software. As Hilbery J said in *Marcel (Furriers) Ltd* v *Tapper* [1953] 1 WLR 49, in finding that a contract for the manufacture and delivery of a fur jacket to the requirements of a customer was a contract of sale:[5]

> . . . a high degree of skill and craftsmanship goes into the making up of a fur jacket such as was to be made for the defendant in this case. . . . I cannot discover anything to distinguish it from the case of an ordinary article which it is part of someone's business to supply and which that person has to make to special measurements for the customer. It requires skill, labour and materials of course, to make it, but the purpose of the transaction is the supply of the complete article for the price.

If, prior to delivery, the software was totally lost in a fire, the customer would surely argue that there had been a total failure of consideration. Thus even with a bespoke contract it may be argued that the purpose of the contract is the supply of goods: namely the transfer to the customer of certain media, which when inserted into his computer enable the computer to operate in a certain way.

To summarise, when cheap standard microcomputer software is supplied by a retailer that is a sale; when other standard software is supplied the transaction is likely to be either a sale or a hiring depending upon whether title to the media

---

4. Per Greer LJ at p. 587.
5. At p. 51.

passes. A contract for the writing of bespoke software might also be regarded as a sale or a hiring since the purpose of the contract is to transfer the media bearing the software, but may also be regarded as a contract for services or for work and materials.

2.2   THE SOFTWARE LICENCE

2.2.1   Why is software licensed?

The original, and still the prevalent, form of contract under which mini and mainframe software is supplied, is the licence.[6] It is, perhaps, somewhat strange that the supply of a functional item – in effect a piece of equipment – should be licensed rather than sold, or hired, as other items of equipment are. The explanation probably lies in the historical evolution of software distribution.

Originally, software was provided free of charge by hardware manufacturers, or at least the cost of it was 'bundled' with the price of the hardware. At the end of the 1960s hardware manufacturers began to unbundle their software and market it separately. At the same time there appeared a new kind of computer company, the software house, specialising in the creation and marketing of software.

Nevertheless, early programs were produced in very small quantities, and were highly expensive. They were viewed as being the embodiment of expensively acquired trade secrets and know-how, rather than as a mass-produced article. Software houses – totally dependent on software for their business – were keen to protect at all costs the intellectual property rights vested in the software, and so adopted the licence as the form of supply. Licences were used for other supplies of expensive technology or know how, so why not software?

It probably also appeared more reasonable and defensible to impose restrictions on the use of software in a licence rather than in a sale contract. The essence of a sale is that full ownership passes, and therefore the right to use the physical object as the purchaser wishes, subject of course to the law regarding infringement of intellectual property. When software was first marketed the subsistence of copyright or any other intellectual property rights in software was a matter of uncertainty, and hence contractual restrictions on disclosure and copying were favoured.

It is now clear that copyright does indeed subsist in computer software, and that the use of software does require the grant of a licence. Accordingly, the approach of granting a licence to use software has been vindicated, although the licence is only one aspect of the supply of software: alongside the licence is a second contract relating to the supply of the physical manifestations of the software. The licence continues to be important, however, because software suppliers continue to be concerned to protect the intellectual property rights

---

6. For a typical software licence see *Conditions for Supply of Licensed Software Packages to Government Users*, published jointly by the Central Computer and Telecommunications Agency and the Computing Services Association.

in their software, and to impose restrictions on the use of the software. Thus even where software is sold without a written agreement (e.g., where it is purchased from a computer store) software producers attempt to impose a shrink-wrap licence on the purchaser. The efficacy of such licences is discussed in 2.7 below.

2.2.2   What property rights are licensed?

A licence is a permission to do something that would otherwise be unlawful. The question arises, therefore, as to what legal permission is granted by a software licence. The answer is, briefly, that in some cases the licence will be a permission to use confidential information, and in virtually all cases it will be a permission to copy a copyright work.

If the software has been kept secret by the producer, or only supplied on conditions of confidentiality and has not been published too widely, then the software licence will be akin to a licence of confidential information or know-how. These conditions will generally be fulfilled where mainframe or minicomputer software is licensed, but it is difficult to see that a mass-produced and widely marketed program for a personal computer could be regarded as confidential information. In any event, pure know-how licensing does give rise to some legal difficulties and, for this reason, the better legal basis for software licensing is the law of copyright.

Since the enactment of the Copyright (Computer Software) Amendment Act 1985 it has been clear that copyright subsists in a computer program. Under that Act not only unauthorised reproduction but also the storage of a program in a computer constituted copyright infringement. This position has been maintained by the Copyright, Designs and Patents Act 1988. In particular, s. 17(2) of the 1988 Act provides that copying a literary work (such as a computer program) includes storing the work in any medium by electronic means. Furthermore, by s. 17(6) copying includes the making of copies which are transient or are incidental to some other use of the work. Since in virtually every case the operation of a program in a computer involves the copying of the program within the computer, this will constitute reproduction for the purposes of the 1988 Act. As the learned recorder said in *Saphena Computing Ltd* v *Allied Collection Agencies Ltd* (1988) 59 Computers and Law 20: 'Whenever an object program is run on a computer, it is thereby copied; and whenever a source program is compiled in a computer it is thereby copied or adapted'. A software licence can, therefore, be legitimately considered to be a copyright licence.

The copyright basis of software licensing is further confirmed by the EC Directive on the legal protection of computer programs (EEC Directive 91/250/EEC — referred to in this chapter as the EC Directive), which will be implemented in the United Kingdom from 1 January 1993. The Directive requires the member states to protect programs by copyright as literary works. Article 4(a) provides that the restricted acts include 'the permanent or temporary reproduction of a computer program by any means and in any form, in whole or in part' and goes on to say that 'insofar as loading, displaying, running, transmission or storage of the computer program necessitate such reproduction, such acts shall be subject to authorization by the rightholder.' This, it will be noted, results in a similar situation to that obtaining under the 1988 Act: a licence is necessary in order to load, run or store a computer program. However, the Directive strikes a blow for users of software by setting out, in Article 5, certain exceptions to the restricted acts which are discussed below.

2.2.3 The licence clause

The licence normally granted by a software licence is the right to use the software on a single computer at a single location. Sometimes the computer is specifically identified, in which case the user will be anxious to ensure that use on a back-up or replacement machine is permitted. Where many computers are networked or clustered together the licence may permit use on any number of computers belonging to the licensee, or some combination of numbers and sites.

The use permitted is also often restricted to the 'internal purposes' of the licensee, a restriction designed to prevent the licensee from operating as a software bureau. However, licensees who are members of a group of companies may find that such wording restricts their ability to process data for their fellow group members and hence may require amendments to the standard wording.

Licence clauses will now, however, have to be read in the light of Article 5 of the EC Directive, particularly Article 5(1) which reads as follows:

> In the absence of specific contractual provisions, the acts referred to in Article 4(a) and (b) shall not require authorization by the rightholder where they are necessary for the use of the computer program by the lawful acquirer in accordance with its intended purpose, including for error correction.

Considerable difficulties arise in trying to understand the meaning of this Article.[7] It is in clear conflict with the preamble to the Directive, which includes the statement that 'the acts of loading and running necessary for the use of a copy of a program which has been lawfully acquired . . . may not be prohibited by contract', although the opening words to Article 5(1) and the omission of any reference to Article 5(1) in Article 9 (which prohibits contracting out of certain provisions of the Directive) suggest otherwise. The legal view of Article 5(1) would seem to be that it is not possible to prohibit loading or running absolutely, although restriction (e.g. as to the location or number of terminals) could be placed on use, and that in the absence of any licence to use, a licence in the terms of Article 5(1) would apply as a matter of law. In any event, the words 'in accordance with its intended purpose' in Article 5(1) are of great importance; software licensors will no doubt attempt to define this in detail in licence agreements, manuals and other literature, and to incorporate restrictions on use in the definition.

---

7. See B. Czarnota and R. Hart, *Legal Protection of Computer Programs in Europe* (London: Butterworths, 1991) (hereinafter Hart & Czarnota), chapter 8; G.P. Smith, 'EC Software Protection Directive – an attempt to understand Article 5(1)', *Computer Law and Security Report* (November–December 1991), p. 148.

A major difficulty arising out of the licence clause for users is that it will almost invariably restrict the licensee from transferring the software to any third party. This may result in difficulties if, for example, the licensee wishes to transfer his computer operations to a facilities management company: the transfer will require the consent of the licensor and will provide an opportunity for the charging of an additional fee. The Copyright, Designs and Patents Act 1988 attempts to address the transfer of copies of programs in s. 56, which gives a transferee of a copy of a program the same right to copy or adapt the program as the transferor had, subject to certain conditions being fulfilled. Those conditions include there being no express prohibitions on the transfer of the copy, or on the assignment of the licence, and the section will therefore rarely apply where there is a full written licence, since such prohibitions are commonplace. Furthermore, the section would seem only to apply where the software was originally sold, and not where it was supplied by way of a hiring or some other form of supply.

This issue is also addressed in the EC Directive. Article 4(a) provides that the holder of the copyright in a program has the exclusive right to distribute the original program, or copies of it, to the public by any means, including rental. However, the article goes on to say that this distribution right is exhausted by the first sale within the European Community of the copy in question except for the right to control further rental of the copy. This could be interpreted as meaning that, when a copy of a program is sold, no restriction on further sale is permissible, although it is not clear that a sale of a single copy by a user would fall within the distribution right since arguably it is not a distribution to the public; if it does not, then a restriction on a user reselling would be permissible, at least so far as the EC Directive was concerned.

Licences have up to now normally prohibited any copying of the program, except as necessary for use. This had the consequence that the user could not make back-up copies of the program for security purposes, although some licences specifically conferred a limited right to make back-up copies. This is now specifically dealt with by Article 5(2) of the Directive, which provides that the making of a back-up copy by a person having a right to use the program may not be prevented by contract 'insofar as it is necessary for that use.' Prohibitions on reverse engineering or decompilation, which have also been commonplace, will now be subject to the provisions of Article 6 of the Directive.

2.3   PRINCIPAL COMMERCIAL TERMS

2.3.1   Delivery

The software will usually be delivered in object code form, with the source code being retained by the licensor. The practical consequence will be that whilst the licensee will be able to use the software, he will not be able to modify or maintain it. He will be dependent upon the licensor for software maintenance, although he may be able to protect himself against the more dire consequences of such dependence by means of an escrow arrangement (see 2.6).

In *Saphena Computing Ltd* v *Allied Collection Agencies Ltd* (1988) 59 Computers and Law 20, the learned recorder expressed the view that if a licensee lawfully has possession of the source code, he cannot be prevented by the licensor from using it to repair the software, since to do so would constitute a derogation from grant contrary to the rule in *British Leyland Motor Corporation Ltd* v *Armstrong Patents Co. Ltd* [1986] AC 577. However:

> there is no further obligation on the [licensor] to facilitate the repair of the software by the [licensee]. If only the object code was supplied under the contract, the [licensor is] under no obligation to supply or license the source code to the [licensee] to enable [him] to repair the object code. If the source code was supplied, the [licensor has] impliedly licensed the [licensee] to copy it for the purposes of [his] business, including repair or improvement of the object code.

The rule in *British Leyland Motor Corporation Ltd* v *Armstrong Patents Co. Ltd* is, therefore, a shield and not a sword, and obtaining access to the source code remains a potent problem for licensees, though one mitigated, so far as error correction is concerned, by Article 5(1) of the EC Directive (see 2.6 and 2.9 below).

Software is usually delivered in the form of a disk or diskette, along with written documentation including the user manual and specification. However, it is technically possible for software to be delivered by transmission over a telephone line (known as downloading) or by a radio or satellite broadcast. The time of delivery will usually be specified in a software licence and as with hardware the time of delivery will generally be of the essence. In the absence of any express provisions delivery will be required within a reasonable time.

2.3.2 Acceptance

Acceptance is a crucial concept in relation to software. As we have seen, software is acquired in order to perform a specified set of functions, within particular timings, on specified hardware. Until the software has been tested the licensee will not be able to assess whether what has been delivered accords with the contract or not. Thus any well-drafted software licence will provide for the software to be subjected to a set of defined tests, on the passing of which the software will be deemed to have been accepted. Acceptance will generally trigger payment of the whole or the final instalment of a lump-sum licence fee, or the commencement of periodic licence fees, and following acceptance the licensee's remedies will be limited to a claim under the warranty provision. On the other hand failure of the acceptance tests will normally signal the premature end of the contract, with the licensee able to return the software in exchange for a refund of any moneys paid.

The nature of the acceptance tests may vary widely. Where a major piece of software is concerned the tests may be detailed sets of tests negotiated and documented as part of the software licence. At the other extreme the acceptance procedure may simply be that if the licensee uses the software for, say, 30 days without rejecting it, he is deemed to have accepted it. A whole range of intermediate possibilities exists. The vital feature of an acceptance procedure, however, is that it should be clear and definitive, setting out the consequences of both the passing and failing of acceptance test, and should be objective.

2.3.3 Payment

The charge made for the use of software is generally called a licence fee. There are two main types: a periodic fee (e.g., monthly or annual) or a single lump sum. With a periodic licence fee the licensee will be concerned about the licensor's rights to increase the fee, and may seek to circumscribe these in some way. For example, only one increase a year may be permitted or rises may be limited by reference to an appropriate index. The licensee may also seek to delay the first payment until after the software has been accepted.

Where lump-sum fees are specified the licensor will be anxious to receive the fee as quickly as possible after signing the licence, while the licensee will not want to pay until the software has successfully passed its acceptance tests. A common compromise would be to provide for instalments of the lump sum to be paid on signature, delivery and acceptance. This arrangement will grant an incentive to the licensor to perform these obligations in accordance with the contractual timetable, while the retention of a significant proportion of the fee until acceptance will give the licensee some security for performance.

By analogy with sale of goods law, the time of payment will generally not be of the essence unless it is expressed as such. Licensors often provide, however, for interest to be payable on overdue amounts.

2.3.4 Term and termination

The licence will often be expressed as perpetual or it will be stated as being for a long fixed term, e.g., 99 years. In the absence of any provision the normal rule is that an intellectual property licence is determinable by reasonable notice although a court might have regard to the consequences of termination for the licensee, and hold that the licence was irrevocable in the absence of a breach of condition by the licensee.[8]

2.4 WARRANTIES

2.4.1 Implied warranties

2.4.1.1 Introduction A software licence may be considered as a sale of goods when title to the medium is transferred, and as a hiring when it is not. If that is the case, then the conditions and warranties as to description and quality implied by the Sale of Goods Act 1979 (sale) and the Supply of Goods and Services Act 1982 (hiring) will apply.

2.4.1.2 Right to sell or grant possession In a contract of sale there is an implied condition on the part of the seller that he has a right to sell the goods (Sale of Goods Act 1979, s. 12(1)). There are also implied warranties under s. 12(2) that the goods are free from any charge or encumbrance not disclosed or known to the buyer before the contract was made, and that the buyer will enjoy quiet possession of the goods. In a hiring there is an implied condition

---

8. See *Martin-Baker Aircraft Co. Ltd* v *Canadian Flight Equipment Ltd* [1955] 2 QB 556 (reasonable notice); *Re Berker Sportcraft Ltd's Agreements* (1947) 177 LT 420 (irrevocable).

that the supplier has the right to transfer possession of the goods by way of hire for the period of the hiring, and an implied warranty that the bailee will enjoy quiet possession of the goods for the period of the hiring (Supply of Goods and Services Act 1982, s. 7(1) and (2)).

These implied conditions and warranties are primarily concerned with title to the physical goods supplied, but nevertheless may be applicable if, for example, the software supplied infringes a third party's rights. Thus if, at the time a copy of some software is sold, the software infringes a third party's intellectual property rights, there will be a breach of the implied warranty that the goods are free from any charge or encumbrance, even though the third party has done nothing to assert his rights. If he does assert his rights, and brings an action against the licensee there will be a breach of the warranty of quiet possession.[9]

It would seem, however, by analogy with the law relating to patent licences, that there is no implied condition or warranty that a licensor has the right to grant the licence to the licensee.

2.4.1.3 Description and quality   In a sale the Sale of Goods Act 1979 implies conditions that the goods will comply with their description (s. 13(1)), that they are of merchantable quality (s. 14(2)), and that they will be reasonably fit for their purpose (s. 14(3)). In a hiring corresponding terms apply by virtue of ss. 8 and 9 of the Supply of Goods and Services Act 1982. If no medium is transferred then no sale or hiring would seem to have occurred. Such a transfer would seem to involve a supply of pure information.

Until recently there did not appear to have been any cases in which the statutory implied terms had been held to apply to software. In *Eurodynamics Systems plc* v *General Automation Ltd* (6 September 1988 unreported) Steyn J refused to decide whether software was goods, or whether the terms implied by the Sale of Goods Act 1979 applied to the software licence in question, as he was able to decide the case without reaching a view on these issues. However, in *Saphena Computing Ltd* v *Allied Collection Agencies Ltd* (1988) 59 Computers and Law 20 the learned recorder decided that 'it was an implied term of each contract for the supply of software that the software would be reasonably fit for any purpose which had been communicated to the plaintiff'. This decision is unsatisfactory, however, since the recorder did not explain the basis on which he found that the term was implied. He did find, however, that the software had been supplied on terms that the software might not be lent, sold or hired to any third party without the licensor's consent, which might suggest a hiring rather than a sale, though this is by no means conclusive. On appeal Staughton LJ stated that 'it was, we are told, common ground that the law governing these contracts was precisely the same whether they were contracts for the sale of goods or the supply of services. It is therefore unnecessary to consider into which category they might come'.[10] On the face of it that is an extraordinary statement since the law relating to goods as against

---

9. *Microbeads AG* v *Vinhurst Road Markings Ltd* [1975] 1 WLR 218
10. *Saphena Computing Ltd* v *Allied Collection Agencies Ltd* (1989) 61 Computers and Law 23.

services is quite different: the only term implied into a contract for services is that reasonable skill and care will be used, not that the result will be fit for any particular purpose or meet any standard of quality.

Where the statutory implied terms do apply a number of considerations need to be taken account of in assessing their application. Programs inevitably contain programming errors or 'bugs' and it is likely that a court will take note of this in determining whether a program is of merchantable quality. Indeed at least two courts have. In *Eurodynamics Systems* Steyn J found that 'Not every bug or error in a computer programme [sic] can . . . be categorised as a breach of contract'. These words were echoed by Mr Recorder Havery QC in *Saphena Computing* when he said that 'even programs that are reasonably fit for their purpose may contain bugs'. Even so only a specific drawing of the licensee's attention to a particular defect will ensure that the implied condition of merchantability is excluded. However, licensors normally seek to exclude the implied condition of merchantability entirely, and sometimes also include statement to the effect that no warranty is given that the program will not contain errors.

So far as the implied condition of fitness for purpose is concerned, it should be remembered that standard package software is not designed for any particular user, and will be unlikely to meet all the requirements of any user. Accordingly, licensors of such software will generally seek to exclude the operation of the implied condition of fitness for purpose but will normally give instead an express warranty that the software will conform with its functional specification, or with the user manual. Where bespoke software is supplied, however, the user may more reasonably expect to receive a warranty that the software will comply with his requirements.

It should be remembered that apart from terms implied by law, terms may also be implied from the facts and circumstances of the particular contract. Here the courts use the 'officious bystander' and 'business efficacy' tests to determine whether the implication of a term is proper. In one case, *Greaves & Co. (Contractors) Ltd* v *Baynham Meikle & Partners* [1975] 1 WLR 1095 the court held, using such tests, that in a contract for the provision of engineering consultancy services there was an implied term that the design which was the subject of the contract should be fit for certain specific purposes. Thus in a software contract that is a mere contract for services (e.g., for programming services) it may be possible to imply a term that the software supplied should comply with particular criteria, over and above the statutory term that the work be carried out with reasonable skill and care.

2.4.2 Express warranties

The existence or otherwise of implied terms in software licences is, as we have seen, a matter of some uncertainty. In reality, such terms are unlikely to be of much assistance to the licensee since they will be pitched in general terms. For example, an implied term that a program be fit for its purpose may help if the software fails to work on the hardware on which the licensee intends, to the licensor's knowledge, to use it. However, if the problem is the failure of the software to perform a particular function the licensee will have no remedy unless he specifically made that requirement known to the licensor. In *Saphena Computing Ltd* v *Allied Collection Agencies Ltd* (1988) 59 Computers and Law 20 the learned recorder found that there was an implied term that the software be fit for all purposes communicated to the licensor before the contract was made, and any further purpose subsequently communicated, provided that in the latter case the licensor accepted the licensee's instructions to make the relevant modification. The consequences of failing to make a requirement known are demonstrated by *Micron Computer Systems Ltd* v *Wang (UK) Ltd*, unreported 9 May 1990 (QBD), in which Micron failed on the evidence to show that it had made its requirement for 'transaction logging' known to Wang. Accordingly, its claim that the system supplied by Wang was defective failed in that respect (see also 2.1.2 above).

A further problem in the real world is that software licences are nearly always written, and nearly always exclude or limit the operation of all implied conditions and warranties. The efficacy of such exclusions and limitations is examined below.

Express warranties given by licensors thus assume considerable importance. Such express warranties normally take one of two forms. First, the warranty may state that the software will comply with its functional specification or user manual, or meet certain specified performance criteria, or the like. Such a warranty has the advantage that compliance or breach can be objectively measured, and is usually the best form of express warranty that a licensee can obtain. The second form of warranty provides that defects in the software will be corrected by the licensor. The disadvantage here is that it begs the question of what constitutes a 'defect'. For example, in the event of failure to perform a particular function there may be a dispute about whether this constitutes a defect. This was precisely what occurred in *Micron Computer Systems*, referred to above.

Whatever the form of warranty, it is likely to be subject to a number of restrictions. First, it will generally be limited to a fairly short period of time, probably between three and 12 months. After this time the software may be covered by the software maintenance agreement, and if so licensees should ensure that there is no overlap, otherwise the value of the warranty is illusory. Secondly, some warranties state that the licensor's only liability is to correct the non-compliance or the defect. The purpose would seem to be to exclude any liability for damages. To the extent that the licensor complies with the warranty this would seem to be effective, but if he fails to remedy the non-compliance or defect, an action for damages would lie for that failure. Thirdly, warranties often state that they cease to apply if the licensee makes any additions or modifications to the software. Licensees will be well-advised to limit the qualification to errors or defects in the software that are actually caused by the addition or modification.

2.5 EXCLUSION AND LIMITATION OF LIABILITY

2.5.1 Common law rules
The common law rules applicable to exclusions and limitations of liability apply to software licences in the same way as to hardware contracts (see 1.10.1).

2.5.2 Unfair Contract Terms Act 1977

So far as the statutory rules in the 1977 Act are concerned, the most important sections to consider in relation to software licences are ss. 6 and 7. Section 6 will apply where there is a sale of goods and s. 7 where the ownership or possession of goods passes, under or in pursuance of a contract not governed by the law of sale of goods or hire-purchase. It would seem, therefore, that s. 6 applies to a software licence if ownership of the physical medium passes to the licensee, whereas s. 7 applies if ownership of the physical medium is retained by the licensor. In either case the effect of the sections is that in a business transaction such terms as may be implied by law as to quality, fitness for purpose and description, may only be excluded or restricted to the extent that it is reasonable to do so. If the software licence constitutes a consumer sale or hiring then those terms may not be excluded at all, and it will be a criminal offence to purport to do so. Section 12(1) of the 1977 Act defines a consumer dealing as one where one party does not make the contract in the course of business, the other does so, and the goods in question are of a type ordinarily supplied for private use. The types of software that meet this third requirement will gradually change – at the time of writing, it is probable that most word processing programs are commonly supplied for private as well as for business use, whereas most desktop publishing programs are not.

The implied conditions and warranties as to title, freedom from charges and encumbrances, and quiet possession cannot be excluded in relation to a sale contract at all, whether the transaction involves a consumer or not. However, in a hiring, whether to a consumer or business customer, the implied terms as to the right to give possession and quiet possession can be excluded to the extent that it is reasonable to do so.

It is sometimes argued that the Unfair Contract Terms Act 1977 does not apply to software licences, because of the provisions of para. 1(c) of sch. 1 to the Act. That paragraph reads as follows:

> Sections 2 to 4 of this Act do not extend to—
> (c) any contract so far as it relates to the creation or transfer of a right or interest in any patent, trade mark, copyright, registered design, technical or commercial information or other intellectual property, or relates to the termination of any such right or interest.

It should immediately be noted that the paragraph only applies to ss. 2 to 4, and not to ss. 6 and 7. Further, the paragraph is in any event qualified in its application to software licences, being limited to 'any contract so far as it relates' to intellectual property. It is submitted, therefore, that while exclusions related to the creation, transfer or termination of intellectual property rights will be exempted from the Act, exclusions as to other matters – such as the quality and performance of the software – will be controlled by the Act.

2.6 SOURCE CODE ESCROW

If the licensor fails to provide software maintenance to the licensee (e.g., the correction of errors in the software or the provision of updates and enhancements) the licensee may be seriously affected. At worst the software may be unusable. The licensor's failure may result from his insolvency or ceasing business, or simply from breach. The licensee may have a right to terminate the licence in these circumstances, but if the software is running important business functions this will be of little comfort to the licensee. If the licensee is only in possession of the object code – which will be the normal state of affairs where the rights to the software are retained by the licensor – self-help will also not be an option for most users, since reverse engineering – or 'decompiling' – the object code to produce the source code necessary for the modification or correction of the software is not a simple process. Until the implementation of the EC Directive there is also a legal obstacle: such decompilation constitutes a breach of copyright in the software since it amounts to making an adaptation of the software, which expressly includes translating a program from one computer langauge or code to another: see Copyright, Design and Patents Act 1988, ss. 21(2) and (4). In addition, decompilation has up to now often been expressly prohibited in software licences. However, the position will now be governed by the Directive, which provides in Article 5(1) that, *inter alia*, adaptation of a program is permitted where it is necessary for the use of the program in accordance with its intended purpose, including for error correction. As we have seen, the meaning of Article 5(1) is somewhat obscure but it would seem that a user cannot be prevented from decompiling programs supplied in object code in order to perform his own error correction, and presumably the user could employ a software house to do this on his behalf. This right is, however, restricted to error correction, and would not cover other forms of maintenance, such as the development of enhancements or new functions.[11]

One solution, it may be thought, would be for the licensee to insist on receiving a copy of the source code as well as the object code. However, this will be fiercely resisted by most licensors as the source code constitutes highly valuable property – the most valuable asset, apart from their staff, of most software houses. They will be reluctant to supply a copy of the source code to most licensees.[12] Furthermore, as we have seen, the licensee's 'right to repair', established by *British Leyland Motor Corporation Ltd* v *Armstrong Patents Co. Ltd* [1986] AC 577 does not give him any right to demand the source code, but merely means he cannot be prevented from using it for the purpose of correcting the software if he lawfully has possession of a copy.

The compromise often adopted in practice is for the licensor to deposit a copy of the source code with an independent third party of impeccable propriety (the escrow agent) and for the licensor, licensee and escrow agent to enter into a tripartite agreement to govern its release. The escrow agreement will provide for the initial deposit of the source code, and for its updating with error corrections and new releases. On the happening of certain specified

---

11. However, it has been suggested that a user may be prevented from carrying out error correction if the supplier offers an error correction service: Hart & Czarnota, p. 65.
12. Sometimes, however, a licensor will supply a copy of the source code as a matter of course as, for example, described in *Andersen Consulting* v *CHP Consulting Ltd*, n. 17 below.

events (e.g., the licensor going into liquidation) certified to him by the licensee, the escrow agent will release the source code to the licensee, for the purposes of maintaining the software. At least two bodies provide an escrow service along these lines, namely the National Computing Centre and the Computing Services Association, and so far it would seem that the arrangements work successfully.

However, the release of such a major asset may not be welcomed by the liquidator, receiver or creditors of an insolvent software house. An attack could be mounted on the basis that the escrow represented a preference under s. 239 of the Insolvency Act 1986 (s. 340 in the case of personal bankruptcy), but this section would only apply where the escrow was set up within six months of the insolvency and where the licensee was a creditor of the licensor. It would seem that in many cases the latter condition would be fulfilled since the licensee would be a creditor with contingent claims in respect of the maintenance obligations of the licensor. Arguments could also, it is thought, be raised that the arrangement breached the *pari passu* rule of distribution enshrined in s. 107 of the 1986 Act; that a liquidator could disclaim the arrangement as an unprofitable contract under s. 178 of the 1986 Act, and that a receiver or liquidator could repudiate the arrangement as a matter of general law. Furthermore it is arguable that the release of the escrow would require a court order under s. 127 of the 1986 Act, which would only be forthcoming if the court was satisfied with the legality of the escrow arrangement itself. Having said all that, however, it would seem that in practice escrow arrangements have worked successfully in many cases.

2.7 SHRINK-WRAP LICENSING

2.7.1 Introduction
Whereas mini and mainframe software is generally supplied directly to the user, microcomputer software is marketed in large quantities, through a distribution chain (or by mail order), in a similar manner to a record or cassette. There is, therefore, no opportunity for a signed licence agreement. Accordingly, software producers have adopted the technique of the 'shrink-wrap licence', a licence agreement the terms of which are set out on the outside of the packaging, visible through clear plastic film, and the terms of which are deemed to be accepted if the packaging is opened.

Such software is normally sold by the software producer to a distributor or dealer, who in turn sells to an intermediate distributor or the customer. The shrink-wrap licence, however, purports to be a direct contract between the software producer and the ultimate customer, quite separate from the contract of sale by which the customer acquired the software. Before examining whether such a contract does exist in law, the terms normally found in a shrink-wrap licence will be examined.

2.7.2 Terms
The terms of the licence will be in a standard form specified by the licensor. The licensee will be granted a licence to use the software, subject to

restrictions; for example, use may be restricted to a single computer. The licensee will be expressly prohibited from copying the software, except perhaps for back-up purposes, and from altering, modifying or adapting it. The licensor may grant a warranty whereby defects in the physical diskette and documentation which are found within a limited time (e.g., 60 or 90 days) will be made good by replacement of the defective item.

All other warranties or conditions, and liability for consequential loss or loss of profits will normally be excluded. In fact, it is difficult to see what warranties or conditions would be implied in the licence, since it would seem to be a pure licence of intellectual property, and the only basis on which the licensor could be liable to the licensee would seem to be negligence, or product liability. The exclusion of liability will be enforceable insofar as it relates to negligence subject to the Unfair Contract Terms Act 1977, s. 2 and will generally be subject to s. 3 of that Act. Product liability, however, cannot be excluded at all, by virtue of the Consumer Protection Act 1987, s. 7. Where the software is of a type normally supplied for private use, the sale of the software by the retailer may constitute a consumer transaction for the purposes of the Consumer Transaction (Restrictions on Statements) Order 1976, as amended. Accordingly, in close proximity to the warranty statement there should be a clear and conspicuous statement that the warranty does not affect the consumer's statutory rights.

Sometimes the licensor will promise to supply updates if a user registration card is returned by the licensee; the card may well provide that the licensee agrees to the terms of the licence, and this aspect of the card is referred to again below.

2.7.3 Enforceability

The typical shrink-wrap licence contains promises by both parties (e.g., a promise by the licensor to replace defective diskettes; a promise by the licensee not to claim consequential loss) and is therefore a *bilateral* contract, if it is a contract at all. Such a contract requires three basic elements: offer, acceptance and consideration. The display of the licence terms clearly constitutes an offer. Consideration is given by the licensee by virtue of his promises in the licence. The difficult question is: does the licensee validly accept the licensor's offer by breaking the seal? Normally, a promisee's acceptance of the promisor's offer must be communicated to the promisor, although it is open to the promisor to waive the requirement for communication. A court anxious to enforce the licence against the licensor may well find that the wording on the licence constituted such a waiver. However, when considering enforcement by the licensor the same considerations do not apply. An offeror cannot unilaterally declare that silence will constitute consent, nor can a party impose a contract by ultimatum. In the absence of clear acceptance by words (e.g., signing a user registration card) or conduct (e.g., returning a defective diskette for replacement), the enforceability of the licence by the licensee is uncertain.

It may be, however, that the enforcement by the licensor of at least some parts of the licence is possible under a completely different legal theory. It is a well-known principle of patent law that a patented article may be sold subject to a limited licence as to the use or resale of the article. This is because the use or sale of such an article will infringe the patent, in the absence of a licence, and it is open to a patentee to grant such licence as he thinks fit. Similar rules would seem to apply in respect of works, such as a computer program, which are protected by copyright, and the use of which may involve reproduction of the work. Section 17(2) of the Copyright, Designs and Patents Act 1988 provides that the storage of a work in any medium by electronic means amounts to reproduction in a material form, and hence it would appear that the running of a program will constitute the restricted act of reproduction. This position has been confirmed by Article 4(a) of the EC Directive, which provides that 'insofar as loading, displaying, running, transmission or storage of the computer program necessitate such reproduction, such acts shall be subject to authorization by the rightholder.' It would seem that, as with a patented article, it is open to a copyright owner to sell a copy of the work subject to a limited licence as to its use. Such limitations will 'run with the goods' and will be enforceable against any subsequent purchaser of the copy by means of a copyright infringement action. Section 56 of the 1988 Act provides that, if there are no express terms prohibiting the transfer of the copy of the software or the assignment of the licence, or providing for the terms on which a transferee may do the things which the purchaser was permitted to do, anything the original purchaser of the copy was allowed to do in relation to copying or adapting the software may also be done by the transferee. The section therefore envisages that the owner of the copyright in the software might only grant a limited licence, or impose conditions on the transfer of the copy. However, the use of a limited licence will not enable the enforcement of limitations on the liability of the licensor, but will only be effective in respect of limitations on the use of the software.

The efficacy of a limited licence must now also be considered in the light of Article 5(1) of the EC Directive. This appears, superficially at least, to remove the ability of a licensor to impose restrictions through a non-contractual licence, given its opening words, 'In the absence of specific *contractual* provisions . . .' (emphasis added).[13] However, there may well be an argument that such restrictions form part of the 'intended purpose' of the program so that the licensee's right to use the program is circumscribed by them in any event.

2.8   BESPOKE SOFTWARE

2.8.1   Introduction
Bespoke software occupies the opposite end of the spectrum from the cheap, standard software for microcomputers that is licensed under a shrink-wrap

---

13. Certainly, this seems to have been the intention of the EC Commission in the first draft of the EC Directive. In the accompanying explanatory memorandum the Commission stated that 'if program producers wish to ensure a greater degree of control over the reproduction, adaptation and distribution of their programs which the system of licences permits, the would-be "purchaser" of a program should be required to read and sign a legally binding licence agreement at the point of sale.'

licence. By contrast, bespoke software is relatively expensive, is by definition non-standard and is supplied pursuant to a direct contract between the software house and the user. Such a contract will have some similarities to the ordinary direct software licence considered above, but it will also have a number of differences resulting from the fact that the software does not exist at the time the contract is made, and is to be written specifically to the requirements of the user. These differences can be conveniently classified as commercial differences and legal differences.

2.8.2 Commercial differences

The essence of a bespoke software contract is that the software is written, or a package is to be tailored, to the requirements of the user. Accordingly, the functional specification of the software becomes a critical document because that specification will set out in detail the user's requirements. It will become the benchmark for the project and will be used to determine whether or not the software house has fulfilled or breached its obligations, is entitled to be paid and, most importantly, whether or not the software actually meets the user's business requirements. In this situation the functional specification is best prepared by the user alone (possibly with the help of outside independent consultants) or by a combination of the user and the software house, with the user maintaining ultimate control of its contents. Indeed, where a large and complex system is proposed there may be a contract with the software house or a consultant, for the production of the specification, quite separate from the contract for the writing of the software.

The successful implementation of a complex piece of software imposes responsibilities not just on the software house, but also on the user. Unlike the supply of a simple package, a bespoke contract is more of a joint effort and, whilst the primary obligation will be on the software house to write and deliver the software, the supplier will depend on the user providing information about his business, testing the software, providing employees to be trained and the like. Crucially, since the user's requirements may change as the project progresses, the contract should provide a procedure for specifying and agreeing changes to the scope of work. These will involve adjustments to the functional specification, the price and probably also the timing of the project. The proper documentation of these changes will avoid disputes later about what the software house's obligation actually was.

Acceptance testing will also occupy a more important role in relation to bespoke software than it does in relation to a package.[14] If package software has been seen working at other users' sites or has been used on a trial basis by the user, the requirement for a formal acceptance test of the package may not be so important. However, in the case of completely new software, acceptance testing is clearly crucial, to determine whether or not the software house has delivered software conforming with the contract and to determine whether or not it is entitled to be paid.

---

14. See S. Charlton, 'Product Testing: Liability, Acceptance, Contract Terms', *Computer Law and Security Report*, (January–February 1989), p. 23.

2.8.3   Legal differences

The first important legal difference between a bespoke contract and an ordinary software licence is that a bespoke contract may vest the intellectual property rights to the software in the user. The property rights that are relevant are primarily copyright and to a lesser extent confidential information, although patent rights cannot be totally ignored. The general rule of English copyright law is that where a person commissions another to produce a copyright work, the copyright in that work vests in the author, and not in the commissioning party.[15] If there is no express provision as to ownership it would be open to the court to imply that notwithstanding the general rule, in equity the copyright belongs to the user, but to reach such a conclusion there would have to be some evidence that this was the intention of the parties. In *Saphena ComputingLtd* v *Allied Collection Agencies Ltd* (1988) 59 Computers and Law 20, a company that had commissioned some software claimed that it owned the software, by reason merely of that fact. This claim was roundly denied by the learned recorder who stated that 'the commissioning of a computer program by a person is not of itself sufficient to vest the copyright in that program in that person', and who went on to find that there was no basis on which to imply a term that the beneficial interest should pass to the commissioning party. It is interesting to note that the recorder was equally firm in denying that there was any trade custom to the effect that copyright as a matter of course vests in the supplier.

The matter will normally (and certainly should) be explicitly addressed in a bespoke software contract, and will often constitute one of the major areas of dispute in the contract negotiations. The user will claim that having paid the software house to develop software to his particular requirements, the software must belong to him, if only to prevent the software house from marketing it to his competitors. The software house will argue that had they intended the user to have ownership of the software, their quoted price would have been much higher, and that because of the nature of their business the work they do for one customer must be capable of forming the basis of work done for another. They will argue that although the software will be written to the particular requirements of the customer, nevertheless it will contain portions of software developed for other customers. The outcome of this debate will usually depend upon the pure negotiating power of the respective parties, but it is interesting to note that in CC 88, the new standard conditions of contract adopted by the government's Central Computer and Telecommunications Agency, ownership of copyright and the other rights in bespoke software for the first time vests in the software house, and not in the government. It should also be borne in mind that even if ownership of the rights in the software vests in the software house, the customer's competitive edge can be preserved by imposing a restriction on the ability of the software house to market the software to competitors of the customer, or at all. The competition law consequences of such a restriction would need to be considered.

---

15. The EC Directive, as finally enacted, is silent on this issue and therefore the general rule still applies. The first draft, however, provided that the commissioner would be entitled 'to exercise all rights in respect of the program, unless otherwise provided by contract.'

The second legal difference revolves around the legal nature of the contract. We have already seen that the supply of package software might amount to a sale of goods (if title to the media passes) or to a hiring (if title does not pass) notwithstanding the fact that the relationship is described as a licence. An agreement for the writing of bespoke software might also be either a sale or a hiring on the basis of the purposive test outlined by Hilbery J in *Marcel (Furriers) Ltd* v *Tapper* [1953] 1 WLR 49. However, the application of the 'substance of the contract' test used by the Court of Appeal in *Robinson* v *Graves* [1935] 1 KB 579 may result in the conclusion that a bespoke software contract is a contract either for services alone, if no materials are transferred, or for work and materials, the major component of which is the provision of services, since the value of the labour expended will be enormous and will far outweigh the cost of the recording medium and other materials delivered pursuant to the contract.

The consequence of the contract falling into one category or another is that a different regime of implied conditions and warranties or other terms will apply. If the contract is one for the sale of goods or a hiring, the implied conditions as to title and compliance with description and sample, fitness for purpose and merchantable quality described in 2.4.1 will apply. If the contract is one for services alone or for work and materials then the Supply of Goods and Services Act 1982 will imply terms that the work must be carried out with reasonable skill and care, and that any materials supplied must be fit for their purpose and of merchantable quality. Thus the quality of the programming would be subject only to a warranty as to reasonable skill and care; the implied terms applicable to the materials would only cover defects in the physical media, and not in the software recorded on the media. In *Saphena Computing Ltd* v *Allied Collection Agencies Ltd* (1988) 59 Computers and Law 20, an implied term as to fitness for purpose was found in a bespoke software contract, although it is not clear on what basis the implication was made. That case is also unsatisfactory because of the statement by Staughton LJ, when the case went to the Court of Appeal, that 'it was, we are told, common ground that the law governing these contracts was precisely the same whether they were contracts for the sale of goods or for the supply of services. It is therefore unnecessary to consider into which category they might come'.[16] With respect to the Court of Appeal, it would seem to make a fundamental difference.

Terms may also be implied from the facts or circumstances of the case. This may mean that a contractor who merely provides a service is nevertheless subject to an absolute warranty that the product of his services will comply with particular requirements or achieve a given result. The facts or circumstances of a bespoke software contract are that a software house is engaged to produce software which conforms with particular requirements set out in the functional specification or some other document, and accordingly it is quite possible that even in the absence of an express warranty a term might be implied that the software will be reasonably fit for its purpose, as that purpose is expressed in the functional specification or other documents.

---

16. (1989) 61 Computers and Law 23.

More normally, however, the user will seek to impose express warranties on the software house. These may be in some general form, for example, that the software will be fit for its purpose but more usefully will be specific, for example, that the software will conform with its functional specification. The software house will not normally object to a warranty along the latter lines since it is really no more than a statement that the software house will meet its primary obligation. The software supplier is more likely, however, to object to a general warranty since it will argue that this goes beyond that obligation and introduces uncertainty.

It remains to consider the extent to which the implied term that the supplier will use reasonable skill and care in the writing of the software may be excluded or restricted. Such a contractual obligation falls within the definition of negligence in the Unfair Contract Terms Act 1977, s. 1(1), and accordingly, under s. 2(2) of that Act, can only be excluded or restricted to the extent that it is reasonable to do so.

2.9 SOFTWARE MAINTENANCE

2.9.1 Definition
Software maintenance usually comprises two elements: the correction of errors or 'bugs' in the software and, secondly, the provision of enhancements and updates to the software. Software maintenance – sometimes also called 'support' – has up to now normally been provided by the supplier of the software because access to the program source code is necessary. This may change since, as described in 2.6 above, Article 5(1) of the EC Directive grants the user a limited right to decompile the object code to produce source code for the purpose of error correction, though not any other form of maintenance such as the development of enhancements or updates. However, sometimes the source code is supplied to the user, either because it is the policy of the software producer to do so[17], or because the intellectual property rights vest in the user. In such a case the user or a third party contracted by the user will be able to maintain the software. The user may also obtain access to the source code through the operation of a source code escrow agreement of the kind described in 2.6.

2.9.2 The maintenance service
The correction of errors is an important element of maintenance, since software almost always contains some errors, and the free error-correction warranty offered by most software suppliers is limited to a period of three to 12 months. The maintenance agreement will normally define the way in which

---

17. In *Andersen Consulting* v *CHP Consulting Ltd*, unreported 26 July 1991 (ChD) the judge described the standard licence agreement of the plaintiffs relating to the program in question, under which the program source code was supplied to licensees for a fee of £125,000. The judge noted that 'the result is that the plain intent of the contract was that the licensee should have the ability, the material and the right to alter and amend the programme (sic) by persons other than those who had written it'.

the maintenance company will respond to a call for maintenance, for example, by telephone assistance initially, followed by a site visit. Faults vary in importance, depending upon the extent to which the functionality and performance of the software is affected, and the supplier may agree to respond more quickly to more important faults. It is evident in practice that the time limits for responding to calls for assistance are less stringent in software maintenance contracts than in hardware maintenance contracts. This is curious, since the consequences of faulty software are at least as serious as those of faulty hardware, if not more so.

Apart from error correction, the maintenance company will agree to supply to the user all enhancements and updates developed by him during the term of the agreement. These fall into a number of categories: corrections of previously reported errors; updates necessitated by changes in the law; variations necessitated by changes in the system software that runs on the hardware in question; and improvements or new functions. The maintenance company is not normally obliged to supply any enhancements or updates, but merely to supply any that it releases to users generally. The user, on the other hand, will usually be obliged to accept and install the enhancements and updates, so that the whole of the maintenance company's customer base is using the same version of the software. For this reason it will often be a requirement of the software licence that the licensee enters into a software maintenance agreement in the first place.

2.9.3 Warranties and liability

A software maintenance agreement is an agreement for the provision of services and accordingly, by virtue of the Supply of Goods and Services Act 1982, s. 13, there will be an implied term that the maintenance company will use reasonable skill and care in carrying out the service.

It is fairly unusual to find express warranties as to the quality of the software maintenance service to be provided, although ideally the maintenance company should agree to maintain the performance of the software at the level laid down in the original acquisition agreement. Although software does not wear out, as a machine may, poorly written error corrections or updates could affect the overall performance of the software.

It will be usual for the maintenance agreement to exclude all implied conditions and warranties and to restrict liability under the contract to a defined amount. The first exclusion purports to exclude the implied term as to the use of reasonable skill and care, and will be effective to the extent that it is fair and reasonable (Unfair Contract Terms Act 1977, s. 2(2)). The second type of exclusion will also be subject to the reasonableness test under the same section and, if the contract is in the maintenance company's standard form, will also be controlled by s. 3 of the 1977 Act.

2.9.4 Duration and charges

A major point arises in relation to the duration of the contract. We have already seen that in normal circumstances the user of the software will only be able to obtain maintenance from the supplier of the software, although an escrow arrangement will provide some security in the event of failure of the software supplier to provide maintenance and Article 5(1) of the EC Directive affords some protection so far as error corrections are concerned. The consequence of this is that the maintenance agreement should be for an indefinite period and either should not be capable of determination by the software producer except in respect of the user's breach, or should be for a fairly long fixed period, equivalent to the user's anticipated period of use of the software.

The maintenance charge will be expressed as an annual or other periodic fee. As with hardware maintenance charges the user should seek some reasonable limit on the frequency and amount of increases. An annual review in line with an index of wages in the computer industry would seem a fair arrangement for both sides.

CHAPTER THREE

Liability

Chris Reed

Computer-controlled processes have become increasingly common, and more and more people are relying on the proper working of their computers to carry out business, and even social activities. Most computer hardware is general purpose, and on its own is incapable of performing any of the functions we have come to expect. The aspect of information technology that has the greatest impact on people's lives is computer software. Software is important because its whole purpose is to produce results – instructions for process control, financial or other information, and even advice – which will be acted upon. These results will almost always be uncheckable (in practice if not in theory) or there would be little point in employing a computer to produce them. Reliance on those results where the results, or the action taken upon them, are in some way defective gives rise to questions of liability. How far is the producer or user of computer software to be held responsible for losses caused by his production or use?

Once it is accepted that liability for losses caused by software requires particular investigation, it should also be clear that the most relevant areas of the law will be contract and negligence. However, recent legislation has imposed strict liability on the producers of products, and it is necessary also to examine that area of liability. It is also important to remember that where there is contractual liability for defective software, the position will be very similar to that in negligence except where this liability arises from the express terms of the contract or the terms implied into contracts for the supply of goods.

3.1 CONTRACTUAL LIABILITY

In liability terms it is important to distinguish between the two different elements of software supply; the licence of intellectual property and the development and/or supply of a copy of the software. So far as licensing is concerned, the only real *contractual* risk is that a third party may possess intellectual property rights which are superior to those of the licensee. The nature and extent of this risk is quite clear, and the drafting of suitable provisions to control it is a comparatively simple matter. By contrast, the development of software under a contract with the user, or the supply of a copy of a package, gives rise to potential contractual liability which is less certain in scope. Liability will arise either from the express terms of the contract or from those implied by law, and the terms in development contracts will be quite different from those in supply contracts.

3.1.1 Software development contracts

If a client commissions a software house to write an application, this will certainly create a contract between them. In almost every case this contract will be in writing, and will normally contain clauses excluding the software house's liability; but what is this liability?

The answer is that the software house has contracted to provide a service – the production of software to the client's specific requirements. Subject to any express contractual provisions setting out the software house's obligations more fully, its liability to the client is governed by the Supply of Goods and Services Act 1982, s.13. This section implies into the contract a term that the provider of the service will take reasonable care in its provision. In the context of software production contracts, the obligation is to take reasonable care to ensure that the software performs the functions specified by the client, together with any other functions which a reasonable software producer would realise to be necessary if the software is to work effectively. This duty should be distinguished from the stricter liability placed on the supplier of goods by ss. 13 and 14 of the Sale of Goods Act 1979. Although that obligation is not absolute, in the sense that goods need only be *reasonably* fit for their common or specified purposes, the supplier is not excused by reason of the fact that he took all reasonable precautions to ensure that the goods were reasonably fit. However, if in our example the software house wrote an application that totally failed to perform, it would not be liable unless it could be proved that the cause of that failure was a lack of care on the part of the software house.

The fact of making a contract establishes the duty to take reasonable care. The defendant will be in breach if he has failed to take as much care in producing his software as a reasonable man in the same position, professing the same expertise, would have done. An attempt to prove that the defendant did not take sufficient care may run into a number of difficulties.

First, the fault may not be self-contained, but due to interaction with the hardware. If the fault is caused by a feature of the hardware which a reasonable software producer would not have expected, then he will not be in breach of his duty. For example, many of the programs written to run on the IBM PC family of computers make 'illegal' calls on the machine's BIOS chip.[1] IBM-compatible 'clones' cannot use the IBM BIOS because it is protected by

---

1. I.e., calls outside the standard established by the operating system.

patent, and so their manufacturers are forced to use a substitute. In some cases the result is that the software fails to recognise the machine, often part-way through execution of the program, and the results can be unpredictable. If the producer should have recognised and dealt with the incompatibility he will be in breach, but in many cases this will be hard to demonstrate, particularly if the hardware in question was not commercially available when the software was designed. The burden of proving breach is on the plaintiff – clearly in some cases it will be difficult to discharge this burden. Of course, the problem will sometimes be entirely due to malfunction of the hardware, but it may be impossible to decide whether this is the case if the fault is one-off or intermittent.

Secondly, much software is, or could be claimed to be, of an experimental nature. Software released as version X.0 is generally updated within a few months as faults are discovered and corrected, and new versions appear on a regular basis.[2] As the duty is to take such care as other reasonable producers would take, it is arguable that, in the current state of the art, perfectly working software is impossible to produce. It may not be careless to release slightly defective software. Again, it will be for the plaintiff to show that the defects are such that a reasonable producer would not have released that version.

Third, the output of the system is in most cases produced by the interaction of the software with data or instructions provided by the user. Before it can be shown that the software is defective, its workings must be disentangled from the data – this will not normally be easy. The problem may arise from a particular combination of circumstances with which the software could not cope – again, should a reasonable producer have foreseen this possibility? It is also conceivable that the use to which the software has been put is not a use that the producer had expected. Should he then be liable? Again, it depends on the foresight of a reasonable producer.

Given these uncertainties, it is essential to establish clearly in the contract the quality standards to be attained, rather than relying on the term implied by the Supply of Goods and Services Act 1982. This can only be done through a combination of careful specification and clear provisions for acceptance testing against that specification. The Institute of Purchasing and Supply provides a precedent, aimed primarily at simple development contracts, in its 'Model Form of Conditions of Contract for Software Development' (1986 version). Clause 12 provides for inspection and testing during the development process, and clause 13 for final acceptance tests. In each case the model clearly provides for the consequences of failing the tests, rather than relying on a general claim for damages. Other model clauses which may be more suitable for large projects can be found in books of computer contracts precedents.[3] Clauses of this type provide at least a starting-point for negotiations.

---

2. For example, the current (1992) version of WordPerfect for DOS is 5.1; version 1.0 first appeared in 1982.
3. E.g., Morgan & Steadman, *Computer Contracts*, 4th ed. (London: Longman, 1991); M. T. M. Rennie, *Computer Contracts Handbook* (London: Sweet & Maxwell, 1985) and *Further Computer Contracts* (London: Sweet & Maxwell, 1989).

Although express warranties of quality are clearly desirable and will be found in most bespoke software contracts, the term implied by s. 13 of the 1982 Act will still be important. Any term which reduces the rights the client would have had under that Act is an exclusion clause,[4] and thus subject to the test of reasonableness by virtue of s. 2(2) or s. 3 of the Unfair Contract Terms Act 1977.

The foregoing only applies, however, to those software development contracts which can be classified as contracts for the provision of services. In most case bespoke or custom software contracts will normally fall into this category as any physical component, such as the manuals or even the media on which the software is supplied, is clearly subsidiary to the main purpose of the contract, which is the design and writing of a unique software package. Problems with the classification of bespoke software will arise, however, where what is contracted for is not a completely new package but one which has already been created and which is modified to meet the customer's requirements. If the modifications are not substantial the main purpose of the contract is the provision of the basic package, and if this is supplied on physical media the contract might well be construed as one for the sale of goods.[5] This point will be increasingly relevant as modular software engineering methods become more common. If all that the software house is doing is combining standard program modules from its library, it will be difficult to discern the same 'service' element as in a complete rewrite.[6] As Hilbery J said, referring to the manufacture of a fur coat:[7]

> I cannot discover anything to distinguish it from the case of an ordinary article which it is part of someone's business to supply and which the person has to make to special measurements for the customer. It requires skill, labour and materials, of course, to make it, but the purpose of the transaction is the supply of the complete article for the price.

3.1.2 The supply of software packages

The legal classification of software is likely to bear little relation to commercial classifications. English law essentially divides the subject-matter of commerce into real property, choses in action, goods and services. Only the last two categories are potentially appropriate for software. The legal regime governing the contract to supply software is thus dependent on which of these categories best fits the software in question. The establishment of the appropriate legal regime is important as it defines the default set of obligations which are

---

4. *Smith* v *Eric S. Bush* [1990] 1 AC 831.
5. By analogy with the 'work and materials' cases such as *Robinson* v *Graves* [1935] 1 KB 579 and *Marcel (Furriers) Ltd* v *Tapper* [1953] 1 WLR 49. See further 2.1.4, 2.8.3 above, 3.1.2 below.
6. To take an example from a different part of the IT industry, every DEC VAX computer is individually configured to the customer's requirements from standard DEC components. There are many thousands of possible configurations – so many that DEC uses an expert system, XCON, to design each VAX. Nonetheless, it would be a brave lawyer who was prepared to argue that the supply of a VAX is a contract for services rather than a sale of goods.
7. *Marcel (Furriers) Ltd* v *Tapper* [1953] 1 WLR 49 at p. 51.

modified by the express contract. We have already seen that bespoke or custom software will usually be classified as services. Package software will normally be goods, as it is supplied on physical media in multiple copies. However, 'telesoftware', downloaded from bulletin boards or similar sources, will probably be treated as services because it has no tangible component.

This classification of software into goods and services is completely illogical, if the normal rules for classifying the products of commerce are followed. These rules are based not on the software's purpose or its format, but on how it is supplied. Goods are defined in the Sale of Goods Act 1979, s. 61, as personal chattels, which requires them to possess some tangible or corporeal element, so it is clear that pure information cannot be goods.[8] Nonetheless, a supplier of standard, packaged software will normally be selling goods. The supply of software is, in part at least, a sale of goods if the main purpose of the transaction is that the purchaser will become the owner of some tangible property[9] containing the software, i.e., the medium on which it is supplied, usually a series of floppy disks. Software which is installed by copying it on to the purchaser's system from a medium that remains the property of the supplier will lack the necessary tangibility.

Software producers might attempt to argue that, even though some tangible medium is supplied, it is only that medium that is goods, so that the software recorded on it is merely information and thus not covered by the Sale of Goods Act 1979. The argument is that, because the value of packaged software subsists mainly in the intellectual property element which is licensed rather than 'sold' to the user, what is supplied is a service and thus subject only to standards of reasonable care. This argument fails to distinguish between the contract *supplying* the package, which is between the dealer and the user and could well be a sale, and the licence of intellectual property rights granted by the *software house* which is clearly not a sale.[10] It is analogous to the seller of a prerecorded cassette tape arguing that the tape is not defective because the only fault is that the music is distorted whilst the tape itself is perfect. The reason that the purchaser pays more for a prerecorded than a blank tape is precisely because it has information (music) on it. This point appears to have been recognised in *Cox* v *Riley*[11] where the defendant was charged with criminal damage. He had erased the programs from a magnetic card that controlled a programmable saw, rendering the card almost valueless. In spite of his argument that he had not damaged the card itself he was convicted, on the ground that he had damaged the 'card as programmed', which was property for the purposes of the Criminal Damage Act 1971.

If this packaged software *is* goods, the seller is obliged under the Sale of Goods Act 1979, s. 14, to supply software that is merchantable and reasonably

---

8. *Oxford* v *Moss* (1978) 68 Cr App R 183.

9. See P. S. Atiyah, *The Sale of Goods*, 7th ed. (London: Pitman, 1985), ch. 2.

10. Where the software house supplies the package directly to the user it will be *both* licensing and supplying; here there is no reason why the supply element of the transaction should not be a sale.

11. (1986) 83 Cr App R 54. See also *R* v *Whiteley* (1991) 93 Cr App R 25. This issue is discussed in greater depth in 8.3.

fit for the purposes the buyer has made known to him. This is assessed in relation either to the common purposes for which software of that type is purchased or by reference to the purpose that the buyer has made known. Software, however, does not have the same degree of homogeneity within its various categories as, say, motor cars. Different word processing or database systems may go about the task in entirely different ways, and prove more or less suitable for entirely different tasks. It is likely that the only clear guidance available to the court will be the claims the producer has made in his advertising and promotional material. This may amount to a description of the goods, or may be some other relevant factor the courts may take into account in deciding if the software is of adequate quality.

It is obviously possible to overcome some of these classification problems by including express provisions as to quality etc. in the contract and providing that these are in substitution for all other rights. However, it must be remembered that if these provisions impose lower obligations on the seller than would be the case under, e.g., the Sale of Goods Act 1979, the term will amount to an exclusion clause and be potentially subject to attack under the Unfair Contract Terms Act 1977.[12]

3.2   EXCLUSION CLAUSES

It is by no means uncommon to find a clause in contracts of US origin providing (a) that the software house warrants only that the media on which the software is supplied are free from defects in normal use, (b) that this warranty is in lieu of all other liabilities, express or implied, whether by statute or otherwise, (c) that liability for breach is limited to rectification of defects in or replacement of the media and (d) that no liability is accepted for consequential loss.

In the light of the Unfair Contract Terms Act 1977 such a clause is almost worse than useless. If the software is goods, the terms that the seller or supplier has the right to sell[13] or supply[14] cannot be excluded at all, and the implied terms as to description and quality cannot be excluded at all if it is a consumer sale or supply, and only subject to the test of reasonableness if not.[15] In the case of bespoke software, the term as to reasonable care under the Supply of Goods and Services Act 1982, s. 13, can only be excluded subject to the test of reasonableness,[16] and exclusions of liability for breach of other terms in the software house's standard-form contract are subjected to the same test by the Unfair Contract Terms Act 1977, s. 3.

The test of reasonableness is set out in the Unfair Contract Terms Act 1977, s. 11, which provides that it must have been fair and reasonable to include the

---

12. Although sch. 2 to the Unfair Contract Terms Act 1977 excludes from the operation of the Act contracts creating or transferring intellectual property rights, the consensus interpretation is that the Act still applies to other parts of the contract, e.g., obligations of quality, delivery dates etc. See 2.5.2 above.
13. Sale of Goods Act 1979, s. 12.
14. Supply of Goods and Services Act 1982, s. 7.
15. Unfair Contract Terms Act 1977, ss. 6 and 7.
16. Unfair Contract Terms Act 1977, s. 2.

clause at the time the contract was made. Schedule 2^{17} sets out a number of factors for the court to take into account – the strength of bargaining position of the parties; whether the party bound by the clause received some benefit (e.g., a lower price) for agreeing to it; how far he knew or ought to have known of the existence and extent of the clause; if the exclusion is contingent on compliance with some condition (e.g., informing the software house of defects in the software within 28 days of the end of acceptance testing) whether it was reasonable to expect the condition to be complied with; and in a sale of goods contract, whether the goods were specially made or adapted to the customer's order. The courts have also held that the question as to which of the parties can most readily insure against the loss is a relevant consideration.[18] In *George Mitchell (Chesterhall) Ltd* v *Finney Lock Seeds Ltd*[19] the evidence was that the buyer would find it impossible to obtain insurance against the consequences of the seller's breach, whereas the seller could easily insure and add less than 1 per cent to the cost of his products. This was the main reason that reliance on the clause was held to be unreasonable. It was also pointed out in that case that a limitation of liability was more likely to be held reasonable than a complete exclusion, though the Act applies in either case. Further clarification of the test can be found in *Phillips Products Ltd* v *Hyland* [1987] 1 WLR 659 where the Court of Appeal examined a clause in the contract for the hire of an earth-moving machine and driver. The clause excluded liability for damage to the hirer's property caused by the driver's negligence, and therefore fell within s. 2(2). At first instance the judge held that there were five factors which were relevant in holding the clause to be unreasonable:

(a)   The defendant was more expert than the plaintiff.

(b)   There was no prior discussion of the clause.

(c)   The plaintiff had no reasonable opportunity to arrange insurance cover against the risks which were excluded (whilst the defendant could easily have insured for third-party liability).

(d)   The factor causing the loss (i.e. the driver) was largely under the defendant's control and not at all under that of the plaintiff.

(e)   The contract was presented to the plaintiff on a 'take it or leave it' basis, as all other hirers of similar machinery used the same contract.

On appeal three further points were held to be relevant:

(a)   Insurance was a particularly important factor.

---

17. In theory sch. 2 applies only to contracts where the possession of goods is transferred; in practice, however, the courts are likely to take its provisions into account when deciding on the reasonableness of other exclusion clauses.

18. At present the insurance market has little experience of the software industry, and insurance may be difficult to obtain on reasonable terms. This fact may make limitations of liability more likely to satisfy the s. 11 test. However, as the claims record of the industry becomes clearer, this position is likely to change.

19. [1983] 2 AC 803. This was a case under the slightly different provisions of the Supply of Goods (Implied Terms) Act 1973 as its facts occurred before the 1977 Act came into force, but it was nonetheless clearly decided with at least one eye on that Act.

(b)   The burden of proving the clause to be reasonable is stated by the Act to be on the person seeking to rely on it.

(c)   A finding of unreasonableness relates only to the *particular* transaction at issue, and does not lay down any general rule about the clause when used in other transactions, even if the contracts are identical.

It is thus important to conduct a proper assessment of the potential consequences of breach, and to construct a clause allocating them in accordance with the financial strengths of the parties and the ability to insure. Whilst it may be tempting to exclude as much as possible, the likely effect is that the software house will be left completely unprotected against claims when the court finds the clause unreasonable. It should also be apparent that there is no point in merely copying a clause used by one's competitors, particularly if (as is often the case) it was drafted with US law in mind. Conversely, when contracting with a US or other foreign client it is essential to take advice on the effect of any standard exclusions under the client's domestic law. Although a clause providing that the contract is to be governed by English law and adjudicated in England may be effective, it may not be so where the contract is to be performed primarily abroad. Again, advice should be taken on the specific circumstances.

3.3   STRICT LIABILITY: THE CONSUMER PROTECTION ACT 1987

Following the EEC Directive on Product Liability (85/374), the Consumer Protection Act was passed in 1987 and came into force on 1 March 1988. The essence of the Act is that producers or suppliers of products in the course of a business[20] should be liable to anyone who suffers personal injury or property damage caused by a defect in that product, irrespective of any fault on the producer's part. As we shall see, however, the effect of the 'state of the art' defence (included largely at the request of the pharmaceutical industry) is to retain the requirement of fault though placing the burden of disproof on the producer.

The main requirements for liability are set out in s. 2(1), which provides that subject to the remaining provisions of the Act,

> . . . where any damage is caused wholly or partly by a defect in a product, every person to whom subsection (2) below applies shall be liable for the damage.

The obvious question raised by this subsection is whether computer software is a 'product', for if it is not the Act is irrelevant to our discussion. 'Product' is defined in s. 1(2) as 'any goods or electricity' including components. 'Goods' are defined in s. 45 as including (amongst other things such as

---

20. Section 4(1)(c).

crops and aircraft which clearly do not cover software) 'substances', and the same section defines 'substance' as 'any natural or artificial substance'. In spite of the circularity of this definition, it is clear that computer software will only qualify as a product if it is a 'substance', which suggests that it must have the tangible quality normally associated with goods. This is supported by the text of the Directive which defines 'product' as any movable. It seems likely, therefore, that the Act applies only to software which is marketed on some form of tangible medium (e.g., a tape or disk) ownership of which is transferred to the purchaser. Software which is installed by copying it on to the purchaser's system from a medium that remains the property of the supplier will lack the necessary tangibility to fall within the definition. The Act is to be interpreted in accordance with EEC law and the Directive, and it has been held that television programmes, which similarly consist of information transmitted as electric signals, are not goods but services.[21]

The Act also limits liability to death or personal injury[22] or damage to property (including land) which is ordinarily intended for private use or consumption and was so intended to be used by the plaintiff.[23] It does not cover damage to the product itself or to any product containing the defective product[24] and the damage must exceed £275.[25] At present the majority of software is purchased by businesses and used solely within the business, so claims can only be expected from outsiders who are injured by the business's activities where the cause was a defect in the software. The most obvious case where the Act might otherwise apply, air traffic control, will not be covered as the software in question is unlikely to be a product. Even so there are a number of situations which will at present fall within the Act – computer-controlled lifts, chips in washing machines etc. – and with the growth in the number of computers in the home, the Act will become increasingly important.

Section 2(1) requires that the damage be caused by a 'defect' in the product, and this is defined in s. 3. A product is defective if it does not provide the level of safety (in respect of property as well as the person) that persons generally are entitled to expect. This raises no problems so far as manufacturing defects are concerned, but if the defect is in the design of the product it has been suggested that this test is little more than the existing test for negligence. The courts are required to consider such matters as the manner of marketing, instructions and warnings, what the producer might reasonably expect to be done with the product, and the time at which it was supplied. This is the kind of risk-utility balancing that is used to decide liability in negligence, and it may

---

21. *Italy* v *Saachi* [1974] ECR 409. Note though that this finding was in the context of the Treaty of Rome provisions on the free movement of goods – whether the same is true in the context of the product liability Directive is a matter of some doubt. It has been argued that some non-UK jurisdictions may take a purposive approach to the definition of 'product', and decide the issue on whether the item in question is effectively mass-marketed or produced only on a one-off basis – see J. Herschbaeck, 'Is Software a Product?' (1989) 5 CL&P 154.
22. Section 5(1).
23. Section 5(1) and (3).
24. Section 5(2).
25. Section 5(4).

well be the case that a manufacturer who would not be liable in negligence will escape liability under the Act as well.[26]

Once the plaintiff has established that he has suffered damage through a defective product, he has a choice of defendants. The obvious person against whom to claim is the producer (defined in s. 1(2)), but he may also claim against any person who holds himself out as the producer or against the importer of the product into the EC if it is produced outside.[27] In some cases, however, it may not be obvious who the producer is, and so the plaintiff is given a right of action against the supplier under s. 2(3). The supplier is only liable, however, if the plaintiff requests from him the name of the producer or importer and the supplier fails to give that name within a reasonable time.

Section 4 contains a number of defences, some of which might be useful to a software producer, but the most relevant by far is the 'state of the art' defence contained in s. 4(1)(e). This provides that the producer can escape liability if he can show that the defect is such that a reasonable producer would not, in the current state of the art in that industry, have discovered the defect. The practice in the software industry is to release software that is not entirely bug-free, on the not unreasonable ground that the use made of the software is not totally predictable and thus exhaustive testing is, commercially at least, impracticable. It has even been suggested that it is impossible to produce bug-free software, though this proposition appears to depend on the mathematical proof that it is impossible to write a program that can be guaranteed to debug another program. Given this practice, it is arguable that a software producer who failed to discover even a quite serious defect in his software would nevertheless be able to take advantage of the defence, so long as the defect is not in an area of the program that would be tested as a matter of course by others in the industry. If this is so, the effect of the defence is merely to permit the producer to *disprove* negligence, a very different matter from the strict liability that the Act apparently introduces.

As the application of the Consumer Protection Act 1987 is so limited in scope and the majority of claims in respect of software will be for financial loss, it seems likely that the Act will have a comparatively small impact on the liability of software producers. Nonetheless, where the claim is for physical injury or property damage the evidential burdens placed on the plaintiff are much lighter than in negligence, and the Act would be the obvious first line of attack. For most claims, however, the common law of negligence will remain the most fruitful hope of recovery.

3.4 NEGLIGENCE

Although the general heading 'tort' covers a wide range of legal wrongs, it becomes clear on closer examination that the only real tortious problems posed by information technology arise in the field of negligence. It is quite possible to imagine situations where a computer might play a part in the commission of

---

26. See, e.g., *Evans* v *Triplex Safety Glass Co. Ltd* [1936] 1 All ER 283.
27. Section 2(2).

another tort, but almost certainly some question of negligence would be involved. Thus in the American case of *Scott* v *District of Columbia* (1985) 493 A 2d 319, where the plaintiff alleged false arrest and wrongful imprisonment against the police, who had relied on a warrant erroneously issued by a computer system, her suit failed because the officers who arrested her had not been negligent in relying on the computer. In other false arrest cases, if there were no question of carelessness in the use of the computer, it would be legally irrelevant that a computer was somehow involved. This is true for other torts – e.g., where the noise from a computer printer constituted a nuisance or an information retrieval system contained defamatory material. These cases would normally raise the same legal problems as noise from a typewriter or defamation in a book.

Before going any further, it is necessary to recognise that the question of liability may be affected by the type of damage suffered by the plaintiff. If this is physical injury or property damage few problems will arise; the test for the existence of a duty of care will be that in *Donoghue* v *Stevenson* [1932] AC 562, and breach and causation will be dealt with as in any other negligence action. The real problems arise when the plaintiff's losses, as is likely to be the case almost every time, are purely economic. If this is so, the question of whether the defendant owes him a duty of care will depend to a large degree on the type of damage that was sustained.

3.4.1 Loss of use of the software

Any producer of software will, to some degree, be aware of the potential that his product has for causing loss to someone who makes use of it. If he fails to take sufficient care when designing the product, and so causes loss to users, his commercial interests will suffer. This does not necessarily mean that he is under a legal duty to take such care. The general principle laid down in *Donoghue* v *Stevenson* [1932] AC 562 that one person owes a duty of care to another if he ought reasonably to have foreseen that his actions or inaction will cause harm to that other, expresses the duty very widely. It might therefore be thought that the producer of software is in the same position as, say, the producer of electric toasters, who clearly owes a duty of care to any person who uses the toaster. In such a case the duty is to take care to design the toaster so as to avoid injuring the user or damaging the user's property. In the case of a software designer the position is rather different. It is unlikely that defective software will cause any loss that is not purely financial,[28] and the attitude of the law towards financial losses is less favourable than towards physical or property damage.

For many years the position appeared to be settled that a plaintiff could only recover for economic loss if it was consequent on physical injury or damage to

---

28. Though common physical processes are increasingly becoming computerised – for example, Honda's four-wheel steering system replaces the physical link between the steering wheel and the road wheels with a computerised link. These types of applications, which include anti-lock braking systems and such mundane things as washing machines, are generally implemented by turning the software into an application specific integrated circuit, i.e., a physical microchip, which is clearly both goods and a product.

property[29] or caused by reliance on a negligent misstatement. However, in *Junior Books Ltd* v *Veitchi Co. Ltd* [1983] 1 AC 520 the possibility of a more relaxed attitude to pure economic loss was recognised. In that case the defendant was a building subcontractor which laid a floor at the plaintiff's premises. The floor quickly proved defective and unsuitable for use. The plaintiff successfully claimed the cost of replacing the floor and lost profits while this was done, in spite of the defendant's argument that these losses were purely financial and thus not recoverable. The House of Lords held that a duty to take care to avoid financial losses could be owed if there was sufficient proximity between plaintiff and defendant, and that in this case, the defendant having been nominated as subcontractor by the plaintiff, a sufficiently close relationship did exist.

However, *Junior Books* has proved a source of worry to the courts, for the fear of opening the floodgates is ever-present. In *Muirhead* v *Industrial Tank Specialties Ltd* [1986] QB 507 the Court of Appeal distinguished it, holding that in that case the plaintiff and defendant (the supplier of a defective pump to the builder of a tank for the plaintiff's lobsters) were not in a sufficiently proximate relationship for the defendant to owe the plaintiff a duty to take care to avoid causing financial loss. Robert Goff LJ explained *Junior Books* as deciding that such a relationship would only arise if the plaintiff relied on the defendant to avoid such losses, and if the defendant could be seen as undertaking responsibility to do so. Similarly in *Simaan General Contracting Co.* v *Pilkington Glass Ltd (No. 2)* [1988] QB 758 the Court of Appeal held that the defendant, which supplied glass to a subcontractor of the plaintiff, owed no duty to the plaintiff to supply glass that was of a consistent colour. There was no reliance on the defendant's expertise and no discussion with it about the nature of the glass to be supplied. Any remedy the plaintiff might have would be in contract against the subcontractor. Finally in *D & F Estates Ltd* v *Church Commissioners for England* [1989] AC 177, a case almost identical to *Junior Books* except for the fact that the subcontractor was not nominated by the plaintiff, the House of Lords refused to follow *Junior Books* and held that it was a case which turned on its own special facts, although the following year the House of Lords refused to disapprove *Junior Books*, recognising that in a few special cases there would be sufficient proximity to give rise to a duty of care in respect of pure economic loss.[30]

There is, then, a strong likelihood that *Junior Books* will not be followed. If it does retain any force, it is in those cases where the software producer is employed to devise software specifically for the user, and where he subcontracts some or all of the work with the knowledge and consent of the user. In such a case, provided there is sufficient discussion between user and subcontractor to show that the user is relying on his expertise rather than the expertise of the main contractor, and provided the subcontractor can be seen to undertake to the user that the software will not be defective, the user will have an arguable case in tort for the cost of replacement or repair. In all other cases,

---

29. *Spartan Steel & Alloys Ltd* v *Martin & Co. (Contractors) Ltd* [1973] QB 27.
30. *Murphy* v *Brentwood District Council* [1991] 1 AC 398.

it seems that the user will have to rely on his contractual rights against his supplier.

3.4.2 Consequential losses caused by reliance on the output of the software

Whether economic loss can be recovered at all appears to be dealt with as a matter of duty, and the test for the existence of a duty of care appears to be a twofold one: first, is the relationship between the plaintiff and defendant sufficiently proximate so that *prima facie* a duty of care is owed? Second, are there any policy reasons why a duty should not be imposed on the plaintiff in this situation?[31] Where, like *Junior Books Ltd* v *Veitchi Co. Ltd* [1983] 1 AC 520, the loss is merely that the software no longer works, the test for proximity is very stringent. It is arguable, however, that if the loss is consequential on reliance on the output of the software a less stringent test should be imposed, a test similar to that used in the cases on negligent misstatements. The results produced by the software are similar to (and in many cases treated by the user as) statements of fact. If reliance on those statements is foreseeable it would seem reasonable to assume that the considerations influencing the courts in negligent misstatement cases will also be relevant in deciding the extent of the duty owed by a software producer. Some indirect support for this proposition can be found in the recent case of *Spring* v *Guardian Assurance plc, The Times*, 10 February 1992, where the basic principle in *Hedley Byrne & Co. Ltd* v *Heller & Partners Ltd* [1964] AC 465 was extended to impose a duty of care on the giver of a reference. This duty was owed not only to the recipient of the reference but also to its *subject*, even though it could not be said that he had relied directly on the misstatement.

It seems likely that reliance losses of this kind may be caused in a number of different ways, and the potential problems may be classified as follows:

(a) Negligence in designing the system.
(b) Negligence in operating the system.
(c) Negligence in relying on the output of the system.
(d) Failure to use a computer system.

3.4.2.1 Negligent design The greatest difficulty that a defendant will have in suing a software producer for losses caused by a negligently designed piece of software is establishing that the producer owed him a duty of care. In *Hedley Byrne & Co. Ltd* v *Heller & Partners Ltd* [1964] AC 465 the plaintiff suffered loss when it gave credit to a firm called Easipower in reliance on a reference given by the defendant bank. The court held that because the plaintiff and the defendant were in such a close relationship, the defendant owed a duty to take care in giving the reference. This case established the possibility of claiming for negligent misstatements. The problem that troubled the court most was the danger of 'opening the floodgates' to litigation. The difficulty with careless words as opposed to careless actions is that the range of those affected is

---

31. *Anns* v *Merton London Borough Council* [1978] AC 728 as explained in *Yuen Kun Yeu* v *Attorney-General of Hong Kong* [1988] AC 175.

potentially very large indeed. The example given by Denning LJ in *Candler* v *Crane Christmas & Co.* [1951] 2 KB 164 of the marine hydrographer is instructive: we are asked to envisage that the hydrographer, in drawing up a chart of a particular part of the oceans, negligently fails to mark in a reef that is a danger to shipping. The chart is published, and is used by the masters of ships sailing in those waters. One or more ships run on the reef, entirely due to the fact that it is not marked on the chart. Should the hydrographer be liable to compensate the master of the ship, the shipowners, and any passengers or cargo owners, all of whom will suffer loss because of his carelessness? Clearly the hydrographer satisfies the test of foreseeability laid down in *Donoghue* v *Stevenson* [1932] AC 562. Clearly, also, his liability is potentially so wide, and extends so far in time (the charts might well be used for many years) that it seems wrong to say that he ought to be held liable.

The solution adopted in *Hedley Byrne & Co. Ltd* v *Heller & Partners Ltd* was to limit the duty of care to those who were in a 'special relationship' with the maker of the statement. This special relationship was variously defined as being 'equivalent to contract' (per Lord Devlin), a voluntary undertaking given to the plaintiff to undertake skill and care (per Lords Morris and Hodson), or knowledge by the defendant that the plaintiff would rely on the statement (per Lord Reid). In any event, it was clear that the mere fact that it was foreseeable that some person in the defendant's position *might* rely on the statement would not be enough to establish a duty of care.

The position has been somewhat clarified in *JEB Fasteners Ltd* v *Marks, Bloom & Co.* [1983] 1 All ER 583, where the defendant accountants negligently overvalued a company's assets in a report prepared for the company. As the defendants knew, the report was intended to be shown to prospective investors in the company. The plaintiff company, which was the eventual purchaser, brought an action against the defendants based on the negligent misstatement in the report. The court held that although the defendants did not specifically know that the report was to be shown to the plaintiff, they did know that the report would be shown to, and relied on by, the class of intending purchasers, a class of which the plaintiff was a member. There was, therefore, sufficient proximity for the defendants to owe the plaintiff a duty of care, though in the event the action failed as the plaintiff had not relied on that statement in deciding to purchase the company.[32] An important element in deciding the proximity question appears to be the purpose for which the advice was produced. In *Caparo Industries plc* v *Dickman* [1990] 2 AC 605 the House of Lords held that a company's auditors owed no duty of care to the shareholders in respect of the accounts because the accounts were not produced for the purpose of being relied on when making investments (even though it was *foreseeable* that they would be relied on[33]). This question is likely to be answered in the affirmative in the case of most software producers – if the output of the software is not intended to be relied on, it is difficult to see why the user bought it.

---

32. See also *Haig* v *Bamford* (1977) 72 DLR (3d) 68 (Canada).
33. See the judgment of the Court of Appeal [1989] QB 653.

Applying these principles to the question of whether a software producer owes a duty of care to the ultimate user, the following position seems a likely one:

(a)   If the software was commissioned by, or modified for, the user, the producer will owe him a duty of care. This appears to follow from *Hedley Byrne & Co. Ltd* v *Heller & Partners Ltd* and is supported by *Junior Books Ltd* v *Veitchi Co. Ltd.*

(b)   If the software was produced for use by a limited class of users, e.g., for a trade organisation which would market the software to its members, then a duty of care would seem to exist following *JEB Fasteners Ltd* v *Marks, Bloom & Co.*, provided it was intended to be used and relied on by that group.

(c)   If the software was produced for release to the general public, then it appears unlikely that the producer owes a duty of care to the user, as the class of users is too indeterminate to satisfy the tests laid down in *Hedley Byrne* and *JEB Fasteners*. It is still the case, however, that the user might have a contractual claim against his supplier.

It should also be recognised that even if the designer of the system does not owe a duty of care in the design itself, if defects become apparent he, or the manufacturer or distributor, may well then owe a duty to users to warn them of the defect. This is well-illustrated by the case of *Walton* v *British Leyland* [1980] Product Liability International 156. Here the plaintiffs were injured when a wheel came off their Austin Allegro car. The defendants had known of this danger for some time, but instead of recalling the model and publicising the danger, they simply instructed their dealers to deal with the problem as the cars came into the dealers' garages. The plaintiffs' car had been purchased from, and was serviced by, a non-Leyland dealer, so it was never modified. The court held that the defendants were liable in negligence, on the ground that once the danger became apparent they were under a duty to warn users, and they had failed to carry out this duty.

Even if a duty of care can be established, it is still necessary for the plaintiff to prove that the defendant was in breach of that duty, and that there is a sufficient causal connection between the breach and the loss that the plaintiff has suffered. The defendant will be in breach if he has failed to take as much care in producing his software as a reasonable man in the same position, professing the same expertise, would have done. The questions which arise here are the same as when a breach of a contractual duty of care is alleged, and have already been examined in 3.1.

The requirement that there be a sufficient causal link between breach and loss may also raise problems. The test for sufficiency is a simple one – is the loss a foreseeable result of the breach? This test was laid down in *The Wagon Mound (No. 1)* [1961] AC 388, where oil that had carelessly been discharged from the defendant's ship was ignited by sparks from the plaintiff's welding operations and burnt down the plaintiff's wharf. On the evidence before it, the court held that fire damage was not a foreseeable consequence of the discharge, and thus the plaintiff's case failed.

More recent cases such as *Anns* v *Merton London Borough Council* [1978] AC 728 and *Junior Books Ltd* v *Veitchi Co. Ltd* [1983] 1 AC 520 have emphasised the close connection between duty and causation. The test for a duty of care is, in part at least, whether the defendant ought to have foreseen that damage of that type might occur. Nevertheless, it is possible to envisage situations where a duty of care is owed but the loss is an unforeseeable consequence of the breach of duty. Let us imagine that, owing to a defect in its design, an accounting program destroys all its data, and that for some reason the user has failed to take back-up copies of the data. Assuming the designer of the program owes the user a duty of care (e.g., the program was specially modified for the user) then it is clear that some loss of data is foreseeable. Nevertheless, it is not foreseeable that all data would be lost, as it is standard practice to take regular back-ups. It follows that further consequential losses – perhaps loss of business, penalties imposed by the Inland Revenue etc. – will also be unforeseeable consequences of the breach.

One final point that should be considered here is that many users of software, in addition to their contract with the supplier, are bound by a licensing agreement entered into between the producer and themselves. This licence operates as a collateral contract,[34] and in many cases will contain clauses excluding the producer's liability for negligent design. It is quite likely that such a clause, insofar as it amounts to a promise by the user not to sue in negligence, will be caught by s. 2(2) or s. 3 of the Unfair Contract Terms Act 1977 and thus fail to protect the producer unless it satisfies the test of reasonableness. The question of whether a clause does satisfy this test can, of course, only be decided by reference to the particular facts of the case, though relevant factors are likely to be the price of the software, how clearly its limitations are spelt out in the documentation, and whether the function performed is innovative or commonplace.[35] Even if the clause fails the test, it may still have a residual importance as a warning to the user of the reliance he may safely put on the results of the software. In *Hedley Byrne & Co. Ltd* v *Heller & Partners Ltd* [1964] AC 465 the bank was in the end held not liable in negligence to the plaintiff because it had issued its reference 'without responsibility', thus making it clear to the plaintiff that reliance could not be placed upon it.

3.4.2.2 Negligent operation The allegation that the plaintiff's loss was caused by the defendant's negligent operation of his computer system will generally give rise to few special legal problems. In most, if not all cases, the defendant will be performing some function affecting the plaintiff, and the computer will merely be the means by which he performs the function – for example, an air traffic controller. The question, 'Did he take sufficient care in operating the computer?' is really part of the larger question, 'Did he take sufficient care in performing that function?'

---

34. If it operates at all when the software is mass-marketed – see chapter 2.7; Smith, 'Tear-open licences' – are they enforceable in England' (1986) 2 CL&P 128; Millard, 'Shrink Wrap Licensing' (1987) 3 Computer Law and Security Report 8.
35. See 3.2 above.

The problem of duty of care was considered in the American case of *Independent School District No. 454, Fairmont, Minnesota* v *Statistical Tabulating Corporation* (1973) 359 F Supp 1095. In that case, a firm of surveyors had been employed by the plaintiff school to value its buildings for insurance purposes. The surveyors employed the defendant corporation to carry out the computational work on their measurements. Unfortunately this work was performed carelessly, with the result that the school was under-insured and suffered losses when buildings caught fire. There was no point in bringing an action against the surveyors as they had performed their work with care and skill, so the school brought an action against the defendant. The court held that the defendant did owe a duty of care to the plaintiff, as it knew that the school would rely on its work in insuring the buildings, and the class of potential plaintiffs was small (in this case, one member). It can be seen that the approach here is similar to that adopted in *Junior Books Ltd* v *Veitchi Co. Ltd* [1983] 1 AC 520, probably because in both cases the losses caused by the negligence were purely financial.

However, it seems fair to say that the courts will be less reluctant to find a duty to take care in operating a computer system than in designing one precisely because the class of plaintiffs will, in the end, be small. The analogy may be drawn with roadworks; although the number of people at risk is potentially very large, in the end only one or two are likely to fall into the hole. Similarly, a negligently *operated* computerised accounting system is likely to cause loss to a few clients only. A negligently *designed* accounting system may cause loss to *all* those potentially at risk (its users) and for this reason a duty of care may be held not to exist.

With regard to the question whether the defendant was in breach of his duty of care, that is, whether he took sufficient care in performing that function, it should be recognised that the introduction of new technology will have an effect on the required standard of performance. The fact that a computer has been used may lead those who are affected by the defendant's performance of his function to expect a higher standard of performance than they would be entitled to expect if a computer had not been used. A failure to perform at this standard may well be evidence of negligence, precisely because proper operation of the computer would produce a higher standard. Thus in the American case of *Southwestern Bell Telephone Co.* v *Reeves* (1979) 578 SW 2d 795, in which the telephone company failed for a year to re-route the plaintiff lawyer's telephone calls to his new number, the jury inferred negligence on the telephone company's part from the fact that the only reasonable explanation was some malfunctioning of the computer or other equipment involved, all of which were under the company's control. The First Court of Civil Appeals, Houston, refused to hold that there was insufficient evidence on which to base this inference.[36]

Nevertheless, it is reasonable to expect 'teething problems' in the introduction of any new technology, and the fact that these problems are foreseeable does not mean that it will be negligent to introduce the new system. The

---

36. See also *County Trust Co.* v *Pascack Valley Bank & Trust Co.* (1966) 225 A 2d 605.

question is whether the new system will, in the end, produce an improvement, and of course whether sufficient care was taken in its introduction and operation, and in curing the initial difficulties. It was for this reason that in the American case of *Gosney* v *State of California* (1970) 89 Cal Rptr 390 the court refused to grant an injunction to force the State to operate its new computerised system of social security payments properly and to introduce new checks and 'fail-safe' procedures. Overall the new system reduced the number of errors; the question of negligence in respect of individual cases could be left to trial of those actions.

3.4.2.3   Negligence in relying on the system's output   We have already seen that a person who relies on the output of a computer system that has been negligently designed or operated may have a claim against the designer or operator. Is it possible, though, that the very act of relying on the system might be negligent?

Clearly the answer to this question must be yes if the defendant who relied on the system knew, or ought to have known, that the system was defective in design or operation. Generally, however, the defendant's reliance will not be negligent if he had no reason to suppose that the output was defective and had acted reasonably in choosing to rely on it. Thus in the *Independent School District No. 454* case discussed in 3.4.2.2 it is clear that the surveyors were not negligent as they had no reason to suspect that the data had been carelessly processed, and had chosen an apparently competent firm to undertake the work. Similarly in *Scott* v *District of Columbia* (1985) 493 A 2d 319 (see 3.4) the police officer who arrested the plaintiff on the erroneous warrant had not been negligent because '[the plaintiff's] protests gave [the officer] no factual basis for questioning the accuracy of a computer system regularly relied on by officers throughout the metropolitan area'. Once there is evidence, however, that the system has produced an incorrect output, reliance on that output will be a breach of duty. This is similar to *Prendergast* v *Sam & Dee Ltd* (1988) *The Times*, 24 March 1988, where a pharmacist misread a doctor's writing on a prescription form and as a result supplied drugs to the plaintiff which caused him to suffer brain damage. The court held that, even on the misreading made by the pharmacist, the prescription was clearly defective (the drug he thought had been prescribed was not made in the strength stipulated on the prescription) and thus the pharmacist was under a duty to check the prescription with the doctor before he dispensed it. His failure to do so was therefore negligent.

It should also be recognised that where a computer system is under the defendant's control the fact that it produced incorrect results may suggest so strongly that the work was undertaken negligently that the doctrine of *res ipsa loquitur* comes into operation. It will then be for the defendant to show that the system of work was sufficiently well-planned and designed that it was reasonable for him to rely on the results. The position is similar to that in *Henderson* v *Henry E. Jenkins & Sons* [1970] AC 282 where a lorry's brakes failed when a brake pipe fractured, injuring the plaintiff. The defendants showed that they operated a safe system of inspection, and argued that this demonstrated that they had taken sufficient care. However, they failed to show that they had no knowledge of special facts that might render their system inadequate (for example, that the brake pipe had been exposed to corrosive agents such as salt water) and as a result were held liable.[37]

It is quite possible to imagine situations where it might be insufficiently careful to rely on the output of the system even though there is no particular reason to suspect that the system has worked incorrectly, because the general possibility of its inaccuracy ought to be in the defendant's mind. One example was suggested in 'Computer horizons' in *The Times* of 1 October 1987, where it was pointed out that auditors of a company's accounts may well be negligent in declaring the accounts to be a 'true and fair' picture of the financial position of the company precisely *because* the accounting system runs on a computer. The dynamic nature of a 'real-time' system, where the information is constantly changing, and the fact that data can simply and untraceably be altered, means that the auditor cannot be certain that the information on which he bases his audit is accurate.

In America, this point has been considered in *Chernick* v *Fasig-Tipton Kentucky Inc.* (1986 unreported). In that case, the defendants were intermediaries in the sale of racehorses. They sold a horse belonging to the plaintiffs to Cloverfield Farm Inc., who intervened in the action. The horse was described in the sale catalogue as 'barren and free from infection', which suggested that the horse would be suitable for breeding purposes. In fact the horse, a mare, had twice spontaneously aborted foals, a fact which substantially affected the horse's value. When Cloverfield discovered this, they complained to the defendants, and eventually a case came to trial in which the plaintiff sellers sued the defendants for the purchase money (which the defendants had refused to hand over) and Cloverfield sued both the plaintiffs and the defendants. It is the action by Cloverfield against the defendants that concerns us here. The defendants had prepared their sale catalogue from information supplied by the plaintiffs, and from information on the Jockey Club computer. It was well-known that the information on the computer was likely to be inaccurate. Nevertheless, the defendants relied on this information to check the plaintiffs' assertions. Not surprisingly, the court at first instance held that the defendants had been negligent, and the Court of Appeals of Kentucky agreed. Unfortunately for Cloverfield, in spite of this negligence, their action against the defendants failed on a technicality.

A similar point was made in *Brown* v *United States* (1984) 599 F Supp 877 where two fishing boats had been lost at sea due to an inaccurate weather forecast. The National Oceanographic and Atmospheric Administration, which produced the forecast, knew that the relevant weather buoy was out of action but nevertheless issued the forecast without adding a warning that it was potentially inaccurate. It was held that this amounted to negligence, and thus the plaintiff's case succeeded.

Another reason why relying on the output of the system might be negligent is that, although the output is accurate, it is not sufficient on its own to justify

---

37. See also *CK Security Systems Inc* v *Hartford Accident & Indemnity Co.* (1976) 223 SE 2d 453.

the reliance that was placed on it. In *The Lady Gwendolen* [1965] P 294 a ship was fitted with the new technology of radar to assist the master in avoiding collisions at sea. In fact, the radar induced the master of the ship to travel at high speeds, even in fog. At the time he collided with another ship, in dense fog and in the restricted channel of the Mersey, he was not only travelling at top speed, but was operating the radar incorrectly. The court was clear that even if the master had operated the radar properly, he would still have been negligent because the radar did not give sufficient warning of other shipping to allow him to proceed at such a speed. Similarly in *Central Maine Power Co.* v *Foster Wheeler Corporation* (1988 unreported) a US power company brought an action in negligence against the designer of a condenser which leaked and damaged other parts of the plant. It was held that the power company was contributorily negligent as its employees had relied solely on the computer system to bring any alarms to their notice, though at the time it was not programmed to do so, and thus failed to prevent the damage.

Problems in this area will often arise when professionals give advice which is based on the output of a computer program. For example, if a solicitor were to undertake a LEXIS search in an attempt to discover the answer to his client's problem, and, having discovered an apparently relevant case, based his advice entirely on the results of the search, he would undoubtedly be liable in negligence if it transpired that the case had been overruled or superseded by statute.

3.4.2.4 *Failure to use a computer system*

The question of when failure to use a computer system might amount to a failure to be sufficiently careful, and thus a breach of duty, will always depend on the particular circumstances of the case. The mere fact that use of a computer would have prevented harm to the plaintiff is not, in itself, proof of negligence, though it must be proved in order to establish the necessary element of causation. If non-use did cause the plaintiff's loss the question will then be whether a reasonable man in the defendant's position would have used the computer so as to avoid the loss. This will be decided by reference, amongst other things, to the 'state of the art' in that particular field.

If the possibility of harm through non-use of the computer is not known at the time of the loss, then it cannot be negligent to fail to use one. For example, it is obvious that a solicitor who advises his client wrongly will cause the client loss. At the time of writing, however, expert systems that might prevent this happening have not been developed to the stage of commercial availability, with the result that it cannot be negligent not to use them. If such systems are developed and prove successful, it will in the end be negligent not to use them, provided that they are sufficiently cheap and easy to use that a reasonable solicitor would provide himself with them. Once the 'state of the art' both recognises the problem and produces usable solutions, it will be negligent not to adopt those solutions even if the custom in that area is not to use them. In the American case of *The T. J. Hooper* (1932) 60 F 2d 737 the plaintiff's barges were lost in a storm at sea whilst being towed by the defendant's tugs. If the tugs had been fitted with radios, they could have received warning of the storm and taken shelter, thus avoiding the loss of the barges. In spite of the fact that it was not common practice to fit radios to tugs, the court held that the defendant was negligent – the technology was easily available, comparatively cheap, and its utility was clear. More recently in *United States Fire Insurance Co.* v *United States* (1986) 806 F 2d 1529 it was held that the actions of the Coast Guard in calculating the site of a navigation beacon by manual rather than computerised means, when the computer system was both available and known to be many times more accurate, was potentially negligent and thus an issue to be decided by the jury at the trial. Similarly, in *Chandler* v *United States* (1988) 687 F Supp 1515 the plaintiff was awarded $1,000 for negligent disclosure of tax return information. The disclosure took place when the IRS instructed Mrs Chandler's employers to deduct arrears of tax from her salary, although a computer search (which was not made) would have revealed that the arrears had already been paid. This was held to be negligent.

The position is much the same at English law. In *General Cleaning Contractors Ltd* v *Christmas* [1953] AC 180, the plaintiff was a window cleaner who was injured when the lower sash of a window suddenly fell. He claimed that his employer had been negligent in not instituting a system of precautions to prevent this from happening. The defence put forward by the employers was that the trade took no such precautions. Lord Reid said: '. . . even if it were proved that it is the general practice to neglect this danger, I would hold that it ought not to be neglected and that precautions should be taken' because the danger was so obvious, and because, although it was not clear exactly what precautions could be taken, it was apparent that the problem could very easily be solved, e.g., by wedging the window.

It follows from *General Cleaning Contractors Ltd* v *Christmas* that there is scope for a court to decide that failure to use also encompasses failure to invent or modify a computer system to prevent harm and such a failure might amount to negligence if the invention or modification would be simple to effect. In order to decide whether a reasonable man would make such an invention or modification, it is necessary to balance the seriousness of the potential loss, the likelihood of its occurrence, and the expense of invention or modification. It should, however, be noted that in the cases that establish this principle[38] there was in each case a precaution that could have been taken that would *certainly* have prevented the plaintiff's loss. Whether the courts would be prepared to hold that a failure to innovate a system which *might* prevent loss (e.g., an expert system) amounts to negligence remains a matter for speculation.[39]

In areas where the new technology has already provided some new service, the question of whether a failure to use it amounts to negligence is greatly exercising the minds of practitioners. For example, is it negligent for a solicitor not to use LEXIS when advising a client? The answer to this question is probably no, if the matter is a straightforward one. If the matter is complex, or is in an area where the law is constantly being modified, then it would seem likely that a solicitor would be negligent if he did not either use LEXIS or take

---

38. E.g., *Paris* v *Stepney Borough Council* [1951] AC 367, *Bolton* v *Stone* [1951] AC 850.
39. See further *Midgen* v *Chase Manhattan Bank* (1981) 32 UCC Rep 937.

counsel's opinion. This again must remain a matter for speculation until the courts have pronounced on it. It is, however, known that many firms of solicitors are insisting that work is checked on LEXIS before it goes out to clients.

3.5 CONCLUSION

As yet the English courts have not been called upon to decide the issues raised in this chapter. The problems, however, lie not so much in the technology as in the application of existing principles to facts that are entirely novel and which have few conceptual similarities with the kind of facts the judiciary are accustomed to encounter. This need not be an insoluble problem; its solution requires the education of the legal profession not merely in how to use the new technology but also in how it works. A lawyer who is entirely ignorant of the processes involved in the creation and running of software can hardly be expected to understand how the principles of negligence, or indeed any other rules of law, should be applied to it. In *Ministry of Housing & Local Government* v *Sharp* [1970] 2 QB 223 Salmon LJ, referring to a proposal to computerise the Land Registry, said, 'Computers might produce an inaccurate certificate without negligence on the part of anyone'. As we have seen, this proposition is unlikely to be true, and the number of judges who would support it is rather smaller than in 1970.

CHAPTER FOUR

Copyright

Christopher Millard

4.1 INTRODUCTION

4.1.1 The nature of copyright

Notwithstanding its considerable and ever-increasing significance to business, intellectual property continues to be one of the law's more obscure and esoteric fields. In popular parlance, confusion often reigns and talk of copyrighting an invention or patenting a trade mark is not uncommon. Such misunderstandings are, perhaps, not surprising given the highly technical nature of much of the law in this area and the scope for overlaps and conflicts between the various rights.

Nevertheless, the effective protection and exploitation of intellectual property rights is crucial to the success, and in some cases the survival, of a growing number of businesses. Nowhere is this more strikingly the case than in the computer industry. For example, the right to manufacture, sell, buy or use a complex product such as a computer system comprising hardware and software may depend on licences of any or all of patents, copyrights, design rights, know-how and trade marks. Similarly, the primary assets of a software house will usually be its copyright works. The focus of this chapter will be on copyright. Other intellectual property rights will be covered later in this book.

What then is copyright? Copyright is, in essence, a right given to authors or creators of 'works', such as books, films or computer programs, to control the copying or other exploitation of such works. In marked contrast to patent rights, copyright begins automatically on the creation of a 'work' without the need for compliance with any formalities. The only prerequisites for protection which apply to all works are that the work must be of a type in which copyright can subsist, and that either the author is a 'qualifying person', or the work has been published or broadcast in an appropriate manner. In the case of certain types of works, including literary works such as books and computer programs, the work must also be 'original' and it must be 'recorded' in some form (e.g., written down or stored in computer memory).

In addition to controlling the making of copies, the owner of copyright in a work has the exclusive right to control publication, performance, broadcasting and the making of adaptations of the work. In certain cases, the author, director or commissioner of a work may be entitled to exercise certain 'moral rights' which may include the right to be identified with a work and to object to distortion or unjustified treatment of the work.

Where any of the various exclusive rights which collectively make up copyright in a work have been exercised without permission, civil remedies may be available to the owner or author. In certain cases criminal sanctions may also be brought to bear, principally where copyright is being infringed with a view to commercial gain. Most of these concepts and terms are discussed in more detail in the rest of this chapter.

4.1.2 Evolution of United Kingdom copyright law

English copyright law has a history going back five centuries and has been regulated by statute for almost three.[1] The first modern copyright law, the Copyright Act 1709 was an attempt to balance the interests of authors and publishers in the face of the leading-edge technology of the day, the printing press. Technology has since moved on and so has the law. The two have not, however, always been in step. Notwithstanding regular piecemeal amendment of the law, the gap between copyright law and new media has periodically had to be closed, or at least narrowed, by means of a radical overhaul of the law. Increased sophistication in the means for commercial exploitation of the economic value of copyright has been a particularly powerful catalyst for change. Cable and satellite broadcasting of films and other works, and the distribution of computer programs and other works in digital form are examples.

A major realignment occurred with the enactment of the Copyright, Designs and Patents Act 1988 ('the 1988 Act').[2] Its predecessor in the copyright field, the Copyright Act 1956 ('the 1956 Act'), had been the subject both of detailed reform discussions[3] and temporary piecemeal amendments[4] for half of its time

---

1. For an interesting historical review see Breyer, 'The Uneasy Case for Copyright: A Study of Copyright in Books, Photocopies and Computer Programs' (1970), 84 Harv LR 281.
2. Royal assent 15 November 1988.
3. A committee set up in 1973 under the chairmanship of Mr Justice Whitford reported in 1977 that the time had come for a general revision of the 1956 Act: *Copyright and Designs Law: Report of the Committee to Consider the Law on Copyright and Designs* (Cmnd 6732) (London: HMSO, 1977). This was followed by two Green Papers which did little to advance the reform process: *Reform of the Law Relating to Copyright, Designs and Performers' Protection* (Cmnd 8302) (London: HMSO, 1981) and *Intellectual Property Rights and Innovation* (Cmnd 9117) (London: HMSO, 1983). The publication in 1986 of a White Paper entitled *Intellectual Property and Innovation* (Cmnd 9712) (London: HMSO, 1986) set the stage for a general overhaul of the law.
4. Design Copyright Act 1968; Copyright Act 1956 (Amendment) Act 1982; Copyright (Amendment) Act 1983; Cable and Broadcasting Act 1984; Copyright (Computer Software) Amendment Act 1985.

on the statute book. The 1988 Act, most of the provisions of which came into force on 1 August 1989,[5] represents an attempt to start again with a clean slate. On this slate are written both a restatement of the general principles of copyright, and also various sets of rules to deal with specific types of copyright work and their commercial exploitation. Although there is considerable scope for criticising the 1988 Act at a detailed level, on the whole it is a far more coherent, comprehensive and accessible statement of the law than the statutes which it replaced.

4.1.3 The Copyright, Designs and Patents Act 1988
The Copyright, Designs and Patents Act 1988, as its name suggests, does not deal solely with copyright. A significant new property right, to be known as 'design right', has been established; the law relating to registered designs has been changed; changes have been made to patent and trade mark law; and the law relating to performers' protection has been reformed and restated.[6] Unless otherwise indicated, references to sections are to those of the 1988 Act.

It is too early to look to the courts for much guidance on interpreting the 1988 Act. In the meantime, some pointers can be obtained from court decisions based on the 1956 Act (as amended), and indeed on earlier statutes, such as the Copyright Act 1911. The extent to which reliance can be placed on such old decisions is, unfortunately, not at all clear. This is because s. 172 of the 1988 Act, given the marginal note 'General provisions as to construction', provides:

(1) This Part restates and amends the law of copyright, that is, the provisions of the Copyright Act 1956, as amended.

(2) A provision of this Part which corresponds to a provision of the previous law shall not be construed as departing from the previous law merely because of a change of expression.

(3) Decisions under the previous law may be referred to for the purpose of establishing whether a provision of this Part departs from the previous law, or otherwise for establishing the true construction of this Part.

Each part of this section seems to introduce a layer of confusion. The first subsection states that the 1988 Act is both a restatement and an amendment of the old law. The second provides that a change in language does not necessarily indicate a change in meaning although, by implication, it may do. The third suggests that we look to court decisions based on the 1956 Act to see whether there has in fact been a change in meaning and generally to assist in understanding the new Act. Thus, even if it can be shown that a particular provision of the 1988 Act 'corresponds' to a provision of the 1956 Act, the fact that the provision has been redrafted in different language may or may not

5. The Copyright, Designs and Patents Act 1988 (Commencement No. 1) Order 1989 (SI 1989) No. 816.
6. For a helpful introduction to the Act as a whole, which incorporates the full text of the statute, see Gerald Dworkin and Richard D. Taylor, *Blackstone's Guide to the Copyright, Designs and Patents Act 1988* (London: Blackstone Press, 1989).

indicate anything about its meaning. It is particularly difficult to see how cases decided under the 1956 Act could illuminate Parliament's intentions in 1988 in including, excluding or substituting specific words in the 1988 Act. There is no reference to the status, if any, of cases decided under older statutes such as the Copyright Act 1911. Taken as a whole, s. 172 should give advocates plenty of scope for argument over semantics, and leave courts with considerable discretion as to whether to rely on or disregard particular precedents as they seek to interpret and apply the new law.

4.1.4   EC Directives and their implementation in the United Kingdom

Differences in the nature and scope of the intellectual property rights available in the 12 EC member States have frequently given rise to trade barriers. In seeking to limit the effects of such restrictions, the European Commission and the European Court have drawn distinctions between the existence and the exercise of intellectual property rights. Ownership of an intellectual property right is not inherently anti-competitive, indeed the Treaty of Rome sanctions import and export restrictions which can be justified as being 'for the protection of industrial or commercial property'.[7] However, attempts to use intellectual property rights as a means of carving up the internal market are vulnerable to challenge under the Treaty. According to the 'exhaustion of rights' doctrine developed by the European Court, goods which have been lawfully put on the market in one of the member States by or with the consent of the owner, must be permitted to circulate freely throughout the Community. Of particular significance to the computer industry is the availability and scope of copyright protection for software products. In June 1988 the Commission published a Green Paper entitled *Copyright and the Challenge of Technology*. In that discussion document the Commission inclined towards the view that copyright is the most appropriate form of protection for computer programs and should provide the foundation for a Directive on software protection. Comments were, however, invited on a number of issues relating to the precise nature and scope of the exclusive rights which member States should be required to grant software owners.

Following a period of consultation which ended in December 1988, a Directive on the legal Protection of Computer Programs ('the Software Directive') was adopted by the Council of Ministers on 14 May 1991.[8] Legislation to implement the Software Directive in the United Kingdom, the Copyright (Computer Programs) Regulations 1992, is expected to be enacted in time for the implementation deadline. Specific aspects of the Software Directive and United Kingdom implementing legislation are discussed later in the chapter.

Additionally, the European Commission has recently adopted a proposal for a Directive on the Legal Protection of Databases.[9] This measure and its

---

7. Treaty of Rome, art. 36.
8. 91/250/EEC, OJ No. L 122, 17 May 1991, p. 42.
9. COM(92). 24 final – syn 393 OJ No. C 156, 23 June 1992, p. 4.

implications for the United Kingdom are also discussed later in this chapter. The Directive requires member States, by 1 January 1993, to adopt whatever legislative measures are necessary to protect 'computer programs' by copyright as literary works.

4.2 IN WHAT CAN COPYRIGHT SUBSIST?

4.2.1 General criteria for protection

4.2.1.1 Works   Section 1 of the 1988 Act provides that:

(1)   Copyright is a property right which subsists in accordance with this Part in the following descriptions of work—
   (a)   original literary, dramatic, musical or artistic works,
   (b)   sound recordings, films, broadcasts or cable programmes, and
   (c)   the typographical arrangement of published editions.
(2)   In this Part 'copyright work' means a work of any of those descriptions in which copyright subsists.

Many products which are protected by copyright do not fit neatly into any single category from this list. On the contrary, by the time they are brought to market, most films, books, software packages, and other composite works comprise a complex bundle of discrete copyright works. Most of the categories of work listed above are of relevance in the computer context. For example, a software product such as a word-processing package could be analysed as a collection of copyright works as follows:

(a)   The program code which, when run on a computer system, provides word processing functions would be a literary work: s. 3(1) of the 1988 Act defines 'literary work' as including 'a computer program'.
(b)   Any documentation or written materials supplied with the package would be one or more conventional literary works.
(c)   Any built-in dictionary, thesaurus, or help-screen files would be literary works, but would probably not be computer programs.
(d)   Artwork included on packaging or in documentation would be one or more artistic works: see s. 4.
(e)   Graphic works or photographs used to produce screen images would be artistic works.
(f)   Copyright would subsist in the typographical arrangement of the documentation supplied with the package: s. 1(1) defines 'the typographical arrangement of published editions' as a separate category of copyright work.

In addition to these six categories of work, three other types of work may be embodied in an audiovisual product such as a video-game:

(g)   The sound track which is produced when the game is run or played might include a recording of one or more musical works: s. 3(1) defines 'musical work' as 'a work consisting of music'.

(h) The sound track would itself be a sound recording: s. 5(1) defines 'sound recording' as '(a) a recording of sounds, from which the sounds may be reproduced, or (b) a recording of the whole or any part of a literary, dramatic or musical work, from which sounds reproducing the work or part may be produced'.

(i) Any set sequence of images which is produced when the program is run would be a film: s. 5(1) defines 'film' as meaning 'a recording on any medium from which a moving image may by any means be produced'.

A further three categories of work may be relevant in relation to a database product:

(j) A database may be protected as a literary work: s. 3(1) defines 'literary work' as including 'a table or compilation'.

(k) Some or all of the items comprised in a database may be protected separately as literary works.

(l) If made available to subscribers to a broadcast videotext or cable service, the video-game would be a broadcast or cable programme: see definitions of 'broadcast' in s. 6(1) and of 'cable programme service' in s. 7(1).

The fact that a software product is not a single work for copyright purposes has a number of significant consequences. For one thing, many different authors, graphic designers, programmers, publishers etc. may be involved in the production and marketing of the product and, as individual authors, may have separate claims to copyright in their respective contributions (see 4.3.1). Secondly, copyright protection will expire at different times in respect of different component parts of the product (see 4.3.3). Thirdly, the scope of copyright protection will not be the same for all of the works which make up a package. For example, unauthorised adaptation of the program code would infringe copyright, whereas there would be no copyright restriction on adaptation of the various artistic works, provided it did not amount to copying or some other restricted act (see 4.4.2.2 and 4.5.2). Fourthly, an author of the text or designer of artwork included in the documentation might be able to exercise moral rights in respect of the works they contributed, whereas a programmer could never make such a claim in respect of the program code (see 4.6).

4.2.1.2 Recording There can be no copyright in a literary, dramatic or musical work 'unless and until it is recorded, in writing or otherwise'. The term of copyright starts to run from the time of such recording (1988 Act, s. 3(2)). 'Writing' is given an expansive definition in the Act as including 'any form of notation or code, whether by hand or otherwise and regardless of the method by which, or medium in or on which, it is recorded, and "written" shall be construed accordingly' (1988 Act, s. 179). Storage in any form of machine-readable media would thus appear to qualify as 'writing'. The words 'or otherwise' would cover fixation in the form of, for example, an analogue recording of sounds or spoken words.

The Act does not contain a definition of 'recording' as such. It is not clear whether a degree of permanence is implied. By analogy with 'sound recording', which is defined, the essence of the concept of recording of a work is probably that there is something from which the work, or part of it, can be reproduced. Presumably, once a work has been fixed in such a form, copyright will continue to subsist in the work notwithstanding the subsequent destruction of the original recording of the work, even where no copy has ever been made in a material form. This issue might be significant if a substantial part of a program, or other work, were to be reproduced from human memory after the author had accidentally or deliberately deleted the original from the memory of the computer on which it was created.

4.2.1.3 Originality Literary, dramatic, musical or artistic works are only protected under the 1988 Act if they are original (1988 Act, s. 1(1)(a)). There is no definition or explanation of the concept of originality. However, the word 'original' was used in both the 1911 and 1956 Copyright Acts and, almost invariably, was interpreted by the courts as relating essentially to origin rather than to substantive considerations such as novelty. Thus, a work will usually be original provided merely that it originates with the author or creator and has not been copied. While some labour and skill must have been expended in creating the work, courts have resisted arguments that the originality requirement should be interpreted as importing connotations of aesthetic quality or innovation.[10]

The low level at which the originality threshold has tended to be fixed by the courts means that even relatively simple and utterly mundane works can be protected by copyright. This is very important in the computer context where programs and other functional works may lack aesthetic appeal and be of minimal creativity yet be of tremendous commercial value. Were a higher threshold to be set for the originality test, it is probable that much computer software and data would fall completely outside copyright.[11] The one area where, until recently, the originality criterion was a particular cause for concern for the United Kingdom computer industry, computer-generated works, has been specifically addressed in the 1988 Act and is discussed in 4.2.2.3.

4.2.1.4 Qualification Copyright will not subsist in any work unless certain 'qualification requirements' are met. The rules, which are set out in Part IX of the 1988 Act (ss. 153 to 162), are complex. For most types of work, however, the general rule is that either the author must be a 'qualifying person' at the time the work is made or, alternatively, the work must be first published in the United Kingdom or some other country to which the Act extends. An author

---

10. See, for example, *Victoria Park Racing & Recreation Grounds Co. Ltd* v *Taylor* (1937) 58 CLR 479; *Football League Ltd* v *Littlewoods Pools Ltd* [1959] Ch 637; *Ladbroke (Football) Ltd* v *William Hill (Football) Ltd* [1964] 1 WLR 273.
11. As has occurred, for example, in West Germany. See Moritz Rottinger, 'The legal protection of computer programs in Germany: renunciation of copyrights?' (1987) 4 CL&P 34.

will be a qualifying person if he or she is a citizen of, or domiciled or resident in, the United Kingdom or some other country to which the Act extends. The qualification requirements will also be satisfied if the author is a citizen of, or domiciled or resident in, or first publication is in, a country to which the Act has been 'applied'.

By virtue of a statutory instrument which came into force along with most of the provisions of the 1988 Act on 1st August 1989, Part I of the Act has been applied to works of different types originating in over 100 specified countries.[12] Special rules apply to certain countries which are not members of either the Berne Copyright Convention or the Universal Copyright Convention but in which the United Kingdom government is satisfied there exists adequate protection for copyright. An order has also been made applying Part I of the Act to works made by officers or employees of the United Nations and certain other international organisations which would otherwise not qualify for protection.[13]

4.2.2 Protection of programs, data, and computer-generated works

4.2.2.1 Computer programs Whereas, in its original form, the 1956 Act contained no reference whatsoever to computers or computing, in the 1988 Act computers make their first appearance in s. 3. Further direct and indirect references are scattered throughout the Act. Section 3(1) of the 1988 Act defines 'literary work' as including '(a) a table or compilation, and (b) a computer program'. This form of words has made it completely clear for the first time that programs are literary works and not merely to be protected as though they were literary works.[14]

What remains unclear is the scope of the term 'computer program' which has still not been defined. Foreign legislatures and international organisations which have defined the term have tended to characterise programs in terms of their information-processing capabilities, with specific emphasis on their ability to cause hardware to perform functions.[15] We have already seen that a software package such as a video-game is in fact a complex collection of separate copyright works. Only some of the works will be computer programs. To take another example, most of the material supplied in printed form or on

---

12. The Copyright (Application to Other Countries) Order 1989 (No. 2) (SI 1989 No. 1293).
13. The Copyright (International Organisations) Order 1989 (SI 1989 No. 989). In force, 1 August 1989.
14. As was the case under the 1956 Act, as amended by s. 1 of the Copyright (Computer Software) Amendment Act 1985.
15. For example, 'A "computer program" is a set of statements or instructions to be used directly or indirectly in a computer in order to bring about a certain result' (United States Copyright Act 1976, 17 USC s. 101); 'A "computer program" is a set of instructions expressed in words, codes, schemes or in any other form, which is capable, when incorporated in a machine-readable medium, of causing a "computer" – an electronic or similar device having information-processing capabilities – to perform or achieve a particular task or result' (World Intellectual Property Organisation, Model Provisions on the Protection of Computer Software, 1978, restated in Memorandum on a Possible Protocol to the Berne Convention, 1991).

disk in a word-processing package will not be 'programs' in the sense of computer code which will cause a computer to process information. The printed materials will be conventional literary and other works. Moreover a great deal of the material supplied on the disk or disks will be digital versions of a dictionary, a thesaurus, and help-screen information, all of which, again, will be conventional literary and possibly artistic works.

The existence of special provisions in the 1988 Act which apply to computer programs but not to literary works in general means that the two terms are certainly not coextensive. Moreover, the inclusion in the Act of many provisions which deal with the use and distribution of conventional works in electronic form makes it clear that a work is not a program just because it is stored digitally. Thus it is arguable that provisions applicable specifically to computer programs, such as the restriction on rental (discussed in part 4.4.2.3), will not apply to a great deal of the material which is typically supplied with program code, even though the whole package may be described for marketing purposes as a 'program' or as 'software'.[16]

Neither the Software Directive nor the draft Copyright (Computer Programs) Regulations 1992 shed much light on the definitional question. The preamble (recitals) to the Directive merely includes a statement that 'the function of a computer program is to communicate and work together with other components of a computer system'. Article 1.1 is somewhat more explicit in stating that 'for the purpose of this Directive, the term "computer programs" shall include their preparatory design material'. The draft Copyright (Computer Programs) Regulations 1992 contain no reference to the meaning of the term 'computer program'. While the term, as used in the 1988 Act, appears susceptible to a very broad construction, it is not clear that it would cover 'preparatory design material'. It is, perhaps, surprising that the draft Regulations do not contain a provision to deal with this point.

4.2.2.2 Data and databases Still more uncertain is the nature of copyright protection for data and databases under the 1988 Act. It is important to distinguish between, on the one hand, the copyright which may subsist in a database as a table or compilation and, on the other hand, copyright in any underlying works. Copyright can subsist in a literary work consisting of a 'table or compilation' (1988 Act, s. 3(1)) quite separately from the copyright which may subsist in any works comprised in the table or compilation. In some cases, numerous authors and owners of copyright may be involved as, for example, where a large number of literary works, such as journal articles, are published collectively as a database. In other cases there may be no underlying works in which copyright can subsist. There is unlikely to be copyright in a single piece of statistical or scientific data, or in the current or historic price of a single

---

16. The term 'software' tends to have broader connotations than 'program'. For example: 'Software [means a] set of computer programs, procedures, and possibly associated documentation concerned with the operation of a data processing system, e.g., compilers, library routines, manuals, circuit diagrams' (United States Copyright Office, Library of Congress, *Compendium of Copyright Office Practices*, 1984, para. 32).

quoted share. Yet a compilation of such data or share prices might be of immense commercial value and would, in principle, subject to the basic originality and qualification requirements already discussed, be capable of protection as a literary work. Since there is no UK statutory definition of 'original', it is necessary to look to case law for guidance.

In the House of Lords case of *Ladbroke (Football) Ltd* v *William Hill (Football) Ltd* [1964] 1 WLR 273, Lord Devlin held that:

> there is copyright in every original literary work, which by definition includes compilations, so that there can be copyright in such productions as timetables and directories, provided always they are 'original'. The requirement of originality means that the product must originate from the author in the sense that it is the result of a substantial degree of skill, industry or experience employed by him.

Thus, in *Independent Television Publications Ltd* v *Time Out Ltd* [1984] FSR 54, and *British Broadcasting Corpn* v *Time Out Ltd* [1984] FSR 64, the court held that the plaintiff's television programme schedules were not mere information (as the defendant had argued), but constituted compilations, requiring a great degree of skill and labour in their preparation. Similarly, in *Express Newspapers plc* v *Liverpool Daily Post & Echo plc* [1985] 1 WLR 1089, the court held that in preparing grids and sequences of letters for the purposes of a newspaper competition, the plaintiffs had expended a great deal of skill and labour and that therefore the grids and sequences were literary works protected by copyright. This was so even though a computer program had been used to prepare the grids and sequences (see 4.2.2.3). The present attitude of the UK courts still, therefore, seems to reflect the findings of the court in *Football League Ltd* v *Littlewoods Pools Ltd* where it was held that:[17]

> . . . there can be no copyright in information or in an opinion *per se*. Copyright can only be claimed in the composition or language which is chosen to express the information or the opinion. . . . where the facts are represented in some special way, it then becomes a question of fact and degree as to whether the skill and labour involved in such special representation of the information is entitled to copyright.

However, it should be noted that although, in this case, a football championship fixtures list was held to be copyrightable, a chronological list of

---

17. [1959] Ch 637 at pp. 651–2. However, recent US cases have cast doubt on the scope for protecting collections of data by copyright. In *Feist Publications Inc.* v *Rural Telephone Service Co. Inc.* (1991) 113 L Ed 2d 358 the Supreme Court held that the data contained in a telephone directory were uncopyrightable facts and that there was 'nothing remotely creative about arranging names alphabetically in a white pages directory' (at p. 380). Consequently, the court ruled that Rural's directory was unprotected as 'it lacks the modicum of creativity necessary to transform mere selection into copyrightable expression' and 'copyright is not a tool by which a compilation author may keep others from using the facts or data he or she has collected'. Compare, however, *Bellsouth Advertising & Publishing Corp.* v *Donnelley Information Publishing Inc.* (1991) 933 F 2d 952 in which the 2nd Circuit considered the copyrightability of a Yellow Pages directory and distinguished *Feist* on the issue of creativity.

fixtures prepared from this entailed insufficient skill, labour or effort to support a claim to copyright.

The World Intellectual Property Organisation (WIPO) has proposed a protocol to the Berne Convention for the protection of literary and artistic works, to extend art. 2(5) of the Convention specifically to include and protect databases (in the wider sense of the word and therefore not just in electronic form) if they constitute intellectual creations by reason of the selection, coordination or arrangement of their contents, provided that it is clear that the protection of collections of data or other unprotected material does not make the data or other unprotected material themselves eligible for copyright protection. The WIPO proposals in relation to databases therefore add nothing to existing UK law, but merely set out expressly the existing approach of the UK courts in their approach to the question of copyright protection for databases and other compilations.

In contrast, the proposed EC Council Directive on the legal protection of databases[18] is likely to have a significant impact on UK law in this area. The proposed Directive would apply only to databases 'stored and accessed by electronic means, and the electronic materials necessary for the operation of the database such as its thesaurus, index or system for obtaining or presenting information', and does not apply to computer programs (art. 1). Article 2(3) provides that an electronic database 'shall be protected by copyright if it is original in the sense that it is a collection of works or materials which, by reason of their selection or their arrangement, constitutes the author's own intellectual creation. No other criteria shall be applied to determine the eligibility of a database for this protection'.[19]

However, the explanatory memorandum to the proposed Directive states that 'even the mere accumulation of facts, statistics, bibliographical information, names and addresses involves considerable commercial activity. Time, labour and organisation of skills are brought to bear, to collect and verify the accuracy of the required volume of data and to create from it a marketable product or service.' The proposed Directive would, therefore, establish limited protection for the contents of databases where such contents are themselves not already protected by copyright. This would be a special, *sui generis,* right to prevent unfair extraction, defined in art. 1 of the proposed Directive to mean 'the right of the maker of the database to prevent acts of extraction and re-utilisation of material from that database for commercial purposes'. The unfair extraction right would apply 'irrespective of the eligibility of that database for protection under copyright. It shall not apply to the contents of a database where these are works already protected by copyright or neighbouring rights' (art. 2(5)). However, compulsory licensing provisions would apply where 'the works or materials contained in a database which is made publicly

---

18. Text as adopted at 29 January 1992. COM(92)24 final – SYN393 OJ No. C156, 23 June 1992, p. 4. For a commentary on the proposed Directive see Millard, 'Comments on the Proposed EC Database Directive' 6 World Intellectual Property Report 76.
19. This seems consistent with the US decision in *Feist Publications Inc.* v *Rural Telephone Service Co. Inc.* (1991) – see footnote 14 above.

available cannot be independently created, collected or obtained from any other source' or where the database is made publicly available by a public body (art. 8). A further inroad on the right to prevent unfair extraction arises in art. 8 which provides that 'the lawful user of a database may, without authorisation of the database maker, extract and re-utilise insubstantial parts of works or materials from a database for commercial purposes provided that acknowledgement is made of this source'. No acknowledgement would be necessary where the extraction and re-utilisation was 'for personal or private use only'.

It is arguable that many on-line databases will be protected as 'cable programmes', listed in s. 1 of the 1988 Act as a distinct category of copyright works. Section 7(1) defines 'cable programme' as 'any item included in a cable programme service'. A cable programme service is 'a service which consists wholly or mainly in sending visual images, sounds or other information by means of a telecommunications system, otherwise than by wireless telegraphy, for reception— (a) at two or more places (whether for simultaneous reception or at different times in response to requests by different users), or (b) for presentation to members of the public'. Various services are excepted from this definition, including 'a service . . . of which it is an essential feature that while visual images, sounds or other information are being conveyed by the person providing the service there will or may be sent from each place of reception, by means of the same system . . . , information (other than signals for the operation or control of the service) for reception by the person providing the service or other persons receiving it' (s. 7(2)(a)). Whether a particular database service falls within the definition of 'cable programme service' will depend on the degree to which it operates interactively. For example, a passive broadcast videotex service (such as Oracle or Ceefax in the United Kingdom) will be a cable programme service, whereas an electronic data interchange facility or home shopping service will be an excepted service. Less clear is the status of an information service which permits a user to issue commands to search a database and perhaps analyse search results or order printouts of documents which have been retrieved.

An unusual feature of on-line or other regularly updated databases is that, arguably, copyright in the database as a whole may continue for an indefinite term. This would be on the basis that every substantial alteration of the material in the database brings into existence a new work and results in a restarting of the clock for copyright purposes. It is debatable whether this outcome is consistent with the underlying principle that copyright in compilations is intended to protect the skill and effort put into preparing the compilation as a whole.[20]

In the proposed EC Directive on the legal protection of databases referred to above, the concept of 'insubstantial changes' is used as a basis for limiting the duration of rights since, by virtue of art. 9, insubstantial changes would not extend the period of copyright and unfair extraction right. This has caused controversy since 'insubstantial change' is defined as any change which is necessary for the database to continue to function in the way it was intended

---

20. The rules as to duration of copyright generally are discussed in 4.3.3.

by its maker to function. A series of 'insubstantial changes' could, however, have the combined effect of changing substantially the nature of the database and it is therefore possible that the unfair extraction right might expire just as the database was becoming a commercially valuable product. If this provision of the draft Directive is left intact, the practical effect is likely to be that database creators may feel obliged to make unnecessary changes to the database in question (e.g., by incorporation of a new category of information or by a change in the database's format) in order to secure extended protection. This is by no means the only controversial provision of the proposed Directive, and the text is likely to be amended before it comes into force.

4.2.2.3 Computer-generated works   As already noted (see 4.2.1.4, above) for copyright to subsist in a work, certain qualification requirements must be met. In most cases, the criterion will be whether the author of a work was 'a qualifying person' at the time the work was made. With the widespread use of programming 'tools' and automated processes for collecting, processing and compiling data, it is likely that an increasing number of works, including computer programs and databases, will have no identifiable human author or authors. Prior to the 1988 Act, there was considerable doubt as to whether such works were eligible for copyright protection.[21]

To ensure that substantial categories of works did not gradually fall out of the realm of copyright, provisions were included in the 1988 Act to enable copyright to subsist in a literary, dramatic, musical or artistic work 'generated by a computer in circumstances such that there is no human author of the work' (ss. 9(3) and 178). The author of such a 'computer-generated' work 'shall be taken to be the person by whom the arrangements necessary for the creation of the work are undertaken' (s. 9(3)). While providing a welcome safety net for useful and valuable works which would otherwise fall outside copyright law, determining whether these new provisions apply to a particular work will still require a careful analysis of the facts.

In particular, care should be taken to distinguish between 'computer-generated' and 'computer-assisted' (or 'computer-aided' works). The latter type of works do not receive special treatment under the 1988 Act. The availability of copyright protection for such works was in effect recognised in a decision under the 1956 Act. In pre-trial proceedings in *Express Newspapers plc* v *Liverpool Daily Post & Echo plc* [1985] 1 WLR 1089, the court ruled that grids of letters produced with the aid of a computer for use in prize draws were authored by the programmer who wrote the relevant software. Rejecting an argument to the contrary advanced by counsel for the defendants, Whitford J stated:[22]

I reject this submission. The computer was no more than the tool by which the varying grids of five-letter sequences were produced to the instructions,

---

21. See C. J. Millard, *Legal Protection of Computer Programs and Data* (London: Sweet & Maxwell, 1985), pp. 25–30.

22. This passage echoes a statement in para. 514 of the Whitford Committee Report (see note 3) in which it was stated that a computer used in the creation of a copyright work was a 'mere tool in much the same way as a slide-rule or even, in a simple sense, a paintbrush'.

via the computer, of Mr Ertel. It is as unrealistic as it would be to suggest that, if you write your work with a pen, it is the pen which is the author of the work rather than the person who drives the pen.

It was perhaps convenient for the court in the *Express Newspapers* case that the programmer was also the person who ran the program on the particular occasion in question and checked the results. The nexus between one person and the finished work was thus very close. It is not clear how the court would have resolved conflicting claims between several programmers, data providers, system operators and so on.

In cases where the association between any individual or individuals and a finished work is so remote that it can fairly be said the work has been created without a human author, there is now the possibility that it will qualify for copyright as a computer-generated work. It is unlikely, however, that the 1988 Act provisions will be dispositive of all doubts as to the subsistence and ownership of copyright in computer output. Disputes may still arise where a number of competing individuals claim to have made the 'arrangements necessary for the creation of the work'. Would, for example, a person using a mass-marketed program generator be entitled to copyright in all such output? Would the author of the underlying software have any claim to copyright in the output? Would two or more identical works produced by different individuals using the same program generator all qualify for protection as original literary works?[23]

4.3 OWNERSHIP AND DURATION OF COPYRIGHT

4.3.1 First ownership

The first owner of copyright in a work is usually the author of the work (1988 Act, s. 11(1)). This is the case regardless of whose ideas underlie the work and of who commissions or pays for the work. This general rule is, however, subject to several significant exceptions. Of widest importance is the special rule that, subject to contrary agreement, the first owner of copyright in a work created by an employee during the course of his or her employment is the employer, not the employee (s. 11(2)).[24] While this rule seems straightforward in principle, in practice its consequences are frequently overlooked.

The most common difficulty arises where a software house or freelance programmer is commissioned to write software under a contract *for* services (as distinct from a contract *of* service, i.e., an employment agreement). Such scenarios are often complicated where contributions to the program development process are made by employees of the company which has commissioned the work and possibly also by independent consultants. The automatic

---

23. For further discussion, see J. A. L. Sterling, 'The Copyright, Designs and Patents Bill 1987', *Computer Law and Security Report*, vol. 3, no. 5 (January–February 1988), p. 2.
24. The other exceptions to the rule relate to Crown and Parliamentary copyright, and the copyright of certain international organisations (1988 Act, s. 11(3)).

operation of the rules as to first ownership may produce results which are contrary to the reasonable commercial expectations of one or more of the parties. For example, the commissioning party may contribute a brilliant original concept and pay all the costs of its subsequent development and implementation, yet end up with no legal rights of ownership in the final product. Even if it had been understood from the start, and possibly even agreed orally, that the commissioner would in all respects 'own' the product, this will not be sufficient to alter the operation of the first ownership rules. This is because, as will be discussed below, assignments of copyright and agreements as to future ownership of copyright will only be enforceable if they are evidenced in writing (1988 Act, s. 90(3) and 91(1); see 4.3.2). It is possible in such a case that the commissioner will be able to persuade a court of equity to order the developer to execute an assignment of copyright. This might be justified on the basis that such an assignment was an implied term of an agreement between the parties.[25] The mere fact that the commissioner paid for the work would not normally be sufficient grounds for inferring such a term, although such an arrangement may be evidence of an implied licence to use the work for the purpose for which it was commissioned (see 2.3.1).

Further potential for dispute arises where there is joint authorship and/or joint ownership of copyright. In the computer industry it is common for several people, sometimes a large number, to be involved in the initial development of a software package. Thereafter, still more people may be involved in the preparation of revised versions and updates. Multiple authorship and divided ownership are, however, by no means uncommon in the copyright field. Section 10(1) of the 1988 Act defines a 'work of joint authorship' as 'a work produced by the collaboration of two or more distinct authors in which the contribution of each author is not distinct from that of the other author or authors.' Thus, where the development of a program really is a joint effort copyright will, subject to the rules governing employee works just discussed, vest in the various contributors jointly. This scenario must be distinguished, however, from that in which a number of people have made separate contributions to a software development project each of which can be identified as such. It may well be that in the latter case there will be a number of quite distinct copyrights in a program or package.

Serious difficulties may arise at the exploitation stage where a software package either has a number of joint owners, or is made up of a number of programs or modules each separately owned. In either case, infringement of copyright will occur if any of the owners seeks to exploit the package as a whole without the consent of all the others. Where the various owners have quite distinct copyrights and one owner refuses to cooperate with the rest, the others may choose to rewrite the relevant part of the package and proceed to market the software without the objecting contributor being involved. This solution

---

25. See, for example, *Merchant Adventurers Ltd* v *M. Grew & Co. Ltd* [1973] RPC 1. The ruling is probably limited to the special facts of that case, however. Where ownership is disputed, a court would be most unlikely to upset the automatic operation of the statutory ownership rules.

will not, however, be available in the case of a single work if various people are joint owners of the whole of it. Unless the rights of the uncooperative party or parties can somehow be severed, attempts to exploit the package may be permanently thwarted.

There are thus many circumstances in which there is a possibility of more than one party claiming copyright and of disagreements about how multiple owners should exercise their rights. Such issues may arise where there is a misunderstanding about ownership of a work which has been commissioned; where a work has been or is likely to be computer-generated; where there are multiple authors; and where ownership is divided. In all such cases, the most satisfactory arrangement for all concerned will usually be for agreement about ownership and exploitation of any rights to be reached in advance and be evidenced in writing. Where the potential for disputes has not been success-fully pre-empted, assignments or confirmatory assignments of copyright may be appropriate to resolve doubts about rights in existing works.

4.3.2 Assignments and licences

A copyright can be given away, be bought and sold, or be left as an inheritance under a will as personal or movable property (1988 Act, s. 90(1)). An assignment, or other transfer, of copyright may be outright or may relate only to certain of the exclusive rights enjoyed by the owner. Thus, for example, an assignee may be given the right solely to translate a software package into a particular language. A transfer may also be limited to any part of the remaining term of the copyright (1988 Act, s. 90(2)). In practice, limited rights, such as to convert a program for use with a particular operating system or for foreign language users, are more often granted by way of licence than by partial assignment. Where such a licence is 'exclusive', the licensee will in effect be treated as the owner in terms of rights and remedies and the distinction between such a licence and a corresponding assignment will, for most purposes, be academic.[26] Assignments of copyright and of 'future copyright' (that is, copyright which will or may come into existence in the future, e.g., in a commissioned work) will only be effective if made in writing and signed by or on behalf of the assignor (1988 Act, ss. 90(3) and 91(1)).

Licences other than exclusive licences can be made informally without being evidenced in writing. Indeed, they may even be inferred from the circumstan-ces of a transaction or the general or specific conduct of the parties. Licences relating to the use of software are generally recorded in a written statement of terms, though frequently there is no signed agreement or contract as such.[27] The 1988 Act provides, in limited circumstances, for there to be deemed licences to use second-hand copies of programs and other works distributed in electronic form (see 4.5.8).

---

26. Section 101(1) of the 1988 Act provides that 'An exclusive licensee has, except against the copyright owner, the same rights and remedies in respect of matters occurring after the grant of the licence as if the licence had been an assignment'.
27. See C. J. Millard, 'Shrink-wrap Licensing' (1987) 4 CLSR 8.

4.3.3   Term of protection

Subject to certain exceptions, copyright in a literary, dramatic, musical or artistic work lasts for 50 years from the end of the year in which the author dies (1988 Act, s. 12(1)). For a work of joint authorship, the 50-year period begins to run at the end of the year in which the last known author dies (s. 12(4)). In the case of computer-generated work, copyright expires after 50 years from the end of the year in which the work was made (s. 12(3)). This latter rule is similar to the rules applying to sound recordings, films, broadcasts and cable programmes (ss. 13 and 14). The typographical arrangement of a published edition, which is itself a work for copyright purposes, is protected for a still shorter term of 25 years from the end of the year of first publication (s. 15). Thus, in the case of a product such as a software package comprising multiple works, copyright in the various component parts will run out on a number of different dates. Duration of copyright may depend, for example, on the life expectancy of various human contributors, the year in which any computer-generated works were made, and the year of first publication of the documentation.

4.4   INFRINGEMENT OF COPYRIGHT

4.4.1   Types of infringing act

Space does not permit a full discussion of all of the acts which can constitute infringement of the copyright in a work. Instead, the focus will be on the principal acts of so-called 'primary infringement', with reference also being made to the various acts of 'secondary infringement'. A primary infringement occurs where a person directly commits an infringing act or authorises someone else to do so. Secondary infringers, as their name suggests, are generally one stage removed from the relevant primary infringing acts, but may be implicated by, for example, importing or distributing infringing copies without the consent of the copyright owner. A crucial distinction between primary infringers and secondary infringers is that those in the former category can be liable for infringing copyright whether or not they realise they are doing so, whereas those in the latter category are only liable if they know, or have reason to believe, that they are committing an act of secondary infringement. Three of the most relevant primary infringing acts (copying, adaptation, and issuing copies to the public) are discussed in 4.4.2 and the various acts of secondary infringement are outlined in 4.4.3.

4.4.2   Primary infringement

4.4.2.1   Copying   Whereas the 1956 Act gave the owner of copyright in a work control over the act of 'reproducing the work in any material form' (s. 2(5)(a)), the 1988 Act contains the much simpler statement that a copyright owner has the exclusive right 'to copy the work' and to authorise anyone else to do so (s. 16(1)(a) and (2)). The 1988 Act provides that control over copying applies in relation to the whole or any substantial part of a work, and regardless of whether copying occurs directly or indirectly (s. 16(3)). As will be seen in 4.5, it may be difficult to establish whether the reproduction of certain structural or other characteristics of a computer program will constitute either direct or indirect copying of a substantial part of the program.

Section 17(2) of the 1988 Act defines copying, in relation to a literary, dramatic, musical or artistic work, as 'reproducing the work in a material form' including 'storing the work in any medium by electronic means'. This provision is reinforced by s. 17(6) which provides that 'Copying in relation to any description of work includes the making of copies which are transient or are incidental to some other use of the work'. As will be seen in 4.5.2, these provisions have significant consequences when applied to computer programs and other works distributed in electronic form.

4.4.2.2 Making adaptations Section 21(1) of the 1988 Act restricts the making of an adaptation of a literary, dramatic or musical work. 'Adaptation' means, among other things, making a translation of a literary work and 'In relation to a computer program a "translation" includes a version of the program in which it is converted into or out of a computer language or code or into a different computer language or code, otherwise than incidentally in the course of running the program' (s. 21(3) and (4)). The draft Copyright (Computer Programs) Regulations 1992 would delete from this definition the words 'otherwise than incidentally in the course of running the program'. The possible implications of s. 21, and the proposed amendment, for the scope of a program copyright owner's control over simple 'use' of software are discussed in part 4.5.2, below.

4.4.2.3 Issuing copies to the public Section 18(1) of the 1988 Act provides that 'The issue to the public of copies of the work is an act restricted by copyright in every description of copyright work'. The act of issuing copies of a work to the public is defined in terms of 'putting into circulation copies not previously put into circulation, in the United Kingdom or elsewhere'. Broadly speaking, this gives the owner of copyright in a work control over publication of the work. Specifically excluded, however, from the ambit of s. 18 are distribution, sale, hiring, loan, or importation into the United Kingdom of copies which have lawfully been issued to the public anywhere in the world. This exclusion is in turn qualified in a most significant respect with the words 'except that in relation to sound recordings, films and computer programs the restricted act of issuing copies to the public includes any rental of copies to the public'.

This restriction on the rental of copies of certain categories of works, including computer programs, was an innovative feature of the 1988 Act. Prior to the 1988 Act no such automatic restriction existed. Copyright owners were, of course, able to restrict rental of their works by agreement and, in addition, the absence of a restriction on rental did not give a person who rented a copy any right to make a further copy from the rented copy. In practice, however, copies of works are often distributed in circumstances such that it is not feasible for appropriate restrictions to be imposed in that way. An obvious example is mass-market distribution of 'shrink-wrapped' software packages.[28] Moreover,

---

28. See C. J. Millard, 'Shrink-wrap Licensing' (1987) 4 CLSR 8.

a theoretical right to restrict the making of further copies from a rented copy is of limited efficacy in the face of widespread private copying of works such as compact discs, videos and software packages. Of far greater use to copyright owners is the new right to prevent, or regulate at source, the rental of copies of such works to the public.

Section 178 of the 1988 Act defines 'rental' expansively as meaning 'any arrangement under which a copy of a work is made available— (a) for payment (in money or money's worth), or (b) in the course of business, as part of services or amenities for which payment is made, on terms that it will or may be returned'. The meaning is expanded still further in sch. 7, paras 6 and 8, to cover lending of sound recordings, films and computer programs by public libraries, whether or not any charge is made for such loans. In the case of computer programs, the right to control rental lasts for 50 years from the end of the year in which copies are first issued to the public in electronic form.[29] During that period, the Secretary of State may order compulsory licensing of programs on payment of royalties to be agreed or, if necessary, fixed by the Copyright Tribunal (1988 Act, s. 66(1)).

4.4.3   Secondary infringement

4.4.3.1   Dealing in infringing copies   Secondary infringement occurs where, without the consent of the copyright owner, a person 'imports into the United Kingdom, otherwise than for his own private and domestic use, an article which is, and which he knows or has reason to believe is, an infringing copy of the work' (1988 Act, s. 22). Infringement also occurs where a person, again without consent, 'possesses in the course of a business' or deals in articles which he knows or has reason to believe are infringing copies. Relevant dealings are selling, hiring, offering for sale or hire, commercial exhibition or distribution of copies of the work, and any other distribution 'otherwise than in the course of business to such an extent as to affect prejudicially the owner of the copyright' (s. 23).

4.4.3.2   Providing articles for making infringing copies   Copyright in a work is infringed where, without the consent of the copyright owner, 'an article specifically designed or adapted for making copies of that work' is manufactured, imported or commercially dealt in by a person who knows or has reason to believe that it will be used for that purpose (1988 Act, s. 24(1)). The scope of this infringing act is not clear. It is not necessary that an article be intended specifically for use in making *infringing* copies, merely that the article is 'specifically designed or adapted' for making copies and that such copies may infringe copyright. Thus, at its broadest, the provision arguably could be construed as covering commonplace articles such as photocopiers, tape

---

29. 1988 Act, s. 66(5). The terms 'electronic' and 'electronic form' are defined in s. 178 of the Act as follows: ' "electronic" means actuated by electric, magnetic, electromagnetic, electrochemical or electromechanical energy, and "in electronic form" means in a form usable only by electronic means'.

recorders, and personal computers which every importer, manufacturer, or dealer should suspect may be used to make infringing copies of works. Such a construction of the section would, however, be absurd. An extremely limited interpretation would probably be nearer the mark. The basis for a narrow construction is the reference to the making of copies of *that* work, meaning that the device in question must have been specifically designed or adapted to make copies of a particular work owned by a particular person, and not merely for making copies of works generally.

4.4.3.3 Facilitating infringement by transmission   As where a copy of a work is rented out and copied by the renter, where a copy of a work is made available by transmission over a telecommunications system, there may in theory be a cause of action against each recipient who stores, and thus copies, the work on reception. However, the practical difficulties inherent in enforcing this right to sue each ultimate infringer render it of little practical use to copyright owners. Section 24(2) of the 1988 Act provides copyright owners with a basis for regulating such dissemination of a work at source, as follows:

> Copyright in a work is infringed by a person who without the licence of the copyright owner transmits the work by means of a telecommunications system (otherwise than by broadcasting or inclusion in a cable programme service), knowing or having reason to believe that infringing copies of the work will be made by means of the reception of the transmission in the United Kingdom or elsewhere.

Accordingly, a supply down a telephone line of software, data, or any other work protected by copyright, may be an act of secondary infringement if done without an appropriate licence.

4.4.3.4 Circumvention of copy-protection   A further area in which the 1988 Act strengthened the rights of owners of works distributed in electronic form relates to devices or information intended to facilitate the circumvention of copy-protection measures. The relevant provision is not grouped with the other sections which deal with secondary infringement but appears quite separately in Part VII of the Act under the heading 'Miscellaneous and general'. Section 296 provides that a copyright owner who issues a work in copy-protected electronic form has the same rights against a person who, with intent, makes available any device or means designed or adapted to circumvent the copy-protection as would be available against a copyright infringer. 'Copy protection' is defined as including 'any device or means intended to prevent or restrict copying of a work or to impair the quality of copies made' (s. 296(4)).

As with the discussion of the restriction on providing articles to be used for making infringing copies (see 4.4.3.2), it is not clear how broadly the circumvention of copy-protection provision will be interpreted by the courts. At its widest, s. 296 could be construed as encompassing any hardware, software, or information intended to facilitate copying of, or access to, encrypted files, or even recovery of corrupted data. Thus, suppliers of bit-copiers and utilities designed to restore garbled or incomplete data might be vulnerable to attack under the provision. Similarly, distributors of hardware devices such as 'ROM blowers', which are designed for copying data from one chip to another, might be caught. However, as with our earlier conclusions regarding secondary infringement, it is likely that a much more restricted analysis would prevail. Thus, a court would probably look for some specific evidence, perhaps based on a special configuration of a device or perhaps based on provocative advertising, to suggest that the manufacturer, importer or dealer intended the device or information in question to be used to circumvent copy-protection. Where a device has multiple potential uses, at least some of which are legitimate, it seems unlikely that s. 296 would be applicable.

4.5   SCOPE OF PROTECTION FOR COMPUTER PROGRAMS AND DATA

4.5.1   Idea and expression, symbolism and functionality

Unlike in the United States, in the United Kingdom there is no statutory rule that bars ideas from copyright protection.[30] However, the EC Directive on the legal protection of computer programs[31] provides in art. 1.2 that 'Ideas and principles which underlie any element of a computer program, including those which underlie its interfaces, are not protected by copyright under this Directive'. The draft Copyright (Computer Programs) Regulations 1992 are silent on this point. In the meantime, there is a number of English, and other Commonwealth, precedents which appear to exclude ideas *per se* from copyright protection.[32] The apparent logic behind the rule was illustrated by the Supreme Court of Canada in *Cuisenaire* v *South West Imports Ltd* [1969] SCR 208 with the observation that 'were the law otherwise, . . . everybody who made a rabbit pie in accordance with the recipe of Mrs Beeton's cookery book would infringe the literary copyright in that book'.[33]

The claimed distinction then is between an idea which cannot be protected by copyright, such as the procedure for making a rabbit pie, and an expression of that idea, such as a written recipe describing the rabbit pie making process, which can be protected by copyright. In the case of a computer program, however, such a tidy analysis is not possible. Indeed, it may be that the statement that ideas can never be protected by copyright is a misleading over-simplification.[34] Take, for example, ideas such as the algorithms on which a program is based, or perhaps the methods or processes which the program

---

30. In the United States, s. 102(b) of Title 17 USC provides 'in no case does copyright protection . . . extend to any idea, procedure, process, system, method of operation, concept, principle, or discovery, regardless of the form in which it is described, explained, illustrated, or embodied in such work'
31. Directive 91/250/EEC.
32. For example, in *Donoghue* v *Allied Newspapers Ltd* [1938] Ch 106, Farwell J stated unequivocally that 'there is no copyright in an idea, or in ideas'.
33. *Cuisenaire* v *South West Imports Ltd* [1969] SCR 208 at p. 212, citing Pape J in *Cuisenaire* v *Reed* [1963] VR 719.
34. This theme is developed in more detail in 4.5.6.

implements. Because of the nature of the interaction between software and hardware, a program, unlike a page from a recipe book, can simultaneously be *symbolic* (i.e., a representation of instructions to be given to the computer) and *functional* (i.e., the means by which the computer is actually instructed to carry out operations). Lines of code which describe an operation or procedure can also be used to implement it. It is as though by putting the relevant pages from Mrs Beeton's cookery book into an oven one could produce a rabbit pie. This special characteristic of computer programs has a number of significant consequences in copyright law. One is that use of a program is almost impossible without infringement occurring (see 4.5.2). Another is that there may be no way to achieve functional compatibility between two or more items of hardware or software without reproducing a substantial amount of code to effect the desired interface or communication (see 4.5.3).

4.5.2 Infringement of program copyright by use of a program
In relation to conventional works, the 'use' of a legitimate copy of a work is not generally restricted by copyright. For example, the simple act of reading a book is not controlled by copyright. It is only on the occurrence of one of the specifically restricted acts, for example, the copying or adaptation of a substantial part of the book, that a question of infringement can arise. However, because computer programs in machine-code form are both symbolic and functional, normal use may necessitate such copying or adaptation. Loading or running a computer program typically entails the copying of part or all of the program from a disk (or other permanent storage medium) to the computer's random access memory (RAM) and central processing unit (CPU). Section 17(6) of the 1988 Act makes it clear that such copying of a work, even though it may be 'transient' or 'incidental to some other use of the work', is nevertheless an infringement of copyright if done without authorisation. Even screen displays generated during the running of a program may constitute infringing copies of copyright material. Because the restriction on copying applies to even simple use of a program, legitimate use can normally only take place pursuant to a licence or permission of some kind. Such a licence may be express or implied. Typically, a software house will seek to attach various conditions to a licence to use. A special provision in the 1988 Act dealing with transfers of second-hand copies of programs is dealt with in 4.5.8.

Section 21(4) provides that 'translation' includes program code conversion, except where such conversion takes place only 'incidentally in the course of running the program'. It is interesting to note that s. 21(5) states that 'No inference shall be drawn from this section as to what does or does not amount to copying a work'. Consequently, the limited exemption set out in s. 21(4) cannot be taken to undermine directly the blanket restriction in s. 17(6) on all copying, including 'transient' and 'incidental' copying. However, it is arguable that the s. 21(4) exception might indirectly undermine the control over use based on the restriction on incidental copying which has just been discussed. With current technology, the process of running a program on a piece of hardware usually entails a combination of copying and adaptation. Prior to execution in the CPU, portions of code will be copied from a permanent storage medium such as a hard or floppy disk, to a temporary and much faster store such as RAM. This initial loading process will constitute copying of a substantial part of the program and will thus be an infringement of copyright if not licensed. Subsequent execution of the code in the CPU is likely to entail a process of code conversion, i.e., translation, which s. 21(4) will probably exempt from the general restriction on making adaptations. Where, however, a particular program can be run by a process of adaptation alone, for example, by interpretation directly from a fast memory store, then it is arguable that no licence will be needed to use the program. If, however, the Copyright (Computer Programs) Regulations 1992 are enacted in their present draft form, this apparent loophole will be closed as the words 'otherwise than incidentally in the course of running a program' would be deleted.

Apart from this special case of use by adaptation alone, United Kingdom copyright law appears to give indirect protection to the ideas underlying a program by making the literal copying inherent in simple use of the program an infringing act. Thus, unlike the ideas and procedures described in a cookery recipe which can be used without infringing copyright in the recipe book, the ideas and procedures embodied in a computer program are regulated by copyright along with the code which implements them whenever the program is used. It is interesting to note, by way of comparison, that under United States copyright law the owner of a copy of a program does not need a licence to make or authorise the making of another copy or adaptation if doing so is 'an essential step in the utilisation of the computer program in conjunction with a machine'.[35]

A similar approach has been adopted in the EC Software Directive,[36] though the deemed right to make copies or adaptations necessary for use seems to be subject to agreement to the contrary. Article 5.1 provides that 'In the absence of specific contractual provisions', copying and adaptation 'shall not require authorisation by the rightholder where they are necessary for the use of the computer program by the lawful acquirer in accordance with its intended purpose, including for error correction'. The words 'in the absence of specific contractual provisions' seem to make it clear that it will remain open to a copyright owner to restrict by contract these acts of copying and adaptation necessary for use.[37] This appears to be the interpretation favoured by the United Kingdom government. The draft implementing regulations would establish a new category of 'fair use' to cover copying and adaptation where necessary for the use of the program by the licensed user in accordance with its intended purpose, including for error correction, *unless the terms of the licensed user's licence specifically prohibit the same* (emphasis added). Whether

---

35. Title 17 USC, s. 117. This derogation from the copyright owner's normal rights to prevent the making of copies and adaptations does not seem to apply where title to the physical copy does not pass to the software user.

36. Directive 91/250/EEC.

37. Confusingly, the relevant recital is inconsistent with art. 5 and provides that 'the acts of loading and running necessary for the use of a copy of a program which has been lawfully acquired, and the act of correction of its errors, may not be prohibited by contract'. Presumably, art. 5 will prevail.

copyright can also be used to prevent non-literal copying, for example, where a person analyses or reverse engineers a program and writes new but functionally equivalent code, is a rather more complex and, in many respects, more momentous issue.

4.5.3 Copying, compatibility and reverse engineering

There may be a limited number of ways, in extreme cases possibly only one, of achieving a particular functional result using a specific configuration of hardware and/or software. Sometimes a single manufacturer can set an almost universal standard or set of standards for carrying out particular operations, perhaps by being there first, by skilful marketing, by dominance in the industry, or sometimes by being truly innovative. Where, for whatever reason, a *de facto* industry standard has emerged, such as the BIOS ('basic input-output system') for IBM-compatible personal computers, the possibility of copyright being used to monopolise the specification of interfaces between hardware and hardware, hardware and software, software and software, and humans and software, has enormous policy implications. Much of the rapid growth and diversity which has characterised the computer industry in the last decade has resulted from the widespread development of hardware and software products which are 'compatible' with those most popular in the market. Such compatible products frequently improve substantially on the products offered by the company which initiated the standard both in terms of price and performance, and often also in terms of innovation. A user who has invested in a particular 'environment' in terms of hardware, software, or training, will often wish to build on that investment without being tied into a particular supplier or suppliers for all future development purposes.

The development of compatible products can, of course, be effected in a number of ways with varying consequences in copyright terms. At one end of the spectrum, a clone may consist of or contain crude copies of key parts, or indeed the whole, of an established product. The maker of such a clone will be vulnerable to be sued for infringement of copyright and a number of other intellectual property rights. Certainly, the literal copying of the whole or a substantial part of an existing program will almost invariably infringe copyright. At the other end of the spectrum, a developer of a compatible product may invest substantial resources in achieving functional compatibility by independent development without making a verbatim or literal copy of any part of the product which is being emulated. To ensure that it can be proved that the competing product is the result of such original labour and skill, a manufacturer may resort to a rigorous and exhaustively documented 'clean-room' procedure. Such a procedure would normally necessitate independent work being undertaken by two discrete groups of software engineers, the first analysing the product to be emulated and producing a functional specification, the second writing code to implement that specification.[38] In between these

---

38. For an interesting discussion of the issues inherent in duplication of the functionality of the IBM BIOS see G. Gervaise Davis III, 'IBM PC Software and Hardware Compatibility' [1984] EIPR 273.

extremes of crude copying and sophisticated reverse engineering, there are various ways in which software may be developed using particular ideas or functions derived from pre-existing software products without any substantial literal copying taking place.

Various tests have been suggested for determining whether products developed using either of the latter two approaches will infringe copyright. So far there has been very little judicial consideration of these issues in the United Kingdom. Indeed, almost all reported cases and current litigation in the area are concentrated in the United States. Much of the argument there has concerned the extent to which copyright law can provide protection against copying of either the 'structure, sequence and organisation' of a program, or of its 'look and feel'. The former concerns the internal structure and workings of a program, the latter its external appearance and user interfaces. Underlying both issues is the fundamental dichotomy in United States law between ideas, which cannot be protected by copyright, and expressions of those ideas, which can. Before looking briefly at some of the American cases, one other general issue should be noted.

4.5.4 Difficulties of proving non-literal infringement
A further consequence of the simultaneously symbolic and functional nature of software is that the traditional tests for establishing that copying of a work has occurred may be wholly inappropriate. It is by no means always the case that functional similarity between two programs is indicative of similarity in the underlying symbolic codes. To extend the rabbit pie analogy one final stage further, just because a rabbit pie looks, smells and tastes very similar to one made by Mrs Beeton is not in itself proof that both have been made from the same recipe. As Megarry V-C put it in *Thrustcode Ltd* v *WW Computing Ltd*:[39]

> ... where, as here, the claim is to copyright in the program itself, the results produced by operating the program must not be confused with the program in which copyright is claimed. If I may take an absurdly simple example, 2 and 2 make 4. But so does 2 times 2, or 6 minus 2, or 2 per cent. of 200, or 6 squared divided by 9, or many other things. Many different processes may produce the same answer and yet remain different processes that have not been copied one from another.

On the facts before it, the court was at a loss to see 'any real evidence of copying'[40] and accordingly dismissed the plaintiff's case. In *LB (Plastics) Ltd* v *Swish Products Ltd* [1979] FSR 145 at p. 149, Lord Wilberforce observed:

> The protection given by the law of copyright is against copying, the basis of protection being that one man must not be permitted to appropriate the result of another's labour. That copying has taken place, is for the plaintiff to establish and prove as a matter of fact. The beginning of the necessary

---

39. [1983] FSR 502 at p. 505.
40. Ibid., at p. 507.

proof normally lies in the establishment of similarity combined with proof of access to the plaintiff's productions.

This issue is of fundamental importance in the context of software copyright infringement. It is not enough for a plaintiff to allege that program code has been copied merely on the basis that a later program is similar to an earlier one in terms of its functionality or its appearance to a user. Actual copying of a substantial part is the key to copyright infringement under United Kingdom law.

4.5.5   Infringement by non-literal copying under United States law

A full discussion of the many reported and pending American cases in the field of software copyright is quite beyond the scope of this chapter. However, a brief consideration of some of the issues which have been raised in the United States may assist, sometimes by analogy, sometimes by way of contrast, in evaluating the position under United Kingdom copyright law.

In its landmark ruling in *Apple Computer Inc.* v *Franklin Computer Corporation* (1983) 714 F 2d 1240, the United States Court of Appeals for the Third Circuit confirmed unequivocally that computer programs in both source and object code are capable of protection as 'literary works' and that such protection extends to programs in machine code embedded in integrated circuit chips. The court then considered whether program copyright extended to operating systems, and in particular whether a merger of idea and expression would prevent Apple from claiming protection for various operating programs supplied with the Apple II microcomputer. The court ruled that 'If other programs can be written or created which perform the same function as an Apple's operating system program, then that program is an expression of the idea and hence copyrightable'.[41] In response to claims by the defendants that there was only a limited number of ways of writing a compatible operating system:[42]

> Franklin may wish to achieve total compatibility with independently developed application programs written for the Apple II, but that is a commercial and competitive objective which does not enter into the somewhat metaphysical issue of whether particular ideas and expressions have merged.'

The court concluded that operating system programs are not *per se* excluded from copyright protection.

Three years later, a different panel of judges in the same Third Circuit Court of Appeals addressed in rather more detail the application to computer programs of the idea – expression dichotomy. In *Whelan Associates Inc.* v *Jaslow Dental Laboratory Inc.* [1987] FSR 1 the plaintiffs alleged that a program developed by the defendant in the PC language BASIC infringed

---

41. 714 F 2d 1240 at p. 1253.
42. Ibid., loc. cit.

their copyright in a similar program written in the minicomputer language EDL. It was accepted that no literal copying had occurred yet the Third Circuit ruled that substantial similarities between the BASIC and EDL programs in terms of their 'structure, sequence and organisation' provided sufficient grounds for a finding of infringement. As regards drawing a line between idea and expression, the court ruled that 'the line between idea and expression may be drawn by reference to the end sought to be achieved by the work in question'.[43] Where the desired purpose can be achieved in more than one way, then any particular means of achieving it will be expression, not idea. On the facts before it, the Third Circuit found that 'the idea of the Dentalab program was the efficient management of a dental laboratory.... Because that idea could be accomplished in a number of different ways with a number of different structures, the structure of the Dentalab program is part of the program's expression, not its idea'.[44]

The Third Circuit's analysis in *Whelan Associates Inc.* v *Jaslow Dental Laboratory Inc.* has been widely criticised by academic writers.[45] A particular concern has been that the court's 'sweeping rule and broad language extend copyright protection too far' by moving towards a degree of monopoly protection previously only given to patent holders.[46] An indication of how widely the *Whelan* ruling could be applied came in *Broderbund Software Inc.* v *Unison World Inc.* (1986) 648 F Supp 1127, where it was cited as 'stand[ing] for the proposition that copyright protection is not limited to the literal aspects of a computer program, but rather that it extends to the overall structure of a program, including its audiovisual displays'.[47] The last part of this statement is rather surprising, given that the *Whelan* case was about infringement of copyright in program code (i.e., a literary work), not infringement of copyright in screen displays (i.e., audiovisual works). Moreover, in place of the structural analysis conducted by the *Whelan* court, the *Broderbund* court was more concerned with whether 'the infringing work captures the "total concept and feel" of the protected work'. Noting 'the eerie resemblance between the screens of the two programs', the court found that infringement had indeed occurred.[48]

An illustration of the flexibility of the 'total concept and feel' or 'look and feel' analysis can be seen in the analysis of an Ohio District Court in *Worlds of Wonder Inc.* v *Vector Intercontinental Inc.* (1986 unreported). The case concerned allegations of infringement of copyright in a talking animated toy bear known as Teddy Ruxpin. The bear was designed to be used with cassette tapes containing a soundtrack together with software to control the bear's movements. The defendants, in competition with the plaintiff, produced

---

43. [1987] FSR 1 at p. 19.
44. Ibid., footnote 28.
45. For example, D. Nimmer, R. L. Bernacchi and G. N. Frischling, 'A Structured Approach to Analysing the Substantial Similarity of Computer Software in Copyright Infringement Cases' (1988) 20 Ariz St LJ 625.
46. Nimmer, Bernacchi and Frischling (see note 45), p. 630. See also, Ganz, '*Whelan* and "work made for hire" threaten job mobility', 4 Computer Law Strategist (1988) 1.
47. 648 F Supp 1127 at p. 1133.
48. Ibid., at p. 1137.

various tapes containing stories and software for Teddy Ruxpin. The court found infringement of copyright in the bear as an audiovisual work on the ground that:[49]

> the general feel and concept of Teddy Ruxpin when telling a fairy tale is the same regardless of whether a WOW or Vector tape is used; the visual effects are identical, and the voices are similar, and the difference in stories does not alter the aesthetic appeal. . . . At least, the work created by the Vector tapes is a derivative work, if not an exact copy.

These and other look-and-feel cases set the scene for an action brought by Lotus against alleged infringers of copyright in the look and feel of the user interfaces of its enormously successful '1-2-3' spreadsheet product.

Before identifying the principal issues at stake in the Lotus case, however, consideration should be given to a move by a District Court in California to limit the breadth of the monopoly given to software copyright owners. In *NEC Corporation* v *Intel Corporation* (1989) 1 CCH Computer Cases 46,020, the court confirmed that microcodes embodied in various Intel chips were protected by copyright as computer programs, yet ruled that the reverse engineering of those programs by NEC did not infringe the relevant copyrights.[50] The court found that 'overall, and particularly with respect to the longer microroutines, NEC's microcode is not substantially similar to Intel's; but some of the shorter, simpler microroutines resemble Intel's. None, however, are identical.' To resolve the issue of whether those of the shorter microroutines which were similar infringed Intel's copyrights, the court placed great emphasis on the possibility of a merger of idea and expression, not as a basis for denying copyrightability but as a justification for the production of substantially similar code:[51]

> In determining an idea's range of expression, constraints are relevant factors to consider. . . . In this case, the expression of NEC's microcode was constrained by the use of the macroinstruction set and hardware of the 8086/88. . . . Accordingly, it is the conclusion of this court that the expression of the ideas underlying the shorter, simpler microroutines (including those identified earlier as substantially similar) may be protected only against virtually identical copying, and that NEC properly used the underlying ideas, without virtually identically copying their limited expression.

It is too early to assess whether *NEC Corporation* v *Intel Corporation* marks a significant shift in the balance between software owners and developers of compatible products.

---

49. Transcript at p.9.
50. In addition, the court ruled that Intel's failure to ensure that chips containing its microcode were properly marked with appropriate copyright notices had resulted in a forfeiture of its copyrights (1 CCH Computer Cases at 60,845).
51. 1 CCH Computer Cases 60,853.

In *Lotus Development Corporation* v *Paperback Software International* (1990)
2 CCH Computer Cases 46,310, the District Court for the District of
Massachusetts was called upon to decide whether the defendant's software
package 'VP-Planner' infringed the copyright in Lotus's '1-2-3' package. Both
products are electronic spreadsheets intended to facilitate accounting and other
processes that involve the manipulation and display of numerical data. District
Judge Keeton identified three elements which appeared to him to be 'the
principal factors relevant to decision of copyrightability of a computer program
such as Lotus 1-2-3'.[52] These were, first, 'some conception or definition of the
"idea" – for the purpose of distinguishing between the idea and its expression'.
Secondly, the court must determine 'whether an alleged expression of the idea
is limited to elements essential to expression of *that* idea (or is one of only a few
ways of expressing the idea) or instead includes identifiable elements of
expression not essential to every expression of that idea'. Finally, 'having
identified elements of expression not essential to every expression of the idea,
the decision-maker must focus on whether those elements are a substantial part
of the allegedly copyrightable "work"'.[53]

Interestingly, the district court judge was fairly dismissive of the 'look and
feel' concept. He did not find the concept 'significantly helpful' because it was
a 'conclusion' rather than a means of reaching a conclusion. Instead, in
applying his three-limb test, Judge Keeton looked at the 'user interface' of the
two programs. He seemed to accept as a basis for analysis the plaintiff's
description of the user interface as including such elements as 'the menus (and
their structure and organisation), the long prompts, the screens on which they
appear, the function key assignments, [and] the macro commands and
language'.[54] Applying his three-stage test to these elements of the user
interface, Judge Keeton found that neither the idea of developing an electronic
spreadsheet nor the idea of a two-line moving cursor menu were copyrightable.
Both elements thus failed to get beyond the first stage. The basic screen display
of a 'rotated L' layout used in most spreadsheet packages to set out columns
and rows failed to pass the second stage as 'there is a rather low limit, as a factual
matter, on the number of ways of making a computer screen resemble a
spreadsheet'. Similarly, the use of a particular key to invoke the menu
command system was found to be 'Another expressive element that merges
with the idea of an electronic spreadsheet'.[55]

One element of the 1-2-3 package did, however, satisfy all three elements of
the copyrightability test. The menu command system itself was capable of
many types of expression and its precise 'structure, sequence and organisation'
was 'distinctive'. Reaching the third element of his test, Judge Keeton found
it to be 'incontrovertible' that the menu command system was a substantial part
of the alleged copyrighted work:[56]

52. 2 CCH Computer Cases 46,310 at 62,264.
53. Ibid., loc. cit.
54. Ibid., at 62,266.
55. Ibid., at 62,268.
56. Ibid., at 62,269.

The user interface of 1-2-3 is its most unique element, and is the aspect that has made 1-2-3 so popular. That defendants went to such trouble to copy that element is a testament to its substantiality. Accordingly, evaluation of the third element of the legal test weighs heavily in favour of Lotus.

The court's conclusion was that it was 'indisputable that defendants have copied substantial copyrightable elements of plaintiff's copyrighted work . . . therefore . . . liability has been established'.[57]

However, in *Engineering Dynamics Inc.* v *Structural Software Inc.* (1991) 785 F Supp 576, although the district court said that the reasoning of *Lotus Development Corporation* v *Paperback Software International* was 'persuasive', it declined to follow the decision and concluded that user interfaces in the form of input and output formats are uncopyrightable ideas. Similarly, in *Brown Bag Software* v *Symantec Corp.* (1992) 960 F 2d 1465 the Ninth Circuit rejected the plaintiff's argument that the *Lotus* approach should be applied in deciding whether the graphical user interface of the defendant's outlining program infringed the plaintiff's copyright. Instead, the court held that it should engage in 'analytic dissection not for the purposes of comparing similarities and identifying infringement, but for the purposes of defining the scope of plaintiff's copyright'.[58] Thus, the court should first determine which elements are uncopyrightable, applying the idea–expression dichotomy and the merger doctrine to each element. Only then should it compare the protectable elements of expression to determine whether infringement may have occurred.

Many district and circuit judges have been critical of the Third Circuit's approach in *Whelan Associates Inc.* v *Jaslow Dental Laboratory Inc.* to the separation of ideas, which may not be protected, from expressions which may be. In *Plains Cotton Cooperative Association of Lubbock Texas* v *Goodpasture Computer Service Inc.* (1987) 807 F 2d 1256 the Court of Appeals for the Fifth Circuit 'declined to embrace' *Whelan*. More recently, the Second Circuit, in *Computer Associates* v *Altai* (1992) 3 CCH Computer Cases 46,505, has commented that the *Whelan* approach to separating idea and expression 'relies too heavily on metaphysical distinctions'. Instead, the *Altai* court suggested that district courts would be 'well advised' to adopt a three-step procedure for determining substantial similarity of non-literal elements of computer programs. First, the court should break down the allegedly infringed program into its constituent structural parts. Secondly, the court should examine each of these parts for such things as incorporated ideas, expression that is necessarily incidental to those ideas, and elements that are taken from the public domain, thus sifting out all non-protectable material. Thirdly, 'left with a kernel, or possibly kernels, of creative expression after following this process of elimination, the court's last step would be to compare this material with the structure of an allegedly infringing program'.[59]

---

57. Ibid., at 62,271.
58. 960 F 2d at 1475–6.
59. *Computer Associates* v *Altai*, transcript (22 June 1992) at 28.

The court concluded that 'we seek to ensure two things: (1) that programmers may receive appropriate copyright protection for innovative utilitarian
works containing expression; and (2) that non-protectable technical expression
remains in the public domain for others to use freely as building blocks in their
own work'.[60] It is interesting to note that the court relied heavily on the
Supreme Court's decision in *Feist Publications Inc.* v *Rural Telephone Service
Co. Inc.* (1991) 113 L Ed 2d 358, noting that '*Feist* teaches that substantial
effort alone cannot confer copyright status on an otherwise uncopyrightable
work' and that 'despite the fact that significant labour and expense often goes
into computer program flow-charting and debugging, that process does not
always result in inherently protectable expression'.[61]

4.5.6   Infringement by non-literal copying under United Kingdom law

The debate may proceed on a somewhat different basis in the United Kingdom.
As already noted, the extent to which ideas are excluded from protection under
United Kingdom copyright law has perhaps tended to be exaggerated. Some
commentators have suggested that there is, on the contrary, considerable scope
for protection of ideas provided merely that they have been reduced to writing
or some other material form. Laddie, Prescott and Vitoria, for example,
identify the 'pithy catch-phrase' that 'there is no copyright in ideas or
information but only in the form in which they are expressed' and comment:[62]

A moment's thought will reveal that the maxim is suspect. For example, in
the case of a book, the ideas it contains are necessarily expressed in words.
Hence, if it were really true that the copyright is confined to the form of
expression, one would expect to find that anyone was at liberty to borrow the
contents of the book provided he took care not to employ the same or similar
language. This is not so, of course. Thus, it is an infringement of the
copyright to make a version of a novel in which the story or action is
conveyed wholly by means of pictures; or to turn it into a play, although not
a line of dialogue is similar to any sentence in the book. Again, a translation
of a work into another language can be an infringement; yet, since the form
of expression is necessarily different – indeed, if it is turned into a language
such as Chinese the translation will consist of ideograms – the only
connecting factor must be the detailed ideas and information.

Laddie, Prescott and Vitoria also note that most of the cases frequently cited
in support of the exclusion of ideas from protection were decided prior to the
1956 Act, many indeed prior to the 1911 Act, and would probably be decided

---

60. Ibid., at 58.
61. Ibid., at 41.
62. Hugh Laddie, Peter Prescott and Mary Vitoria, *The Modern Law of Copyright* (London:
Butterworths, 1980), para. 2.52, footnotes omitted.

differently today.[63] Similar scepticism about the blanket exclusion of ideas from copyright has been expressed in judicial circles. In *LB (Plastics) Ltd* v *Swish Products Ltd* [1979] FSR 145 Lord Hailsham of St Marylebone LC observed:

> . . . it is trite law that there is no copyright in ideas. . . . But, of course, as the late Professor Joad used to observe, it all depends on what you mean by 'ideas'. What the respondents in fact copied from the appellants was no mere general idea.

More recently, in *Plix Products Ltd* v *Frank M. Winstone (Merchants)* [1986] FSR 63, a case concerning infringement of artistic copyright, Pritchard J of the High Court of New Zealand has suggested that the so-called 'idea–expression dichotomy' can perhaps best be understood by distinguishing two different kinds, or levels, of 'ideas'. The first type of idea, 'the general idea or basic concept of the work', cannot be protected by copyright. Copyright can, however, subsist in the second type, namely 'the ideas which are applied in the exercise of giving expression to basic concepts'. As Pritchard J then observed (at pp. 93–4):

> The difficulty, of course, is to determine just where the general concept ends and the exercise of expressing the concept begins. . . . The basic idea (or concept) is not necessarily simple – it may be complex. It may be something innovative; or it may be commonplace, utilitarian or banal. The way the author treats the subject, the forms he uses to express the basic concept, may range from the crude and simplistic to the ornate, complicated – and involving the collation and application of a great number of constructive ideas. It is in this area that the author expends the skill and industry which (even though they may be slight) give the work its originality and entitle him to copyright. Anyone is free to use the basic idea – unless, of course, it is a novel invention which is protected by the grant of a patent. But no one can appropriate the forms or shapes evolved by the author in the process of giving expression to the basic idea. So he who seeks to make a product of the same description as that in which another owns copyright must tread with care.

This analysis has interesting implications for the debates relating to the development of compatible software by means of reverse engineering, and the emulation of the look and feel of the user interfaces of popular software packages. A court in the United Kingdom may, like the High Court of New Zealand, be concerned more with whether a significant amount of an author's labour and skill has been misappropriated, than with whether what has been taken is 'merely' an idea.

At the time of writing, there has been no reported full trial decision on any question of infringement of software copyright under the 1988 Act or its

---

63. Ibid., paras 2.50 to 2.54.

predecessor the 1956 Copyright Act, though there have been a number of reported interlocutory (pre-trial) rulings relating to alleged infringements.[64] To a large extent, it is necessary to rely on the basic principles just discussed to assess the scope of non-literal infringement of software copyright under English law. However, two of the interlocutory decisions, one under the 1956 Act and one under the 1988 Act, give some indication of the arguments which may sway English courts in such cases, though neither is of significant precedential value.

In *MS Associates Ltd* v *Power* [1988] FSR 242, the plaintiff alleged that one of its ex-employees was marketing a program called 'B-tran' and that substantial parts of that product were copied from one of the plaintiff's established products, 'C-Gen'. Falconer J was satisfied that there was an arguable case of infringement. This was based on evidence of similarities between the programs coupled with the fact that in working on part of C-Gen before he left the plaintiff's employment Power had access to the plaintiff's source code. Evidence of literal copying was limited. However, the court was satisfied that the plaintiff had an arguable case and a real prospect of succeeding in obtaining a permanent injunction at trial because of certain 'striking' line similarities and various 'similarities in structure' between the programs.[65]

By way of contrast, in *Total Information Processing Systems Ltd* v *Daman Ltd* [1992] FSR 171 the acting judge (Paul Baker QC) was not prepared to find prima facie evidence of infringement notwithstanding admitted copying. He gave a preliminary ruling that there was no arguable case that the plaintiff had infringed copyright by copying various field and record specifications in the defendant's costing program. The plaintiff admitted having copied those parts of the defendant's interface file which were necessary to link its payroll program to the defendant's costing program. The defendant claimed, first, that the three-program package was a compilation, copyright in which was infringed when the plaintiff substituted its payroll program for the defendant's. Secondly, the defendant claimed that the copying of the specification of the files and records from the costing program infringed copyright in that program. The judge rejected the argument that the compilation was protected, partly because:[66]

> . . . to accord it copyright protection would lead to great inconvenience. It would mean that the copyright owners of one of the components could not interface with another similar program to that of the other components without the licence of the compiler.

64. *Gates* v *Swift* [1981] FSR 57; *Sega Enterprises Ltd* v *Richards* [1983] FRS 73; *Systematica Ltd* v *London Computer Centre Ltd* [1983] FSR 313; *Thrustcode Ltd* v *WW Computing Ltd* [1983] FSR 502; *MS Associates Ltd* v *Power* [1988] FSR 242; *Leisure Data* v *Bell* [1988] FSR 367; *Total Information Processing Systems Ltd* v *Daman Ltd* [1992] FSR 171.
65. [1988] FSR 242 at p. 248. Notwithstanding these findings, when it applied the 'balance of convenience test', the court refused to grant an interlocutory injunction, principally it seems on the ground that the likely effect of such an order would be to put the defendants out of business (ibid. at pp. 250–2).
66. [1992] FSR 171 at p. 179.

Regarding the specification which had been copied, he ruled that:[67]

> The part copied can be likened to a table of contents. It would be very unusual that that part of a book could be described as a substantial part of it. The specification in high-level language of fields and records in the data division tells one little or nothing about the costing program and so, in my judgment, cannot be regarded as a substantial part of it.

Both of these conclusions are curious. Regarding the first, it has never been a criterion for copyright protection that the partial monopoly afforded by a copyright must not lead to 'great inconvenience'. Regarding the second, it seems quite likely that a detailed table of contents for a book could constitute not only a substantial part of a work but might even be a work in its own right. Similarly, a program specification could qualify as either a substantial part of a work or as a discrete work.

There are currently three trends which might result, generally, in a weakening of copyright protection for software. One trend which, if developed, would significantly weaken the scope of copyright protection for software is reliance on the principle of non-derogation from grant as a basis for permitting what would otherwise be infringing acts. The limited 'repair right' recognised by the House of Lords in *British Leyland Motor Corporation Ltd* v *Armstrong Patents Co. Ltd* [1986] AC 577 has been applied by the Official Referee's Court in *Saphena Computing Ltd* v *Allied Collection Agencies Ltd* (1988) 59 Computers and Law 20 to permit acts necessary for software maintenance which would normally infringe copyright.[68]

A second basis for a weakening of the monopoly given by copyright would rest on a development of competition law principles. How would a United Kingdom court respond if asked to decide on the scope of copyright protection in circumstances where, for example, a single set of machine instructions is the only way to achieve a particular functional result, such as interfacing with a particular item of hardware or software? In such a case, it might be possible for the court to conclude that the subject-matter in question is not protected by copyright due to lack of originality. However, a particular interface specification or procedure may be highly original and the result of considerable labour and skill. As has already been established, United Kingdom courts cannot invoke a 'merger doctrine' as a justification for excluding material from copyright on the ground that idea and expression have merged. In practice, however, a person who sought to use copyright as a basis for monopolising a *de facto* industry standard might be vulnerable to challenge under United Kingdom or EC competition law (see 12.3.3).

---

67. [1992] FSR 171 at pp. 180–1.
68. *British Leyland Motor Corporation Ltd* v *Armstrong Patents Co. Ltd* concerned the protection of the designs of functional objects, spare parts for cars, through artistic copyright in the underlying design drawings. This basis of claim has been severely restricted by the 1988 Act. In *Saphena Computing Ltd* v *Allied Collection Agencies Ltd* the Court of Appeal (1989) 61 Computers and Law 23 did not comment on the official referee's finding. For a more detailed discussion of the concept see chapter 2, para. 2.3.1.

A third, and related, development is the EC Directive on software protection. Article 1.2 of the Directive requires all EC member States to protect programs as literary works but to exclude from protection 'Ideas and principles which underlie any element of a computer program, including those which underlie its interfaces'. The draft Copyright (Computer Programs) Regulations 1992 contain no reference to the exclusion of ideas from copyright protection. This is presumably because the UK government believes that ideas are already excluded from protection as a result of judicial pronouncements to that effect. However, even if English law is already consistent with art. 1.2, there will remain considerable scope for dispute about what constitutes an 'idea' for the purposes of the exclusion. Moreover, the Directive's much debated 'decompilation' right is so hedged about by restrictions as to give developers of compatible products limited comfort regarding risks that their reverse engineering activities may infringe copyright.

4.5.7 Decompilation of computer programs

During the Software Directive's turbulent passage through the EC legislative process, by far the most contentious issue concerned the new right to be given to users permitting them to decompile a program where necessary to achieve the interoperability of that program with another program. The complex compromise agreed by the principal protagonists, after many months of heated debate and lobbying, is now enshrined in art. 6 of the Directive. The draft Copyright (Computer Programs) Regulations 1992 follow the text of art. 6 quite closely and provide that a program may only be decompiled where four criteria are met. First, the decompilation exercise must be 'indispensable to obtain information necessary . . . to achieve the interoperability of any independently created program with the original program'. Secondly, only a licensed user, or that person's agent may carry out the decompilation exercise. Thirdly, the required information must not already be readily available. Fourthly, only those parts of the program necessary to achieve interoperability may be decompiled. Exercise of the decompilation right would be hedged about by three further restrictions. It would be an infringement of copyright to use the information obtained by decompilation for any purpose other than achieving interoperability; to supply such information to any other person (except where necessary to achieve interoperability); or to use the information to develop, produce or market a program substantially similar to the one which had been decompiled.

Consistently with art. 9.1 of the Directive the draft regulations would render 'void and of no effect' provisions having the effect of prohibiting or excluding the decompilation right.

4.5.8 Back-up copies of computer programs

Article 5.2 of the Software Directive provides that 'The making of a back-up copy by a person having a right to use the computer program may not be prevented by contract insofar as it is necessary for that use'. The draft Copyright (Computer Programs) Regulations 1992 would implement art. 5.2 as follows. The proposed new s. 29B(1) of the 1988 act would permit the making of an additional copy of a program by a licensed user where '(a) the making of the additional copy is for the sole purpose of ensuring that a copy is available for use in the event that a copy is lost, destroyed or rendered unusable; and (b) the making of an additional copy is necessary for the licensed use'. In practice, most PC software must be loaded on to the hard disk of a PC before it can be run. The loading process often entails the 'explosion' of compressed files and the installation of the package for a particular configuration of hardware and software. The making of a back-up copy, in the sense of a verbatim copy of the original disks, is quite unnecessary as the original disks are available for back-up purposes. Thus, the new back-up exemption may be of limited application.

4.5.9   Infringement of copyright in data and databases

Copyright in a work may be infringed by its inclusion in, and distribution as part of, a database. In addition to the copying, or adaptation, which occurs on incorporation of a work into a compilation, the definition of 'commercial publication' of a work in s. 175(2) of the 1988 Act covers expressly the act of 'making the work available to the public by means of an electronic retrieval system'. Thus, to avoid copyright infringement, a database provider may need to obtain licences from owners of copyright in works which are to be incorporated in a database.

As stated in 4.2.2.2, the database itself may qualify for copyright protection, provided that the arrangement or presentation of the compilation is the result of a sufficiently substantial degree of skill and labour. This copyright will be infringed not only where a facsimile copy is made, but also, under UK law, where the infringer uses the compilation as a 'short-cut', thus gaining an unfair advantage by avoiding the effort and skill used by the author. An example is the case of *Waterlow Publishers Ltd* v *Rose* (1989) *The Times*, 8 December 1989 which related to Waterlow's 1984 edition of *The Solicitors' and Barristers' Directory and Diary* to which the defendant had initially resorted for his information in preparing the rival publication, *The Lawyers' Diary*. The Court of Appeal held that an infringement had occurred even though there had been no copying of the layout or arrangement of the material, and even though much of the information had been independently checked by the rival with the data subjects. This, therefore, introduces an element equivalent to the notion of 'fair dealing' into the question of database copyright infringement in the UK, in that the court focused on whether the copying 'was for the purposes of overcoming difficulties and was of benefit to the defendant'.

Similarly, in the case of *Elanco Products Ltd* v *Mandops (Agrochemical Specialists) Ltd* [69] (which related to a label and leaflet sold with herbicide), the court observed that 'the defendants were fully entitled to make use of any information which was available to them in the public domain for the purposes of compiling their trade literature, but they were not entitled to copy the plaintiffs' trade literature thereby making use of the plaintiffs' skill and

---

69. [1979] FSR 46. Recently upheld in interlocutory proceedings in *Dun & Bradstreet Ltd* v *Typesetting Facilities Ltd* [1992] FSR 320.

judgment and saving themselves the trouble and cost of assembling their own information and thereby making their own selection of material to put into that literature'.[70] However, this case concerned interlocutory proceedings and the substantive questions of copyright subsistence and infringement were not considered in detail, it being merely held that there was an arguable case.

This general approach by the UK courts contrasts with the US decision in *Feist Publications Inc.* v *Rural Telephone Service Co. Inc.* (1991) 113 L Ed 2d 358, where the 'sweat of the brow' doctrine of copyrightability was repudiated in favour of copyright protection for expression not effort. The US approach accords with the principles underlining the proposed Council Directive on the legal protection of databases (see 4.2.2.2). Under the proposed Directive factual contents of electronic databases that are not already protected by copyright would be protected by means of a new *sui generis* right to prevent for a period of ten years unfair extraction of the contents for commercial purposes (art. 2(5)).

As far as database copyright infringement is concerned, the proposed Directive provides that the owner of the copyright in an electronic database has the exclusive right to do or authorise the reproduction, translation, adaption, arrangement or alteration of the database; the reproduction of results of such acts; the communication or performance of the database to the public; and any form of distribution to the public, including the rental of the database or of copies thereof (art. 5).

Under current United Kingdom law, whether a database is characterised as a literary work or cable programme, or both, the scope of the primary infringing act of copying the whole or a substantial part of the work can be difficult to assess. A database may be accessed remotely, for example, by telephone dial-up, or directly from a local storage medium, such as a compact disc. In either case, a user is only likely to copy a small part of the whole database in the normal course of viewing pages. Indeed, with a user searching for information of perhaps only a few characters in length in a database consisting of millions or billions of characters, the proportion will often be minuscule. It is difficult to see how such selected viewing or searching would infringe any rights in the compilation. It is, however, possible that such normal use would infringe rights in one or more of the literary works or cable programmes which comprise the database. Moreover, a user who deliberately downloaded a sizeable portion of the material contained in a database might infringe copyright in the database as a whole.

4.5.10   Second-hand copies of works in electronic form
Section 56 of the 1988 Act contains a complex and somewhat convoluted statement of the rights to be enjoyed by a person taking a transfer from the original purchaser of a copy of a program or other work in electronic form. The provision is applicable where a copy of such a work 'has been purchased on terms which, expressly or impliedly or by virtue of any rule of law, allow the purchaser to copy the work, or to adapt it or make copies of an adaptation, in connection with his use of it'. Subject to any express terms to the contrary,

---

70. [1979] FSR at p. 57.

where the copy is transferred to a third party, that person is entitled to do anything with the copy which the original purchaser was permitted to do. From the moment of transfer, however, any copy or adaptation retained by the original purchaser will be treated as an infringing copy. The same rules apply to any subsequent transfers made by the new owner and that person's successors in title.

Section 56 is not a model of clarity. Taking its application to computer programs, packaged software is typically distributed with a licence 'agreement' in which the software producer purports to retain title to part or all of the product. Where title to the physical copy of the program does not pass, it will make no sense to speak of the 'purchaser' of the copy. Moreover, the scope for inferring licences in this area is quite uncertain and thus the reference to terms which the purchaser has the benefit of 'impliedly or by virtue of any rule of law' is not particularly illuminating. In practice, quite apart from the theoretical question of whether or not there is a 'purchaser', it is likely to continue to be the norm for software, and most other works published in electronic form, to be distributed with an express prohibition, or at least restriction, on transfers to third parties. In all such cases, the operation of s. 56 will be completely pre-empted.

4.6 MORAL RIGHTS

4.6.1 The nature of moral rights

The Berne Union, of which the United Kingdom is a member, provides for its members to give authors various 'moral rights'. Such rights are to be personal to the author or creator of a work and are to be capable of exercise independently of the economic exploitation rights in the work. For the first time in the United Kingdom, the 1988 Act gives the author of a work or director of a film the right, in certain circumstances, to be identified as such (s. 77). Relevant circumstances include commercial publication of the work or any adaptation of it. This right is otherwise known as the right of 'paternity'. Authors and directors also have the right to object to 'derogatory treatment' of their works (s. 80(1)), which right is otherwise known as the right of 'integrity'. Treatment of a work will be deemed derogatory 'if it amounts to distortion or mutilation of the work or is otherwise prejudicial to the honour or reputation of the author or director' (s. 80(2)). Two other moral rights give protection against false attribution of a work,[71] and the right to privacy of certain photographs and films (s. 85). With the exception of the false attribution right, which expires 20 years after a person's death, all of the moral rights continue to subsist for as long as copyright subsists in the work in question (s. 86). The rest of the discussion here will be focused on the rights of paternity and integrity as they apply to literary, dramatic, musical and artistic works.

4.6.2 Restrictions on scope

The right of paternity must be asserted in writing and will in most cases only bind third parties who have notice of it (1988 Act, s. 78). In the case of works

---

71. I.e., the right not to have a work wrongly attributed to one (s. 84).

created in the course of employment, the copyright in which vested automatically in the employer, the right does not apply to anything done by, or with the
authority of, the employer or any subsequent owner of copyright in the work
(s. 79(3)). The right of integrity is also severely cut back in relation to works
created by employees, copyright in which originally vested in their employers
(s. 82(1)).[72] Neither right applies, in any event, in relation to computer
programs and computer-generated works (ss. 79(2) and 81(2)).

These exclusions appear, at first sight, to abrogate moral rights as they apply
to works produced by the computer industry. Moral rights will, nevertheless,
have significant implications for the computer and related industries and those
who work in them. As already noted in this chapter, software packages, for
example, are much more than computer programs for copyright purposes.
While moral rights will not be available in respect of any programs and
computer-generated works incorporated in a package nor any work owned
automatically by an employer, moral rights will be available in respect of many
other works produced on a commissioning basis. For example, a freelance
technical author would be able to assert the right of paternity and object to
unjust modification of published manuals or other technical documentation,
and a freelance artist may make such claims with regard to published artwork.
Moreover, moral rights will be applicable to many works which are included
in databases and in that context it is difficult to see how the right of paternity
could be exercised without becoming unduly cumbersome. Protection against
false attribution applies to all categories of works but is less likely to cause
problems in practice.

4.6.3 Consents and waivers

Although moral rights are 'inalienable' and thus cannot be assigned like the
economic rights in a work,[73] a person entitled to moral rights can forgo the right
to exercise the rights in part or completely. In general, it is not an infringement
of moral rights to do anything to which the right-holder has consented.
Moreover, any of the moral rights 'may be waived by instrument in writing
signed by the person giving up the right'. Such waivers may relate to specific
works or to works generally, may be conditional or unconditional, and may be
made subject to revocation (1988 Act, s. 87). Given the potential difficulties
which were identified in 4.6.2, it is probable that many organisations will
include express consents or waivers of moral rights in their standard terms of
business for commissioned works.

4.6.4 Remedies

Infringements of moral rights are actionable as breaches of statutory duty
owed to the person entitled to the right (1988 Act, s. 103(1)). In relation to

---

72. The right will only apply if the author '(a) is identified at the time of the relevant act, or (b)
    has previously been identified in or on published copies of the work; and where in such a case
    the right does apply, it is not infringed if there is a sufficient disclaimer.' (s. 82(2)).
73. Although they do form part of an author's estate on death and consequently can pass to third
    parties under a will or on intestacy (s. 95).

infringement of the right to object to derogatory treatment of a work, a court may grant an injunction requiring a disclaimer to be given, for example, on publication, dissociating the author from the treatment of the work (s. 103(2)). In relation to the right of paternity, a court must, in considering what remedy should be given for an infringement, take into account any delay in asserting the right (s. 78(5)). Both of these qualifications on remedies have the effect of further limiting the potential commercial leverage which moral rights may confer on an author. Where, for example, a publisher has incurred considerable expense over a period of time in preparing a work for publication, instead of stopping publication because of derogatory treatment a court may merely order that a disclaimer be printed. Likewise, the author's right of paternity may effectively be undermined as a result of any delay in asserting the right.

4.7 CIVIL REMEDIES, CRIMINAL SANCTIONS AND PROCEDURAL MATTERS

4.7.1 Civil remedies
Copyright is a property right, and where infringement has been proved, the copyright owner can, subject to certain special rules, benefit from 'all such relief . . . as is available in respect of the infringement of any other property right' (1988 Act, s. 96). In practice, the principal remedies are injunctions to prevent further breaches of copyright, damages for breach of copyright and orders for delivery up of infringing copies. Other remedies include accounts of profits (used relatively rarely because of the difficulty of proving the precise profits made) and orders for disposal of infringing copies which have been seized or delivered up to a plaintiff (see generally ss. 96 to 106 and 113 to 115).

Various court orders can be obtained at the pre-trial stage, in some circumstances without the alleged infringer being given any warning or opportunity to make representations to the court. One such *ex parte* order which has been used with particular success against audio, video and software pirates is the '*Anton Piller*' order.[74] Such an order can authorise a plaintiff to enter a defendant's premises, without prior warning, to seize evidentiary material which might otherwise be tampered with or disappear before trial. This is obviously a powerful remedy capable of abuse in the hands of overenthusiastic plaintiffs and its use is now quite strictly supervised by the courts.[75]

---

74. So called after the case in which it was first obtained, *Anton Piller KG* v *Manufacturing Processess Ltd* [1976] Ch 55. For an example of the grant of such an order in a case of alleged software piracy, see *Gates* v *Swift* [1981] FSR 57.

75. In another software copyright case, *Systematica Ltd* v *London Computer Centre Ltd* [1983] FSR 313 at p. 316, Whitford J observed that 'A situation is developing where I think rather too free a use is being made by plaintiffs of the *Anton Piller* provision'. Subsequently, in *Columbia Picture Industries* v *Robinson* [1986] FSR 367 at p. 439, Scott J commented 'that the practice of the court has allowed the balance to swing too far in favour of the plaintiffs and that *Anton Piller* orders have been too readily granted and with insufficient safeguards for respondents'. The court laid down a number of procedural safeguards which should be complied with to ensure minimum protection for defendants.

While a final injunction may be granted at trial, it is quite common in cases of alleged software copyright infringement for an 'interlocutory' injunction to be granted in pre-trial proceedings. An injunction may be prohibitory, for example, enjoining a defendant from copying or in any way dealing with the material which is the subject of the dispute.[76] Alternatively, or in addition, an injunction may be mandatory, for example, requiring delivery up of source code pending trial.[77]

As a general rule, damages for copyright infringement are intended to compensate a plaintiff for actual loss incurred as a result of the infringement. This might typically be calculated on the basis of royalties which would have been payable to the plaintiff had the defendant, instead of infringing copyright, obtained a licence for the acts in question.[78] The 1988 Act specifies one set of circumstances in which damages must not be awarded, and one in which they may be increased beyond the compensatory level. The former arises where it is shown that the defendant did not know and had no reason to believe that copyright subsisted in the work in question at the time of infringement. In such circumstances, 'the plaintiff is not entitled to damages against him, without prejudice to any other remedy' (s. 97(1)). In other cases, however, the court may award 'such additional damages as the justice of the case may require' in all the circumstances, with particular reference to '(a) the flagrancy of the infringement, and (b) any benefit accruing to the defendant by reason of the infringement' (s. 97(2)).

4.7.2 Criminal sanctions

The 1988 Act sets out a number of categories of criminal copyright infringement which, in general, are intended to penalise those who deliberately infringe copyright with a view to commercial gain. Specifically, it is an offence, if done without a licence, to manufacture for sale or hire, import into the United Kingdom other than for private and domestic use, distribute in the course of business or otherwise 'to such an extent as to affect prejudicially' the rights of the copyright owner, an article which the offender knows to be, or has reason to believe to be, an infringing copy of a work (1988 Act, s. 107(1)(a), (b), (d)(iv) and (e)). On summary conviction the penalties for such an offence are imprisonment for up to six months and a fine not exceeding the statutory maximum, or both (s. 197(4)(a)).[79] On conviction on indictment the maximum penalties are imprisonment for up to two years or a fine.[80]

It is an offence, if done without a licence, to possess in the course of a business with a view to committing an infringing act, or in the course of

---

76. For example, *Gates* v *Swift* [1981] FSR 57.
77. For example, *Raindrop Data Systems Ltd* v *Systematics Ltd* [1988] FSR 354; *Leisure Data* v *Bell* [1988] FSR 367.
78. For example, *Redwood Music Ltd* v *Chappell & Co. Ltd* [1982] RPC 109.
79. At the time of writing, the statutory maximum was £5,000.
80. Section 107(4)(b). There is no statutory limit on the fine which may be imposed on conviction for one of these offences on indictment. In practice, however, the amount will be governed by the general principle that a fine should be within an offender's capacity to pay (*R* v *Churchill (No. 2)* [1967] 1 QB 190).

business to sell or let for hire, to offer or expose for sale or hire, or exhibit in public, an article which the offender knows to be, or has reason to believe to be, an infringing copy of a work (s. 107(1)(c), (d)(i), (ii) and (iii)). It is also an offence to make or possess 'an article specifically designed or adapted for making infringing copies of a particular copyright work' if the offender knows or has reason to believe that the article will be used to make infringing copies for sale or hire or use in the course of a business (s. 107(2)).[81] These latter categories of offences are only triable summarily and the maximum penalties are imprisonment for up to six months or a fine not exceeding level 5 on the standard scale, or both (s. 107(5)).[82]

Where a person is charged with any of the criminal offences under the 1988 Act, the court before which proceedings are brought may order delivery up of any infringing copy or article for making infringing copies (s. 108). The 1988 Act also provides for a magistrate, if satisfied that one of the offences which are triable either way has been or is about to be committed and that relevant evidence is in specified premises, to 'issue a warrant authorising a constable to enter and search the premises, using such reasonable force as is necessary' (s. 109). Moreover, where any of the offences is committed by a company 'with the consent or connivance of a director, manager, secretary or other similar officer . . . or a person purporting to act in any such capacity' that person is also guilty of the offence, and liable to be prosecuted and punished accordingly (s. 110).

Taken as a whole, these criminal offences set high stakes for commercial copyright infringement and are intended to provide an effective deterrent against commercial infringement of copyright in software and other works. Moreover, a software pirate who fraudulently uses a trade mark may be convicted of a new counterfeiting offence, the maximum penalty for which is 10 years' imprisonment.[83]

4.7.3 Presumptions

A prerequisite to a successful action for copyright infringement, whether in civil or criminal proceedings, is proof of authorship and ownership of the relevant copyright(s). For practical and procedural reasons, proof of such facts can sometimes constitute a substantial hurdle to a plaintiff or prosecutor, as the case may be. The 1988 Act provides that various presumptions will apply in proceedings relating to various types of copyright work. These include a presumption that where a name purporting to be that of the author of a literary, dramatic, musical or artistic work appears on published copies of the work, the named person shall, until the contrary is proved, be deemed to be the author. It is, moreover, presumed that the special rules as to first ownership of works created during the course of employment, etc. were not applicable and thus that the named person was the first owner (s. 104).

---

81. Interpretation of the equivalent civil infringement is discussed in 4.3.2.
82. At the time of writing, level 5 on the standard scale was £5,000.
83. Section 300. An offender convicted on indictment may also be liable to pay an unlimited fine. The penalty limits for summary conviction are six months' imprisonment and a fine not exceeding the statutory maximum.

A special rule applies to copyright notices appearing on copies of computer programs. In litigation relating to program copyright, 'where copies of the program are issued to the public in electronic form bearing a statement— (a) that a named person was the owner of copyright in the program at the date of issue of the copies, or (b) that the program was first published in a specified country or that copies of it were first issued to the public in electronic form in a specified year, the statement shall be admissible as evidence of the facts stated and shall be presumed to be correct until the contrary is proved' (s. 105(3)). This special presumption is likely, on occasions at least, to be of major assistance to plaintiffs in civil cases and the prosecution in criminal proceedings. As a result, program copyright owners should ensure that they affix appropriate copyright notices to all copies of a program they publish and that any licensees are obliged to do likewise.

CHAPTER FIVE

The patentability of computer software

Gerald Dworkin

5.1 THE PATENT SYSTEM

Patents for inventions go back a very long way; long before 1624, when the system was accorded specific statutory recognition in England by the Statute of Monopolies. A patent confers upon the inventor of some new or improved industrial product or process a monopoly right over that invention for a certain number of years to enable him to exploit it, and to stop others from exploiting it without authority. The emphasis is upon 'industrial application'; mere discoveries or theories without any immediate industrial relevance are excluded from the system, as are, for example, writings or artistic works, which are more properly regarded as within the scope of copyright.

The relevant United Kingdom legislation today is the Patents Act 1977 and patents are granted for inventions which are 'novel' and 'not obvious' to those familiar with the state of the art in question. Most countries grant patents for inventions and there are international and regional conventions designed to promote the system around the world. In Europe, the European Patent Convention ensures that the patent laws of most of the European States are more or less in harmony with each other and that inventors can obtain patents in all or any of those States by complying with similar conditions. In due course, it should be possible for an inventor to obtain *one* patent valid throughout the European Community, rather than, as now, having to apply for a number of separate patents in each of the member States for which patent protection is sought.

Patent rights can last, normally, for up to 20 years. The justifications for conferring such a long monopoly upon an inventor are many. The prospect of the grant of a patent monopoly is said to provide an incentive to some inventors to invent and also to disclose the details of that invention to the public,[1] whereas if there were no incentive the inventor might not find it worthwhile to invent or would do all that was possible to keep information to himself and so inhibit the advance of scientific, technical and industrial knowledge. It also acts as a stimulant for the inventor, and those associated with him, to invest in the development of the new invention. Thus, the law is said to serve an important social purpose in assisting the innovative process and furthering industrial and economic welfare.

It has always been difficult to quantify the economic importance of patents. They are essential to some industries, notably the pharmaceutical industry, and of varying degrees of importance, directly or indirectly, to most others. Although there are some who criticise the patent system and put forward various proposals for improving it, or enhancing it by providing alternative or complementary rights such as 'petty patents' or 'innovation warrants', there is little doubt that governments today recognise its importance in the dynamics of industrial innovation.

Innovative forms of computer *hardware* clearly fall within the scope of, and can be protected by, the patent system. At first sight there seems to be no reason why the same rules should not apply to innovative *software*. On further analysis, though, the situation is far from simple.

Computer specialists maintain, with cause, that lawyers and other policy makers involved with software often do not understand the relevant technologies. One can sympathise with the difficulties faced by those who seek to place computer software into an, or the, appropriate legal framwork. The failure to analyse the nature of computer software (and firmware) carefully enough adds to the difficulty of deciding whether software is more akin to copyright or to patentable subject-matter. Much of the expression and information involved in and produced by computer software has a copyright feel about it; much else, starting from its initial appearance as a kind of machine, looks more like the subject-matter of patent law.

In the early stages there were countless discussions as to whether patent or copyright law should be the preferred method of protection. There was even the prospect, because software did not seem to fit naturally into either system, of creating a new *sui generis* computer software right. Today there is general international consensus that computer software protection should be achieved primarily through copyright law rather than through any other legal regime; although, as Chapter 4 illustrates, there are recurring doubts about whether copyright law protection is always adequate or appropriate.

Yet there has always been some scope for the use of patent law to protect software-related inventions and algorithms: the problem has always been; how much scope?

---

1. A patent applicant must make a sufficient disclosure of the invention, but it is not always easy in this area to determine what is required. The EPO Guidelines state 'it is necessary that the invention is described not only in terms of its structure, but also in terms of its function, unless the functions of the various parts are immediately apparent. Indeed in some technical fields (e.g., computers) a clear description of function may be much more appropriate than an over-detailed description of structure'. However, for an example of a rejection of a computer-related invention for insufficient explanation, see *IBM* [1989] 3 EPOR 157.

5.2 ARE COMPUTER PROGRAMS PATENTABLE SUBJECT-MATTER?

Why should there be any difficulty in accepting that innovative computer software can be just as patentable, if the relevant patent rules are satisfied, as any other industrially applicable invention?

The answer, to some extent, lies in the need to distinguish between an industrially applicable innovation which involves the use of a computer program – a computer-related invention – and an innovative computer program, where the only invention and the only product involved is the computer program itself. It is the nature of a computer program *alone* which poses the problems.

Although neither English patent nor English copyright law provides any statutory definition of a computer program there have been many authoritative attempts to define the term. Thus the WIPO Model Provisions on the Protection of Computer Software (1978) defined a computer program as 'a set of instructions capable, when incorporated in a machine-readable medium, of causing a machine having information-processing capabilities to indicate, perform or achieve a particular function, task or result'.

It was the emphasis upon the 'instructional' aspects of programs which led some to deny that they could be patentable subject-matter; inventions are usually understood to be solutions to technical problems which use scientific principles in the fields of physics, chemistry or biology. However, so-called 'instructions to the human mind' are not normally considered to be inventions. An allied consideration was that computer programs involved algorithms and mathematical formulae, and the proper scope of patents would be as much exceeded if monopoly rights were granted over such fundamental matters as it would be, for example, if Einstein could have obtained a monopoly right over his theory of relativity. Thus, in 1970, the Banks Committee report on the British patent system[2] declared that computer programs are basically methods of mathematical calculation or sets of instructions for carrying out such calculations. 'Methods of mathematical calculation have never been held to be patentable and there is no reason to recommend a change in this position.'[3]

To skilled patent practitioners, form is at least as important as substance. The skilled draftsman may often be able to frame his patent claims in such a way that what at first seems to be unpatentable subject-matter is reformulated into the standard stuff of patents. The significance of careful drafting was adverted to by the Banks Committee:

> The position on program patents seems to be that they are granted by the Patent Office when the claims are drafted so that they relate to a piece of machinery or apparatus, e.g., a computer when programmed in a certain way; a tape or card with a certain configuration of holes; a computer-controlled process, such as a power station or steel works, provided that the invention claimed shows novelty [and inventive step].

---

2. Cmnd 4407 (London: HMSO, 1970).
3. Cmnd 4407 (see note 2), para. 483.

The Committee then pertinently remarked:

> Whether or not there can be said to be a real distinction between a program
> invention claimed in this rather roundabout way and a claim to the program
> itself is at least open to doubt.[4]

These themes – namely that computer programs are somewhat different to
other inventions in that they relate to information, instructions, mathematical
formulae etc. and yet, notwithstanding this, there may be *some* scope for
patentability of certain kinds of computer software linked to industrial activity
– recur through most of the case law in those jurisdictions which have been
called upon to examine the issue. The patent offices and courts of most
countries have displayed a remarkably similar trend, moving from initial
hostility to patenting computer program innovations to a much more relaxed
and flexible approach.

This can be illustrated by comparing the way in which vacillating developments in the United States foreshadowed similar vacillations in the United
Kingdom and Europe. Even now, patent law, or at least patent office practice,
does not yet appear to achieve identical results in all jurisdictions.

5.2.1 Developments in the USA

In the 1970s the US Patent Office was not in favour of patenting computer
programs. The courts of the United States were also unreceptive to those
arguing for patents for most kinds of computer programs although they were
not prepared to strike down all computer programs as unpatentable subject-
matter.

Thus in *Gottschalk* v *Benson* (1972) 409 US 63 the Supreme Court held that
a method for converting numerals expressed as binary-coded decimal numerals
into pure binary numerals, which was useful in devising programs for digital
computers, could not be patented as a 'process'. The uneasy reasoning in the
judgment was fairly characteristic of many other decisions in the area:

> It is conceded that one may not patent an idea. But in practical effect that
> would be the result if the formula for converting binary code to pure binary
> were patented in this case. The mathematical formula involved here has no
> substantial practical application except in connection with a digital com-
> puter, which means that [if accepted] the patent would wholly pre-empt the
> mathematical formula and in practical effect would be a patent on the
> algorithm itself.

This kind of analysis came in for severe criticism:[5]

> The statement as to 'pre-empting the mathematical formula' is nonsense.
> [The applicants] were claiming a certain means and that means only. They

---

4. Cmnd 4407 (see note 2), para. 474.
5. Donald S. Chisum, *Patents* (New York: Matthew Bender, looseleaf), vol. 1, sect. 1.03[6].

did not claim all means of converting BCN to pure binary . . . The method they claimed was to a prescribed series of steps for manipulating information (data) – not a 'mathematical formula' in the conventional meaning of that term. Many patents have in effect 'pre-empted' all the then known practical applications of a newly discovered 'principle' or truth.

A line of 'anti-patent' decisions reached its zenith before the Supreme Court in *Parker* v *Flook* (1978) 437 US 584. This case concerned a patent application for a method for updating 'alarm limits' during a chemical process. The levels of temperature, pressure and flow rates have to be constantly monitored and when any of these 'process variables' exceeds a predetermined 'alarm limit' there is an abnormal condition indicating either inefficiency or danger. During transient operating situations it may be necessary to 'update' the alarm limits periodically.

The method for which a patent was sought consisted of three steps: first, the initial step which measured the present value of a process variable (for example, temperature); secondly, an intermediate step which used an algorithm (a procedure to solve a mathematical problem) to calculate an updated alarm-limit value; and then a final step whereby the actual alarm limit was adjusted to the updated value.

It was argued by the applicants that they were seeking a patent for something more than a computer program alone; it was not simply a formula for computing an alarm limit but much more, namely the 'transformation and reduction of an article to a different state or thing' and so patentable subject-matter. The Supreme Court disagreed; the discovery of a 'phenomenon of nature or mathematical formula' cannot 'support a patent unless there is some other inventive concept in its application'; and it did not look kindly on attempts by draftsmen to dress up applications to make them look something more than computer program claims:

> The notion that post-solution activity, no matter how conventional or obvious in itself, can transform an unpatentable principle into a patentable process exalts form over substance. A competent draftsman could attach some form of post-solution activity to almost any mathematical formula; the Pythagorean theorem would not have been patentable, or partially patentable, because a patent application contained a final step indicating that the formula, when solved, could be usefully applied to existing surveying techniques.

Thus, an unpatentable mathematical formula did not become patentable subject-matter by the addition of 'conventional post-solution applications'.

In many respects *Parker* v *Flook* marked the end of an era. Shortly afterwards another case, not factually dissimilar to *Parker* v *Flook*, reached the Supreme Court. *Diamond* v *Diehr* (1981) 450 US 175 concerned a patent application relating to use of a mould for shaping uncured synthetic rubber into cured precision products. (A 'cure' is obtained by mixing curing agents into uncured polymer in advance of moulding, and then applying heat over a period of time. If the synthetic rubber is cured for the right length of time at the right temperature, it becomes a usable product.)

The background was as follows: it was possible, using well-known time, temperature and cure relationships to calculate by means of the 'Arrhenius equation' when to open a cauldron (press) and remove the cured product. But the industry had not previously been able to obtain uniformly accurate cures because the temperature of the moulding press could not be precisely measured.

The new method for obtaining accuracy also comprised three steps. First, there was a known process of constantly measuring the actual temperature inside the mould; secondly, temperature readings were then automatically fed into a computer which repeatedly recalculated the cure time by use of the 'Arrhenius equation'; and, finally, when the recalculated time equalled the actual time that had elapsed since the press was closed, the computer signalled a device to open the press.

Once again the court had to decide whether this was simply a formula for computing an alarm limit, which would involve unpatentable subject-matter, or the 'transformation and reduction of an article to a different state or thing', which might then involve patentable subject-matter. This time, it decided that there was patentable subject-matter: the claims were not directed to a mathematical algorithm or an improved method of calculation but rather recited an improved process for moulding rubber articles by solving a practical problem which had arisen in the moulding of rubber products. This conclusion was not affected by the fact that in several steps of the process a mathematical equation and a programmed digital computer were used. The court distinguished *Parker* v *Flook* by emphasising that a mathematical formula does not become patentable subject-matter merely by including in the claim for the formula 'token post-solution activity'; in this case it would appear that the final step in the process, involving a device which opened the press, was something more than token post-solution activity.

It is difficult to appreciate the significance of the factual distinction between these two cases. It seems fairly clear that the majority of the court provided an unconvincing distinction because of a change of approach: it was now prepared to be much more favourably disposed towards accepting the patentability of computer programs which were related to technical processes.

Since *Diamond* v *Diehr*, the US Patent Office has ceased to resist issuing patents for computer program-related inventions. Its Guidelines outline a two-stage analysis. First, it is necessary to determine whether a scientific principle, law of nature or idea, which may be represented by a *mathematical* algorithm, is either directly or indirectly recited by the claim being analysed. If so, the second step is to determine whether the claim *as a whole* merely recites a mathematical algorithm or method of calculation. If it does, the claim would wholly pre-empt others from using the algorithm in its entirety, and so is unpatentable. However, if the mathematical algorithm is implemented in a specific way (to define structural relationships in machine claims or to refine or limit steps in process claims) it is patentable provided it is novel and inventive:[6]

---

6. Sherman, Sandison and Guren, *Computer Software Protection Law*, vol. 2 (1989).

Ultimately, the criterion derived from *Diehr* is that for software to be patentable subject matter, it must be a dynamic part of a larger, computer-implemented process, tied to and affecting the result thereof, rather than simply a calculation of numbers or data according to a mathematical algorithm without any resulting, non-token application. It is this teaching which has subsequently been explored by the lower courts.

The increased interest in filing patent applications for computer-program-related inventions[7] has resulted in patents being issued for linear programming algorithms, spell-checking routines, logic-ordering operations for spreadsheet programs, brokerage cash-management schemes and bank college-saving systems.

Critics of the extensive use of patents to protect computer-program-related inventions and 'non-mathematical' algorithms have claimed that, since *Re Iwahashi* (1989) 888 F 2d 1370, virtually *any* algorithm can be patented if the claims are skilfully drafted.[8] In that case, the invention related to an improvement in a system for voice-pattern recognition. The improvement lay in the computer program eliminating a series of computer-intensive multiplication steps and substituting a less expensive system of addition and use of squares.

The claim recited a series of interconnected means for doing the various steps of the algorithmic calculation, such as means for calculating a sum, together with a read-only memory (ROM) in which was stored a list of squares or numbers (a so-called 'look-up ROM'). The Patent Office was not impressed by the fact that the algorithm was stored in a ROM. It considered the use of pseudomachine format immaterial; the claim in effect wholly pre-empted 'any and every means for performing the functions'. The court disagreed, regarding the ROM as 'a specific piece of apparatus'. The claim did not wholly pre-empt the use of the algorithm because any use without a ROM or its equivalent would not infringe the claim. Accordingly, the court held that the claim was directed to statutorily permissible subject-matter.

The US Patent Office has cautioned against the view that the *Iwahashi* decision, literally interpreted, would enable virtually any computer algorithm to be patented. In an official notice it interprets the decision to rest on the Court's finding that Iwahashi's claim was 'truly drawn to specific apparatus', and that a ROM was not the same thing as a means for storing data. The policy of the Patent Office will be to treat apparatus limitations in other patent applications on a case-by-case basis. If apparatus limitations appear to the Office to enable the claim to encompass 'any and every means for performing' the functions involved, the Office will deny a patent unless the applicant proves that the claim is actually narrower than that in scope.

The issue of claim scope should be treated as a matter of burden of proof . . . [and it will be the applicant's] burden to show that the functionally defined

---

7. In the first half of 1989, 2,600 patent applications on software related inventions were filed.

8. See Stern, 'Patenting Algorithms in America' [1990] EIPR 292 and 321.

disclosed means do not encompass any and every means for performing the recited function.

Nevertheless, one commentator has concluded:

Inserting a nominal hardware limitation into the middle of a computer-algorithm claim written otherwise in means-for format would appear to make the claim satisfy the *Iwahashi* test for patentable subject-matter. By the same token the way is now paved for patenting computer-related algorithms in almost all cases. The ROM limitation alone, if insinuated into the middle of the claim, will suffice in a great many cases. For the others, the ingenuity of patent draftsmen should suffice to find an innocuous or nominal hardware limitation.[9]

5.2.2 Developments in the UK prior to the European Patent Convention

In the United Kingdom the precise boundaries of patentable subject-matter were left very much to the courts. Before the Patents Act 1977 the definition of 'invention' was very general and harked back to 1624:

any manner of new manufacture the subject of letters patent and grant of privilege within section 6 of the Statute of Monopolies 1624 and any new method or process of testing applicable to improvement or control of manufacture (Patents Act 1949, s. 101(1)).

The courts did not take the view that computer programs or computer-related inventions could never be patentable subject-matter. Instead, they struggled with fundamental patent law principles in attempting to decide which computer-related inventions could, and which could not, be patentable. Their approach changed over the years, in line with a general tendency to widen the scope of patentable subject-matter, but it was difficult to obtain from the various decisions very clear guidance as to the nature of the dividing line between what was and what was not acceptable.

There was still the same reluctance, as we have already seen was the case in the USA, to accept for patentability innovations relating, for example, to discoveries, scientific principles, mathematical formulae and matter more appropriate for copyright protection; the patent monopoly must not be carried too far. The courts also clung to a preference for inventions which were or related to 'manners of manufacture', namely inventions which provided 'end or vendible products'.

However, a more relaxed approach was evidenced in *Burroughs Corporation (Perkins') Application* [1974] RPC 147 where a claim to a method of controlling a computer (via the interruption by a slave computer of a central computer's routine operations) was allowed. Graham J was critical of a number of the arguments against accepting computer programs as patentable subject-matter.

---

9. Ibid.

First, the requirement of a vendible product as patentable subject-matter was rapidly becoming outmoded:

> We . . . consider that it is not enough to take a narrow and confined look at the 'product' produced by a method. Of course, if a method is regarded purely as the conception of an idea, it can always be said that the product of such a method is merely intellectual information. If, however, in practice, the method results in a new machine or process or an old machine giving a new and improved result, that fact should . . . be regarded as the 'product' or the result of using the method, and cannot be disregarded in considering whether the method is patentable or not.

Secondly, he was not well disposed to allowing the form of a patent claim to override the substance of the innovation:

> [The Patent Office] view is that a line, albeit a thin one, can be drawn between claims to 'methods of programming a computer' on the one hand and, for example, claims for methods 'of transmitting data' or 'for controlling a computer' on the other, on the basis that the product of the former is a computer programmed in a particular way, while the product of the two latter is merely intellectual information. The desirability of such a line being drawn is said to be that the Office will otherwise logically be compelled to allow claims which will, for example, monopolise simple methods of operating the buttons of an ordinary office calculator, and even, possibly, methods for the solution by a schoolmaster of quadratic equations. . . .
>
> As a matter of common sense . . . [this distinction] seems, prima facie, to be a matter of words only and to have no substance. It is difficult to see what real difference there is between a claim to 'conditioning and operating' a computer and a claim to 'controlling' a computer.
>
> The question does not depend upon fine distinctions of words. Looking at the matter from the common-sense point of view, why should a claim which starts 'a method of programming a computer' be allowable, but one which starts 'a method of controlling a computer' be not allowable, when the result of each method in practice is precisely the same.

5.2.3   The European Patent Convention
The European Patent Convention ushered in a new patents era. Article 52(2)[10] expressly declared what could *not* be regarded as inventions for the purposes of patent law:

> . . .
>
> (a)   discoveries, scientific theories and *mathematical methods*;
> (b)   aesthetic creations;

---

10. These provisions are enacted in more or less the same form in the national patent laws of the member States. In the UK, the relevant provision is the Patents Act 1977, s. 1(2).

    (c)   *schemes, rules and methods for performing mental acts, playing games or doing business, and* **programs for computers;**
    (d)   *presentations of information.*

At first sight, the die seemed to have been well and truly cast; not only is it now possible to discount computer programs on the grounds that they are mathematical methods, presentation of information etc., but there is also an express exclusion of computer programs themselves. The copyright lobby had triumphed and computer programs had been removed completely from the sphere of patents!

Of course, closer analysis of the above provisions, as they stand, could have supported arguments that not all software-related inventions were excluded from being patentable-subject matter, but clearer support for that view came from the proviso in art. 52(3):

The [foregoing provisions] shall exclude patentability of the subject-matter or activities referred to . . . only to the extent to which a European patent application or a European patent *relates to such subject-matter or activities* **as such.**

The early indications from the European Patent Office were that there would be a fairly strict approach towards accepting computer-software-related inventions. However, in response to pressure from the computer industry for a more liberal approach, the European Patent Office issued revised and more relaxed Guidelines in 1985.[11] These have influenced European Patent Office practice and its Boards of Appeal and merit detailed attention.

General
In considering whether the subject-matter of an application is an invention within . . . art. 52(1), there are two general points the examiner must bear in mind. Firstly, any exclusion from patentability . . . applies only to the extent to which the application relates to the excluded subject-matter as such. Secondly, the examiner should disregard the form or kind of claim and concentrate on its content in order to identify the real contribution which the subject-matter claimed, considered as a whole, adds to the known art.

If this contribution is not of a technical character, there is no invention within art. 52(1). Thus, for example, if the claim is for a known manufactured article having a painted design or certain written information on its surface, the contribution to the art is as a general rule merely an aesthetic creation or presentation of information. . . .

Programs for computers
The basic patentability considerations here are exactly the same as for the other exclusions listed in art. 52(2). However, a data-processing operation

---

11. These have no legal force, but are helpful in establishing practice.

can be implemented either by means of a computer program or by means of special circuits, and the choice may have nothing to do with the inventive concept but be determined purely by factors of economy or practicality. With this point in mind, examination in this area should be guided by the following approach:

A computer program claimed by itself or as a record on a carrier, is not patentable irrespective of its content. The situation is not normally changed when the computer program is loaded into a known computer. If however the subject-matter as claimed makes a technical contribution to the known art, patentability should not be denied merely on the ground that a computer program is involved in its implementation. This means, for example, that program-controlled machines and program-controlled manufacturing and control processes should normally be regarded as patentable subject-matter. It follows also that, where the claimed subject-matter is concerned only with the program-controlled internal working of a known computer, the subject-matter could be patentable if it provides a technical effect. As an example, consider the case of a known data-processing system with a small fast working memory and a larger but slower further memory. Suppose that the two memories are organised under program control, in such a way that a process which needs more address space than the capacity of the fast working memory can be executed at substantially the same speed as if the process data were loaded entirely in that fast memory. The effect of the program in virtually extending the working memory is of a technical character and might therefore support patentability.

Where patentability depends upon a technical effect the claims must be so drafted as to include all the technical features of the invention which are essential for the technical effect.

The practice of the European Patent Office and the decisions of the European Boards of Appeal have been based upon these guidelines and, to a large extent, they are being used in the national patent offices of the member states of the Convention.

They are by no means easy to apply, though, and it is far from clear that all the relevant adjudicatory bodies are applying the rules in a consistent way. The United Kingdom courts, for example, have stressed that in the interests of harmony, European Patent Office decisions, though not binding, should be taken into account.[12]

Sometimes seeming inconsistencies in approach are said to turn upon the ways in which particular patent claims are drafted. The courts adopt an ambivalent approach to patent drafting. They recognise, of course, that in patent law the validity and scope of monopoly rights are highly dependent upon the way in which patent claims are drafted; drafting being one of the most

---

12. *Gale's Application* [1991] RPC 305 per Nicholls LJ at p. 322. Yet, as examiners in the UK Patent Office have pointed out, when faced with 'English case law which does not sit very happily' with EPO decisions, they are bound by the decisions of their own courts and cannot freely follow the EPO, e.g., *Sharp's Application* (1992) IPD 14171.

important skills of the patent practitioner.[13] Occasionally, however, it is emphasised that the form of a claim must not be allowed to obscure the substance of what is being claimed:

> ... the examiner should disregard the form or kind of claim and concentrate on its content in order to identify the real contribution which the subject-matter claimed, considered as a whole, adds to the known art.[14]

Sometimes inconsistencies are explained away on the basis that each application must turn upon its own facts.

What is usually missing from all the discussions, however, is any detailed examination of the underlying rationale for the line which is being drawn between those computer-program-related inventions which constitute patentable subject-matter and those which do not, apart from applying the words of art. 52 or the equivalent national legislation. Do the decisions make any practical or economic sense?

There are an increasing number of reported decisions on the patentability of computer-program-related inventions. These can be analysed in a number of ways: by country, chronologically, or by the particular types of subject-matter. The main rules are relatively clear, although their detailed application is less so. A closer examination of some of these rules should demonstrate how difficult it is to see clearly where the boundaries of patentability should really be.

5.2.3.1   A computer program claimed by itself is not patentable, irrespective of its content   That is the classic 'as such' exclusion. Patents cannot be granted for computer programs alone; protection for computer programs *simpliciter* is a matter for copyright or other laws. For patentability there must be an invention comprising a computer program *plus* something else; a computer-program-related invention.

5.2.3.2   A computer program which is recorded on a carrier is not patentable, irrespective of its content   It would be too easy to link a computer program to an additional feature – some form of hardware – and claim that there is now an invention which goes beyond the computer program itself. The simplest example is one which has already been referred to; a computer program *plus* its carrier. As in the USA, so in Europe, it has been emphasised that it would be nonsense to forbid the patenting of a computer program, and yet to permit the

---

13. Some of the leading examples of computer-program-related invention applications were accepted as involving patentable subject-matter only after amendments were made to the original claims: *Vicom* (T208/84) [1987] 2 EPOR 74; *Merrill Lynch's Application* [1989] RPC 561.

14. European Patent Office Guidelines quoted above. See Nicholls LJ in *Gale's Application*: '. . . it is convenient and right to strip away, as a confusing irrelevance, the fact that the claim is for "hardware". It was, *in substance*, a claim to a series of instructions which incorporated the improved method.'

patenting of a floppy disk containing a computer program.[15] Here, the substance of the claim is no more than a patent for the program as such. Something more than a carrier is required.

The European Patent Office Guidelines explain the situation thus:

> . . . if a computer program is claimed in the form of a physical record, e.g., on a conventional tape or disk, the contribution to the art is still no more than a computer program. In these instances the claim relates to excluded subject-matter as such and is therefore not allowable. If, on the other hand, a computer program in combination with a computer causes the computer to operate in a different way from a technical point of view, the combination might be patentable.

Immediately, problems of classification arise; when is a carrier more than a carrier? When can a computer program and its carrier be regarded as something more, inventive hardware, and so patentable subject-matter?

This was the issue which was addressed in *Gale's Application* [1991] RPC 305. Here the applicant discovered a method of calculating the square root of a number with the aid of a computer, which eliminated the prior art needed for a division stage. He put the necessary instructions into a ROM (a 'read-only memory' chip) and applied for a patent claiming '*Electronic circuitry* in the form known as "ROM", to provide controlling means whereby [the computer program] shall . . . eliminate recourse to the process of division'.

The Patent Office refused the application but Aldous J allowed an appeal, holding that the ROM was an article with one dedicated function whose structure had been altered during manufacture so as to perform the method of the function as defined by the claim. This was something more than a computer program and a carrier; there was a difference between a claim relating to a disk containing a program and a ROM with particular circuitry. In the former the disk carried the program and was in effect a claim relating to the program, whereas in the latter the program was used as the basis for altering the structure of the ROM, which could be used to carry out the program or method.

The Court of Appeal, perhaps more alive to the consequences of upholding this claim, disagreed and held that the ROM was no more than a carrier.[16] The distinction drawn by Aldous J between a disk containing a program and a ROM with particular circuitry was incorrect since it was 'exalting form over substance'. The ROM did become a dedicated piece of apparatus, but the position remained that the only respects in which the structure of the ROM had been altered were those necessary to embody, in conventional form, a particular set of instructions. It would be nonsense if a floppy disk containing a program was not patentable but that a ROM characterised only by the instructions in that program should be.

---

15. See, e.g., Dillon LJ in *Genentech Inc.'s Patent* [1989] RPC 147.
16. Not without considerable hesitation, however. Parker LJ confessed that he had been swayed from time to time in favour of patentability, which was supported by earlier dicta and cases in the UK and also by EPO decisions.

It appears to have been established, then (contrary, possibly, to *Re Iwahashi* (1989) 888 F 2d 1370 in the USA), that a computer program remains excluded matter whether it is on a software carrier (a disk) or in hardware (a ROM).

One then moves, inevitably, from computer programs plus carriers to computer programs employed in conventional computers, and a similar result is reached.

5.2.3.3 The situation is not normally changed when the computer program is loaded into a known computer   The view of the European Boards of Appeal, which has been approved by the UK courts, is that since the only conceivable use for a computer program is the running of it on a computer, the exclusion from patentablity of programs for computers would be effectively undermined if it could be circumvented by including in the claim a reference to conventional hardware features, such as a processor, memory, keyboard and display, which in practice, are indispensable if the program is to be used at all.[17]

At first sight, even were it to be accepted that there is patentable subject-matter whenever a computer program is made to work with a computer, this would not necessarily lead to a vast increase in claims for computer-program-related inventions; most would be unable to surmount the barriers of novelty or inventive step. However, there would be problems if novelty and inventivenesss resided only in the computer program itself. Accordingly, there is some superficial attraction in excluding the combination without more of computer programs and conventional computers. Conventional computers are treated as carriers for programs, as was indicated by Nicholls LJ in *Gale's Application*:

> ... [o]nce it is accepted, as it must be, that if Gale's discovery or method or program were embodied in a floppy disk (software) neither the disk nor a computer into whose RAM that program has been inserted could be patented, it must ... follow that the silicon chip with its circuitry embodying the program (hardware) cannot be patented either.

5.2.3.4 The invention must be considered as a whole   One of the reasons why a combination of an inventive computer program and conventional computer is not regarded as patentable subject-matter is because the inventiveness resides in the program alone, which is excluded subject-matter. Should this apply in all cases, for example, in cases where there is some more significant interaction between the program and the conventional computer? In *Merrill Lynch's Application* [1988] RPC 1, an important decision relating to a computerised trading system in stocks and shares, Falconer J felt that he was obliged to assess where the inventive step resided; if it resided in the excluded matter alone, and the non-excluded features were already known or obvious, there was no patentable subject-matter. This was surprising, since the learned judge had purported to follow the reasoning in *Vicom* (T208/84) [1987] 2

---

17. See *IBM/Document abstracting and retrieving* (T22/85) [1990] EPOR 98; *IBM/Text processing* (T65/86) [1990] EPOR 181; referred to with approval in *Gale's Application* [1991] RPC 305.

EPOR 74 where a European Technical Board of Appeal had emphasised that it was immaterial where novelty and inventiveness resided; the invention *as a whole* had to be considered.

Falconer J's reasoning was criticised in the genetic engineering decision *Genentech Inc.'s Patent* [1989] RPC 147, where the judgments of the Court of Appeal ranged widely over many fundamental areas of patent law. Dillon LJ pointed out that to insist that an invention must have some additional novelty and inventiveness beyond the excluded subject-matter could limit considerably the availability of patents. This reasoning, if similarly applied to a discovery (which is also not patentable 'as such'), would suggest that the application of the discovery is only patentable if the *application* is itself novel and not obvious, altogether apart from the novelty of the discovery. That would have a very drastic effect on the patenting of new drugs and medicinal or microbiological processes. It would also represent a drastic change from English law as previously understood.

When the Court of Appeal became seised of *Merrill Lynch's Application* [1989] RPC 561 it had the benefit of the reflections of the court in *Genentech* concerning Falconer J's judgment and so, even though the claim was rejected on other grounds (which will be discussed later), it adopted the approach that a claim must be viewed 'as a whole'.

Normally, of course, the invention as a whole will have to show something more than the normal interaction between the inventive computer program and the conventional computer, although what this 'something more' comprises is not always clear. In *Wang Laboratories Inc.'s Application* [1991] RPC 463, for example, an invention relating to digital processing and 'expert systems' involved programming a conventional computer. The court held that the machine, the computer, remained the same even when programmed. The computer and the program did not combine together to produce a new computer. They remained separate and amounted to a collocation rather than a combination making a different whole. The contribution was made by the program and no more.

5.2.3.5 The invention must be of a 'technical' character

The EPO Guidelines state that if the inventive contribution is not of a *technical* character, there is no invention within art. 52(1).

Curiously, the word 'technical' does not appear in the European Patent Convention or in the UK Patents Act 1977 in this context, although it has been argued that rules 27 and 29 of the EPC support the view that a patentable invention (a) must relate to a *technical field;* (b) must be concerned with a *technical problem*; and (c) must be characterised in the claims by means of *technical features*.[18] Nevertheless, the 'technical' aspect is now one of the key factors in assessing the patentability of certain types of computer program-related inventions. It is easy to understand how this requirement crept into the system. As has been noted earlier, just as inventions at one time were concerned primarily with 'manufactures' and 'vendible products', so today we are

---

18. G. D. Kolle, 'Patentability of Software-Related Inventions' (1991) 22 IIC 660.

concerned with a wider range of inventions susceptible of *industrial* application. These tend to be technical, in a very general sense, whereas the specific exclusions from patentability mostly seem to relate to inventions of a non-technical kind. Thus in many of the critical cases, it has to be established whether the claim relates to one of the excluded items, a computer program, discovery, mathematical method etc., or whether there is an additional technical element involved.

The problem, however, is that whilst there is no difficulty in understanding the general meaning of the word 'technical' it is nowhere satisfactorily defined. In *Wang Laboratories Inc.'s Application* [1991] RPC 463 Aldous J complained that 'technical':

has become a word of art. Thus the arguments tend to concentrate on whether or not the invention has a technical result or is useful in solving a technical problem or makes a technical contribution. This creates difficulties in that the word 'technical' is open to a number of meanings, depending upon its context.

He was referring to a decision which had held that the claimed functional interrelationship between the computer program and the computer did not define a new way of operating the computer in a *technical sense*.

It is difficult to understand what is meant by a 'technical sense', but its decision is consistent with the view that the invention was no more than a computer program to carry out a mental act, being the production of an abstract.

The EPO Guidelines and reported decisions refer to a range of other expressions, some, but not all, of which are synonymous: 'technical character', 'technical effect', 'technical process', 'technical means', 'technical benefit', 'technical advance', 'technical interaction' and 'technical features'.

The influential decision in *Vicom* (T208/84) [1987] 2 EPOR 74 focused emphasis upon the technical factor. There, the patent application related to methods and apparatus for improving the quality and speeding up the processing of pictures. There was no new end-product; instead there was a process involving the physical manipulation of electrical signals representing the picture in accordance with steps expressed mathematically in the form of an algorithm. One of the benefits conferred by this 'invention' was a substantial increase in processing speeds.

Essentially, the case was analysed in the following way. First, could the application be rejected on the ground that the essence of the development was a mathematical method, as such? No, said the board, it was something more than that, namely a technical process:

There can be little doubt that any processing operation on an electrical signal can be described in mathematical terms. The characteristics of a filter, for example, can be expressed in terms of a mathematical formula. A basic difference between a mathematical method and a technical process can be seen, however, in the fact that a mathematical method or a mathematical algorithm is carried out on numbers (whatever these numbers may represent) and provides a result also in numerical form, the mathematical method or algorithm being only an abstract concept prescribing how to operate on the numbers. No direct technical result is produced by the method as such. In contrast thereto, if a mathematical method is used in a technical process, that process is carried out on a physical entity (which may be a material object but equally an image stored as an electric signal) by some technical means implementing the method and provides as its result a certain change in that entity. The technical means might include a computer comprising suitable hardware or an appropriately programmed general-purpose computer.

The board, therefore, is of the opinion that even if the idea underlying an invention may be considered to reside in a mathematical method a claim directed to a technical process in which the method is used does not seek protection for the mathematical method as such.

Secondly, if it was not a mathematical method, could it nonetheless be rejected on the ground that the invention was a computer program? No, said the board. Applying the same reasoning, there was something more, a technical process, and so the claim was not for a computer program *as such*:

[A] claim directed to a technical process which process is carried out under the control of a program (be this implemented in hardware or in software) cannot be regarded as relating to a computer program as such within the meaning of art. 52(3) EPC, as it is the application of the program for determining the sequence of steps in the process for which in effect protection is sought.

The *Vicom* decision was followed in *Koch & Sterzel/X-ray apparatus* (T 26/86) [1988] EPOR 72, where it was argued in connection with a computer-related X-ray apparatus that, as there was no constant technical interaction between the inventive program and the (well-known in the prior art) X-ray apparatus and that a technical effect was produced only at the end of a computing operation, the conventional X-ray apparatus and the computer program had to be looked at quite separately. The board, however, emphasised that it was irrelevant when the technical effect occurs, nor was there any need to weigh up the technical and non-technical features before coming to a conclusion.[19]

... an invention must be assessed as a whole. If it makes use of both technical and non-technical means, the use of non-technical means does not detract from the technical character of the overall teaching.

---

19. [1988] EPOR 72 at pp. 75–6. The Technical Board of Appeal refused to refer the decision to an Enlarged Board of Appeal to give it an opportunity to reconsider *Vicom* and the Guidelines. For a further reiteration of these principles, see *Sternheimer* (T366/87) [1989] 3 EPOR 131.

5.2.3.6   Achieving an external technical effect   There is less difficulty when it can be shown that there is some kind of *external*, as opposed to internal, technical feature. Thus, the EPO Guidelines state that 'program-controlled machines and program-controlled manufacturing and control processes should normally be regarded as patentable subject-matter'.

5.2.3.7   Internal technical effect   The real difficulty in applying tests based upon 'technical' features is that, by some standards, any software operating a conventional computer could be described as being of a technical character; technical things must be happening within the machine.

The EPO Guidelines recognise that some internal technical effects might satisfy the patentability requirements:

> Where the claimed subject-matter is concerned only with the program-controlled *internal* working of a known computer, the subject matter could be patentable if it provides a technical effect. As an example, consider the case of a known data-processing system with a small fast working memory and a larger but slower further memory. Suppose that the two memories are organised under program control, in such a way that a process which needs more address space than the capacity of the fast working memory can be executed at substantially the same speed as if the process data were loaded entirely in that fast memory. The effect of the program in virtually extending the working memory is of a technical character and might therefore support patentability.

What the Guidelines fail to do, however, is to provide satisfactory guidance as to when the internal activity of a software-related apparatus will *not* be regarded as sufficiently technical. The result has been a series of applications in the EPO and the United Kingdom Patent Office in relation to text-processing which has led to hair-splitting, and arguably inconsistent, decisions. A few examples on either side of the line should demonstrate the difficulties.

Most of the cases in this area find against there being patentable subject-matter on 'technical' and other grounds. Thus *IBM/Document abstracting and retrieving*[20] concerned an application for a system for automatically abstracting documents, storing them and enabling them to be retrieved easily. The EPO Board of Appeal found that although the functional interrelationship of the hardware elements figuring in the claims differed from those previously known, it did not define a new way of operating the computer in a technical sense, but rather was the logical consequence of a set of rules and only expressed the algorithm underlying the required program. Whilst it was true that the information was stored through electrical signals this, in itself, did not qualify as a technical process since there was no change in the document as a technical entity.

---

20. (T22/85) [1990] EPOR 98. Followed by the Court of Appeal in *Gale's Application* [1991] RPC 305. See also *Apple Computer Application* (1992) IPD 15001.

In *IBM/Semantics related expressions* (T52/85) [1989] EPOR 454, there was an application for a system for automatically generating a list of expressions semantically related to an input linguistic expression and a method for displaying such a list of expressions. IBM argued that the claimed invention was a technical solution of a technical problem. This was rejected. As regards the problem, the finding of semantically related linguistic expressions had to do with the linguistic significance of words and was thus a linguistic problem. No technical problem of the computer was to be solved. As regards the solution, technically the computer did not seem to work in an unusual way. The solution claimed was the straightforward automation of the linguistic problem.

Contrasts were then drawn between the technical functioning of the equipment producing a non-technical result. It was the result which counted:

> It remains . . . true that internally a computer functions technically and this applies also to its display device. However, the effect of this function, namely the resulting information about the existence of semantically related expressions, is a purely linguistic, that is, non-technical result. [IBM] agrees that the claimed system can be implemented by pure software and this implementation is the only one described and preferred. No new reconfigured hardware has been shown to be used in this case. . . . this new reconfiguration by software is not a technical contribution here.

A similar problem arose before the UK Patent Office in the *Hitachi* [1991] RPC 415 decisions. These applications related to a type of computer program known as a 'compiler', the purpose of which is to assist a program writer by translating a program written in a high-level language into a form that is directly executable by a specific computer. The innovation claimed was an increase in program execution speed. The applicant asserted that the claims produced a technical result because each caused a computer to execute a source program more quickly. Reliance was placed upon *Genentech Inc.'s Patent* [1989] RPC 147, *Vicom* (T208/84) [1987] 2 EPOR 74 and *Merrill Lynch's Application* [1989] RPC 561, where Fox LJ had said that in *Vicom* the decisive technical contribution in the form of a new result was the substantial increase in processing speed. Nevertheless, the applications were refused. The increase in program execution speed was thought not to be sufficient in itself. In *Vicom*, the board allowed the claims to proceed not because the algorithm involved achieved an increase in processing speed but because the claims related to a technical process producing a technical result, the process being some form of enhancement performed upon images represented by arrays of numbers, one feature of the result being that the operations were effected more quickly. The examiner argued that Fox LJ could not have meant that a mere increase in processing speed was sufficient to secure patentability, since if this were the case the original claims in *Vicom*, being claims to an algorithm giving rise to an increase in processing speed, would not have been rejected by the EPO Board of Appeal. If followed, this reasoning demonstrates a more restrictive interpretation of the technical factor.

In *Siemens/Character form* T(158/88) [1992] EPOR 69, the application related to a process for displaying on a visual display unit characters which have different forms depending on whether they are used in isolation, or at the beginning, middle or end of words, as in Arabic. This, too, was rejected. The statement that technical means (e.g., a visual display unit) were to be used to carry out the claimed process was not alone sufficient to render patentable a process which in essence constituted a computer program as such. A computer program was not considered part of a technical operating procedure if the claimed teaching merely modified the data and produced no effects beyond information processing.[21]

Whether or not one agrees with the conclusions, these EPO cases appeared to provide a reasonably consistent approach; for these and other reasons to be considered later, text-processing innovation does not constitute patentable subject-matter. Two other decisions in the same fields of activity, however, have found in favour of patentable subject-matter, so blurring that consistent approach.

In the first, *IBM/Computer-related invention* (T115/85) [1990] EPOR 107, the application was for a method of displaying one of a set of predetermined messages in response to an event using conventional computer hardware operated by a suitable program. The board held that this was patentable subject-matter. Giving visual indications automatically about conditions prevailing in an apparatus or system was basically a technical problem.

In *Wang Laboratories Inc.'s Application*[22] Aldous J expressed some perplexity at this decision, as did members of the Court of Appeal in *Gale's Application* [1991] RPC 305. He confessed that it was 'difficult to understand the full reasoning of the board without recourse to the specification . . . [and also] what the board meant by the word "technical". However, the board seems to have concluded that the invention was more than a computer program, in that it related to a machine which carried out a function useful for industrial application by providing a visual indication of conditions in the machine.' Nicholls LJ accepted the decision since the instructions solved a 'technical' problem lying within the computer, although he confessed to difficulty in identifying clearly the dividing line.

In the second decision, *IBM/Data-processor network* (T06/83) [1990] EPOR 91, it was held that:

> . . . an invention relating to the coordination and control of the internal communication between programs and data files held at different processors

---

21. See also T38/86-1989: a method of proofreading a text-document and automatically detecting and replacing linguistic expressions; T121/85-1989: a spell-checking arrangement for use in word-processing systems; *IBM/Text processing* (T65/86) [1990] EPOR 181: a method for automatically detecting and correcting contextual homophone errors in a text document; *Apple Computer Application* (1992) IPD 15001: improved performance was not of itself a technical result; the improved performance had itself to occur in a technical field; *Sharp's Application* (1992) IPD 14171: if an invention is argued to be patentable because it achieved a technical effect, that effect had to be over and above any technical effect present as a consequence of the use of functionally defined means of the type that were to be found in a conventional computer.

22. [1991] RPC 463 at p. 470.

in a data processing system having a plurality of interconnected data processors in a telecommunication network, and the features of which are not concerned with the nature of the data and the way in which a particular application program operates on them, is to be regarded as solving a problem which is essentially technical.

Again, Aldous J in *Wang Laboratories Inc.'s Application* [1991] RPC 463 attempted valiantly to reconcile this decision with the others:

[The claim here is for] an invention for a series of computers interconnected so as to coordinate and control internal communications between programs and data files in different computers. Thus the claim had as the basis for the invention a computer program, but it related to a series of computers connected together. It was, therefore, not surprising that the Board held that the invention was not confined to a computer program as such.

5.2.3.8   The technical result must not itself be excluded by art. 3(2)   One would have thought that if a patent application satisfies the appropriate technical requirement that would suffice to establish that there was patentable subject-matter. However, a further important, though dubious, additional control was established by the Court of Appeal in *Merrill Lynch's Application* [1989] RPC 561. In its view, the claim to the trading system, even when viewed as a whole, was nothing more than 'a method of doing business' also excluded as such under the Patents Act 1977, s. 1(2).

Fox LJ stated:

Now let it be supposed that claim 1 can be regarded as producing a new result in the form of a technical contribution to the prior art. That result, whatever the technical advance may be, is simply the production of a trading system. It is a data-processing system for doing a specific business, that is to say, making a trading market in securities. The end result, therefore, is simply 'a method . . . of doing business' and is excluded by section 1(2)(c). The fact that the method of doing business may be an improvement on previous methods of doing business does not seem to me to be material. The prohibition in section 1(2)(c) is generic; qualitative considerations do not enter into the matter. The section draws no distinction between the method by which the mode of doing business is achieved. If what is produced in the end is itself an item excluded from patentability by section 1(2), the matter can go no further. . . . A data processing system operating to produce a novel technical result would normally be patentable. But it cannot . . . be patentable if the result itself is a prohibited item under section 1(2). In the present case it is such a prohibited item.

This reasoning is suspect and unnecessarily restrictive. The court seemed prepared to accept that the law since the Patents Act 1977 may now be less generous than that which applied earlier, for when *International Business Machines Corporation's Application* [1980] FSR 564, a case said to be on all fours with the present case but one where a patent claim was allowed, was cited to it, all that Fox LJ could say was that 'it was decided under the 1949 Act which is not in the same form as the 1977 Act'. Had the court adopted a better approach this lame distinction need not have been made. The fact that the claim involves a method of doing business should no more create an automatic exclusion from patentability than should the fact that a computer program is involved. A business scheme, taking into account the technical process, when looked at as a whole, could be patentable subject-matter. It is not a method of doing business *as such*. The better approach, if the court is anxious to prevent a patent grant from being obtained in this case, is to strike it down at a later stage on the ground that it is not novel or that it is obvious. This is a matter to which it will be necessary to return shortly. Ironically, not only was a patent for this innovation obtained in the USA[23] but also subsequently in the UK simply by revised claims in a form directed to the operation of a programmed computer!

Nevertheless, there is an increasing number of decisions which support this view; the presence of a technical contribution may be foiled if the result is excluded subject-matter even if it is not that subject-matter 'as such'! Thus, if the claim is essentially one or more of the following: a mathematical method[24] or a scheme, rule or method for performing mental acts[25] or doing business[26] or a program for a computer[27] or the presentation of information, then, notwithstanding any technical contribution, the application will be suspect. Yet, as we have seen, some claims involving a technical contribution relating to excluded subject-matter will be acceptable![28]

5.2.3.9 Drafting   Where patentability depends upon a technical effect the claims must be so drafted as to include all the technical features of the invention which are essential for the technical effect.

5.2.3.10 Conclusions   What conclusions can be drawn from this lengthy survey? First, in general there is a generous approach to the patentability of software-related inventions in the United Kingdom, Europe and most other countries. However, in the text-processing type of case there is a clear reluctance to grant patents. This objective has been achieved by curtailing the scope of the required 'technical contribution' and limiting the operation of the

---

23. *Paine, Webber, Jackson & Curtis* v *Merrill Lynch* (1983) 564 F Supp 1369.
24. *Gale's Application* [1991] RPC 305.
25. *IBM/Document abstracting and retrieving* (T22/85) [1990] EPOR 98; T38/86-1989: a method of proofreading a text-document and automatically detecting and replacing linguistic expressions; *Wang Laboratories Inc.'s Application* [1991] RPC 463: the expert system is no more than a claim to a monopoly for a computer program which will carry out a method for performing a mental act, namely, producing expert advice; the claim is to a scheme or method for performing a mental act using a computer program; *Sharp's Application* (1992) IPD 14171: a claim to a conventional computer running a novel program which performed a mental act – as was the case here – was not allowable irrespective of any technical advance on the prior art.
26. *Merrill Lynch's Application* [1989] RPC 561.
27. *Gale's Application* [1991] RPC 305.
28. *IBM/Document abstracting and retrieving* (T22/85) [1990] EPOR 98.

'as such' provision. The price paid for this, at the very least, has been inconsistency and consequential uncertainty. It is still not possible to state with confidence where the patentability lines are drawn, and little attention has been given to the broader practical and economic implications of what is becoming a legal maze.[29]

5.3 NOVELTY AND INVENTIVE STEP

As already emphasised, even were there to be a more relaxed policy of accepting 'technical' computer software as patentable subject-matter, patent offices are unlikely to be flooded with applications. Apart from factors such as cost and delay, the most obvious deterrent would be that many would fail at the next two hurdles; namely showing that the invention is novel and inventive. Logically these are all distinct issues, although the reported decisions show that the novelty and inventiveness requirements are sometimes influential in dealing with the question of whether there is patentable subject-matter.[30]

Whether the problems of novelty and inventive step in relation to computer-related inventions present any greater difficulties in practice than in other areas of technology or biotechnology in the UK and the European Patent Community is a matter which yet has to be explored. There are problems in the USA which will be examined soon.

5.4 EXCLUSIVE RIGHTS AND INFRINGEMENT

It has already been noted that, in some respects, the exclusive rights conferred on a patentee are as strong as, if not stronger than, copyright, which is the usual, preferred means of protection. The patent grant confers a true monopoly and so a patentee does not have to prove to a court that the defendant has, directly or indirectly, 'copied' the patentee's invention. The exclusive rights can be used to prohibit virtually all types of *commercial* manufacture, use, importation or other dealing with the invention. With non-commercial activity, however, patent rights are weaker; it is a defence for a person to make, use or deal with a patented invention if it is done privately and for purposes which are not commercial (Patents Act 1977, s. 60(5)(a)), whereas there is no similar sweeping exemption for private, non-commercial use in copyright law.

'Contributory infringers' are those persons who supply primary infringers with the means to infringe. They are often far more desirable targets, from a commercial point of view, than the primary infringers themselves, and ought to be accountable to rights holders. Yet copyright law provides very little protection against them. *CBS Songs Ltd* v *Amstrad Consumer Electronics plc*

---

29. For recent discussions of some of the current decisions, see Sherman, 'The Patentability of Computer-related Inventions in the United Kingdom and the European Patent Office' [1991] EIPR 85; G. D. Kolle, 'Patentability of Software-related Inventions in Europe' (1991) 22 IIC 660; Cutforth, 'Patents for Software: Off-course again?' (1991-92) 21 CIPA 4.
30. For a recent example of a decision where the different hurdles are analysed interchangeably rather than sequentially, see *Esswein/Automatic programmer* (T579/88) [1991] EPOR 120.

[1988] AC 1013 demonstrates that it is not sufficient to impose copyright liability on somebody who supplies another with the means of committing an infringing act, even if he has knowledge or intends those means to be used for infringement. The contributory infringer must *authorise* an infringement; he must grant, or purport to grant, the infringer authority to infringe before he too incurs liability. A contributory infringer in patent law, however, would be liable in such circumstances if he supplies or offers to supply another 'with any of the means, relating to an essential element of an invention, for putting the invention into effect when he knows, or it is obvious to a reasonable person in the circumstances' that an infringement will occur (Patents Act 1977, s. 60(1) and (2)). In the case of the supply by a contributory infringer of items in common commercial use ('staple commercial products') it is necessary to show that the product has been supplied for the purpose of 'inducing' infringement (Patents Act 1977, s. 60(3)). Two US cases where liability for contributory infringement was established would be similarly decided in the UK: *Magnavox Co.* v *Mattell Inc.* (1982) 216 USPQ 28 concerned the production and supply of components for a computerised video game; and *Re Certain Personal Computers and Components Thereof* (1984) 224 USPQ 270 related to the sale of 'unstuffed motherboards', or ROM-less computers, specifically designed to be fitted with non-infringing copies of computer programs which would, when made up, infringe a patent.

The full extent of protection for computer programs under copyright law is a matter which is presently exercising the minds of the computer industry and, increasingly, the courts. Once a person moves away from making a more or less exact copy of a computer program, it becomes less clear whether there is liability for 'copying' or 'reproduction'. In some cases, the defendant may be liable because there has been an 'adaptation' (e.g., a translation) of the copyright program. In other cases, the issue will be whether the defendant has copied the 'expression' of the plaintiff's copyright computer program or has taken the 'idea' of that program which, under copyright law, he is free to take. Here, American courts have played havoc with logic by categorising 'idea' as 'expression' in a bold attempt to widen the scope of copyright; although there are recent signs that the protection offered by copyright law is becoming more limited. Where the courts draw the line between what is 'expression', and so protected, and what is 'idea', and so not protected, will determine how far copyright law will protect those who use and develop essential aspects of the plaintiff's computer program. This is a matter discussed in detail in chapter 4.

Similar problems may arise where inventions involving computer programs are patented, but here also the courts have not yet had the opportunity of probing the full scope of patent protection.

Although the Patents Act 1977 does not refer expressly to ideas, concepts or principles, patent law has never purported to confer monopoly rights on these alone. We come back to the exclusion from patentability of 'a discovery, scientific theory or mathematical method' *as such*. In all these cases, as we have seen, it is necessary to show that the idea or concept has been used to produce some technical advance. Provided there is some technical contribution, there is greater scope for protection of ideas under patent law than under copyright law, even after any judicial distortions of the idea–expression dichotomy in copyright law. It is likely to be easier, and more appropriate, to protect certain fundamental computer programs, which can be applied technically, through the patent system, although these are likely to represent only a small proportion of the total number of applications filed relating to computer programs.

Under patent law generally, the patentee has exclusive rights only over the invention as defined in the patent claims and so it is permissible for anybody to make use of the patent specification, even whilst the patent subsists, to 'patent around' and come up with a computer-related invention which falls outside the claims.[31] The approach to the construction of patent claims has changed. At one time, the courts employed a fairly 'literal' approach so that unless the patentee marked out all aspects of his invention by careful drafting, a competitor could well avail himself of the essence of the patentee's invention by doing something just outside the scope of the patent claims. Today, the courts are more sympathetic to patentees. Under United Kingdom law the courts now adopt a more 'purposive approach', and the protocol to art. 69 of the European Patent Convention adopts a similar stance, so that the construction of a patent claim should combine 'fair protection for the patentee with a reasonable degree of certainty for third parties'. The need to balance the competing interests of the patentee and third parties will mean, though, that in this respect we are almost brought back to the same problem in patent law as the idea–expression problem in copyright law! It will normally be for the patentee to state expressly what he regards as the essential elements of the invention; where a competitor does not take all the essential elements, he may escape liability. On the other hand, if all the essential elements are taken and a competitor does not copy exactly but uses inessential equivalents, patent infringement may still occur. For example, in the American case of *Decca Ltd v United States* (1976) 191 USPQ 439 the defendants' Omega system for positioning ships and aircraft which was operated by a digital computer was held to infringe the plaintiff's patented analogue-computer-related invention. The plaintiff's claim was not limited to a specific analogue mechanism; it was not an essential aspect of the patented invention.

In the United Kingdom, a great deal of uncharted territory has to be explored.[32] The courts in the United States are a little further advanced.

5.5   EMPLOYER/EMPLOYEE RIGHTS

Where computer programs are developed by employees in the course of their employment, any copyright in them will ordinarily vest in the employer.[33] There is no provision in copyright law for any employee rewards for

---

31. Where a person comes up with a patentable invention which involves infringement of the prior patent, then a patent licence must be sought from that patentee before the derivative patent can be exploited.
32. For a recent infringement decision of the Court of Appeal see *Willemijn Houdstermaatschappij BV v Madge Networks Ltd* (1992) IPD 15068.
33. Copyright, Designs and Patents Act 1988, s. 11(2).

outstanding developments. The usual problem arises when computer programs are commissioned from outside agencies and it is frequently not appreciated that, in the absence of contractual provision to the contrary, the copyright remains with those agencies. In some circumstances it may be difficult to know whether the author of a program is, in law, an employee or independently commissioned and various tests are used to attempt to differentiate between the two.

However, where an employee produces a computer-related invention there may well be additional benefits to which the employee is entitled resulting from the success of the invention. The Patents Act 1977 provides that where a patented invention is of outstanding benefit to an employer and it is 'just' that an employee should be awarded compensation, the employee may be entitled to a fair share of the benefit which the employer has derived, whether or not the invention belonged originally to the employer or whether it was an invention owned by an employee but subsequently assigned to the employer (Patents Act 1977, ss. 39 to 43). Little guidance has yet been provided as to the level of compensation an employee may expect.

5.6   PATENTS, COPYRIGHT AND POLICY

Much of this chapter has been concerned with the way in which the legal rules relating to patentability operate. Little attention has been paid to the more fundamental question; what scope should the patent system provide for software and software-related inventions?

The case for patents is, superficially at least, straightforward. Any innovation which is susceptible of industrial application is prima facie worthy of being patentable subject-matter. All the theoretical arguments which justify patent protection generally should apply. If a purpose of the patent system is to stimulate industrial innovation, there is no reason why such an important industry as the software industry should be excluded from its proper scope if it wishes to come within it. Supporters of patents would maintain that copyright protection alone is not sufficient for software innovation. Patent protection is stronger; it confers exclusive rights against anybody who, without authority, makes, uses or deals with a patented software-related invention for commercial purposes, whether or not that person is actually copying; whereas the exclusive right of a copyright owner is simply to prevent copying and does not preclude anybody else from coming up with the same invention independently. In any event, the software industry may not always be assessing whether it is better to have copyright or patent protection; the 'either–or' approach is misconceived. The two systems may protect different aspects of computer programs and computer-program-related inventions and, in some cases, it will be of value for two complementary rights to coexist. The case against the patent system becoming too prominent in the software world operates at both the practical and the conceptual level.

In comparison with the ease of obtaining copyright protection, there are the standard disincentives to those seeking to use the patent system: the cost and time involved in obtaining registered patents in all those countries where it is commercially important to have them; the uncertainties in assessing the validity and full scope of the registered rights; the difficulties inherent in the detection and proof of infringement; and the cost of renewals and infringement litigation. These factors in most cases would inhibit all save the large computer companies from using a body of law which requires public disclosure of their new developments.[34]

There are further practical objections. In the United States, in particular, there has been a long-standing problem in that its Patent Office does not have an effective system for the examination of computer program technology. In *Gottschalk v Benson* (1972) 409 US 63 the US government maintained that it was highly questionable whether an effective system for the examination of computer programs could be developed. That was in 1972 yet, surprisingly, there are still difficulties. A recent study[35] concluded that:

> the published literature does not completely embody software and computer science prior art. Much prior art exists only in product form without publication in journals, and it is virtually impossible to find, let alone count or profile, all software-related or algorithmic patents because they are not classified and indexed in a way that permits effective search and study.

This is a surprising, ironic, and surely temporary finding in view of the fact that computer technology has been responsible for the development of electronic databases providing virtually instantaneous and complete information about everything![36] Nevertheless, the problem has been said to explain why the Patent Office has long sought to find that claims involve non-patentable subject-matter rather than accept the invention and then have to consider issues of novelty and obviousness.[37]

Although there are some who favour granting patents even to mathematical algorithms[38] and others who argue that decisions such as *Re Iwahashi*[39] enable this to be achieved indirectly, there is a growing literature which questions any

---

34. Contrast, for example, the fierce debates prior to the European Community Directive on Copyright and Software (91/250/EEC) between those computer industry interests which opposed any right for reverse engineering by competitors and sought to prevent unauthorised access to their source codes by using copyright, trade secret and contract laws, and others who maintained that access to such information should be freely available in the interests of the industry and free and fair competition.

35. US Congress Office of Technology Assessment: *Computer Software and Intellectual Property – Background Paper* (1990). See Stern, 'Patenting Algorithms in America' [1990] EIPR 292 at p. 296.

36. For a critical commentary on the failure of the US PTO to adopt an automated patent search system that will enable it effectively to search the prior art, see Antton and Feitshans, 'Is the United States Automating a Patent Registration System for Software? A Critical Review of Information Management in the US Patent and Trademark Office' [1990] EIPR 470.

37. It has been estimated that less than 1 per cent of all computer programs in the USA are sufficiently inventive to meet the standard invention requirements. J. E. Brown, 'International Trends in Computer Program Protection' (1987) 3 CL&P 157.

38. D. S. Chisum, 'The Patentability of Algorithms' (1986) 47 U Pitt L Rev 959. Cf. A. Newell, 'Response: the Models are Broken, the Models are Broken!' (1986) 47 U Pitt L Rev 1023.

39. 888 F 2d 1370 (1989).

further liberalisation of software patent law. Indeed, there are powerful, and occasionally shrill, voices that would remove most forms of computer innovation from the reach of patents. This is the view of Richard Stallman, President of the League of Programming Freedom, though that body goes to the opposite extreme in seeking to remove computer programs from all forms of monopoly control.[40]

Samuelson favours a *sui generis* approach in preference to copyright and patents, since both areas of law have to be distorted to accommodate software.[41] Her analysis of the US scene is equally applicable to Europe. First, the case law on program patentability and recently issued Guidelines lacks a sound theoretical basis and relies heavily upon indefensible distinctions. Secondly, she perceives conflicting views: those of patent attorneys who seem strongly to favour patent protection for computer program innovations and who have succeeded in transforming Patent Office policy; and those of the industry itself which is expressing concern about software-related patents.

If the software industry neither wants nor needs the patent system in order to be a vital and innovative industry then, as a matter of public policy, it is sensible not to use the patent system for the protection of program-related innovations.

It is difficult to know, however, what *the* view of the software industry is. As with the debates preceding the Community Software Copyright Directive (91/250/EEC), the industry is likely to contain opposing views. Many of the reported decisions point to the demand coming from large companies which are heavily involved in research and innovation. Their smaller competitors are prone to complain that patent protection for industry development is too strong, and that the development of copyright law without the aid of patent protection is powerful evidence that the latter is not necessary for the software industry to thrive. It is possible that the extensive use of patents might disrupt the balance that has been achieved in the industry through developments in copyright law.

There are several reasons why those in the software industry who seek properly to take advantage of the patent system should not be restricted from doing so. First, any discrimination against the software industry, or any other industry, has to be clearly justifiable as a matter of policy. The initial premise must be that innovation in the software industry should be treated, prima facie, in the same way as innovation in any other industry. There will always be complaints from competitors that monopoly rights are anticompetitive, but from the point of view of the rights holders that is what monopoly protection is about. Abuse of monopoly power can be controlled from within the system itself or through properly framed competition laws. The exclusion of computer

---

40. Stallman, 'Against Software Patents' (1991) Managing Intellectual Property (August-September 1991) 20.
41. P. Samuelson, '*Benson* Revisited: the Case against Patent Protection for Algorithms and other Computer Program-Related Inventions' (1990) 39 Emory LJ 1025.

programs 'as such' from patent law, if sensibly operated, should be acceptable since it conforms with basic patent law principles, and the expansion of copyright protection should cope with most of the problems of simple software piracy. Significant sectors of the industry have a legitimate interest in patenting the practical applications of software. It invests heavily in software research and is not persuaded that copyright protection is sufficient. What it is looking for in many cases is protection for *other* computer-related aspects of the relevant development, rather than for the program alone. A second reason for using patents is that the European software industry should not be placed at a competitive disadvantage *vis-à-vis* its American and Japanese competitors.

In spite of some assessments that the levels of protection are more or less comparable in all these countries,[42] this is questionable. It appears, at present, that US law at least is affording more generous protection to some of the text-processing types of program. There should be a harmonised approach; either the US has gone too far or the EPO and the member States of the European Patent Convention have not gone far enough.

A recent important American Office of Technology Assessment (OTA) report[43] has even cast doubt on whether its current range of laws are adequate for protecting software. Although the extensive use of patent law to protect software-related inventions and algorithms demonstrates that patent protection is of importance to some sectors of the US software industry, it was noted that the law is controversial and there are conflicting views on how effective it is. The OTA report then posed important questions:

> Congress might wish to consider whether the trend towards more use of patent protection, absent alternatives to protect program functionality, affects the public-interest 'balance' in terms of equity for small/large software firms and for those with many/few legal and financial resources. What will be the effect on end users and the public at large? Will 'stronger' protection for software spur innovation, stifle it, or have no real effect overall? Will it disproportionately disadvantage individuals and small firms versus large (or rich) corporations?

These issues then led the OTA to suggest that:

> . . . there may be a point where it is in the public interest to develop new law(s) either to *complement* the existing framework or to *substitute* for copyright and/or patent protection for software. It might be appropriate for Congress to consider periodically giving limited *sui generis* rights for incremental software advances that are not patentable, or for aspects of program functionality that fall outside copyrightable subject-matter (with a

42. 'Patentability of Computer-Related Inventions. A Comparative Study Prepared by the European Patent Office in September 1989 in Connection with the Trilateral Cooperation Between the EPO, JPO and USPTO.' (1990) 21 IIC 817.
43. Office of Technology Assessment, *Finding a Balance: Computer Software, Intellectual Property and the Challenge of Technological Change* (1992).

shorter-term, lower criteria for inventiveness and/or special exemptions for infringement).

The case for a further appraisal, which has been made out in the USA, applies equally to Europe. Whether it comes may depend upon how the various patent offices and courts continue to develop and apply relevant legal principle and how satisfactory it is to all branches of the software industry. There seems little doubt that there is much activity in this area yet to come.

CHAPTER SIX

Design right and semiconductor chip protection

Robert J. Hart and Chris Reed

Prior to the Copyright, Designs and Patents Act 1988 (the 1988 Act), industrial designs were protected by a complex set of interacting legislative provisions.[1]

The 1988 Act set out to reform the law by introducing a new design right to replace several aspects of the pre-existing regime of protection. The system of rights in designs is now rather simpler, though several different types of right are still involved:

(a) If the design is for an artistic work, it is primarily protected by copyright.

(b) If the design is non-functional (i.e., appealing solely to the eye and not dictated by the functions the article made to the design is to perform) it is registrable under the Registered Designs Act 1949. This gives the proprietor of the right a monopoly protection of the design for a term extended to 25 years by the 1988 Act.

(c) If the design is to be used for manufacturing functional items, the design itself (i.e., the drawing plus any associated text) will still attract copyright as an artistic or literary work, so that directly copying it will be an infringement. However, under s. 51 of the 1988 Act copyright in that design is

---

1. For a brief description of the position before the 1988 Act see G. Dworkin and R. Taylor, *Blackstone's Guide to the Copyright, Designs and Patents Act 1988* (London: Blackstone Press, 1989), pp.138–45.

not infringed by manufacturing items to the design. Instead, protection is given by means of the new design right (see 6.1). Design right can subsist in parallel with registration of the design.

So far as the computer industry is concerned, the new design right is likely to be the most important method of protecting designs. It would potentially cover such matters as the layout of circuit boards, component designs, designs for paper paths in laser printers etc. The area in which it will have the greatest impact, however, is in the design and manufacture of semiconductor chips. These were previously protected under a *sui generis* topography right, but for chips designed after 1 August 1989 this right disappeared and protection now subsists under an amended version of design right.

6.1   DESIGN RIGHT

This is a property right which, under s. 213(1) of the 1988 Act, subsists in original designs. 'Design' is defined in s. 213(2) as: 'the design of any aspect of the shape or configuration (whether internal or external) of the whole or part of an article'.

'Originality' has a somewhat more restricted meaning than for copyright, and not only must the design not be copied, but it must not be commonplace in the design field in question when it was created (s. 213(4)).

There are three aspects of designs in which by virtue of s. 213(3) no design right can subsist:

(a)   A method or principle of construction.

(b)   What have been described as the must-fit/must-match exceptions. It is not an infringement to copy aspects of the design which are essential to ensure that another article will connect with or fit against the original article, or which are dependent on the appearance of the original article where the new article is intended to form an integral part of it. A good example of the working of this exception would be the design of a paper output tray to attach to a printer. Here, it must fit to the printer and so can copy features of the printer's design which are essential for that purpose, and as it is intended to become an integral part of the printer it can copy design features which allow it to match the printer's appearance.

(c)   Surface decoration (this is potentially registrable under the 1949 Act).

Design right comes into existence at the moment the design is recorded in a design document by a qualified person,[2] and normally belongs to the designer. However, if the design is made in the course of employment it belongs to the employer, or if it is commissioned then, unlike the position in relation to copyright, the commissioner is the proprietor (s. 215). In each case, though,

---

2. Who is a qualified person is defined in orders made under s. 221, but it is essentially the same as for copyright.

this is subject to any agreement in writing to the contrary.[3] If the design is computer-created, the designer is the person who made the arrangements necessary for its creation (s. 214(2)).

Design right has a shorter term than copyright. Under s. 216 it lasts for 15 years from the end of the year of creation or 10 years from the end of the year in which articles made to the design are made available for sale or hire, whichever is the shorter period. The right may be assigned in the same way as copyright, except that licences of right are available during the last five years of the term (s. 237).

Infringement is dealt with in ss. 226 to 228 of the 1988 Act. These provide that the owner of the design has the exclusive right to reproduce it for commercial purposes, which means:

(a)   to make articles to the design, or
(b)   to make a design document for the purpose of enabling such articles to be made.

Secondary infringement is essentially the same as for copyright, by importing, possessing for commercial purposes or trading in infringing articles (i.e., articles manufactured to the design). However, even though the unauthorised making of a design document is an infringement, importation of or commercial dealing with such a document is not (s. 228(6)). The remedies available to the proprietor of the right are also similar, and in addition to injunctions, damages or an account of profits, the owner of the right can also apply for an order for delivery up of infringing articles and for orders for their destruction (ss. 229 to 235).

Although these general principles of design right will apply to many aspects of computer technology, it is important to note that their application to semiconductor chip designs is substantially different. The regime of semiconductor chip protection will be examined in 6.2 in some detail, highlighting these differences.

6.2   SEMICONDUCTOR CHIP PROTECTION

Semiconductor chips are formed from layers of semiconductor material such as silicon, germanium or gallium arsenide, with insulators of various compositions that combine to form the components required to make up an electronic circuit. The layers are 'doped' in predetermined places with traces of other elements, and sandwiched together with insulating and metallic layers to form the chip. The configuration of these layers is determined by directing a pattern of light on to a photosensitive surface, either through a physical 'mask' or via a computer-controlled light beam which traces out the circuit, and it is the circuit thus produced which determines the chip's functionality. The investment in establishing these

3. Design Right (Semiconductor Topographies) Regulations 1989, reg. 5, amending s. 215 of the 1988 Act.

configurations is extremely high, and the development of a new family of semiconductor chips can cost over £10 million. A chip can be copied, however, for less than £100,000, as the physical technology is in most cases standard in the industry. It is thus clear that the aspect of semiconductor chips which requires protection from unauthorised copying is their design.

Until recently, no country's intellectual property regime provided specific protection for semiconductor products. Although it was generally thought that designs for chips received some protection under the intellectual property laws of the UK,[4] the position was never very clear. In 1984, however, the US passed the Semiconductor Chip Protection Act (the US Act) which introduced a new form of protection for 'mask works'. These are defined in s. 901(a)(2)(A) as:

> a series of related images, however fixed or embodied, having or representing the predetermined three-dimensional pattern of metallic, insulating or semiconductor material present or removed from the layers of a semiconductor chip product.

If the work is original (i.e., not staple, commonplace or familiar in the industry: s. 902(b)) and first exploited in the US or exploited elsewhere by a US national or domiciliary, the designer of the mask work receives the exclusive right to reproduce or to import or distribute the work or products containing the work (s. 905). This right lasts for 10 years from the earlier of the mask work's registration or its first commercial exploitation (s. 904(b)).

The US Act also provides that reverse engineering will not be an infringement if the work produced by such engineering is itself original, not substantially similar to the first work, and involves significant toil and investment (s. 906(a)). When considering the acts which are permitted under 'reverse engineering' it is important to recognise that the US legislators attempted to codify so-called established industry practice, so that a second chip designer could reproduce and use the designs of a protected chip for the purposes of research and development, resulting in the design of a second chip with the same electrical and physical performance characteristics as the protected chip. During the House debate on the US Act this was identified as achieving 'form, fit and function' compatibility.

The intention of the reverse engineering exception was to permit the making of improvements on or alternatives to existing chips by incorporating substantial parts of the first design into the second chip. If the second chip is the result of substantial study and analysis and not the result of simple plagiarism, the creation of a second mask work whose layout is 'in substantial part similar to the protected mask work' is permitted.

In addition to the originality requirement, the existence of a 'paper trail', which will substantiate the level of study and analysis embarked on by the reverse engineer, is important in separating the pirate from the legitimate engineer. In *Brooktree Corporation* v *Advanced Micro Devices Inc.* (1988) No. 88-1750-E (cm) (SD Cal 13 December 1988), the court noted that both parties

---

4. See R. Hart, 'Questions Raised on Legally Protecting Semiconductor Chips' (1986) 2 YLCT 93.

agreed that if the defendant could produce an adequate paper trail establishing reverse engineering the appropriate standard for infringement would be that the two masks were 'substantially identical'; if no independent creation through reverse engineering was established, the appropriate standard would be that the two mask works were 'substantially similar'.

The importance of this Act outside the US lies in its reciprocity provisions, for s. 902 provides that mask works from countries outside the US are only protected within the US if that country has signed a mask work protection treaty with the US and provides equivalent protection for mask works in its own domestic legislation. As a result, many developed countries have introduced legislation along the lines of the US Act, and the Council of the EEC issued Directive 87/54/EEC[5] (the Directive) to ensure that member States amended their legislation to qualify for reciprocal protection. Initially this was done in the UK by the Semiconductor Products (Protection of Topography) Regulations 1987 (SI 1987 No. 1497, the 1987 Regulations).

The 1987 Regulations differed somewhat from the US Act by creating a new intellectual property right, 'topography right', which was the exclusive right to reproduce the whole or a substantial part of an original topography, or to deal in a reproduction of it or in a semiconductor product incorporating such a reproduction (reg. 4(1)). 'Topography' was defined as the design of the pattern fixed or intended to be fixed on a layer of a semiconductor product, or on a layer of other material (e.g., a mask) to be used in the manufacture of such a product, and included the arrangement of the layers of semiconductor product.[6] To satisfy the requirement of originality, reg. 3(3) provided that the topography must be the result of the creator's (or creators') intellectual efforts, and must not be commonplace among creators or manufacturers of topographies and semiconductors. However, a work that consisted of non-original elements would still be original if the *combination* of those elements satisfied the two-part test of originality.

Topography right is now replaced by a modified version of design right, implemented by the Design Right (Semiconductor Topographies) Regulations 1989 (SI 1989 No. 1497, the 1989 Regulations). These regulations amend and extend the 1988 Act's application to semiconductor products, and references in this chapter to the 1988 Act are to the Act as amended. It is worth saying at the outset that the overall reaction of the semiconductor industry is that, as so much adaptation was required to make design right conform with the Directive, it would have been better to remove semiconductor topographies from design right altogether and to re-enact the 1987 Regulations. However, the industry has always been seriously concerned that the 1987 Regulations had major flaws, and some of these are overcome in the 1989 Regulations.

6.2.1 Creation and subsistence of the right

Regulation 2(2) of the 1987 Regulations provided that 'the creation of a topography occurs upon its first expression in a form from which it can be

---

5. OJ No. L 24, 27 January 1987, p. 36.
6. 1987 Regulations, reg. 2(1). This regulation also defines the term 'semiconductor product'.

reproduced'. This complied with art. 7(1)(c) of the Directive. Although the US Act only provides protection for 'mask works fixed in a semiconductor chip product' the effect is much the same, as that Act's definition of 'fixed' includes the requirement that 'its embodiment in the product is sufficiently permanent or stable to permit the mask work to be perceived or reproduced from the product'.

Regulation 2(1) of the 1989 Regulations defines a 'semiconductor topography' to be a design falling within s. 213 of the 1988 Act which is a design of either of the following:

(a)   the pattern fixed, or intended to be fixed, in or upon—
   (i)   a layer of a semiconductor product, or
   (ii)   a layer of material in the course of and for the purpose of the manufacture of a semiconductor product, or
(b)   the arrangement of the patterns fixed, or intended to be fixed, in or upon the layers of a semiconductor product in relation to one another.

Even though a design has been made, s. 213(6) of the 1988 Act provides that design right 'does not subsist unless and until the design has been recorded in a design document or an article has been made to the design'. A design document is 'any record of a design, whether in the form of a drawing, a written description, a photograph, data stored in a computer or otherwise' (s. 263(1)). Design documents for topographies are given more protection than other design documents, as their importation or commercial dealing is a secondary infringement (see 6.2.2).

It would seem, therefore, that a design document for a semiconductor product is defined much more broadly than a mask work under the US Act or a topography under the Directive. Both of these latter definitions include the requirement that it be a series of related images which represent the three-dimensional pattern of the product's layers. Contrast this with the definition of a design document above. This does not restrict protection to a series of related images, and so a list of the functional requirements of a complex application-specific integrated circuit (ASIC) held in a computer which operates a chip design program would probably qualify as a design document.

6.2.2 Infringement

If a competitor wants to emulate the original ASIC, and his analysis and evaluation produces a similar list of functions and requirements, this would potentially be an infringement of design right in the original list. However, the competitor is relieved of liability by reg. 8(1) and (4) of the 1989 Regulations. Paragraph (1) of reg. 8 provides that the design right owner's rights are not infringed by reproducing the design privately for non-commercial aims, or by reproducing it for the purpose of analysing or evaluating the design, or for analysing, evaluating or teaching the concepts, processes, systems or techniques which are embodied in it. This permits direct copying of the topography for those limited purposes only. Indirect copying by *using* the analysis to create a *new* design is excused by reg. 8(4), so that it is not an infringement to:

(a)   create another original semiconductor topography as a result of an analysis or evaluation of the first topography or of the concepts, processes, systems or techniques embodied in it, or

(b)   reproduce that *other* topography. (Emphasis added).

The important thing to note is that the US Act and the Directive only provide protection against the unauthorised reproduction etc. of mask works and topographies. 'Reverse engineering' is expressly permitted, and incidental copying in the reverse engineering process is not an infringement of design right.

A significant amendment to the 1988 Act is the removal of the words 'for commercial purposes' from s. 226(1) so far as topographies are concerned. As a result, the owner of design right in a topography has the exclusive right to make chips to the design, or to make a design document recording the topography, for both commercial and non-commercial purposes. This is, of course, subject to the exceptions contained in reg. 8(1) and (4) of the 1989 Regulations. The net effect is that non-commercial manufacture of chips to the design is forbidden, whilst copying for the purpose of reverse engineering is permitted. This overcomes the problem that manufacture for in-house use would otherwise not have been an infringement, since s. 263(3) of the 1988 Act defines an act done for 'commercial purposes' as an act done with a view to the article being sold or hired in the course of business.

Indirect infringement of design right under s. 227 of the 1988 Act occurs when an infringing article is imported into the UK for commercial purposes, or where a person has an infringing article in his possession for commercial purposes or, in the course of a business, sells or lets it for hire or exposes it for sale or hire. When the Directive was drafted the Commission was keen to ensure that protection was given to the topography itself, so that design houses producing topographies would be provided with protection for those products separate from their incorporation in a chip product. For this reason, s. 228(6) does not apply to semiconductor topographies, thus indirectly including topography design documents in the definition of infringing articles.[7] This is clearly an important issue, as already design houses are providing an ASIC design service which will produce for a customer the design information (i.e., masks) which can then be used by a separate silicon fabrication house to produce the ASIC.

It should also be noted that under reg. 8(5) of the 1989 Regulations any of the above acts will amount to an infringement if done in relation to a *substantial part* of the topography as well as in relation to the whole. It is not clear whether this adds anything to s. 213(2) of the 1988 Act, under which 'design' means the design of the whole or part of an article. Both these provisions apply to topography designs, and s. 213(2) may be broader in scope than reg. 8(5).

Because topography protection is subject to EC law, the doctrine of exhaustion of rights applies. Once the article in question has been lawfully sold or hired within the EC, its further importation into or dealing in the UK is not prohibited by s. 227.[8]

---

7. 1989 Regulations, reg. 8(3).
8. 1989 Regulations, reg. 8(2).

6.2.3 Originality
The Directive calls for 'the creator's own intellectual effort', though this may be shown by the original combination of elements of the design which are not themselves original. This restrictive definition of originality was included in the 1987 Regulations, but is *not* found in the 1988 Act. The only qualification is that a topography design will not be original if it is commonplace in the design field (s. 213(4)), and a similar qualification is found in the US Act. This is an important issue for semiconductor topographies as they are, in the vast majority of cases, new compilations of well-known (i.e., commonplace) elements. A topography will be protected by design right if the combination is not commonplace, and there will be no need to show 'intellectual effort' (which might be difficult given the use of design teams, and the fact that the principles of assembling the elements of a design are fairly well-established, though the effort involved in successfully doing so might be substantial). The inclusion of computer-generated designs in the scope of design right is particularly important, especially in respect of ASICs produced by computer–aided design techniques.

6.2.4 Design right exclusions
Neither the US Act nor the Directive contain provisions equivalent to s. 213(3) of the 1988 Act (see 6.1). These exclusions from the protection of design right have the potential to limit substantially the protection offered to semiconductor topographies. It seems probable that the configuration of the interfacing area of the topography of a semiconductor chip would fall within the 'must-fit' exclusion of s. 213(3)(b)(i). More serious is the exclusion in s. 213(3)(a) of a 'method or principle of construction', since it is arguable that the topography, when held in electronic form, defines the principles of the construction of the chip and may well also define the method (i.e., doping requirements) to be used to create the chip. If this is so, much of the protection which the 1989 Regulations were intended to provide will be lost under this exception. It is possible that we might find ourselves in a position where advances in technology outstrip the law's provisions (in this case before they came into force!) as older methods of chip production such as physical masks will attract protection whereas computer-controlled light or electron beam scanning may well fall within this exception.

6.2.5 Duration of the right
Design right normally subsists for 15 years from the end of the year in which the design was first recorded in a design document or in which articles were first made to the design, or 10 years from the end of the year in which articles made to the design were first made available for sale or hire, whichever is the shorter period. Design right in a topography is capable of subsisting for nearly 26 years. This is because s. 216 of the 1988 Act as amended by reg. 6(1) of the 1989 Regulations follows the Directive, which does not limit the subsistence of the right to the shorter of these two periods. Thus if a topography were created on 1 January 1989 but not commercially exploited, under the amended s. 216(b) the right would not expire until midnight on 31 December 2004. If it

was first made available for sale or hire on that date, the right would continue under s. 216(a) until 31 December 2014. Design right in topographies also differs from other design rights in that there is no provision for compulsory licences of right in the last five years of the term, as reg. 9 of the 1989 Regulations provides that s. 237 of the 1988 Act does not apply to semiconductor topographies.

6.3   THE WIPO TREATY

The WIPO Treaty concerning integrated circuit design protection was adopted by WIPO at a diplomatic conference in Washington on 26 May 1989. Articles 2 to 8 deal with the issue of protection for integrated circuit designs, whilst arts. 9 to 20 deal with administrative issues; only the former are examined in this chapter.

6.3.1   Definitions

The Treaty provides definitions in art. 2 for 'integrated circuit' and 'layout-design (topography)'. It also defines who is the holder of the right and the requirements for a layout-design to be protected.

The definition of integrated circuit differs from that used in the US Act and the Directive, but the essence is a layout-design (topography) which has been integrally formed in or on a piece of material and is capable of an electronic function. It should be noted that the definition envisages only one active element, and it may well be that protection for discrete components of a design could be included under a law which conforms with the Treaty.

The definition of 'layout-design (topography)' also differs from the equivalent definitions in the US Act and the EC Directive. It is defined as: 'the three-dimensional disposition, however expressed, of the elements, at least one of which is an active element, and some or all of the interconnections of an integrated circuit'. Because the definition includes the words 'however expressed', computer-held information will fall within the scope of the definition. It should also be noted that there is no need for the design to have been implemented in physical form as the words 'or such a three-dimensional disposition prepared for an integrated circuit intended for manufacture' have also been included in the definition. This is an important issue since, in Europe at least, there are specialist design houses which will prepare the layout design or topography of an ASIC for a customer, the topography being implemented by a separate semiconductor foundry. Clearly it is important for the design to be protected at this stage, and not merely after its implementation in a semiconductor chip product as is the case under s. 902(a)(1) of the US Act.

6.3.2   Subject-matter

Article 3(1) of the WIPO Treaty obliges each contracting State to secure intellectual property protection in respect of layout-designs which meet the requirements of art. 3(2), i.e., if they are the result of the creator's own intellectual efforts and are not commonplace. This is very similar to art. 2(2) of the EC Directive. It should be noted that the question of whether computer-generated designs satisfy these requirements has been left open.

6.3.3 The scope of protection

Article 6(1) of the WIPO Treaty identifies two acts which are unlawful if performed without the authorisation of the right holder:

(a) Reproducing, whether by incorporating in an integrated circuit or otherwise, the whole or any part of a protected layout-design.

(b) Importing, selling or otherwise distributing for commercial purposes a protected layout-design or an integrated circuit incorporating the protected layout-design.

Only the second of these acts is prohibited under the US Act and the Directive, though of course the manufacture of a chip inevitably requires the reproduction of its design. The question of whether innocent infringement (i.e., performance of one of the prohibited acts by a person who does not know or have reasonable grounds for knowing that a right subsists in the design) should be unlawful is left to be decided by each signatory (art. 6(4)).

Article 6(2) contains exceptions for teaching and research, and more importantly a reverse engineering exception, reproduction for the sole purpose of evaluation, analysis and research. The reverse engineering exception also permits the creation of a second layout-design, if it complies with the originality requirements of art. 3(2), on the basis of evaluation or analysis of a protected layout-design.

The Treaty also permits signatories to provide for compulsory non-exclusive licences (art. 6(3)) and for the exhaustion of rights (art. 6(5)). The compulsory licensing provision was one of the main reasons why the US and Japan voted against adoption of the Treaty.

6.3.4 Duration of protection

Under art. 8 of the WIPO Treaty protection is to last for at least eight years. As most existing legislation sets a longer period (usually 10 years) for protection and contains reciprocity provisions, it is likely that any signatory which wishes to obtain effective international protection for its nationals' designs will adopt a 10 year period. However, the adoption of norms in an international treaty of this type might eventually lead to international pressure to reduce the length of protection in countries which already have semiconductor chip protection legislation, and this provision was also objected to by the US and Japanese delegations.

6.3.5 Adoption and ratification

The Treaty was adopted by 49 votes to two (US and Japan) with five abstentions. The Treaty has been signed by eight states (China, Egypt, Ghana, Guatemala, India, Liberia, Yugoslavia and Zambia) but so far only ratified by Egypt. Under art. 16(1) five ratifications are necessary for the Treaty to enter into force.

6.4 CONCLUSIONS

Although the UK regime of protection for semiconductor topographies is in theory just a special case of design right, in practice it will be best to treat it as a separate type of intellectual property right. Because of the Directive, any decision of the European Court will be binding on UK courts, and the 1989 Regulations will need to be interpreted in the light of EC law. It should also be noted that because the right was devised in response to US legislation, any changes in the US Act are likely to be implemented in this country and the other EC member States.

On an international level an increasing number of countries have adopted semiconductor chip protection legislation since the first edition of this book, and a table showing the position in selected countries is reproduced as table 6.1 on page 172. The effect of the WIPO Treaty on the position remains to be assessed.

So far as other computer products are concerned, design right will in some circumstances provide a useful form of protection for hardware manufacturers. This right, together with other forms of protection such as registered designs, trade marks and the tort of passing off, offers manufacturers some protection for their efforts in entering or creating new markets. The pace of innovation in the computer industry is so great, however, that the protection offered is likely to be of short duration in practical terms. The best form of protection of one's competitive position, as the most successful manufacturers have demonstrated, is the quality of the product and its technical excellence.

Table 6.1 International semiconductor topography legislation

Country	Term	Originality	Registration Requirements	Reverse engineering	Innocent infringement	Non-voluntary licence	Date of implementation
	10 years from:						
Australia	1st c/e	(1)	None	Y	Y		1989
Austria	1st c/e	(2)	(4)	Y	Y		1/10/88
Canada	1st c/e + f	(1)	(4)	Y	Y	Y	27/6/90
Finland	1st c/e	(1)	None	(5)			
Hungary	1st c/e + f	(1)	(4)	(5)	Y		1/1/92
Japan	Registration	(3)	(4)	Y	Y		May 1985
Sweden	1st c/e	(3)	None	(5)			1/4/87
Switzerland	1st c/e + e	(1)	(4)	(5)	Y		
US	1st c/e + r	(1)	(4)	Y	Y		1984
EC							
Belgium	1st c/e	(2)	None	Y	Y		5/2/90
Denmark	1st c/e	(2)	(4)	Y	Y	Y	3/3/88
France	1st c/e + f	(2)	(4)	Y	Y	Y(6)	6/11/87
Germany	1st c/e + f	(2)	(4)	Y	Y		1/11/87
Greece							
Ireland	1st c/e	(2)	None	Y	Y		13/5/88
Italy	1st c/e + f	(2)	(4)	Y	Y		21/2/89
Luxembourg	1st c/e + f	(2)	(4)	Y	Y	Y(6)	30/12/88
Netherlands	1st c/e + f	(2)	(4)	Y	Y		7/11/87
Portugal	1st c/e + f	(2)	(4)	Y	Y		30/6/89
Spain	1st c/e + f	(2)	(4)	Y	Y		5/9/88
UK	1st c/e	(2)	None	Y	Y	Y(7)	7/11/87 (8)

1st c/e   First commercial exploitation
1st c/e + f   First commercial exploitation plus filing
1st c/e + r   First commercial exploitation plus registration
(1) Not commonplace in the industry
(2) Creator's own intellectual effort
(3) Not defined
(4) Two years from first commercial exploitation
(5) Not as such, but exceptions for teaching, analysis or research
(6) For purposes of State security
(7) For Crown use
(8) Replaced by 1989 Regulations

CHAPTER SEVEN

Protecting confidential information

Allison Coleman

One of the main features of computers is their ability to store, manipulate and transmit data in ways that could not be achieved with manual records and storage systems. A result of this is to focus attention on data and on information and to follow this with questions about their position within the protective regime of the law. For example, to what extent is information treated as a commodity in its own right? How can or does the law control its use or abuse? The questions are legion and the answers varied.

In this chapter we shall narrow the discussion and look at the extent to which the law protects one special category of information which might be stored on a computer, namely confidential information. This category is traditionally given special treatment in law, but the advent of computing has aggravated the risks of its unauthorised use, disclosure or manipulation. The computer hacker is potentially a more intrusive animal than the burglar or more traditional spy.

Information processed by computers can be of many types; for example, it can be personal, business or governmental information, or perhaps a mixture of these. Similarly, information learned by computer operators and program-mers can fall into any of these groups. Once information in any of those groupings is classified as confidential, certain general legal principles govern its use or disclosure by a confidant. In this chapter we shall look at these general principles, but within the general framework there are sometimes special rules which apply to different types of confidential information. Where the rules diverge we shall look at the law relating to trade secrets rather than the rules which apply to the other categories of secrets, for this chapter is aimed primarily at managers and computer scientists working in industry rather than at civil servants and governmental agencies and the confines of space make complete coverage impossible.

In the world of high technology it is unduly insular to consider only English law, for computers and modern telecommunications links allow information to be moved around the world and across jurisdictional boundaries in but the blink of an eye. Lawyers and information managers therefore need to be familiar with themes and developments in other countries. While the basis of this chapter will be the law of England and Wales we shall also make reference to the laws of other countries, notably the United States and Canada, and also to proposals for law reform, for the law is never static and new concepts introduced into other legal systems often have an impact on our own.

It would also be remiss to look only at the civil action for breach of confidence. When a valuable asset such as commercial information is misappropriated, e.g., by industrial espionage, the question arises whether a crime has been committed. We shall therefore look at the criminal laws of various countries and shall see that often, and rather surprisingly, the criminal law intervenes very little if purely information is 'stolen' or interfered with, as opposed to the tangible asset on which it is stored. This is an area which is ripe for reform, and in this context a draft statute produced by a law reform body in Canada may provide a useful precedent.

In other chapters it has sometimes been much easier to describe the law in its direct application to computers. For example, it is possible to analyse statutes and cases on copyright in computer programs. In the field of confidential information the law is generally old and computers are new, and there are not all that many English cases dealing specifically with computers and even fewer statutes. Thus it is necessary to describe the law of confidence in other contexts and to apply it to computers by way of analogy. However, there has been a steady trickle of cases in the United States in the last few years. Many of these apply comparable principles to those of English law and they also provide useful factual examples. They will therefore be cited at appropriate points.

7.1 THE CIVIL ACTION FOR BREACH OF CONFIDENCE

In English law three conditions must be satisfied before a civil action for breach of confidence can succeed:[1]

(a)   The information must be confidential.
(b)   The information must have been disclosed in circumstances which give rise to an obligation of confidence.
(c)   There must be an actual or anticipated unauthorised use or disclosure of the information.

A fourth factor is sometimes added, namely that the plaintiff must suffer detriment. However, it is uncertain whether this is an element of the action or whether it is something which the court takes into account when deciding the appropriate remedy. In any event its significance was reduced by Lord Keith

---

1. *Coco* v *Clark (Engineers) Ltd* [1969] RPC 41 per Megarry J.

of Kinkel in *Attorney-General* v *Guardian Newspapers Ltd (No. 2)* [1990] 1 AC 109, who said:[2]

> ... I would think it a sufficient detriment to the confider that the information given in confidence is to be disclosed to persons whom he would prefer not to know of it, even though the disclosure would not be harmful to him in any positive way.

Each of the three main elements of the action for breach of confidence will now be considered in turn.

7.1.1   What is confidential information?
Lord Greene MR in *Saltman Engineering Co. Ltd* v *Campbell Engineering Co. Ltd* (1948) 65 RPC 203 described confidential information as something which is not public property and public knowledge. This means that there is no need for absolute secrecy before information can qualify as confidential. Relative secrecy may suffice. Thus information may be confidential if it is inaccessible or if it is not readily available to the public. For example, programs developed to drive robots on a production line and known only to the employees of a particular firm may be confidential, as may be novel software methodologies[3] or even information which a journalist has gleaned by searching through old newspapers and publicly available documents such as birth certificates and wills. In the last example there is a new compilation of information or even a rediscovery of information which has ceased to be generally known. Either way, the law will protect the fruits of the journalist's labours until he chooses to put them into the public domain or until someone else does the same work and then puts the results of his own research into public circulation.

The extent of disclosure which will be needed before information comes into the public domain is a matter for determination by the court in the light of the facts of the case. However, once information is in the public domain it cannot be protected under confidentiality laws, as was decided in the UK *Spycatcher* case[4] and in the US case of *Public Systems Inc* v *Towry and Adams* (1991) WL 184452 where the Alabama Supreme Court ruled that a commercially available spreadsheet program using public data could not be protected under Alabama trade secrecy laws.

The fact that relative secrecy is all that is needed before information can qualify as confidential contrasts with the requirement of absolute novelty in patent law where any prior publication, no matter how obscure, will destroy novelty and deny patentability.

The test of relative secrecy would seem to be an objective one, the matter being looked at by the court in the light of all the relevant circumstances. A different and more subjective test of confidentiality was suggested in *Thomas*

---

2. [1990] 1 AC 109 at p. 256.
3. *Healthcare Affiliated Services Inc.* v *Lippany* (1988) 701 F Supp 1142.
4. See *Attorney-General* v *Guardian Newspapers Ltd (No. 2)* [1990] 1 AC 109, but cf. *Schering Chemicals Ltd* v *Falkman Ltd* [1982] QB 1.

Marshall (Exports) Ltd v *Guinle* [1979] Ch 227 by Sir Robert Megarry V-C, a judge whose decisions will feature prominently in this chapter. He said that there were four elements which might be of assistance in identifying confidential information in a trade or industrial setting:

(a)   The information must be information the release of which the owner believes would be injurious to him or of advantage to his rivals or others.

(b)   The owner must believe the information is confidential or secret, i.e., not already in the public domain.

(c)   The owner's beliefs under the previous two heads must be reasonable.

(d)   The information must be judged in the light of the usage and practices of the particular industry concerned.

This test concentrates very heavily on the views of the 'owner' of the information. However, these views are objectively assessed under the third requirement that they must be reasonable, thus preventing overzealous protection of information which by objective standards is not the true subject-matter of an action for breach of confidence.

7.1.2   Categories of confidential information

Any sort of information may be classified as confidential, but in practice confidential information tends to fall into three categories, personal information, governmental secrets and trade secrets. While it is public policy to protect confidential information generally, each of these categories of information is also protected for special reasons which may not apply equally to the other classes. For example, the protection of personal information is closely tied up with the maintenance of privacy. Thus in *Argyll* v *Argyll* [1967] Ch 302 the Duke of Argyll was not able to publish in a newspaper the secrets of his marriage to the Duchess of Argyll. But English law, unlike, for example, the laws of North America, is remarkably reluctant to develop a full-blown action for the protection of privacy[5] and the extent to which the action for breach of confidence can fulfil this role is very limited.

The protection of governmental secrets gives rise to yet other public policy issues such as preservation of national security, international diplomacy, politics and the reputations of governments and of public figures; plus questions of the freedom of the press to publish information in their own commercial interests and/or in the interest of free and informed debate. One issue which has been highlighted is the attitudes of different governments to freedom of information and the preservation of secrecy. This is appositely illustrated by the pursuit of Mr Peter Wright through the courts of the world by the representatives of the Thatcher government in an attempt to prevent the publication of his book, *Spycatcher*.[6] This should be contrasted with the abandonment of a case by the Wilson government after they lost at first

---

5. See, e.g., *Kaye* v *Robertson* [1991] FSR 62.
6. See note 4.

instance in an action for breach of confidence against Richard Crossman for publishing Cabinet secrets.[7]

Trade secrets are valuable commercial assets and to a large extent they are protected for the same reasons as other intangible commercial assets such as patents and copyrights. These include rewarding innovation and effort, allowing recoupment of expenditure on research and development and curtailing unfair competition by limiting the opportunities for piracy. In the context of computing, trade secrets may include software or hardware specifications as well as more standard business information such as pricing policies, lists of customers and suppliers, the company's payroll, quotations and investments, any or all of which may be kept on an in-house computer or may be held on behalf of a client on the computer of a specialist bureau.

Because the protection of trade secrets will feature quite prominently in this chapter a definition should be attempted. It has proved notoriously difficult to define a trade secret, but one fairly recent attempt at a non-exhaustive definition comes from the report of the Alberta Institute of Law Research and Reform and Federal Provincial Working Party, *Trade Secrets* (Report No. 46, 1986) as amended in a draft statute adopted by the Canadian Uniform Law Conference in 1988.[8] This definition has the advantage of reflecting case law in England and Wales and in the United States of America, and thus can serve as an indicator of elements in all three jurisdictions. The draft statute states that:

> . . . trade secret, means information that
>   (i)   is, or may be, used in a trade or business,
>   (ii)   is not generally known in that trade or business,
>   (iii) has economic value from not being generally known, and
>   (iv)   is the subject of efforts that are reasonable under the circumstances to prevent it from becoming generally known.
>   (2)   For the purposes of the definition, trade secret 'information' includes information set out, contained or embodied in, but not limited to, a formula, pattern, plan, compilation, computer program, method, technique, process, product, device or mechanism.

7.1.3   When will an obligation of confidence be imposed?

Generally an obligation of confidence will be imposed whenever confidential information is disclosed for a limited purpose. The recipient of the information will then be under a duty to use the information for the limited purpose only, and if he discloses or uses the information for any other purpose he will be in breach of his obligation and is liable to be restrained by injunction or subject to other appropriate remedies. For example, in *Saltman Engineering Co. Ltd* v *Campbell Engineering Co. Ltd* (1948) 65 RPC 203 the plaintiffs gave to the defendants confidential designs for tools which the defendants were to manufacture solely for the plaintiffs. When the defendants manufactured the

---

7. *Attorney-General* v *Jonathan Cape Ltd* [1976] QB 752.
8. References in this chapter will be to the amended version. For the full text see Coleman, *The Legal Protection of Trade Secrets* (ESC/Sweet and Maxwell, 1992), App. 2(a).

tools on their own account they were held to be in breach of an obligation of confidence. The court held that the designs had been handed over for a limited purpose only and the defendants were not entitled to use them or the information contained in them for any other purpose.

More recently the same principles were applied in *Fraser* v *Thames Television Ltd* [1984] QB 44 where the plaintiffs had disclosed in confidence to a television company an idea for their own show. When the company tried to use the idea for a series featuring other actresses without first obtaining the plaintiffs' consent, it was held to be in breach of its obligation of confidence. A good example of the imposition of an obligation of confidence in the field of computers might be where a consultant programmer is brought in to develop programs which will be integrated with other programs devised in-house. Details of these programs will have to be disclosed to the consultant, but this disclosure is clearly for the sole purpose of work for that organisation and he or she will not be free to use the information in work for other clients.

Problems can sometimes arise in determining the issue of whom a duty of confidentiality is owed to. In *Fraser* v *Evans* [1969] 1 QB 349 the plaintiff, Fraser, wrote a report for the Greek government. His contract stated that he was to keep confidential any information that he acquired while compiling the report, but the Greek government did not enter into a reciprocal obligation to keep confidential information supplied by Fraser to them. After its delivery to the Greek government Fraser's report was leaked by an unknown source to a newspaper, which proposed to publish an article about it. Fraser thought that the article might damage his reputation and he sought to restrain its publication on the ground of breach of confidence. The court held that, on the facts, no one owed a duty of confidentiality to Fraser despite his own categorisation of the information as being sensitive. Similarly, in the US case of *Bush* v *Goldman Sachs & Co.* (1989) 544 So 2d 873, Bush had developed a computer model to restructure government bond debt through refunding. Bush was hired by one company to become part of its team tendering for the contract to restructure the bond debt of the city of Birmingham, Alabama. Bush's computer model was submitted to the city authorities as part of the tendering process. However, the contract was given to another company, Goldman Sachs. Goldman Sachs subsequently made use of Bush's model without his consent. However, an action for breach of confidence failed, first because Bush had failed to take positive steps to protect the confidentiality of the model, e.g., by express notice of confidentiality in the tendering documentation; and secondly the court held that the city authorities, which had undoubtedly passed on the information to Goldman Sachs, owed no duty of confidentiality to Bush. Because they owed no duty to Bush they did not act in breach of duty in passing on the information to Goldman Sachs, which likewise could also not be held liable.

Precedent has not limited the range of circumstances in which an obligation of confidence can arise; it is a question of fact to be decided in each case but there are guidelines. For example, in the commercial context a useful statement was made by Megarry J in *Coco* v *A. N. Clark (Engineers) Ltd* [1969] RPC 41. He said that where information of commercial or industrial value is given on a businesslike basis or with a common object in mind such as a joint venture or the manufacture of articles by one party for another, the recipient is under a heavy burden if he seeks to refute the contention that he is bound by an obligation of confidence. Where confidential information falling into the other categories is disclosed this dictum is obviously not directly applicable, but use of the limited-purpose test described above should overcome any difficulties.

In *Coco* v *A. N. Clark (Engineers) Ltd* Megarry J gave another test for the circumstances giving rise to an obligation of confidence. He said that an obligation would lie when a reasonable man standing in the shoes of the recipient of the information would realise on reasonable grounds that the information was being given to him in confidence. It will be remembered that in *Thomas Marshall (Exports) Ltd* v *Guinle* [1979] Ch 227 Megarry V-C (as he later became) had defined information which could be classified as confidential. There he viewed the situation from the standpoint of the 'owner' of the information, but now when faced with the other side of the coin he said that the circumstances which give rise to an obligation were to be viewed from the position of the reasonable recipient. This shift in emphasis from the 'owner' to the recipient reflects the bilateral nature of the obligation of confidence and the mixed elements of subjectivity and objectivity in the various tests. These take into account not only the views of the parties to the action but also the public interest in the maintenance of confidentiality. In certain circumstances even if information has been classified as confidential an obligation of confidence will not arise if, for example, it would be against the public interest to keep the information confidential or if such a restriction would prevent an ex-employee using the general knowledge and skill acquired in his former employment. The special position of employees will be considered in a later section of this chapter, but we shall now look in greater detail at the public interest which permits disclosure even of information which is otherwise classified as being confidential.

7.1.4   The public interest in disclosure
The cases show that there is a clear public policy in favour of protecting confidential information. However, in certain circumstances that policy is overturned by one which holds that it is in the public interest that even confidential information should be disclosed, either to the public as a whole, e.g., through the media, or to the appropriate authorities such as the police. For example, suppose a scientist has discovered a cure for AIDS or for cancer. Should he be allowed to lock it in his safe or store it on his computer with the intention of keeping it a secret for the rest of his life? If one of his employees proposes disclosing the secret in a medical journal, to a national newspaper or at a scientific conference, should the discoverer be able to restrain him from so doing by an action for breach of confidence? The answer in morality is clearly no, but what is the position in law?

The test for determining the public interest in disclosure has varied over the years. An early and much-quoted dictum comes from the case of *Gartside* v *Outram* (1857) 26 LJ Ch 113, where Wood V-C said 'there is no confidence as to the disclosure of an iniquity'. From this there arose what became known as the 'iniquity rule', which basically meant that a confidant was justified in breaching confidentiality and disclosing information in the public interest if it was related to some misconduct, and the closer this misconduct came to criminal or unlawful activity the better. But this is a rather narrow basis on which to permit disclosure and it may not, for example, permit the disclosure of the cure for cancer referred to in the previous example, for there the discoverer who wishes to keep the information out of the public domain is guilty of no criminal or unlawful conduct even though most would probably castigate his intentions as immoral.

Lord Denning led a movement away from the iniquity rule in *Initial Services Ltd* v *Putterill* [1968] 1 QB 396, *Fraser* v *Evans* [1969] 1 QB 349 and *Schering Chemicals Ltd* v *Falkman Ltd* [1982] QB 1, but there remained uncertainty about the status of the old rule or the extent of any new rule until *Lion Laboratories Ltd* v *Evans* [1985] QB 526, where the Court of Appeal held that confidential information may be disclosed in circumstances where there was 'just cause or excuse', which is obviously a much broader notion than that of an iniquity.

In *Lion Laboratories Ltd* v *Evans* the plaintiff company manufactured computerised electronic equipment known as the Lion Intoximeter which was used by the police to measure the level of alcohol in the breath of people suspected of drunk driving. Readings from the machine were used as a basis for prosecution. Confidential internal memoranda produced by the company indicated that readings from the machines were often inaccurate. Two of the plaintiff's employees gave copies of the memoranda to a national newspaper, the *Daily Express*, which at that time was conducting a campaign against the use of the intoximeter by the police. The plaintiff sought an injunction to restrain publication of the information by the newspaper on the grounds of breach of confidence and breach of copyright. The actions failed as the Court of Appeal held that there was a public interest in the disclosure of the information, as it might lead to the reappraisal of a device which had the potential for causing wrongful conviction for a serious offence. The court said that the defence of public interest was not limited to cases involving disclosure of an iniquity, iniquity being just one example of the public interest exemption and not therefore an essential ingredient. The court based the defence on the wider ground of 'just cause or excuse' for disclosure, with the caution given by Griffiths LJ that the decision should not be treated as a 'mole's charter'. The court also made it clear that there was a difference between matters which, on the one hand, it was in the commercial interest of newspapers to publish and which might merely be of public interest to read and, on the other hand, matters which it was in the public interest to disclose. Only in the latter cases would the public interest permit disclosure of confidential information. Furthermore, the press might not always be the appropriate medium for a disclosure. In other cases it might be more appropriate to disclose the information to the police or other authorities. That was not, however, the case here where disclosure through the press would be allowed.

Two other cases which have contrasting results but which illustrate the application of the doctrine of public interest are *Cork* v *McVicar* (1984) *The Times*, 31 October 1984 and *Francome* v *Mirror Group Newspapers Ltd* [1984] 1 WLR 892. In *Cork* v *McVicar*, Cork, a former detective sergeant in the

Metropolitan police, agreed to supply information about police corruption to McVicar who was planning to write a series of articles on that topic. Under the terms of the contract between them conversations were to be tape-recorded, but when Cork wished to supply confidential information off the record the tape recorder was to be switched off. McVicar agreed to use only legitimately recorded information as the basis for his articles and also to submit manuscripts to Cork for approval prior to publication. Unknown to Cork, McVicar had strapped to his leg a secret tape recorder which he used to record the entire conversations between himself and Cork including therefore information which was expressed as being confidential and off the record. McVicar then used the information from the secret tape recordings to compile a manuscript which was to be serialised in the *Daily Express* newspaper. Cork had not approved this manuscript and he sought an injunction to restrain the disclosure of the information and publication of the articles. The *Daily Express* was joined as a party to the action. They knew of the agreement between Cork and McVicar. In this case Scott J refused to grant the injunction on the ground that it was in the public interest that the information be disclosed. Furthermore, disclosure to the press was justified because the information related to alleged police corruption and disclosure to the police might not suffice.

By way of contrast, in *Francome v Mirror Group Newspapers Ltd,* another national newspaper proposed to publish information obtained from unauthorised tape recordings of telephone conversations between a jockey, Johnny Francome, and his wife. These telephone conversations revealed that Francome had breached Jockey Club regulations and possibly committed criminal offences. In this case, however, the plaintiff's application for an interlocutory injunction succeeded. The court held that the information imparted in the course of the telephone conversations was confidential,[9] and on the facts of the case there was no public interest in the disclosure of the information through the pages of a national newspaper. Here disclosure to the police or to the Jockey Club would have been sufficient. The court also seemed to place considerable weight on the fact that the information had been obtained as a result of an illegal telephone tap contrary to s. 5 of the Wireless Telegraphy Act 1949, and this breach of the criminal law gave to the plaintiff at least an arguable case that he had private rights against the offenders which he was entitled to protect by an injunction prior to a full trial of the action. Each case therefore depends on its facts, including the extent of the disclosure proposed.

Looking now to the law in other countries, in the United States there is no reference in the Uniform Trade Secrets Act to either a defence of disclosure in the public interest or to the public interest in disclosure being a factor which the court will take into account when assessing whether information is protectable in the first place. In the US this is something considered by the courts when exercising their discretion to grant a remedy. It is thus a function of the remedial process rather than a question of the attachment of liability or the availability of a defence. However, public interest does not seem to be unduly limited in its ambit either by the words of a statute or by case law.

---

9. Cf. *Malone v Metropolitan Police Commissioner* [1979] Ch 344, discussed later.

There have been no Canadian cases on the point, but in the report of the Alberta Institute of Law Research and Reform (see 7.1.2) it was recommended that henceforth public interest should be a defence to an action for improper disclosure or use of a trade secret. Unfortunately the Institute defined public interest very narrowly as 'the interest of the public at large in being made aware of the existence of a crime, fraud or other unlawful conduct or of a matter affecting public health or safety in relation to the creation, composition or utilisation of a trade secret'. It is therefore unclear that facts such as those of *Lion Laboratories Ltd* v *Evans* would fit within this defence, and in this instance it is arguable that the Canadian report errs too much on the side of caution. The multiplicity of circumstances in which an action for breach of confidence can arise warrant much greater flexibility, otherwise the action could be distorted by too great an emphasis on confidentiality at the expense of other countervailing policies which also fulfil necessary roles in the structure of modern information law.

7.2 JURISDICTION

There has been much debate about the jurisdictional foundation of the action for breach of confidence, but quite remarkably the courts seem free to draw on most of the available jurisdictional bases – contract, equity, property and tort. In many instances the facts will lead quite naturally to the application of one of these bases, in others there may be several possibilities. We shall now look at various jurisdictional bases and indicate the areas where they are most frequently employed in practice.

7.2.1 Express contractual obligations of confidence
Parties who are aware that information is confidential and that its unauthorised use or disclosure would be disadvantageous to them would be well advised to enter into express contracts of confidentiality with their confidants before making a disclosure. As well as setting out the terms on which the information is disclosed, the contract will also serve as a warning of both confidentiality and the serious intent of the discloser.

An express contract may be oral or in writing, although writing is clearly advantageous for evidential reasons. No particular form is necessary so long as the intent is clear, and it is common for the obligation of confidence to be set out in a letter or deed which, in practice, follows a fairly standard pattern. In return for the release of the information the confidant agrees to treat it as confidential and to use it only for the limited purpose intended. However, it is normal to qualify the agreement by providing that in three cases the obligation shall cease:

(a) If the information subsequently comes into the public domain other than by breach of confidence on the part of the confidant.

(b) If it was lawfully in the confidant's possession before the agreement.

(c) If it was acquired by the confidant after the agreement from a third party who was not also bound by an obligation of confidence to the present discloser.

Confidentiality clauses are also commonly found in contracts dealing with an array of other matters such as contracts for the supply or maintenance of hardware or software, consultancy contracts, and agreements for the provision of data services.

It is not necessary to define in the contract all of the information which is to be regarded as being confidential, and indeed this will rarely be possible in practice. But if an injunction is sought to restrain breach of an obligation of confidence, it is important then to define carefully for the purpose of the proceedings information which is believed to be confidential and which it is alleged is, or is thought likely to be, improperly used or disclosed. For example, in *Amway Corporation* v *Eurway International Ltd* [1974] RPC 82 the plaintiff alleged that all of the material in all of its sales promotion literature was confidential. The claim failed. The court held that the plaintiff had not disclosed the information to the defendant under an obligation of confidence, but even if it had, an injunction could not be granted to restrain use of such a generalised body of information or what the judge referred to as 'mere know-how'. The distinction between protectable confidential information and 'mere know-how' which cannot be protected is an important one, and is relied on heavily in employment cases as will be shown in a later part of this chapter.

Another useful device for protecting confidential information is what can be described as a 'black box' contract. In *K.S. Paul (Printing Machinery) Ltd* v *Southern Instruments (Communications) Ltd* [1964] RPC 118 the plaintiff supplied a telephone answering machine to one of the defendants under a contract for hire, which specified that the defendant was not to remove the machine from the address and position at which it was installed nor interfere in any way with the machine or with any of its electrical connections. In breach of this agreement one of the defendants allowed another defendant to remove it, take it apart and examine it. Damages would obviously not have been an appropriate remedy as the plaintiff clearly wanted to preserve the 'secrets in the box'. As a result the court granted an interlocutory injunction restraining the defendants from using or disclosing confidential information gleaned from the unlawful inspection.

This type of contract is obviously useful in the supply of computers or other technologically advanced equipment where the secret parts can be shielded from view. In the absence of such agreement the law of confidence will not prevent the purchaser of equipment from reverse engineering a machine or disassembling a program.[10] Even copyright laws do not prevent a competitor from taking the ideas behind, e.g., a computer program, copyright being aimed at protection of the form in which material is laid out rather than the ideas on which it is based.[11]

7.2.2 Implied contractual obligations

An obligation of confidence may also be implied into a contract. An implied term can provide the entire obligation of confidence or it may supplement an

---

10. See, e.g., *Acuson Corp.* v *Aloka Co. Ltd* (1989) 257 Cal Rptr 368, 209 Cal App 3d 1098, 209 Cal App 3d 425.
11. See further chapter 4.

express term. An example of its supplementary role is *Thomas Marshall (Exports) Ltd* v *Guinle* [1979] Ch 227 where an employee was subject to an express clause prohibiting the disclosure of confidential information belonging to his employer. However, on the facts of the case the employee had been *using* the information for his own purposes and not *disclosing* it to others. The court held that the express term against disclosing confidential information could be supplemented by an implied term prohibiting its use.

Another case on the implied obligation of confidence, and one to which we shall return later, is *Schering Chemicals Ltd* v *Falkman Ltd* [1982] QB 1. The facts were that the plaintiff was a drug company which manufactured a drug called Primodos. It had been suggested that the drug could have harmful effects on unborn children, and as a result the plaintiff suffered bad publicity. It engaged the first defendant to train its executives in television techniques and to put across effectively the plaintiff's point of view. This first defendant engaged the second defendant to help with the training courses. The plaintiff supplied a large amount of information on the drug to the first defendant and that in turn was passed on to the second defendant. It was acknowledged that the first defendant had received the information in confidence, but it was never established whether the second defendant gave an express undertaking of confidentiality.

Shortly after the training course the second defendant proposed making a television programme about the drug for Thames Television. Much of the information which was to be included in the film had been supplied by the plaintiff for the training course but, importantly, most of it was already available from public sources. The plaintiff sought an injunction to restrain use of the information, arguing that it had been obtained in circumstances imposing an obligation of confidence and to use it in the film would amount to breach of confidence.

Lord Denning MR, who dissented, refused to imply an obligation of confidence on the ground that the information was publicly available. Shaw and Templeman LJJ disagreed. Shaw LJ said that the second defendant owed a fiduciary duty to the plaintiff and described his conduct as a 'flagrant breach of an elementary duty to honour confidences'. He said that the law did not grant 'a licence for the mercenary betrayal of business confidences'. As for the argument that the information was in the public domain and thus not confidential, he said this was 'at best cynical; some may regard it as specious'.

Templeman LJ also held that the second defendant was under a duty of confidence, but instead of describing it as a fiduciary duty, he said, most importantly in the present context, that it was based on an implied promise. He said that the information had been given for one purpose only, and when the second defendant had agreed for reward to take part in the training course and had received the information from the plaintiff he came under a duty not to use that information, and in particular he impliedly promised not use it for the very purpose which the plaintiff sought to avoid, namely bad publicity or publicity which it reasonably regarded as bad. Rather unusually, although the information was already in the public domain it remained confidential as between the parties to the action, and as the second defendant could not republish or recycle it without causing further harm he would be in breach of his obligation of confidence if he used the information for another purpose. Furthermore, as Thames Televison had acted with full knowledge of the facts they could be in no better position than the second defendant, and they too would be restrained from using or disclosing the information.

7.2.3 The different obligations of confidence owed by employees and consultants

7.2.3.1 Employees Employees both generate and acquire confidential information in the course of a contract of employment. The general principle is that the employee holds the confidential information for the benefit of the employer.

Employment contracts do, however, present special problems, as here the contractual obligation of confidence is subject to the qualification that an employee is, after the termination of his contract of employment, free to use his general knowledge and skill either for his own benefit or for the benefit of others. As a result, the confidential character of information is probably more closely scrutinised in these cases than in almost any others. One of the most difficult questions in this area of the law is to determine the dividing line between confidential information and general knowledge and skill. For example, is the knowledge acquired by a computer systems expert in the course of his employment his own to use as he pleases or is it an asset belonging to his employer? What is the position of firms of head-hunters who seek to persuade highly skilled personnel to leave their present employment and to use their expertise for the benefit of others in return for greater reward? In today's competitive environment, expertise is a valuable commodity, but to what extent is it really readily saleable?

An employee's obligation of confidence may be found in the express or in the implied terms of his contract of employment. This was illustrated earlier by the case of *Thomas Marshall (Exports) Ltd* v *Guinle* [1979] Ch 227, where it will be remembered that an express term prohibiting the disclosure of confidential information was supplemented by an implied term preventing the employee using that information. In employment cases the implied obligation of confidence is part of the more general implied obligation of good faith and fidelity which every employee owes to his employer. This obligation exists during the term of the contract, but, very importantly, it also continues after employment ceases. It is at its clearest and strongest during the subsistence of the contract, for here as Gurry argues[12] the employee's interest in enhancing his knowledge and skill 'interlocks' with his duty to develop and improve his employer's business. At this stage Gurry shows that the obligation of fidelity owed by an employee to his employer can be expressed in three propositions:

(a) An employee is bound not to disclose or use confidential information which he receives in the course of his employment for purposes which are against the interests of his employer.

---

12. Francis Gurry, *Breach of Confidence* (Oxford: Clarendon Press, 1984), p. 179.

(b)   An employee must not compete with his employer or work for any of his rivals.

(c)   The employee is bound to disclose to his employer any valuable information which he receives in his capacity as an employee and which is unknown to his employer, and this will include any confidential information which would further his employer's trade.

The first two propositions are illustrated by *Hivac Ltd* v *Park Royal Scientific Instruments Ltd* [1946] Ch 169, where five people who were employed by the plaintiff were working in their spare time for the plaintiff's rivals, the defendant. If this had continued they were almost certain to have disclosed to the defendant confidential information belonging to the plaintiff. As a result, the plaintiff succeeded in its action to restrain the defendant from continuing to employ the plaintiff's employees. Moonlighting is therefore discouraged.

After the contract of employment has been terminated the employee's implied duty of good faith and fidelity continues and he will still be required to keep confidential those secrets which he learnt during his former employment. However, at this stage the interest of the employee in using and developing his general knowledge and skill usually diverges from his former employer's interest in his own business. To return to the previous example, the computer systems expert whose skills have been head-hunted by a rival concern or who wishes to set up in business on his own account may not be prepared to make less than full use of all of the knowledge that he possesses, including knowledge of information classified by his former employer as being confidential, or indeed his new employment may be conditional on the full use of such knowledge. Here a number of policies conflict, namely the public policy in the maintenance of confidences as against policies favouring mobility of labour, the free flow of information and free competition. As a compromise, the first policy holds sway to the extent that a former employee is under a continuing obligation not to use or disclose confidential information belonging to his former employer, but the other policies ensure that he is free to use his general knowledge and skill.

There are a number of tests for determining the dividing line between confidential information and general knowledge and skill. In *Printers & Finishers Ltd* v *Holloway* [1965] 1 WLR 1, Cross J said the question was whether the information could 'fairly be regarded as a separate part of the employee's stock of knowledge which a man of ordinary honesty and intelligence would recognise to be the property of his old employer, and not as his own to do as he likes with'. More recently the Court of Appeal laid down guidelines in *Faccenda Chicken Ltd* v *Fowler* [1987] Ch 117. Neil LJ, giving the judgment of the court, said that in order to determine whether information could be classified as so confidential that an employee should not be allowed to use or disclose it for the benefit of a subsequent employer it was necessary to consider all the circumstances of the particular case, but the following were among those to which attention must be paid:

(a)   The nature of the employment: employment in a capacity where confidential information is habitually handled may impose a high obligation of confidentiality because the employee could be expected to realise its sensitive nature to a greater extent than if he were employed in a capacity where such material reached him only occasionally.

(b) The nature of the information itself: in order to be protected the information must be of a highly confidential nature; no other information could be protected even by a covenant in restraint of trade. The court said it would clearly be impossible to provide a list of matters which would be protectable as trade secrets. Secret processes of manufacture were obvious examples, but innumerable other pieces of information were capable of being trade secrets even though the secrecy of some information may only be short-lived. In addition, the fact that the circulation of certain information was restricted to a limited number of individuals may throw a light on the status of the information and its degree of confidentiality.

(c) Whether the employer impressed upon the employee the confidentiality of the information.

(d) Whether the relevant information can be easily isolated from other information which the employee is free to use or disclose: this factor should not be regarded as conclusive, as might have been suggested in earlier cases, but like the other matters listed above it was one of the factors which the court should take into account.

The result of this is that if information is not categorised as confidential under these criteria then it forms part of the employee's general knowledge and skill, and it may be easier to apply the factors listed in *Faccenda Chicken Ltd* v *Fowler* to employees in high-technology industries than it is to apply more general statements such as that in *Printers & Finishers Ltd* v *Holloway*. However, there are still many difficulties and each case must inevitably turn on its facts.

Neil LJ also made it clear that he was stating principles which would apply only when the ex-employee wanted to earn his living from use of the information in question. He left open the question whether additional protection should be afforded if an ex-employee proposed not to use it in order to earn his living but merely to sell it to a third party. Such a distinction, if drawn, would be new to English law. It would also necessitate the development of a new set of principles of a complexity hitherto unforeseen. For example, what would be the position of a person who sold information in return for a consultancy for one day a week, or for one day a month, or for one day a year, or for just one day?

An alternative approach to reliance solely on an obligation to respect confidentiality, and hence a way around some of the difficulties described above, might be to use a contractual term to restrain the employee from working for competitors after he leaves his employment. However, the courts view such restrictions unfavourably and they will only be enforced if they are no wider than is reasonably necessary to protect the employer's interests in terms of the activities covered, the geographical area to which the restriction extends and the length of time it lasts.[13] For example, a hardware manufacturer

---

13. *Nordenfelt* v *Maxim Nordenfelt Guns & Ammunition Co. Ltd* [1894] AC 535.

whose business consisted solely of producing automatic teller machines for use in the banking industry in the UK would be unable to restrict one of its programmers from working for any other hardware manufacturer in the world for 10 years after leaving. It is important to note that if the restriction is too wide it is likely to be totally ineffective, thus allowing the employee to work for a direct competitor[14] and directing reliance back on the uncertain obligation of confidence. A better restriction would be against working on the production of automatic teller machines and connected hardware for any business marketing its equipment in the UK. The length of time of the restriction should not last beyond the date when the employer's secret technology is likely to become obsolete.

7.2.3.2 Consultants   An increasing number of people are now working in the computing industry as consultants, i.e., as independent contractors rather than as employees. It is therefore necessary also to consider their position in relation to confidential information generated and acquired in the course of their work.

A well-drafted contract for services to be provided by a consultant should always deal with the ownership of intellectual property rights generated in the course of the work and with the question of confidentiality. This is in the interests of both the consultant and the firm for which the work is to be done.

In the absence of express agreement it is necessary to fall back on ordinary principles of law. So far as confidential information is concerned this will be governed by implied contractual terms, as in the case of a contract of employment. A consultant should hold for the benefit of the firm for which he works all trade secrets generated or acquired in the course of the work and he should not use or disclose these trade secrets for any unauthorised purpose. Counterbalancing this is the principle that a consultant, like an employee, is entitled to use for his own benefit and for the benefit of others his general knowledge and skill. Thus again we meet the thorny issue of what is a trade secret and what is general knowledge and skill. Where does the dividing line lie?

In the case of an employee, *Faccenda Chicken Ltd* v *Fowler* [1987] Ch 117 laid down guidelines as to which information could be used for the benefit of the employee and others after termination of a contract of employment and which should be kept secret. However, there is nothing in *Faccenda Chicken Ltd* v *Fowler* to indicate that those guidelines would apply equally to a consultant. If they do not apply, consultants are therefore in a different position to employees. Cases such as *Schering Chemicals Ltd* v *Falkman Ltd* [1982] QB 1, discussed above, *Deta Nominees Pty Ltd* v *Viscount Plastic Products Pty Ltd* [1979] VR 167, and *Surveys & Mining Ltd* v *Morrison* [1969] QdR 470 have taken a rather hard line with consultants who have acquired confidential information whilst working for one client then subsequently used that information for their own benefit or for the benefit of others. In each of these case the courts have held that the consultant has acted in breach of an obligation of confidence.

---

14. *Mason* v *Provident Clothing & Supply Co. Ltd* [1913] AC 724.

If employees and consultants are treated differently several propositions follow. For example, while both consultants and employees can use their general knowledge and skill for the benefit of others, more information is likely to be held to be confidential and protectable in the case of consultants than in the case of employees. Viewing this from the point of view of a firm deciding to take on additional labour, it might be desirable therefore to take on independent contractors or consultants rather than to employ employees under short-term contracts.

7.2.4   The equitable obligation of confidence

There are many circumstances in which confidential information is disclosed and yet there cannot be said to be any contract between the discloser and his confidant. This will normally be the case when personal confidences are exchanged between friends, and it will often be so when an inventor discusses his invention with potential financiers and business partners. In these circumstances any obligation of confidence will almost always be equitable. For example in *Coco* v *A. N. Clark (Engineers) Ltd* [1969] RPC 41, the plaintiff who had designed the 'Coco Moped' sought cooperation from the defendant in its development. The parties quarrelled before any agreement was reached, but features of the Coco Moped were later found in the defendant's mopeds. The court found that the information which the plaintiff gave to the defendant was not confidential but, had it been, Megarry J said that an equitable obligation would have been imposed if, applying the test which we met earlier, the circumstances were such that a reasonable man standing in the shoes of the recipient of the information would have realised on reasonable grounds that the information was being given to him in confidence.

Another example is *Seager* v *Copydex Ltd* [1967] RPC 349 where the plaintiff, in the course of negotiations for marketing one type of carpet grip which he had invented, disclosed his design for a second grip and suggested the name 'Invisigrip'. This disclosure would seem to have been unsolicited. Negotiations foundered and the defendant decided to develop and market a carpet grip of its own. This it also called 'Invisgrip' and its design closely resembled the second grip described to it by the plaintiff. The plaintiff succeeded in an action for unauthorised use of confidential information. The court said that even if the plagiarism by the defendant was unconscious there were too many coincidences and too many similarities for the court to conclude that there had been anything other than a misuse of information given to the defendants by the plaintiff. Equitable principles were also applied recently by the Irish courts in *House of Spring Gardens Ltd* v *Point Blank Ltd* [1985] FSR 327 where because there were no Irish cases in point the courts applied the doctrines of English law.[15]

7.2.4.1   Unsolicited disclosures   Cases on the equitable obligation of confidence highlight the problems which can arise from unsolicited disclosures.

---

15. See further A. Coleman, '*House of Spring Gardens* v *Point Blank Ltd:* "A Maze of Deception"' [1988] EIPR 218.

Some firms regularly receive ideas from outsiders about new products or improvements to their existing ranges, and while it is not proper that they should make free use of all confidences that come their way, their subsequent activities should not, at the other extreme, always be inhibited by a prior unsolicited disclosure. Strong representations were made to the Law Commission on this point.[16] Evidence to the Commission showed that many firms adopted elaborate procedures in order to avoid an obligation of confidence. Some firms required the person submitting the information to sign a form recognising that no obligation of confidence existed in relation to the information, the person submitting the information being limited to such rights (if any) which he may have to patent, copyright or design rights. Other firms were content to ensure that the person submitting unsolicited information appreciated that the recipient would remain free to exploit ideas involved if they had already been, or were in the future, independently discovered by the recipients or if they were in the public domain. In other words those firms who understood their legal position modified their relationship with the discloser of confidential information by express contract, whereas those who did not know the law often found themselves bound to respect confidentiality. To ameliorate the position of persons in the latter category the Law Commission recommended[17] that the law be changed, and that an obligation of confidence should come into existence only when the recipient of the information had given an express undertaking of confidence or where an undertaking could be inferred from the relationship between the parties or from the conduct of the recipient. However, this is arguably going too far and represents an unnecessary change. It is better to prefer confidentiality and to refute the obligation if necessary than to place barriers in the way of it arising in the first place.

7.2.5 Tortious obligations of confidence

So far tort has not featured very prominently in the cases on breach of confidence, but it assumes an important role in proposals for reform in three common law jurisdictions, England and Wales, Canada and the United States.[18]

In each of these jurisdictions it has been suggested that henceforth, at least in certain areas, the action for breach of confidence should be based on tortious liability. In 1981 the English Law Commission recommended[19] that the present action for breach of confidence should be abolished and that it should be replaced by one new statutory tort of breach of confidence covering the unauthorised use or disclosure of confidential information. In contrast to the reforms in the United States and Canada, the English Law Commission recommended that the new action should apply to all categories of confidential

16. Law Commission, *Breach of Confidence* (Law Com. No. 110, Cmnd 8388) (London: HMSO, 1981), para. 5.3.
17. Law Commission, *Breach of Confidence* (see note 16), para. 6.14.
18. See further Coleman, *The Legal Protection of Trade Secrets* (see note 8), ch. 2.
19. Law Commission, *Breach of Confidence* (see note 16), para. 6.2.

information. In the US and Canada the various categories of information are now often treated separately. There, for example, the law of privacy has burgeoned in recent years, affecting the protection of personal confidences, and reform bodies now suggest that trade secrets should also be treated separately, recognising the different interests involved and their greater affinity with the policies of intellectual property and unfair competition law than with the issues underlying, e.g., privacy and governmental information. In this section we shall be looking at the reforms of trade secrets law, following once again the theme of trade where the law diverges as between the different categories of confidential information.

In the US and Canada the problem is that confidentiality is a matter for state or provincial law, unlike patents and copyrights which are regulated federally. As a result, although there is a common core of principles underlying the action for breach of confidence, laws do diverge across the country. There have been two main sets of proposals for uniform laws for the United States. The first came in the *Restatement of the Law of Torts* published in 1939. Like the later English Law Commission Report, this recommended that it should be a tort for a person to use or disclose a trade secret without privilege to do so. However, when the 1939 Restatement was updated the legal protection of trade secrets was omitted. The American Law Institute, which produces the Restatements, said that trade secrets had become a subject of such importance in its own right that it no longer belonged in that volume of the Restatement and that it should receive independent treatment in a separate Trade Practices Restatement, but regrettably this was never produced.

In a separate development in 1979 the US National Conference of Commissioners on Uniform State Laws recommended the adoption of another set of uniform laws on trade secrets set out in a Uniform Trade Secrets Act, which could be enacted by individual state legislatures. This has now been adopted (sometimes with amendments) in at least 35 states.

The latest set of proposals for reform come from Canada in the joint Report of the Alberta Institute of Law Research and Reform and a Federal Provincial Working Party (7.1.4 above). The reforms suggested there reflect to a far greater extent the recent changes in US law than those recommended by the English Law Commission. This reflects a desire on the part of the Canadians to harmonise laws in North America, but it also means a break from Commonwealth jurisprudence which has traditionally been reflected in Canadian laws. At the date of writing no province of Canada has enacted the reform proposals, but the matter is by no means dead, and changes are likely.

For present purposes one of the main differences between the various sets of proposals for law reform lies in the number of torts which each recommends. Both the Restatement and the English Law Commission recommend one; the Alberta Institute and the US Commissioners recommend two. Common to all was the suggestion of a tort of unauthorised use or disclosure of a trade secret; but additionally the US Commissioners and the Alberta Institute recommend a second tort of improper acquisition of a trade secret. This latter tort is very important as it characterises as a separate tort the act of industrial espionage. Under the Restatement and the Law Commission proposals, improper acquisition *per se* is not a separate tort. No liability attaches until information improperly acquired is used or disclosed, although an injunction can of course be obtained to restrain anticipated use or disclosure. However, the improper acquisition of trade secrets is such an important issue that it is considered in much greater detail below where we shall look at both the civil and the criminal aspects of the subject. For the purposes of this section, it can be concluded that although tort is not an important jurisdictional base for the action for breach of confidence at the moment it is likely to become so in the future, and in some instances it may even supersede the contractual and/or equitable obligations of the current law.

7.2.6   Confidential information as property
A fourth jurisdictional base for the action for breach of confidence is in property. So far this has not featured prominently in English civil cases, although it has been used quite often in US cases. However, there have been many attempts to classify confidential information as property for the purposes of the criminal law in order to found charges of theft and other property-based offences. These will be considered later in the section on the criminal law. In the view of the present author, property in its traditional sense is not an ideal jurisdiction for the action for breach of confidence. Contract, tort and equity are more appropriate in that they focus on entitlement rather than ownership and this more accurately reflects rights over information than does property.

7.3   THE SPECIAL PROBLEM OF CONFIDENTIAL INFORMATION ACQUIRED BY IMPROPER MEANS

Before discussing the criminal law we shall consider first one rather surprising gap in the protection of confidential information by the civil law. This occurs where confidential information is acquired by improper means by a person such as a spy or computer hacker who is under no pre-existing obligation of confidence. As we have seen, the emphasis of the English action is on breach of an obligation of confidence. In cases where there is an obligation to respect confidentiality there are few problems in founding liability provided all the other elements of the action are present. To use the familiar example, an employee or ex-employee who misappropriates his employer's confidential information, e.g., in order to use it himself or to disclose to a trade rival, will be acting in breach of confidence and can be restrained by injunction or be subject to the other remedies of damages, an account etc.; and any third party who acquires information from the employee knowing that it has been disclosed in breach of an obligation will be similarly liable. Thus the employee who gleans secrets from unauthorised use of a sector of his employer's computerised database can be made liable.

By way of contrast, where there is no obligation of confidence there can be no breach and no action. This causes problems, for example, where a spy gleans a secret from reading a confidential document, tapping a telephone or gaining unauthorised access to a computer network. The spy or hacker cannot, without a high degree of artificiality, be said to have voluntarily undertaken an obligation to respect the confidentiality of the information he has improperly acquired. Any obligation must be imposed involuntarily by the law but here the law seems remarkably reluctant to intervene. A similar problem arises in the law of trusts. A trustee who misappropriates trust property acts in breach of a fiduciary obligation owed to a beneficiary under the trust. Breach of fiduciary duty allows the beneficiary to trace the property through other forms and into other hands. But if a thief who is not a trustee or other fiduciary misappropriates trust property, he breaks no fiduciary obligation and there is no right to trace in equity.

It is surprising that there have been few civil cases on the improper acquisition, use or disclosure of confidential information by persons who have no pre-existing obligation of confidence. After all, espionage is not particularly rare. For the lawyer looking for a precedent there are few guiding principles, only some broad-ranging statements, but these are not necessarily helpful even though they are often cited in this context. For example, in *Millar* v *Taylor* (1769) 4 Burr 2303 it was said that an injunction would be granted to prevent:

Surreptitious or treacherous publishing of what the owner never made public at all, nor consented to the publication of. . . . Ideas are free. But while the author confines them to his study, they are like birds in a cage which none but he have a right to let fly.

Millar v *Taylor* was, however, a case on the common law right of property in the copyright in an unpublished work and although sometimes cited in the context of breach of confidence and information law it cannot be relied on as authority in this particular field. Another broad statement is to be found in *Ashburton* v *Pape* [1913] 2 Ch 469, where Swinfen Eady LJ said:

The principle on which the Court of Chancery has acted for many years has been to restrain the publication of confidential information improperly or surreptitiously obtained or of information imparted in confidence which ought not to be divulged.

Also, in *ITC Film Distributors Ltd* v *Video Exchange Ltd* [1982] Ch 431, Walton J referred to a general rule that where A has improperly obtained possession of a document belonging to B the court will, at the suit of B, order A to return the document to B and deliver up any copies of it that A has made, and will restrain A from making use of such copies or the information contained in them. But again, although the dictum seems to be relevant, both *Ashburton* v *Pape* and *ITC Film Distributors Ltd* v *Video Exchange Ltd* involved obtaining documents by a trick in order to use them in legal proceedings and arguably they are not directly applicable to the action for breach of confidence.

More recent cases have not clarified the position. In *Malone* v *Metropolitan Police Commissioner* [1979] Ch 344, the plaintiff's telephone was tapped by the Post Office at the request of the police. The plaintiff sought a declaration that he had a right of confidentiality in the information conveyed in the course of his telephone conversations and that recordings thereof were made in breach of confidence.

Megarry V-C, delivering the judgment of the court, drew a distinction between misuse of information (a) by a person to whom the information was intended to be communicated (where presumably the obligation of confidence would be governed by contract or by the normal equitable principles described above), and (b) by someone to whom the plaintiff had no intention of communicating anything. It is of course into this latter category that the spy and the telephone tapper fall. However, Megarry V-C did not distinguish those who deliberately set out to acquire information and those who come across it accidentally, which is arguably very important in deciding whether to attach liability, and in the course of his judgment many of the examples given were of those who accidentally overhear and maybe these examples even unfairly trivialise the problem.

He said that a person who utters confidential information must accept the risk of any unknown hearing that is inherent in the circumstances of communication. Those who exchange confidences on a bus or a train run the risk of a nearby passenger with acute hearing or a more distant passenger who is adept at lip-reading; those who speak over the garden wall run the risk of the unseen neighbour in a tool-shed nearby; office cleaners who discuss secrets in the office when they think everyone else has gone home run the risk of speaking within earshot of an unseen member of staff who is working late; those who give confidential information over an office intercommunication system run the risk of some third party being connected to the conversation.

His lordship then went on to say that he did not see why someone who has overheard some secret in such a way should be exposed to legal proceedings if he uses or divulges what he has heard. Furthermore, he said that no doubt an honourable man would give some warning when he realised that what he heard was not intended for his ears, but the court had to concern itself with the law and not with moral standards. Here he said he was dealing with only a moral precept and not with one that was legally enforceable.

Applying those general principles to telephone conversations, Sir Robert argued that a speaker takes such risks of being overheard as are inherent in the system. By way of illustration he said that users of the telephone system knew that they might be overheard when using extension lines, private switchboards or as a result of 'crossed lines'. A more modern example not given by his lordship would of course be tapping into an electronic mailing system. Megarry V-C said that in recent years so much publicity had been given to the deliberate tapping of telephone lines 'that it is difficult to envisage telephone users who are genuinely unaware of this possibility'. As a result he concluded that he did not see how it could be said that an obligation of confidence could be imposed on those who overhear a conversation 'whether by means of tapping or otherwise'. How, one might ask, would his lordship have viewed a case of computer hacking?

So far as tapping telephones was concerned, Megarry V-C expressly stated that he was only dealing with a case of authorised tapping by the police in connection with the detection of crime and his dicta on tapping must be limited accordingly,[20] but the judgment does remain disturbingly general on other

---

20. Cf. *Francome* v *Mirror Group Newspapers Ltd* [1984] 1 WLR 892, discussed earlier.

methods of improper acquisition of confidential information and on the failure of the law to impose an obligation of confidence even where the improper acquisition is deliberate and for monetary gain.

In 1972 the Younger Committee (Cmnd 5012) concluded on the basis of the earlier cases that in English law it is highly uncertain whether a person who uses or discloses confidential information which he knows to have been improperly obtained can be made liable in an action for breach of confidence. The Committee recommended that the law should be clarified and that an obligation of confidence should be imposed if the user or discloser of confidential information knew or ought to have known that it was obtained by illegal means. This was also the recommendation of the Law Commission in their preliminary Working Paper,[21] although there they referred to acquisition by unlawful means which they envisaged covering information obtained by means prohibited by the criminal law; taking without authority any object from which the information was obtained; and possibly also information obtained by means of a trespass to land. The Law Commission changed their minds on this after consultation, and in their Final Report[22] they said that improper acquisition should be only one of those circumstances which gave rise to an obligation of confidence and that obligation would be broken only by unauthorised use or disclosure; and they also defined improper means much more narrowly than before. It is important to note in the present context that neither the Younger Committee nor the Law Commission in their final Report suggested that the improper acquisition of confidential information in itself should be a tort, as is provided by the US Uniform Trade Secrets Act, recommended in Canada and discussed in 7.2.5. It is recognised that in most circumstances it is the use or disclosure of the information which causes the greatest harm, and this may be the rationale of the conclusions of the Law Commission, but in the view of the present author the earlier in the chain of activity the liability attaches the better.

The Law Commission proposals have, of course, never been enacted and hence the problem remains in English law of trying to control the improper acquisition, use or disclosure of confidential information obtained in circumstances where there is no obligation of confidence remains. An obvious example of the difficulty is where a defendant uses a decompiler to create a partial or complete pseudo-source code for a software package distributed in object code only. The information contained in the pseudo-source code may well have been kept secret by the producer and it has clear commercial value. It is, however, extremely doubtful whether the method used to discover that information would be 'improper'. For this reason many software licences attempt to place an obligation on the buyer of the software not to decompile it, and a further obligation not to use the code other than as part of the marketed package.

One decision which could solve the dilemma, if it were followed here, is the Australian case of *Franklin* v *Giddins* [1978] Qd 72. The facts were that the defendant stole budwood cuttings from the plaintiff's genetically unique

---

21. Working Paper No. 58.
22. Law Commission, *Breach of Confidence* (see note 16), para. 6.4 and App. A, cl. 5.

nectarine trees. An action was brought for the improper acquisition by the defendant of the confidential information embodied in the genetic coding in the wood. Dunn J in the Supreme Court of Queensland accepted that:

> The parent tree may be likened to a safe within which there are locked up a number of copies of a formula for making a nectarine tree with special characteristics . . . when a twig of budwood is taken from the tree, it is as through a copy of the formula is taken out of the safe.

Having thus classified it as a misappropriation of confidential information he went on to hold that the defendant had breached an obligation of confidence owed to the owner of the tree. He said, 'I find myself quite unable to accept that a thief who steals a trade secret, with the intention of using it in commercial competition with its owner, to the detriment of the latter, and so uses it, is less conscionable than a traitorous servant'.

Thus unconscionability was brought into play to found an action, but this is no less vague a term than many others which have been used as bases of the action for breach of confidence in equity in other circumstances. As Professor Gareth Jones has argued,[23] equity should not be past the age of child-bearing, and the action for breach of confidence should be capable of extension to protect confidential information obtained by improper means regardless of whether there is a pre-existing relationship of confidence. This is particularly important now that information is assuming a greater role in technologically advanced communities. The defects of the present civil law leave a huge gap in the protection of confidential information in English law. This problem does not arise in the US and would not arise in Canada if the reform proposals were enacted. In the next section we shall see that English criminal law also fails to punish the misappropriation of confidential information. There is an obvious need for reform.

7.4 THE CRIMINAL LAW

The analysis in this part of the chapter inevitably cuts across the divisions drawn in preceding sections, for information can be misappropriated not only by persons who have never been bound by an obligation of secrecy, such as by strangers engaged in industrial espionage, but also by those already under an obligation of confidence, such as employees who disclose the trade secrets of their employers to trade rivals. In the latter example, the prospect of making employees and ex-employees liable for misappropriating trade secrets shows perhaps even more poignantly than ever the need to distinguish carefully between an employee's general knowledge and skill, which he is of course entitled to use for the benefit of himself and others, and his employer's trade secrets which he cannot use or disclose, for in some legal systems the distinction could represent the line between criminal and legitimate activity.

---

23. (1970) 86 LQR 463, at pp. 482–3.

Once again this account will concentrate mainly on the misappropriation of trade secrets. There are very different policy issues underlying the question of criminalising the acquisition of other categories of confidential information, and for reasons of space as well as emphasis no mention is made of the Official Secrets Acts and the problems they bring in their wake.

7.4.1 English law

In English law, if there is intentional interference with a tangible object such as damage to or permanent deprivation of a computer disk or a piece of paper, or unauthorised entry on to land with intent to do specified acts in relation to tangibles or people, then various criminal offences may be committed. But if only information is 'taken' or interfered with by reading, memorising or photographing the tangible object on which the confidential information is stored, then no crime may be committed unless of course it is a case of computer hacking which is now regulated by the Computer Misuse Act 1990.[24]

In English law, 'theft' of a trade secret is not a criminal offence. The main case is *Oxford* v *Moss* (1978) 68 Cr App R 183, where an undergraduate improperly obtained the proof of an examination paper before the examination was held. He read the paper and then returned it, retaining the information for his own use. He was charged with theft but was acquitted. Two reasons were given: first, for the purposes of the Theft Act 1968 information is not property, and only property can be stolen; and secondly, the university had not been permanently deprived of the tangible asset which had been taken, namely the piece of paper, and borrowing does not amount to theft. *Oxford* v *Moss* was followed in *R* v *Absolom* (1983) *The Times*, 14 September 1983, where a geologist was acquitted of a charge of theft after he had obtained and tried to sell to a rival company details of Esso Petroleum's oil exploration off the Irish coast, information which was valued in evidence as worth between £50,000 and £100,000.

The emphasis in English law is clearly on the interference with a tangible asset, and because in neither *Oxford* v *Moss* nor *R* v *Absolom* was the owner of the information permanently deprived of such an asset there could be no successful prosecution for theft. However, even if a tangible asset such as a piece of paper or a computer disk is taken, the value of the tangible asset may in no way reflect the value of the information either in terms of damage to a business, if the secret is a trade secret, or of unwanted publicity if the information is of a personal nature; and if we look at the attitude of society towards crime, a charge of theft of a piece of paper worth pence is regarded as of far less importance than a charge of theft of information worth maybe thousands of pounds. Furthermore, when confidential information is misappropriated its owner loses the advantage of the exclusive right to control its use, yet this is not an asset protected by the English law of theft. All this is very strange.

Other criminal charges may of course be relevant. For example, in *Cox* v *Riley* (1986) 83 Cr App R 54 the defendant was successfully prosecuted for

---

24. See further, 8.6.

criminal damage after he had erased computer programs from a plastic circuit card used to operate a computerised saw. The court held that even though the Criminal Damage Act 1971 required damage to tangible property, the circuit card was useless without the programs and, as it would cost time and money to restore the programs, the property in the card had been damaged. But again, the emphasis of the law is on the tangible asset rather than on the effect of the defendant's actions on the information itself.

Under the Computer Misuse Act 1990, s. 3, a person is guilty of an offence if he does any act which causes an unauthorised modification of programs or data held on a computer, provided he has the requisite intent and knowledge. This offence was drafted to overcome a number of problems in the application of the Criminal Damage Act 1971 to computers and computerised information. But the offence is not addressed towards any particular classification of programs or data, i.e., it covers any programs and data and not just confidential matters. It does not apply when data storage media other than computers, such as filing cabinets, are accessed without authorisation, nor does it apply to damage to programs or data which are, e.g., on disks lying on a shelf in an office. Presumably s. 3 would now apply to the facts of *Cox* v *Riley*, for that involved a computerised saw, but again, as the examples show, the wrong to which s. 3 is directed is a wrong against a particular storage medium which contains information, namely a computer, rather than being a wrong directed specifically and exclusively towards information as a commodity in its own right.

7.4.2   Scots law
A similar approach has been taken in Scotland. In *Grant* v *Procurator Fiscal* [1988] RPC 41 the High Court of Justiciary said that there was no crime in Scots law of dishonest exploitation of the confidential information of another. Also, the court refused to exercise the inherent powers of the Scottish courts to create a new crime. In that case the defendant had made copies of computer printouts belonging to his employer and then offered to sell them to a rival concern. The printouts contained confidential information about the employer's customers. In the course of his judgment the Lord Justice-Clerk said that while the defendant may have breached an express or implied obligation of confidence owed to his employer under the civil law it would be quite another thing to categorise such behaviour as criminal. If it was to be criminalised it was a matter for Parliament and not for the courts.

7.4.3   Reforms
Surprisingly, there have been few calls for the reform of English law. In 1972 the Younger Committee[25] specifically rejected the suggestion that there should be a new offence of theft of information, and when the Law Commission[26] were asked to consider the law relating to breach of confidence their terms of reference limited them to the civil law alone. They made no recommendations for reform of the criminal law. By way of contrast the New Zealand Committee

---

25. Cmnd 5012 at p. 149.
26. *Breach of Confidence* (see note 16), para. 4.10.

for Torts and General Law Reform said that the chief weakness of the New Zealand law relating to trade secrets was the lack of specialised criminal provisions. However, no specialised offence has been enacted in New Zealand or indeed in any other Commonwealth country, whereas in the United States many states have criminal statutes expressly protecting trade secrets; and in Europe there are criminal offences in a number of Codes, for example art. 17 of the German Unfair Competition Law of 1909.[27] This states that an employee who wrongfully communicates an industrial or commercial secret is liable to be imprisoned for up to three years and to pay a fine; and similar provisions are to be found in art. 418 of the French Penal Code and art. 162 of the Swiss Penal Code. Interestingly, the civil laws of Japan dealing with the misappropriation of trade secrets have recently been reformed but there have been no changes to the criminal laws. Prosecutions have, however, been obtained under general criminal laws such as larceny and embezzelment.

7.4.4   Canadian cases

There have been some interesting developments in Canada in recent years. In *R* v *Offley* (1986) 28 CCC (3d) 1, the Alberta Court of Appeal followed the English decision of *Oxford* v *Moss* (1978) 68 Cr App R 183 and held that confidential information could not be stolen. It specifically rejected the reasoning of the Ontario Court of Appeal in *R* v *Stewart* (1983) 42 OR (2d) 225. There the defendant had been asked by the representative of a union to obtain the details of the employees of a hotel. This information was contained in the employees' personal files and computer records held by the hotel company. They were regarded as being strictly confidential and were protected by the hotel's security arrangements. The defendant had contacted an employee of the hotel and asked him to copy the confidential information without removing or affecting the records themselves. The defendant was charged with three offences, namely counselling an employee of the hotel to commit fraud, theft and mischief to the private property of the hotel. The accused was acquitted on all three counts and the Crown appealed against the acquittals on the charges of counselling theft and counselling fraud. By a majority of two to one the Ontario Court of Appeal allowed the appeal and a conviction was entered for counselling theft.

Interestingly, the Ontario Court of Appeal in *Stewart*, in contrast to the Alberta Court of Appeal in *Offley*, held that confidential information was property for the purposes of the offences of theft and fraud in Canadian criminal law. For example, Houlden JA said that while clearly not all information was property he could see no reason why confidential information that had been gathered through the expenditure of time, effort and money by a commercial enterprise for the purposes of its business should not be regarded as property and hence entitled to the protection of the criminal law. In *Offley* and *Stewart* we therefore have two contrasting decisions of two Courts of Appeal of Canadian provinces, the outstanding question being whether confidential information is property for the purposes of the criminal laws of

---

27. See Coleman, *The Legal Protection of Trade Secrets* (see note 8), ch. 7.

Canada with its obvious implications also for the jurisdictional foundation of the civil obligation to respect confidentiality. The decision of the Supreme Court of Canada in *Stewart* (1988) 50 DLR (4th) 1 was therefore anxiously awaited.

On appeal, the Supreme Court of Canada rejected the notion that confidential information could be property. First it said that although 'anything' (using that term in its technical sense in the Canadian Criminal Code) whether tangible or intangible could be the subject-matter of a charge of theft, it must be of such a nature that it can be the subject of a proprietary right; and secondly, the property must be capable of being taken or converted in a manner that results in deprivation of the victim. Taking each of these elements in turn Lamer J, giving the judgment of the court, said that it had not been settled that property was the basis of the civil action for breach of confidence, but even if it had been it would not automatically follow that it would be so classified for the purposes of the criminal law. If it was property under the criminal law a large number of provisions of the Criminal Code would potentially apply to acts in relation to confidential information and a whole host of practical problems would ensue. He recognised that information of commercial value was in need of some protection under the criminal law, but this was a matter for Parliament and not for the courts. For policy reasons the court held that confidential information was not property for the purposes of the Canadian Criminal Code.

Secondly, the Supreme Court held that an intangible could not be 'taken' as such; nor could it be converted, as conversion required deprivation of its use and possession and if merely information was misappropriated (as opposed to the tangible on which the information was stored) then the alleged owner was not deprived of the information: henceforth, the information was merely shared. The only 'thing' that the victim would be deprived of was the confidentiality of the information and in the view of the court confidentiality could not be the subject of theft because it did not fall within the meaning of 'anything' as previously defined. Confidentiality could not be property, as it could not be owned only enjoyed. Furthermore, the Court rejected the argument of Cory JA in the Ontario Court of Appeal that there was a right of property in confidential information which was the subject of copyright, as were the employer's confidential lists in this case. Lamer J explained that copying a list constitutes an infringement of copyright under the Copyright Act, but the rights provided in that Act could never be taken or converted as required by the theft provisions as their owner would never suffer deprivation. Once again, there would only be sharing and this was not enough.

The result of the Canadian Supreme Court decision in *Stewart* is that the question of criminalising the misappropriation of confidential information was referred back to the Canadian legislature. Those countries which do not already criminalise this type of conduct will inevitably have to consider doing so sooner or later, for with the growth in the use of computers and the development of information as a commodity in its own right the pressures will grow to afford information the same degree of protection as other valuable assets. In Canada there is already a set of proposals for legislative reform of this area of confidentiality. In 1986 the Alberta Institute of Law Research and Reform and the Federal Provincial Working Party recommended not only changes to the civil law but also the creation of new criminal offences relating to the misappropriation of trade secrets. These new offences have the advantage of being custom-built and hence avoid the difficulty of fitting intangible assets into an inappropriate conceptual framework which was developed to accommodate tangibles. Thus the report rejects the approach of the Ontario Court of Appeal in *Stewart* and argues that property should not form the basis for liability. We shall look at these proposals, as it is possible that they will be enacted in Canada in the next few years, albeit with amendments, and they also form a good starting-point for reform in other common law jurisdictions.

7.4.5 Proposals for the reform of Canadian criminal law
It was decided that in order to achieve uniformity the same information should be protected under both the civil and the criminal law. Thus the definition of a trade secret is set out in the earlier section of this chapter describing various categories of confidential information. Secondly, it is recommended that the new criminal offences should proscribe the non-consensual acquisition, use or disclosure of a trade secret, that term being used in the sense both of what might otherwise be called 'theft' of a secret and also of acts where the consent was fraudulently obtained, e.g., where the victim was duped. Thus there are two offences in the draft Bill covering the two aspects of non-consensual conduct. First a new s. 301.3(1) of the Criminal Code would provide that:

> Everyone who fraudulently and without colour of right acquires, discloses or uses the trade secret of another person, without the consent of that other person, with intent to deprive that other person (a) of control of the trade secret or (b) of an economic advantage associated with the trade secret is guilty of an indictable offence and is liable to imprisonment for 10 years, or of an offence punishable on summary conviction.

Secondly a new draft s. 338.1(1) would provide that:

> Everyone who, by deceit, falsehood or other fraudulent means, whether or not it is a false pretence within the meaning of this Act, induces any person to disclose, or to permit another person to disclose or use, a trade secret, is guilt of an indictable offence and is liable to imprisonment for 10 years, or of an offence punishable on summary conviction.

It was hoped that, by clearly defining the mental element which the accused must be shown to have, only the most reprehensible of conduct would be caught by the new provisions. As an additional safeguard, it is proposed to provide that no one commits an offence under s. 301.3 in respect of an acquisition, disclosure or use of a trade secret if:

> (a) the trade secret was acquired by independent development or by reason only of reverse engineering; or

(b)   the information was acquired in the course of that person's work, and the information is of such a nature that the acquisition amounts to no more than an enhancement of that person's personal knowledge, skill or expertise.

The proposed amendments to the Criminal Code contain two further offences aimed at, for example, the industrial spy who goes on what may be described as a 'shopping expedition' in order to acquire information, the precise character of which he does not know but which he thinks he may be able to sell or otherwise use. Subsequent reports suggest that these offences are not popular among those responsible for legislation and may be dropped from any draft Bills which come forward.

The Canadian proposals illustrate the moves in many countries to criminal-ise the misappropriation of trade secrets. So far English law has not followed this lead. But inevitably pressures will mount to reform the law in this area, and the idea of adopting custom-built offences rather than extending existing property-based offences in order to found liability is a sound one, and indeed one suggested by individual judges in England, Scotland and Canada. But there are strong reasons favouring the free flow of information and requiring the disclosure even of confidential information, and any shift in the balance needs to be carefully considered, hence the delays in introducing legislation in Canada and maybe the silence in the United Kingdom.

CHAPTER EIGHT

Computer crime

Ian Lloyd

8.1 INTRODUCTION

The topic of computer crime generates much publicity in terms both of its financial and legal impact. To an extent, however, the mass of published material is more a cause of confusion than of enlightenment. The most difficult task facing any analyst is to separate myth from reality, whilst the lawyer's task is to decide whether and to what extent particular forms of conduct might be regarded as criminal under existing legal formulations. Dependent upon the result of this latter exercise, further questions may arise whether a case can be made out for the introduction of computer-specific legislation and, if so, about the form that this should take.

In view of the wide range of activities which may come within the ambit of the topic an essential prerequisite is the adoption of a scheme of categorisation. A leading American commentator, Donn Parker, identified four forms of computer abuse distinguished in each case by the role played by the computer. Thus, the computer might:[1]

(a) serve as the victim of crime;
(b) constitute the environment within which a crime is committed;
(c) provide the means by which a crime is committed; or
(d) symbolically be used to intimidate, deceive or defraud victims.

In a general sense the definition is worthy of consideration but its practical utility is limited in that many of the examples of conduct cited could equally

---

1. *Crime by Computer* (New York: Scribner, 1976).

well be located within two or more of the categories. An example can be taken from what was perhaps the most notorious instance of computer-related fraud, that involving the Equity Fund Insurance Company. Over a number of years, the directors and senior managers of the company perpetrated a sustained and substantial fraud on the company. As part of their efforts to prevent the detection of their activity, arrangements were made for the creation of fictitious insurance policies. Much of the data relating to these policies was maintained on computer and it can be argued that the computer served to fill Parker's roles of environment, means and symbolism. By processing and storing the data involved, the computer provided the necessary environment. Next, the means criteria would be satisfied by the fact that but for the computer's processing capabilities the scheme could not have been perpetrated on such a scale (the losses caused were estimated at $2 billion and it was eventually discovered that of the company's claimed 97,000 policies no fewer than 64,000 were fictitious) or for such a period of time (nine years elapsed between the start of the fraud and its exposure). Finally, the involvement of the computer appeared to inhibit the company's auditors from fully investigating its financial position.

Within recent years the question of the response of the criminal law to instances of computer misuse has come under active consideration in the United Kingdom. Initial investigations were conducted by the Scottish Law Commission which published a consultative memorandum in 1986[2] and a report in 1987.[3] A similar exercise was subsequently carried out by the Law Commission with a working paper appearing in 1988[4] and its final report in 1989.[5] Legislative action followed quickly with a Computer Misuse Bill based on the Law Commission's recommendations being introduced under the private members' procedure, receiving the Royal Assent in June 1990 and entering into force on 1 August 1990.

In terms of time, the United Kingdom can be seen to have lagged behind many other major States in introducing computer-specific legislation. The United States was among the first countries to introduce such legislation with provisions operating on both a State and federal level. In Europe, Austria, France, Denmark, Finland, Italy, Luxembourg, the Netherlands, Norway, Portugal, Spain, Sweden and West Germany enacted computer crime statutes during the 1980s. Parallel to these national developments came an increasing recognition, comparable to that identified in the field of data protection, that the operation of many computer systems transcended national boundaries with the merger of computer and communications technologies permitting a user located in one State to access computer systems almost anywhere in the world. These international aspects have prompted the involvement of agencies such as the Organisation for Economic Cooperation and Development, the Council of Europe and the European Community in an ongoing debate about the need for and form of legislative intervention.

---

2. Consultative Memorandum No. 68, Computer Crime.
3. Scot. Law Com. No. 106, Cm 174.
4. Working Paper No. 110.
5. Law Com. No. 186, Cm 819.

Almost inevitably, each agency or legislature involved in the topic has set out its own agenda for action. Although the particular categorisations adopted may vary, three common threads can be identified in their work. These encompass the topics of:

(a) computer fraud,
(b) damage to data or programs,
(c) 'theft' of information.

This chapter will consider each of these topics in more detail, linking them to a discussion of the provisions of the Computer Misuse Act 1990 and to relevant statutory and case law developments within other jurisdictions. It should also be stated that the chapter is concerned solely with the question whether particular forms of conduct are, or should be, met with criminal sanctions. The fact that conduct may not be regarded as criminal does not necessarily imply that the perpetrator will not be subject to some form of penalty. Many instances of computer misuse are reportedly committed by employees. In such an event disciplinary sanctions may be applied by the employer. In other situations where conduct results in some form of loss to a computer owner a civil law action seeking recompense may be available against the perpetrator.

8.2 COMPUTER FRAUD

Consideration of the topic of computer fraud raises three major questions: What is it? How extensive is it? Is it illegal? In common with most aspects of the topic, definitional problems abound. In the United Kingdom the Audit Commission has conducted four triennial surveys of computer-related fraud based on a definition referring to: 'any fraudulent behaviour connected with computerisation by which someone intends to gain financial advantage'. Such a definition is clearly capable of encompassing a vast range of activities some of which may have only the most tenuous connection with a computer. The Council of Europe, in its report on computer-related crime[6] advocates the establishment of an offence consisting of:[7]

> The input, alteration, erasure or suppression of computer data or computer programmes [sic], or other interference with the course of data processing, that influences the result of data processing thereby causing economic loss or possessory loss of property of another person, or with the intent of procuring an unlawful economic gain for himself or for another person.

Again, this definition is broad in scope. It would appear for example that the proposed offence would be committed by a person who wrongfully uses another party's cash dispensing card. The advantage of the Council of Europe

---

6. Recommendation No. R (89) 9 adopted by the Council of Ministers on 13 September 1989.
7. Ibid., p. 28.

approach is, however, that it directs attention to the crucial aspect of the topic, the manipulation of data with a view to obtaining some form of financial advantage at the expense of another party. This may take one of two forms. The first is the attempt to secure direct pecuniary benefit, e.g., to cause £500,000 to be transferred to the perpetrator's bank account. The alternative form of advantage occurs when the perpetrator is relieved of payments that he or she would otherwise be obliged to make. An example might see the perpetrator making unauthorised use of a third party's password in order to secure free use of a database with any bills being sent to the third party.

The next issue to be considered is the scale of the fraud problem. Here it is scarcely an exaggeration to suggest that there are as many estimates as there are commentators on the topic. Surveys resulting in findings of significant levels of fraud have been made by the Stanford Research Institute in the United States and by a number of computer security consultants in the United Kingdom. The latter cannot be regarded as entirely impartial in the field and the methodology of the Stanford organisation has been subjected to trenchant criticism.[8] Perhaps the most official estimates in the United Kingdom are those which have been made by the Audit Commission. Four surveys have been conducted by this organisation, in 1981, 1984, 1987 and 1990. The most recent survey covered the period 1987–90 and identified 73 cases of computer fraud with a total cost of £1.1 million.

If the Audit Commission's figures were to reflect the total amount of computer fraud the topic would not be worthy of further discussion. To put the figure into perspective, it has recently been estimated that annual losses from bicycle thefts amount to some £2.4 million in the Glasgow area alone. Extrapolated on a national basis, this would suggest losses in the region of £100 million and yet there appears to be little pressure for a bicycle-specific statute. The Audit Commission is totally dependent upon users voluntarily reporting instances of fraud, and it may be significant to note that when respondents were asked in the 1984-7 survey to give their estimation of the total losses resulting from computer fraud those respondents who had themselves been the victim of computer fraud proffered a considerably lower estimate (£200 million) than those who had not been victims (£330 million). Few of the incidents referred to in their reports concern financial institutions and those that do often refer to relatively unsophisticated and trivial actions. The average fraud reported to the Audit Commission involved a loss of some £21,000.[9]

Although there is no conclusive evidence that large-scale computer fraud exists, the dependence of the financial sector upon the computer is such that the consequences of any successful crime could be dramatic. Literally billions of pounds are transferred every day between banks making use of computerised payment and electronic funds transfer systems. Not only do the transactions represent vast amounts of money, their speed is also significant. It has, for

8. J. K. Taber, 'On Computer Crime (Senate Bill s. 240)' (1979) 1 Computer/Law Journal 517 and M. Wasik, 'Surveying Computer Crime' (1985) 1 CL&P 110 at p. 113.
9. For a discussion of the various estimates relating to the scale of computer fraud, see Wasik, *Crime by Computer* (Oxford: Clarendon Press, 1991) at pp. 34–68.

example, been estimated that all of the United Kingdom's foreign currency reserves could be transferred abroad within 15 minutes. Under international protocols agreed between the participating banks such transfers are regarded as irrevocable. To this extent, therefore, an electronic signal transferring funds from one account to another represents more than just evidence of the payee's entitlement to the specified assets. The ex head of Scotland Yard's Computer Crime Unit has commented:[10]

> The prevention of crime here is important. No, it's not important, it's vital. These days money is not the pound in your pocket; it's the $234 billion worth of transactions which go out from the City of London and back every day. All that money really amounts to is electronic digits travelling down wires. That's real money.

To use the terminology of the Data Protection Act 1984, this is an area where the prevention of crime is more important than its detection.

The third question posed relating to incidents of computer fraud was whether such conduct can be regarded as criminal. A perception does appear to exist that substantial problems face any prosecution for computer fraud. During the passage of the Computer Misuse Bill, reference was made in Parliament to the results of a Department of Trade and Industry study indicating that of 270 instances of computer misuse identified, only six prosecutions were brought and three convictions for fraud secured. Such statistics sit uneasily with the findings of the Audit Commission whose latest survey found that 37 out of 63 instances of computer fraud had led to a prosecution. In only 6 per cent of cases was no action taken against an identified perpetrator.

The high success rate reported in the Audit Commission's survey offers an optimistic prognosis for the prosecution of instances of computer fraud. Two specific difficulties may, however, be identified; the first concerning the moment in time at which an offence may be considered to have been committed and the second the question whether a machine may be the victim of deception. To an extent, these difficulties may have been resolved with the passage of the Computer Misuse Act 1990, but an account of the problems encountered prior to its passage remains relevant.

In terms of the time at which an offence is committed, the case of *R* v *Thompson* [1984] 1 WLR 962 furnishes a helpful illustration. Thompson, a computer programmer, was employed by a bank in Kuwait. Whilst so employed, he devised a plan to defraud the bank. Details of customers' accounts were maintained on computer. A number of these accounts were dormant, i.e., no transactions had taken place over a significant period of time. Thompson devised a program which instructed the computer to transfer sums from these accounts to accounts which he had opened with the bank. In an effort to minimise the risks of detection, the transfers were not to be made until Thompson had left the bank's employ and was on a plane returning to England.

---

10. *Guardian*, 8 January 1987.

On his return to England, Thompson opened a number of accounts with English banks and wrote to the manager of the Kuwaiti bank instructing him to arrange for the transfer of the balances from his Kuwaiti accounts. This was done but subsequently his conduct was discovered and Thompson was detained by the police. Charges of obtaining property by deception were brought against him and a conviction secured. An appeal was lodged on the question of jurisdiction. Whilst not denying any of the facts recited above, Thompson argued that any offence had been committed in Kuwait and, therefore, that the English courts had no jurisdiction in the matter.

This plea did not commend itself to the Court of Appeal which held that the offence was committed at the moment when the Kuwaiti manager read and acted upon Thompson's letter. At this stage Thompson was subject to the jurisdiction of the English courts. Delivering the judgment of the court, May LJ stated:[11]

> Discard for the moment the modern sophistication of computers and programmes [sic] and consider the old days when bank books were kept in manuscript in large ledgers. In effect all that was done by the appellant through the modern computer in the present case was to take a pen and debit each of the five accounts in the ledger with the relevant sums and then credit each of his own five savings accounts in the ledger with corresponding amounts. On the face of it his savings accounts would then have appeared to have in them substantially more than in truth they did have as the result of his forgeries; but we do not think that by those forgeries any bank clerk in the days before computers would in law have thus brought into being a chose in action capable either of being stolen or of being obtained by deception.

In the particular case the effect of this approach was to confer jurisdiction upon the English courts and to sustain the conviction. Recalling, however, the speed with which large sums of money may be transmitted, the effect of the decision may be considered to deprive those financial institutions which rely on computers in the course of their operations of a significant element of the criminal law's protection.

The second problem which might arise in relation to a scheme of computer fraud occurs where the perpetrator's only communication is with a computer. In the case typified by the example of the theft of a card for use in a cash dispensing machine and its subsequent use to obtain money, it would appear that a prosecution for theft might be brought. More significant problems occur in the situation where the effect of the conduct is not to obtain direct pecuniary advantage but rather to obtain services whilst avoiding the charges normally levied for their provision. An example is to be found in the facts of the case of *R* v *Gold* [1988] AC 1063. Gold, together with his co-accused Schifreen, was a computer hacker who, in pursuance of what they regarded as a hobby, sought to obtain unauthorised access to computer systems. By means of what the law report refers to as a 'dishonest trick' they obtained a password issued by British

---

11. [1984] 1 WLR 962 at pp. 967–8.

Telecom to one of its engineers allowing use of its 'Prestel' system. This system offers subscribers access to a variety of database services. Upon agreeing to pay rental charges plus further charges dependent upon the nature and extent of usage, users would be allocated a password. Use of the engineer's password enabled Gold to obtain access to the 'Prestel' services without incurring any charges.

After some time British Telecom became suspicious about Gold's activities and made arrangements for details to be recorded of the telephone numbers called from Gold's own telephone. Scrutiny of these records, coupled with information retained on the 'Prestel' computer, revealed the nature and extent of Gold's predatory activities. The question then arose what, if any, offence had been committed. In the event that Gold had been resident in Scotland there would have been little dispute concerning the competence of a charge of obtaining services by means of a false pretence. In determining whether this offence has been committed attention is paid to the conduct of the perpetrator. A different approach prevails under English Law. The comparable offence would be that of obtaining property or services 'by deception'. Although the point has not been definitively settled, the assumption has been that only a human being can be the victim of deception.[12] Such a view finds support in the eighth report of the Criminal Law Revision Committee which recommended a shift from offences involving the concept of false pretence on the basis that the word 'deception':

> has the advantage of directing attention to the effect that the offender deliberately produced on the mind of the person deceived, whereas 'false pretence' makes one think of what exactly the offender did in order to deceive.

Although the proposition that a machine may not be deceived rests on *obiter* statements rather than binding precedent, the prosecution in *R* v *Gold* eschewed the opportunity to obtain a definitive ruling on this point, turning instead to the provisions of the Forgery and Counterfeiting Act 1981. This provides in s. 1 that:

> A person is guilty of forgery if he makes a false instrument, with the intention that he or another shall use it to induce somebody to accept it as genuine, and by reason of so accepting it to do or not to do some act to his own or any other person's prejudice.

By s. 10, attempts to induce a machine to accept the instrument are equated with attempts so to induce a person.

The critical issue before the courts was whether any false instrument had been made. One reason why the 1981 Act had proved attractive to the prosecution was that it had been produced following a report by the Law

---

12. See *Davies* v *Flackett* [1973] RTR 8; *Director of Public Prosecutions* v *Ray* [1974] AC 370; *R* v *Laverty* [1970] 3 All ER 432; *R* v *Royle* [1971] 1 WLR 1764 and *R* v *Kovacs* [1974] 1 WLR 370.

Commission[13] which had sought to update the law, *inter alia*, to take account of technical developments. To this extent the Act's definition of 'instrument' sought to move away from the traditional concentration on paper-based documents, providing[14] that the word's definition should include:

> any disc, tape, soundtrack or other device on or in which information is recorded or stored by mechanical, electronic or other means.

Where in the present case was the instrument? Consideration of this issue requires an examination of the nature of the Prestel system's operations. By dialling the Prestel telephone number a user would initiate communications with the system. Contact would be made initially with an area of the computer called the 'user segment'. The purpose of the user segment was to receive data from the user, channel it to an appropriate sector of the computer for processing and transmit the reply to the user. A user seeking access to the system would cause to be transmitted details of his allocated password. This data would be received by the user segment and held there momentarily whilst the information was passed on to that portion of the computer holding data relating to subscribers. If the password was valid, the instruction to allow access would be given. At this stage the information would be deleted from the user segment's memory. The entire log-in procedure would occupy a very short period of time, normally less than 1 second.

An initial candidate for the role of false instrument might appear to be the password details as transmitted by the user in the form of electronic impulses. This possibility was not pursued by the prosecution which conceded that any instrument had to be *eiusdem generis* with the devices listed in s. 8. These all required that the instrument be a physical object. Obviously signals being transmitted along a telephone line have no physical existence.

In the event, the prosecution based their claim on the contention that the 'user segment' in its state as repository of the password details constituted the false instrument. This submission was clearly accepted by the trial jury which convicted both accused. These convictions were reversed by the Court of Appeal on the basis that the user segment was not capable of constituting a false instrument, a view which was shared by the House of Lords. A variety of reasons were advanced by the various appellate judges for this conclusion. Two are of particular significance. First it was held by Lord Lane CJ that:[15]

> ... neither [the Law Commission report nor the Forgery and Counterfeiting Act 1981], so it seems to us, seeks to deal with information that is held for a moment whilst automatic checking takes place and is then expunged. That process is not one to which the words 'recorded or stored' can properly be applied, suggesting as they do a degree of continuance.

---

13. Law Commission, *Criminal Law Report on Forgery and Counterfeit Currency* (Law Com. No. 55) 1973.
14. Section 8(1).
15. [1987] QB 1116 at p. 1124.

A further reason related to the nature of the Prestel system's operations. The user segment both received the data and transmitted them onwards to the computer's subscriber database. To this extent the user segment was both victim and deceiver, a somewhat schizophrenic state of affairs.

Finally, both tribunals were critical of the attempt to invoke the 1981 Act. The Lord Chief Justice concluded:[16]

We have accordingly come to the conclusion that the language of the Act was not intended to apply to the situation which was shown to exist in this case. . . . It is a conclusion which we reach without regret. The Procrustean attempt to force these facts into the language of an Act not designed to fit them produced grave difficulties for both judge and jury which we would not wish to see repeated.

The appellants' conduct amounted in essence . . . to dishonestly obtaining access to the relevant Prestel databank by a trick. That is not a criminal offence. If it is thought desirable to do so that is a matter for the legislature rather than the courts. We express no view on the matter.

In large part, the enactment of the Computer Misuse Act 1990 can be seen as a response to the failure of the prosecution in *R* v *Gold*, and it must be likely that repetition of the conduct at issue could result in a successful prosecution under this statute. The case remains relevant, however, as an illustration of the definitional problems which may be encountered in seeking to apply even legislation which has been specifically designed to regulate developing technology.

8.3 DAMAGE TO DATA OR PROGRAMS

It is stated frequently that developments in information technology are serving to bring about a second industrial revolution. Just as iron and coal served as the raw materials and the driving force of the first industrial revolution, so information or data and computers serve the same roles today. In the same fashion that a steam engine is fit only for display in a museum if no coal is available to power it, so a computer is useless without data.

The general term 'data' can be used in two contexts. First it will include the sequence of instructions which constitute a computer program. Second, it includes information which is more recognisable to the lay person, those details – whether concerning individuals, companies, commodities or anything else – which will be stored or processed in a computer.

In both contexts the data may constitute a valuable asset for its holder. Again, the value may arise in a number of ways. A commercially produced computer program may sell for several hundred or even thousand pounds. Where a program has been produced by or to the order of a user the costs may be even greater. In 1988 it was estimated that the United Kingdom market for software stood at £1.7 billion. The acquisition of data to be processed or stored

16. Ibid., loc. cit.

will also be an expensive task and, in many cases, the data will also possess a monetary value. Destruction of software or data or the impairment of the functioning of a computer system may, therefore, result in a user incurring costs in replacing the data and also losses in production or the efficient functioning of their business pending recovery.

One of the features of information which makes it a unique commodity is that it cannot be destroyed or used up. What can be affected is its representation on some form of storage device such as a floppy disk. A person who secures access to a computer system may be able to cause the deletion of large amounts of data from the computer's memory. Such conduct may well result in the computer owner sustaining substantial financial damage. Another form of conduct which receives considerable publicity today involves the introduction to a computer system of some form of 'virus'. A variety of forms of virus exist capable of causing a variety of consequences for the computer owner. Some species which are relatively benign may cause a message to appear on the computer monitor. The 'stoned' virus for example, causes the message 'I am stoned' to appear when an infected computer is first switched on. The effects of other viruses may be largely cosmetic. The 'ping-pong' virus, for example, causes the display of a ball which travels continually across the screen. Many viruses, however, are capable of much more damaging consequences including the deletion of large portions of the data held on the computer. Referring to the possible damage which might be caused by a virus, one computer consultant has commented: 'It's quite simple. If I wanted my competitor to go bankrupt I would just anonymously send someone in that company an infected games disk.'

Conduct of the kind described above, when the result of a deliberate act, might well be regarded as a form of electronic vandalism. In both Scotland and England, precedents exist to suggest that such conduct may be successfully prosecuted as a species of damage to property.

In Scotland, although no cases have been concerned directly with conduct affecting computer data, the decision of the High Court in *Her Majesty's Advocate* v *Wilson* 1984 SLT 116 furnishes a useful precedent. The case concerned an incident at a power station in which Wilson, an employee of the electricity company, maliciously pressed an 'emergency stop' button. The effect of this was to stop the generation of electricity. Once stopped, it took 28 hours for the power station to resume normal operations. Although no equipment suffered any form of damage, the exercise cost the power station owners some £147,000.

Wilson was charged with malicious mischief. The sheriff dismissed this charge as irrelevant, holding that physical damage to corporeal property was an essential element of the offence. An appeal was brought by the procurator to the High Court which, by a majority, held that the conduct causing purely economic loss could nonetheless constitute malicious mischief. The Lord Justice-Clerk (Wheatley), after surveying the institutional writers' comments on the nature of the offence, held that:[17]

---

17. 1984 SLT 116 at p. 119.

If the malicious intention improperly to stop the production of electricity is established, and the achievement of that had the effect of rendering inoperative a machine which should have been operating productively and profitably, then in my view that is just as much damage to the employer's property as would be the case in any of the more physical acts of sabotage.

The implication of the Lord Justice-Clerk's ruling would appear to be that if data are altered with the intention of adversely affecting the operation of a computer, the offence of malicious mischief will have been committed.

Such a conclusion might be open to criticism. In particular, the approach advocated by the Lord Justice-Clerk can be criticised as extending undesirably the scope of the offence. On the basis of his comments it might be argued that a person who placed wheel clamps on a motor vehicle (without damaging it in any way) might be charged with malicious mischief. Although many motorists may well be sympathetic to such a proposition it is difficult to accept that the conduct could properly be regarded as malicious mischief.

As will be discussed, the passage of the Computer Misuse Act 1990 may well have rendered otiose discussion of the relevance of malicious mischief. Once again, however, the underlying issues remain relevant in assessing whether and to what extent damage to an individual's economic well-being can be equated with that which is more physical in nature.

Equivalent issues concerning the applicability of existing offences involving damage to property arose in the later English case of *Cox* v *Riley* (1986) 83 Cr App R 54, which was directly concerned with 'damage' to a computer program. The appellant, Cox, was employed to operate a computerised saw. The equipment in question consisted of a powered saw whose operations could be controlled by means of the insertion of a printed circuit card containing a number of computer programs. The equipment contained a program cancellation facility. This was used by Cox, deliberately and without due cause, to erase programs. This rendered the saw useless until it was reprogrammed, a task which required its owner to expend 'time and effort of a more than minimal nature'.

Cox was charged under s. 1(1) of the Criminal Damage Act 1971. This provides:

A person who without lawful excuse destroys or damages any property belonging to another intending to destroy or damage any such property ... shall be guilty of an offence.

The word 'property' is defined in s. 10 as 'property of a tangible nature whether real or personal'.

The crucial question before the court was whether any property had been damaged or destroyed. Counsel for Cox argued that his conduct had only affected the electronic impulses making up the computer programs. These did not fall within the definition of property. This contention was rejected by the Divisional Court which held that the crucial factor was that as a result of Cox's conduct, the saw's owner was required to expend time and money in restoring the saw itself to its original condition, i.e., as a device which could be used to cut wood in accordance with instructions transmitted from a computer program.

Although the two cases arrived at the same result the reasoning adopted in *Cox* v *Riley* is, it is submitted, to be preferred to that of the High Court of Justiciary. An analogy may fairly be drawn with more traditional forms of conduct such as the spraying of slogans on the wall of a building. In such a situation there is no dispute that the offence of criminal damage may have been committed yet it cannot be argued that the building has suffered structural damage, nor will it be the case that the owner is unable to use it. The essence of the offence is, surely, that time, effort and money will require to be expended in order to restore the building to its original unblemished condition.

In the event, whilst the Scottish Law Commission remained satisfied that *Her Majesty's Advocate* v *Wilson* constituted an acceptable precedent for the computer context, the Law Commission, despite the successful invocation of the offence of criminal damage in a small number of subsequent prosecutions, came to the conclusion that *Cox* v *Riley* had not confronted fully the point that the dictionary definition of damage required 'some injury to a thing'. This, it was argued, had posed problems for the police and prosecuting authorities which reported: 'recurrent (and understandable) difficulty in explaining to judges, magistrates and juries how the facts fit in with the present law of criminal damage'. Accordingly, they recommended that the Criminal Damage Act 1971 should be amended, effectively to reverse the decision in *Cox* v *Riley* by making it clear that damage to programs or data would not constitute the offence of criminal damage. Parallel to this, a new computer-specific offence should be established. Paradoxically, no sooner was this view applied within the Computer Misuse Act 1990 than the Court of Appeal decision in the case of *R* v *Whitely* (1991) 93 Cr App R 25 declared unequivocally that the offence of criminal damage would be applicable in the situation where damage was caused to computer data.

8.4   THEFT OF INFORMATION

The third category of computer misuse identified at the beginning of this chapter is that involving the 'theft' of information. In the event that information is held on some tangible storage device, e.g., a piece of paper or a computer disk, the theft of the device will constitute the offence and, in determining the gravity of the perpetrator's conduct, account will be taken of the value of any information held therein. In the United States case of *Hancock* v *Texas* (1966) 402 SW 2d 906, for example, a quantity of computer disks were stolen. Under Texan law, theft of property valued at less than $50 constituted a misdemeanour rather than the more serious felony. Although the value of the disks was less than $50, the court accepted evidence that several thousands of dollars had been expended in the creation of the informational content of the disks and held that this was the appropriate value to be used in determining the nature of the offence. There would appear no doubt that this approach would be adopted in similar proceedings before a court in the United Kingdom.

A variety of forms of behaviour will fall to be discussed under the present heading. Initially, consideration will be given to the fundamental question whether information, separated from any physical objects, might constitute the subject-matter of a charge of theft. Subsequently, a variety of other forms of dealing in information will also be considered with a view to determining whether these might constitute criminal offences of any description.

In Scotland, theft is a common law offence. A variety of definitions can be found in the works of the institutional writers. Hume, for example, defines it as encompassing 'the felonious taking and carrying away of the property of another'. In England, the offence of theft is contained in s. 1 of the Theft Act 1968. This states that a person is guilty of theft who: 'dishonestly appropriates property belonging to another with the intention of permanently depriving the other of it.' 'Property' is defined in s. 4 as including: 'money and all other property, real or personal, including things in action and other incorporeal property'.

Two difficulties face any attempt to invoke the law of theft in the informational context. First, unless the information is held on some storage device which is also removed, it is difficult to see how the Scottish requirement of 'taking and carrying away' or the English equivalent of 'appropriation' can be satisfied as the holder will still possess the information. It is possible that this argument could be countered with the proposition that the holder has lost exclusive possession or knowledge of the information. Even if this argument were to be accepted – and it could clearly apply only to information that was in some way confidential – a second objection relates to the question whether information might be regarded as property for the purpose of the law of theft. Although it was suggested in Parliament during the passage of the Theft Act 1968 that the above definition would encompass the theft of a trade secret, such an interpretation does not appear compatible with the decision of the Divisional Court in *Oxford* v *Moss* (1978) 68 Cr App R 183. Moss, a university student, obtained access to a proof copy of an examination paper which he was due to sit and determined to remove and copy the paper prior to returning the original. Upon his conduct being discovered, the question arose whether any criminal offence had been committed. As it was an integral part of his scheme that the original paper should be returned he could not be charged with the theft of the paper. In the event, the charge related to the theft of the confidential information contained in the paper.

Moss was acquitted by the Liverpool magistrates on the basis that confidential information could not be regarded as property. This conclusion was upheld by the Divisional Court which declared that whilst the holder of information might be given limited rights in respect of information which could be upheld at civil law, the information itself was not property and hence could not be stolen.

Further support for the view that information cannot be regarded as property for the purposes of theft can be taken from the decision of the House of Lords in *Rank Film Distributors Ltd* v *Video Information Centre* [1982] AC 380. In the course of civil proceedings involving an allegation of breach of copyright, the appellants sought discovery of a variety of documents in the possession of the respondents. In resisting this application, the latter claimed that disclosure would expose them to the risk of criminal proceedings for, *inter alia*, theft of the appellants' copyright interests, and would therefore infringe their privilege against self-incrimination. Although the Copyright Act 1956 makes frequent reference to 'ownership' of copyright, the respondents' plea was rejected on this point, Lord Fraser commenting that:[18]

> The risk of prosecution under the Theft Act 1968 may, I think, be disregarded as remote, because that Act applies to theft of 'property' which is defined in a way which does not appear to include copyright but only, so far as this appeal is concerned, to the physical objects such as tapes and cassettes which are of small value by themselves.

Although the Copyright Designs and Patents Act 1988 specifically states in s. 1 that: 'Copyright is a property right which subsists in accordance with this Part in the following descriptions of work', it would not appear that this will make any change to the status of copyright. Such a view finds support in the judgment of Oliver LJ in *Paterson Zochonis & Co. Ltd* v *Merfarken Packaging Ltd* [1986] 3 All ER 522. Dismissing a claim that the respondents owed a common law duty of care to avoid actions which might result in an infringement of the appellants' copyright interests he held that:[19]

> the plaintiffs' case ultimately depends upon the existence, alongside the statutory duty not to infringe copyright, of a parallel common law duty owed to the copyright owner to take reasonable care not to infringe copyright. For my part I am wholly unable to accept the existence of such an additional or parallel duty.

Such a conclusion is in conformity with the principle of intellectual property law constituting an exception to the general rules against acts restricting competition. As such, the extent of copyright protection is to be found in the copyright legislation.

An unfortunate feature of the English cases dealing with the property status of information is the absence of any detailed discussion of the issues involved. In view of this it is relevant to look at the recent Canadian case of *R* v *Stewart* where these questions were extensively considered. Stewart sought to obtain details of the names and addresses of hotel employees. This information was sought by a trade union which wished to recruit members from amongst the employees. The information was contained in personnel files held on the employer's computer. Stewart's scheme was to persuade an employee to copy the data from the computer without, however, removing any tangible objects. The scheme being discovered, Stewart was charged with the offence of counselling the offence of theft 'to wit: to steal information, the property of the . . . Hotel contrary to section 283 of the Criminal Code'.

---

18. [1982] AC 380 at p. 445.
19. [1986] 3 All ER 522 at p. 531.

Section 283 provides that:

Everyone commits theft who fraudulently or without colour of right takes, or fraudulently and without colour of right converts to his use or the use of another person, anything whether animate or inanimate.

Although the word 'anything' appears in the above provision, all the courts dealing with the case were agreed that the word had to be interpreted in the sense of 'any property'.

At trial, Stewart was acquitted by the judge (Krever J) who held that information, even confidential information, could not be regarded as property:[20]

... confidential information is not property for the purpose of the law of theft in Canada. . . . If this interpretation should be thought to be inadequate to meet the needs of modern Canadian society, particularly because of its implications for the computer age, the remedy must be a change in the law by Parliament. It is not for a court to stretch the language used in a statute dealing with the criminal law, to solve problems outside the contemplation of the statute. If an accused person's conduct does not fall within the language used by Parliament, then, no matter how reprehensible it may be, it ought not to be characterised as criminal.

This view was supported by Lacourcière JA in the Court of Appeal but the majority were in favour of conferring at least a limited property status upon confidential information. Cory JA argued:[21]

Compilations of information are often of such importance to the business community that they are securely kept to ensure their confidentiality. The collated, confidential information may be found in many forms covering a wide variety of topics. It may include painstakingly prepared computer programs; . . . meticulously indexed lists of suppliers. . . . For many businessmen their confidential lists may well be the most valuable asset of their company. . . . The importance of confidential information will increase with the growth of high-technology industry. Its protection will be of paramount concern to members of industry and the public as a whole.

In similar vein, Houlden JA stated:[22]

While clearly not all information is property, I see no reason why confidential information that has been gathered through the expenditure of time, effort and money by a commercial enterprise for the purposes of its business should not be regarded as property and hence entitled to the protection of the criminal law.

---

20. 138 DLR (3d) 73 at p. 85.
21. 149 DLR (3d) 583 at pp. 599–600.
22. 149 DLR (3d) 583 at p. 595.

The Court of Appeal decision was subjected to considerable criticism[23] and ultimately was overturned in the Supreme Court on grounds similar to those adopted by Krever J. In particular, it was held that the Court of Appeal's decision marked an extension to the law of theft. As such this constituted a usurpation of the power of the legislature, especially in the situation where competing interests existed between those seeking the preservation of confidentiality and those wishing to promote the free flow of information. A further indication of the issues involved can be taken from the report of the Canadian House of Commons Standing Committee on Justice and Legal Affairs which argued:

> For reasons of public policy the exclusive ownership of information which, of necessity, would flow from the concept of 'property', is not favoured in our socio-legal system. Information is regarded as too valuable a commodity to have its ownership vest exclusively in any particular individual.

In the United Kingdom both Law Commissions recognised that the issue of the property status of information was assuming, and would continue to assume, greater significance. As indicated in the Canadian report quoted above, the significance of the point extended beyond the computer field. Given their limited remit to consider the criminal aspects of computer misuse it was considered inappropriate to make any in-depth examination of the topic or produce any proposals for reform. Although this conclusion may be supported in the light of the Law Commissions' remits, the issue is clearly of enormous significance to the development of our 'information society' encompassing concepts such as data protection, intellectual property and freedom of information in addition to purely criminal aspects.

8.5   THE REPORTS OF THE LAW COMMISSIONS

Reference has previously been made to the activities of the Law Commissions in the area of computer misuse. The initial investigations were conducted by the Scottish Law Commission whose consultative memorandum was published in 1986. This identified no fewer than eight forms of computer-related behaviour, considering first, the extent to which the conduct might be regarded as criminal under existing criminal provisions, and second, in the event that the conduct was not so regarded, whether a case could be made out for the extension of the criminal law. Following upon its survey, the Scottish Law Commission reported in 1987 and recommended the enactment of a Computer Crime (Scotland) Act. This should be a short measure which would create one new criminal offence, that of obtaining unauthorised access to a program or data stored in a computer but only where this was done in order to:

---

23. See R. Grant Hammond, 'Electronic Crime in Canadian Courts' (1986) 6 Oxford J Legal Stud 145.

inspect or otherwise acquire knowledge of the program or the data or to add to, erase or otherwise alter the program or the data with the intention—
    (a)   of procuring an advantage for himself or another person; or
    (b)   of damaging another person's interests.

It was further proposed that the offence should be committed where the perpetrator acted in a reckless fashion. Penalties for the offence would have been dependent upon whether proceedings were summary or solemn. In the former case a sentence of up to six months' imprisonment might be imposed; in the latter a term of up to five years would be sanctioned.

The Law Commission's investigation of the topic began somewhat later in time. It was not until 1988 that a working paper was published. The tone of this document was similar to that of the Scottish report. Although it did not come to any definite conclusions, it proposed that a new offence of unauthorised access should be created and sought views on the particular form which the offence should take. The Law Commission's final report was published in 1989 and displayed significant differences from the working paper. Whilst the former had been almost dismissive of the problems of computer abuse, the final report, based in part on confidential consultations with computer users, took a much more serious view of the problem and of the need for reform.

Once again the issue of unauthorised access was at the core of the recommendations. Whereas the Scottish Law Commission had proposed to make such access an offence only when it served as a precursor to further acts, the Law Commission were influenced by commentators who argued that a computer owner who became aware that a party had secured unauthorised access would have to proceed on the assumption that further damage had been caused and would be put to considerable expense in checking data and perhaps replacing programs or data with back-up copies. Accordingly the Law Commission proposed that the act of obtaining unauthorised access should be made unlawful regardless of whether the perpetrator possessed any ulterior motive. Effectively, therefore, the activity of computer hacking would be declared criminal even where hackers acted out of a sense of curiosity or from the desire to test their computing skills by overcoming security devices intended to prevent unauthorised persons from obtaining access to a computer system.

During 1989 there was considerable discussion of the possibility that the government might introduce legislation in the field. Such a possibility prompted the Law Commission to accelerate the production of their final report to such an extent that time did not permit them to follow their normal practice of including a draft Bill. In the event governmental action was not forthcoming, but the main proposals of the Law Commission formed the basis of the Computer Misuse Bill introduced by Michael Colvin MP. The Bill was widely welcomed in Parliament although concern was expressed that the mechanisms for its enforcement might not prove sufficient. The measure received the royal assent on 29 June 1990 and entered into force on 1 August.

8.6   THE COMPUTER MISUSE ACT 1990

8.6.1   Introduction

The Computer Misuse Act 1990 creates three new criminal offences. The basic offence specified in the Act is that of obtaining unauthorised access to a program or data held on a computer. In addition to constituting an offence in its own right this conduct may serve as the preliminary to a second offence, that of obtaining access with intention to facilitate the commission of a further offence. Finally, the unauthorised modification of data or programs is declared to be criminal.

In the case of the first offence, a prosecution may only be brought on a summary basis with a maximum penalty of six months' imprisonment and/or a fine of up to £2,000.[24] The remaining offences are regarded as more serious; proceedings may be on the basis of an indictment and a jail term of up to five years may be imposed.

8.6.2   Obtaining unauthorised access to computer material

Section 1(1) of the Computer Misuse Act 1990 provides:

A person is guilty of an offence if—
(a)   he causes a computer to perform any function with intent to secure access to any program or data held in any computer;
(b)   the access he intends to secure is unauthorised; and
(c)   he knows at the time when he causes the computer to perform the function that that is the case.

These requirements are cumulative. First of all an accused must seek to obtain access to a program or data held on a computer. The offence may be committed equally well by a person who obtains direct access to a computer system itself or by the more archetypal hacker who secures access by means of a telephone connection.[25] The question next arises what level of contact will require to be made. The offence requires more than the obtaining of access to any hardware involved but calls for at least an attempt to cause the computer to 'perform a function'. This phrase receives a wide definition, s. 17 providing that it encompasses the acts of altering or erasing the program, the copying or moving of the program or data either to another location in the computer's memory or to some other storage device, e.g., the perpetrator's own computer,

---

24.   Level 5 on the standard scale.
25.   In the first prosecution brought under s. 1, the defendant was accused of obtaining unauthorised access to a computer belonging to his employer. The defendant was acquitted when the judge ruled that the phrase 'any computer' was to be interpreted in the sense of any computer other than the one with which the accused was in direct contact. This ruling was subsequently overturned by the Court of Appeal (*Attorney-General's Reference (No. 1 of 1991)* [1992] 3 WLR 432) which held that the 'plain and ordinary' meaning of the phrase 'any computer' included instances where direct access was obtained to a computer. The case does however, provide further evidence of the problems encountered in prosecuting instances of computer misuse.

or causing it to be displayed or otherwise output from the computer. This last provision is exceptionally broad and it may well be the case that the act of switching on a computer or making initial telephonic contact, which will cause a 'log-in' screen to appear or even a command prompt, will suffice.

It is not required that the perpetrator should seek access to any particular computer. It is frequently reported, for example, that hackers will dial telephone numbers almost at random in an attempt to discover those which will provide contact with a computer system. The first requirement for commission of the s. 1 offence will be satisfied when such efforts are successful even though the hacker may not be aware of the identity of the 'victim' computer at this stage.

The second element of the basic offence requires that the access be unauthorised. This occurs where access is not sanctioned by a person who is entitled to control access to the program or data in question. The question whether access is authorised or unauthorised can only be determined by reference to the actions and intentions of the computer owner. By referring to 'programs' and 'data' rather than a computer system, the Act recognises that access rights may be themselves divided into a number of categories. The operator of, for example, a bulletin board may be quite willing to allow anyone to see certain categories of information but may reserve other categories for a more limited class of user.

In order for the offence to be committed it is necessary, finally, that the user should be aware of the fact that access is unauthorised. Only intentional acts are susceptible of punishment under this statute. In practical terms, if a computer owner wishes to be able to establish that a particular user has acted in an unauthorised manner he will be required to take steps to bring any use limits to a user's notice. If, for example, upon making initial contact with a computer system a user is asked to supply a password or identification code, it might be assumed that a party who does not possess such information should be aware that he is not authorised to attempt to proceed further. Where users have limited access rights, it will be necessary for such limits to be brought to their notice. Whereas the recommendations of both the Council of Europe and the OECD refer to the overcoming of security measures as a prerequisite to the commission of the basic unauthorised access offence no such limitation is included in s. 1. However, difficulties might be encountered in establishing the requisite *mens rea* in the event that the operator of a computer system took no steps to indicate to unauthorised users that their presence was unwelcome.

A further scenario might also be identified. User A has been allocated a password by the computer owner. A discloses his password to B and encourages B to use the password to obtain access to the computer. In the event this occurs B's access will be unauthorised, as although A is entitled to access the computer he is not entitled to 'control' access and therefore cannot transfer his rights to a third party. The question which may require to be determined by a court is whether B could possess the necessary *mens rea* for commission of the unauthorised access offence.

One final point deserves consideration as relevant to all of the offences established under the Act. No attempt is made to define the word 'computer'.

This is very much in line with the approach adopted in other statutes (such as the Data Protection Act 1984) operating in the area. The offences, it will be recalled, relate to dealings in respect of programs or data and may be triggered by an act causing a program to perform its function. Many modern appliances, ranging from washing machines to motor cars, make extensive use of simple computers, often consisting of a single semiconductor chip, to control their operations. In such a situation, it might be argued that an unauthorised person using the washing machine would be guilty of an offence under s. 1. Such a result would appear not a little bizarre and in general terms the operation of the unauthorised access offence does seem to conflict with the Scottish Law Commission's recommendation that the unauthorised use of a computer should not *per se* be made unlawful.

The introduction of the unauthorised access offence has been criticised in many quarters. On a point of principle, its scope may be contrasted with the recommendation of the Scottish Law Commission which would have required unauthorised access plus an intent to cause harm to the interests of the computer owner and with the Council of Europe's recommendation that the commission of the offence should require the overcoming of security measures. Although the act of obtaining unauthorised access to a computer system may be regarded as a form of electronic breaking and entering, it may also be compared with the acts of eavesdropping on a private conversation (or detecting and deciphering the electromagnetic emissions generated by a computer), watching a person's movements or reading the contents of a private letter. Unless such conduct is accompanied by other illegal acts no criminal sanctions may currently be invoked against the perpetrator. It might therefore be suggested that the effect of s. 1 is to place the computer, together with programs and data held thereon, in a special and privileged position.

A further argument against the imposition of criminal sanctions was advanced by the Data Protection Registrar. In his fifth report, he posited the possibility of a hacker gaining access to a system 'with no intent of abusing its contents and who causes no damage' and argued:[26]

> There seems to be a consensus that this is often juvenile 'hobby' behaviour. The Registrar recognises the undesirability of 'criminalising' juveniles and the concern that young people should not be introduced to the criminal justice system unless necessary.

As was stated earlier, the Law Commission were ultimately persuaded that the consequences of hacking were not as innocuous as suggested by the Registrar. A computer owner, it was suggested, becoming aware that unauthorised access had been obtained, might well feel compelled to assume that the system had been compromised and expend considerable energy in checking for signs of damage. This analysis may well be accurate but once again comparison with other forms of conduct gives cause for concern. A relevant example might concern a houseowner who becomes aware that house keys have

---

26. Pages 30–1.

been missing for a short period of time before reappearing. In such a situation, the fear may well be that the keys have been removed, a copy made and that a visit may be expected from a burglar. Faced with such a prospect the householder may reasonably expend energy in altering the compromised locks. Under this scenario it is difficult to identify any criminal offence which has been committed and yet the parallel with the conduct rendered criminal under s. 1 is very close.

Beyond the argument whether there should be an unauthorised access offence, the question arises whether there is any realistic prospect of its being enforced. The problem is especially acute in the situation where the 'hacker' has no connection with the computer owner and accesses the systems by means of a telephone connection. The only manner in which the identity of the hacker is likely to be detected is by the monitoring of telephone calls. Such conduct (involving no more than the recording of the numbers called and the duration of a connection) is of course carried out as a matter of routine by the telephone companies. The Act, however, contains no provision for them to be required to pass such details to the police to aid investigation of an alleged offence. Although there is no prohibition against the data being supplied on a voluntary basis, statements made during the Act's passage would suggest that such cooperation is not always given.

In the event that suspicion falls on a particular individual it is possible for a search warrant to be issued. In respect of England and Wales this power is provided in s. 14 and enables a constable to seek a warrant from a circuit judge empowering a search of premises in which it is believed that a s. 1 offence has been or is about to be committed together with the concomitant power to remove any relevant evidence, except for items defined as privileged, excluded and special procedure material under the provisions of s. 9(2) of the Police and Criminal Evidence Act 1984.

Although the powers in respect of a physical search are extensive it has been suggested that, in the absence of a further power to require the disclosure of data relating to use of a telephone, it will be difficult to establish 'reasonable grounds' for the belief that search of particular premises might be justified.

In addition to the unauthorised access offence the Computer Misuse Act 1990 creates two more serious offences. In many situations the commission of the s. 1 offence will serve as a precursor to the commission of the more serious s. 2 and s. 3 offences. This relationship is illustrated by s. 13 which provides that a person charged with an offence under s. 2 or s. 3 may be acquitted on such a charge yet convicted of a s. 1 offence even though no such charge was specified in the original complaint or indictment.

8.6.3   The ulterior intent offence

Section 2 of the Computer Misuse Act 1990 creates what is referred to as the ulterior intent offence. This offence is committed by a person who secures unauthorised access to a computer system with the intention of using that access to facilitate the commission of a further serious criminal offence. An offence will be so regarded when the sentence is fixed by law (most notably in cases of murder) or where a first offender aged 21 or over might be sentenced to a five-year term of imprisonment.[27] For the purpose of the offence it is irrelevant whether it would, in fact, be impossible to commit the further offence, e.g., an attempt to transfer funds from a bank account which does not have any funds in it.[28]

To a considerable extent, this provision will serve to overcome the difficulties identified in cases such as *R v Thompson* [1984] 1 WLR 962. Although a repetition of the conduct at issue in that case could still not be prosecuted on the basis of theft or the obtaining of property by deception at any earlier stage in the proceedings, the ulterior intent offence would be committed at the stage where the perpetrator obtains access to the data with the intention of amending the data so as to facilitate the commission of such offences.

It may, of course, be the case that conduct falling short of the completion of the criminal act in question will constitute a criminal attempt. A distinction is drawn, however, between conduct which is preparatory to the commission of a crime and that which constitutes part of the perpetration of the criminal act. In *R v Thompson*, for example, the appellant's conduct in amending the accounts on the bank's computer would be regarded merely as preparatory to the offence of obtaining property by deception and would not, therefore, constitute a criminal attempt. In the event of a repetition of this conduct the effect of s. 2 will be to bring forward the moment in time at which a serious criminal offence is committed. The requirement that the unauthorised access offence be committed as a prerequisite to that of the ulterior intent offence may give rise to some difficulties. Most instances of computer fraud, it would appear, are committed by employees. In such a situation it may not be the case that the access was unauthorised, although clearly any access rights may have been used for an unauthorised purpose.

In advocating the creation of the ulterior intent offence the Law Commission referred to two forms of conduct which they felt would not constitute an offence under the existing law but which were considered deserving of such a fate. The first example cited concerned a hacker who secured access to a bank's computer system, the system being used for electronic fund transfers. In order to accomplish a transfer a password would require to be transmitted. The hypothesis was that the hacker might attempt to transmit a large number of combinations in the hope of finding the correct one. In the Law Commission's view, no offence of attempt would be committed at the stage of transmitting the passwords.

A second illustration referred to an intending blackmailer who obtained access to data held on a computer in order to obtain confidential personal information to be used for the purpose of blackmail. Once again it is unlikely that conduct of that nature could, at the stage of obtaining the data from the computer, constitute a criminal attempt.

Although a case can certainly be made out for suggesting that conduct of the kind hypothesised by the Law Commission should be rendered criminal it may be arguable how far the examples given support their case. Although the

---

27. Section 2(2).
28. Section 2(4).

legislation imposes no obligation upon a computer owner adequately to safeguard access to and use of the machinery, it may be considered unlikely that any banking system would permit a 'casual' outsider to obtain access and attempt to transmit permutation after permutation of password in the hope of discovering a valid combination.

Although the particular example chosen by the Law Commission can be criticised, the misuse of electronic fund transfer systems is a cause for concern and constitutes a compelling justification for the creation of the new offence. The case for applying the new offence to the second form of behaviour is more problematic. Once again, the problem is genuine. An instance has been reported from France of access being obtained to computerised medical records in order to identify and subsequently to blackmail patients suffering from AIDS. That the conduct is reprehensible is beyond question but in this situation it is difficult to distinguish between the conduct of a person who secures access to information held on computer and one who accesses information held in paper-based records. There appears little justification for holding one party to be guilty of a serious criminal offence at the stage of obtaining, or attempting to obtain, access to information whilst the other faces no such sanction.

In such cases it may be that any inconsistency results from the Act's failure to distinguish between two categories of unauthorised user. The first category encompasses those who are entitled to access to the premises within which the computer is located but have no right of access to the computer together with those who, whether operating the computer directly or accessing it by telephone, possess limited rights in respect of their usage. In the event that such persons either access the computer or exceed their access rights their actions might well be considered equivalent to that of an employee or third party who makes unauthorised use of any other piece of equipment, and are not deserving, therefore, of more extensive criminal sanctions. The second category of user is one who has no entitlement either to be on the premises or, acting remotely, to make any use of the computer. Such a person, when operating in a non-computer environment, will be likely to commit burglary-related offences in obtaining access to information held on the user's premises. The unauthorised access and ulterior intent offences can be regarded as establishing a new offence of electronic burglary and thereby bringing the criminal sanctions into line with those applicable to the comparable form of non-computer-related conduct.

8.6.4   Unauthorised modification of computer material

The rather bland phrase 'unauthorised modification of computer material' encompasses some of the most damaging forms of behaviour occurring within the computer field. Although most publicity is today given to so-called computer viruses, these represent but one manifestation of the problem. Anyone obtaining access to a computer system may well, by means of a few commands, delete large amounts of data, and even the introduction of a magnet in close proximity to computer equipment may produce a similar effect. In addition to the situation where programs or data are deleted from a computer's memory, the perpetrator may seek to modify the contents by adding data – perhaps in the form of comments. In *R* v *Gold* [1988] AC 1063 the perpetrators' activities on Prestel included the act of obtaining access to the contents of an electronic mailbox allocated to the Duke of Edinburgh and inserting a number of jocular remarks to the sparse contents found therein.

Although the prosecution was unsuccessful in *R* v *Gold*, cases such as *Cox* v *Riley* (1986) 83 Cr App R 54 indicated that at least some forms of conduct might be prosecuted under existing provisions of criminal law. As previously indicated, however, the application of the offence of criminal damage was considered to be uncertain. The effect of s. 3 of the Computer Misuse Act 1990 is twofold. First, it provides a computer-specific offence analogous to that of criminal damage, and second, it modifies the definition of damage found in the Criminal Damage Act 1971 to make it clear that damage to data will not *per se* constitute the offence.

The basis of the s. 3 offence is the unauthorised attempt to modify the contents of any computer. Once again, liability will only be incurred in respect of an intentional act. The act must be intended to impair the operation of a computer or to prevent or hinder access to any programs or data, to impair the operation of any program or the reliability of any data. It is not necessary that the conduct be directed at any particular computer, thus a person causing a computer virus to enter into circulation might be prosecuted under this section even though he may not have targeted any specific computer(s). On this basis, the originator (or any other party who deliberately causes the dissemination of the virus) will be held responsible for the modification of any computer which is infected even though he may not be directly responsible for the infection of any particular machine, this being brought about by an unsuspecting (or even reckless) authorised user. To this extent the phrase 'to cause' must be interpreted in two senses; in respect of the act which causes the effect and also of the act which is proximately responsible for its occurrence. In pursuing this point, a further scenario might also be considered. An individual, being aware that data of a particular kind are held on computer, may seek to bring about a change in the information. A simple example might involve an individual giving false information with a view to causing the modification of an unfavourable entry on a credit reference agency's files. It might be argued that such conduct will constitute an offence under s. 3.

It is clear from the Act's definitions that the mere act of adding data to a computer will constitute an unauthorised modification. An example might concern an employee who types a private letter using his employer's computer. As s. 2(5) states that the fact that a modification is permanent or temporary is immaterial, it would not even appear that there is a necessity for the text of the letter to be stored on the computer. It is, however, to be recognised that the act of making an unauthorised modification constitutes only one element of the new offence and that the prosecution are required additionally to establish that its effect was to impair the operation of the computer (s. 2(2)). In the event that a portion of text is stored on a computer's hard disk utilising only a minuscule fraction of the disk's storage capacity, it will be difficult to establish that the operation of the computer has been impaired. It may be noted, however, that the Act does not require that the degree of impairment be substantial or significant.

In the event that a computer is infected with some form of virus which has the effect of destroying data held thereon it will be relatively straightforward to establish that its operation has been impaired. A more difficult situation may arise where the modification causes the alteration of the screen display without affecting the contents of the computer or its processing capability. Although the word 'impair' is not defined in the Act, its dictionary definition refers to a diminution in 'quantity, value or strength'. It may be the case that the computer's value has not been diminished by such conduct, but the point is at least arguable.

8.6.5 Jurisdiction

The capability of many computer systems to transmit and receive data takes no account of national boundaries. Operation of the legal retrieval system Lexis in the United Kingdom, for example, involves the transfer of data between here and the United States. In the event that a user and a computer are located in different countries and conduct which might be regarded as criminal occurs, the question arises which legal system might have jurisdiction. The Computer Misuse Act 1990 introduces the concept of a 'significant link' with one or other of the United Kingdom's legal systems. In the case of s. 1 or s. 3 offences, an English, Northern Irish or Scottish court will have jurisdiction if either the offender or the victim computer was located in that territory.[29] The position is slightly more complex with regard to a s. 2 offence. Here the domestic tribunal will only have jurisdiction where the further acts intended would constitute an offence in the country in which it was intended that they should occur.[30]

8.7 INTERNATIONAL DEVELOPMENTS

To date, the most significant international actors in the field of computer crime have been the Organisation for Economic Cooperation and Development and the Council of Europe. In 1986 the former published a survey of existing national provisions. Identifying the need for an international consensus it identified a basic catalogue of offences involving the 'input, alteration erasure and/or suppression of computer data and or computer programmes' [sic] with the intention of causing an illegal transfer of funds, to commit a forgery or with the intention of hindering the operations of a computer system. Additionally, the act of obtaining unauthorised access to a computer system either by overcoming security measures or with dishonest or harmful motives was identified together with the infringement of copyright interests for commercial gain.

In 1989 the Council of Europe's Committee of Ministers adopted a recommendation on the topic of computer crime. The approach adopted was similar to that advocated by the OECD with the identification of a minimum

---

29. Sections 4 and 5.
30. Section 4(4).

list of measures which it was suggested should be incorporated into the criminal laws of member States. Eight specific forms of conduct were represented in this list: computer fraud and forgery, damage to data or programs, computer sabotage, unauthorised access (again involving the overcoming of security measures), the unauthorised interception of data transmissions (whether internal to a system or otherwise), the unauthorised reproduction of a computer program or of a topography.

8.8 CONCLUSIONS

With the passage of the Computer Misuse Act 1990, the United Kingdom has joined the ranks of States which have recognised that computer crime requires specific legislation. As the measure only entered into force in August 1990 and at the time of writing has yet to be properly tested in the appellate courts, any comment regarding the success or failure of the Act's approach must be speculative.

In 1982, guidelines were prepared by the Home Office outlining principles which should be taken into account in determining whether new criminal provisions should be introduced. First, it was stated, the behaviour must be so serious that it cannot satisfactorily be dealt with on the basis of civil law remedies, e.g., damages. Second, criminal sanctions should only be created where other less drastic means of control would be ineffective, impractical or insufficient. A final principle required that any new offence should be susceptible of enforcement.

Applying these principles in the context of acts of computer misuse it must be acknowledged at the outset that virtually every form of behaviour discussed throughout this chapter will expose the perpetrator to the very real risk of a civil action brought by the computer owner or user whose equipment is affected. On this assumption, the Computer Misuse Act 1990 must face scrutiny on three counts. First, has the case been made out for the application of the criminal law? Second, has the optimum approach been adopted? Finally, is there a reasonable prospect that the legislation can be enforced adequately?

That certain forms of computer misuse are deserving of criminal sanctions may scarcely be disputed. The argument that fraud should not be prosecuted in the situation where a computer was involved is one which is likely to prove attractive only to the most hardened computer fraudster. A significant distinction exists between conduct which would be criminal in the absence of the computer and that which could not be so regarded. Prior to the Act's passage, the criminal law extended little protection to the holder of information. In certain situations infringement of intellectual property rights might constitute a criminal offence, although the practical impact of these provisions was limited largely to instances of video and software piracy. It is perhaps significant that whilst initially these criminal offences were introduced in technology-specific legislation, the opportunity was taken with the passage of the Copyright, Designs and Patents Act 1988 to extend their application to all forms of copyright protected works.

In many instances the effect of the Computer Misuse Act 1990 will be to create offences which are analogous to those currently in existence. The behaviour which may form the subject of the unauthorised access offence has frequently been referred to as a form of 'electronic burglary'. Sometimes the equivalent of obtaining forcible and unauthorised entry to premises may be present, but in other cases the conduct may be more analogous to a trespass, a matter which generally comes within the ambit of the civil law. The point has previously been made that the provisions of s. 1 are more extensive than those recommended by either the OECD or the Council of Europe.

In respect of the more serious offences established by the 1990 Act the parallels with existing forms of criminal behaviour are stronger, although again there may be situations where conduct will be punishable in situations where a computer is involved where the same conduct would not be considered criminal in its absence.

Assuming that a case for legislation has been made out, the next question to be considered is whether the optimum approach has been identified. A significant difference can be identified between the reports of the Law Commissions, which can be only partially explained by reference to developments in technology between their reports. The more limited reform advocated by the Scottish Law Commission is based upon a relatively optimistic view of the flexibility and applicability of the general principles of the criminal law. Such an approach may be more feasible in Scotland where many of the criminal offences remain rooted in the common law than in England where the equivalent offences are often statute-based with consequential limits upon the flexibility of judicial interpretation. Although the United Kingdom is following a widely adopted approach in introducing special computer crime legislation, the major advantage of the alternative approach of applying general offences – such as criminal damage or obtaining property or services by deception – coupled where necessary with definitional amendments, is that computer-related conduct will be clearly and unequivocally linked with its non-technological equivalent. Even the advantage of specificity undoubtedly possessed by the Computer Misuse Act 1990 is minimised by the understandable failure of the legislation to essay any definition of core terminology such as 'computer', 'programs' and 'data'. The proliferation of computer technology has resulted in many common objects being wholly or partly controlled by such devices. Many automobiles, for example, make extensive use of computers even to the extent of controlling the operation of the vehicle's locking system. In such an event it may be that any attempt to pick the locks will also involve the commission of at least the unauthorised access offence under the Computer Misuse Act 1990. Although it may be doubted whether any prosecution will proceed on such a basis, the absence of definitions may well face the courts with just the problems that the statute was intended to avoid. *R v Gold* [1988] AC 1063 provides eloquent testimony to the difficulty which the application of a seemingly obvious phrase such as 'recorded or stored' might face given the involvement of a computer.

The final issue to be considered is whether the new prohibitions can be enforced. That the task may be difficult is not in question but the same comment may be made in respect of many criminal offences. The real issue is whether the difficulties facing enforcement of the new offences are so significant as to render nugatory any deterrent effect that might otherwise be anticipated from the legislation and, indeed, serve to bring the criminal law into disrepute. It must certainly be the case that the owner of a self-contained system will be better able to assist any police investigation than a party whose computer system may be accessed remotely and where much of the evidence of abuse will be controlled by telecommunication undertakings rather than by the victim. In respect of the ulterior intent and unauthorised modification offences, the Act empowers the police to seek a warrant under the provisions of the Interception of Communications Act 1985 requiring the service provider to monitor specified communications and to provide them with the results of such activity. The form of monitoring required in such a situation would normally be 'call logging' with a record being made only of the telephone numbers called from a particular phone together with details of the time and duration of the calls. Such information will, of course, be required for the service provider's own billing procedures. No comparable provision applies in respect of the basic unauthorised access offence. The inclusion of such a provision in the legislation was rejected on the basis that it would represent too Draconian a response to what is to be considered a comparatively minor offence. It was, however, suggested that there was no legal impediment prohibiting the supply of the information on a voluntary basis. Attention must, however, be drawn to the provisions of the European Convention on Human Rights concerning the protection of the right to privacy. The uses to which call-logging data might be put were considered by the Court of Human Rights in the case of *Klass* v *Federal Republic of Germany* (1978) 2 EHRR 214. Although the court ultimately gave approval to German practices in this regard, it did so with a deal of reluctance and in respect of a system where reasonably stringent controls existed concerning the circumstances under and procedures by which such data could be released for the purposes of criminal investigations. It may be argued that the voluntary release of data in respect of investigations of a minor criminal offence and with no legal safeguards or requirements would be considered to constitute a breach of the Convention. Nonetheless, the difficulties facing the prosecution of the Computer Misuse Act 1990's offences do not appear sufficient to suggest that it is not capable of being enforced.

CHAPTER NINE

Evidence

Michael Silverleaf

9.1 INTRODUCTION

The law of evidence is a subject which presents considerable difficulty and complexity. Much of the complexity arises from the piecemeal way the rules of evidence have grown up in English law. Many rules, such as the blanket bar on the admission of hearsay evidence which made perfect sense in a society where little was written, have no useful place in a modern legal system. Yet they have not been removed. The law has rather sought to evolve by limiting their application and overriding them in many circumstances. The result is a system in which it is impossible to have a clear picture of what is and is not evidence without some appreciation of the essentially obsolete principles from which it has arisen.

It might be thought that when applying such a system to modern technology the problems would be insoluble. In fact this is not the case. In principle the application of the law of evidence to cases involving information technology, and computers in particular, poses no unique problems. A sound grasp of the law of evidence is essential to understanding how technological disputes are best presented to the courts and resolved. And a straightforward approach to the basic evidential rules is essential to a proper grasp of the law. Evidence is often found to be a difficult subject by those who study it because they fail to pay sufficient attention to the basic rules. The reason for this is that the basic rules have little obvious application in the modern context. However, they are the key to the application of all the modern practices. The first purpose of this chapter is to outline the basic rules so as to explain how the modern rules fit into them. This is not a textbook on the law of evidence; it is simply a guided tour. It is intended to equip the reader with sufficient knowledge and understanding to use such a textbook in the context of technological and computer litigation.

In practice, unfortunately, the absence of any essentially novel difficulties does not mean that the courts have absorbed computer disputes without discomfort. The major problem is that the courts are in general ill-equipped to deal with complex technological disputes. Lawyers and judges, who usually have an arts background, find technological jargon and problems difficult to come to terms with, and are as a result often misled into believing that there is something magical about technical expressions or formulae simply because they are unfamiliar with them.

The result of this is that the quality of the presentation of evidence to the courts in technological cases assumes a greatly increased importance. The court cannot be relied upon to fill in for itself any gaps which are left, or to make intuitive leaps from the evidence which is presented to the general rule which it represents. This is in direct contrast to non-technical cases where the courts readily apply their own knowledge and understanding to the problems before them.

The second purpose of this chapter is to examine the evidential problems which arise in technological cases and give general guidance in meeting them. It concentrates on evidential matters in civil disputes, in particular the hearsay rule, documentary evidence and discovery, and expert evidence. Also included is a section concerned with the manner of assembling and presenting evidence to best effect in court. The chapter concludes with a note on criminal evidence by Chris Reed, which concentrates on the problems of admissibility and the hearsay rule.

9.2 THE NATURE OF EVIDENCE

The meaning of the word evidence in its legal context is given in the *Oxford English Dictionary* as:

> Information, whether in the form of personal testimony, the language of documents, or the production of material objects, that is given in legal investigation, to establish the fact or point in question.

This definition is both concise and complete. Evidence is the means by which the court is put in possession of the facts upon which it has to adjudicate. Unless there is a dispute as to particular facts there need be no formal evidence of them. Many potential disputes in actions can be resolved before evidence is required by appropriate pleadings,[1] thus highlighting the real areas of dispute and shortening the trial.

---

1. This includes both the principal pleadings (the statement of claim, defence, counterclaim, reply and defence to counterclaim) and any further particulars given of them, as well as admissions sought and given as a result of notices to admit facts (see 9.6 below). The power of concise pleadings to direct and limit cases cannot be overstated.

9.3 DIRECT AND HEARSAY EVIDENCE

Evidence in English law is categorised as falling into two main classes, direct and hearsay. The basic common law principle is that direct evidence is admissible, that is, receivable by the court, whilst indirect or hearsay evidence is not. Direct evidence is that given by a witness of things he or she has actually seen. Hearsay or indirect evidence is that which is reported by a witness from some other source. Much confusion arises from this distinction, it often being thought that evidence from A of what B said can never be received by the court because it is hearsay. This is not so. It is only correct if the evidence is tendered to demonstrate that what B said had occurred did occur. Then A's evidence of what occurred is hearsay; it is no more than a report from A of what B said occurred. However, it is often the case that what B said is relevant not because its truth is being asserted but because B said it. For example, there may well in a contractual or copyright claim be an allegation that certain things were agreed during the course of a meeting between A and B. A's evidence of what was said by B is then plainly direct evidence of what A heard and saw relating to the crucial facts. Evidence from A of what he heard B say is therefore hearsay only if it is tendered to prove the truth of B's statement. The same is true of documents. A proper understanding of this distinction is essential in dealing with all questions of evidence.

Once there is a dispute, the court can only resolve it in the light of the evidence. Evidence in English proceedings is primarily direct oral evidence. In all technological cases, as in many civil proceedings, direct oral evidence is not necessarily the most important part of the evidence. The contemporary documents often speak more loudly and clearly than any personal recollection of events. Strictly, though, only very limited classes of documents are admissible as evidence of themselves.[2] Most documents, including all private documents, have to be proved by production and attested to. In the case of documents of record, it is now the case that the originals are no longer required to be produced and their contents can be proved in evidence by the production of appropriately certified copies. The above requirements are those for direct evidence.

Under the scheme of the Civil Evidence Acts 1968 and 1972 a wide range of hearsay or indirect evidence is now admissible. The scheme permits hearsay statements to be admitted in evidence provided that the rules of court made under the scheme are followed. The purpose of these is to ensure that any hearsay statements to be relied on are precisely identified before the trial so that they may be properly investigated and challenged by the opposite party. The Civil Evidence Act 1968 covers general hearsay statements. The Civil Evidence Act 1972 is concerned with expert opinion evidence. Both are of considerable importance in litigation involving computers. It is also important to keep firmly in mind that although the scheme of the two Acts makes such material admissible in evidence, it says nothing about the weight the court

---

2. Essentially public records within the Public Records Act 1958 and certain categories of published works of a public nature such as dictionaries and public maps.

should give to that evidence in its deliberations. The court is therefore at liberty to determine that such evidence is of little or no weight or to find that it is unacceptable in the face of contradictory direct evidence. In practice, the court accords the utmost weight to the evidence afforded by contemporary documents and records (provided it is satisfied that they are genuine) whether they are admissible in evidence as documents or not.

9.4   CIVIL EVIDENCE ACT 1968

The Civil Evidence Act 1968 applies to a variety of categories of statements made outside the ambit of the proceedings in question. The Act covers oral and written statements whether made by persons called as witnesses or others,[3] previous statements made by a witness to the proceedings whether for the purpose of showing their inconsistency or for rebutting an allegation that his evidence has been fabricated,[4] records compiled by persons acting under a duty,[5] statements produced by computers,[6] and statements which go to the credibility of a person who has made a statement which is admissible under s. 2.

The procedural rules made under the 1968 Act are set out in Order 38[7] of the Rules of the Supreme Court 1965, and it is beyond the scope of this chapter to do anything more than summarise their operation. In any case, notice must be served of intention to rely on a statement[8] and the rules provide for the contents of such a notice. The notice must always identify the source and content of the statement and the circumstances in which it was made.[9] A party on whom a notice is served may serve a counter-notice[10] requiring the maker of the statement named in the notice to be called as a witness at the trial. It is a reason for not doing so that the maker is dead, mentally or physically unfit to attend as a witness, beyond the seas or cannot be identified or found,[11] and if any of these reasons is alleged to apply the original notice must state this.

The rule relating to admissibility of statements held on a computer is of particular interest here, if only to demonstrate that it will never be applicable to any case in which the functioning of a computer system is in issue. For a statement contained in a document produced by a computer to be admissible the notice must state whether the computer was operating properly throughout the material period and, if not, whether any malfunction was such as to affect the production of the document in question or the accuracy of its contents.[12] It must also contain particulars of a person who occupied a position of responsibility in relation to the operation and supply of information to the

---

3. Section 2.
4. Section 3.
5. Section 4.
6. Section 5.
7. Rules 20 to 34.
8. RSC 1965, Ord. 38, r. 21.
9. RSC 1965, Ord. 38, rr. 22 to 24.
10. RSC 1965, Ord. 38, r. 26.
11. RSC 1965, Ord. 38, r. 25.
12. RSC 1965, Ord. 38, r. 24(2).

computer who is available to be called at the trial to give evidence.[13] It can be seen from this that the exception to the hearsay rule is directed to making general business records kept on a computer admissible. It is not concerned with disputes about the functioning of the computer itself.

9.5 CIVIL EVIDENCE ACT 1972

This is far more directly relevant to technological disputes as it regulates the giving in evidence of matters of opinion. For practical purposes this is expert evidence which, although it in principle consists of inferences of fact, is treated as opinion evidence as the inferences can only be drawn by those possessing the necessary skill and expertise in relation to the facts in question.[14]

In any action[15] in which expert evidence is sought to be adduced the party wishing to adduce the evidence must apply to the court for directions.[16] Those directions will normally include a direction that the expert must make a report of his evidence and that this report is disclosed before the trial.[17] The court may decide not to order that the expert's evidence be disclosed in this manner if it thinks that there is sufficient reason to do so, and in determining whether this is the case the court must have regard to particular circumstances. These are essentially where the evidence is based on a version of events which is in dispute or upon facts not ascertainable by the expert himself, either because he cannot discern them by observation or because they are outside his sphere of competence.[18] In practice disclosure is nearly always ordered. The court may also direct that the parties' expert witnesses meet without prejudice to see if they can identify those parts of their evidence which are in dispute and produce a joint report of those parts which are not.[19]

The order for disclosure of experts' reports will always provide that the expert may not give any evidence not in substance disclosed in his report, and usually provides for mutual exchange of opposing reports where there is no preliminary meeting. In such cases, the parties often seek to supplement their experts' reports in answer to the opposite party's initial expert report. This is usually done without objection although the orders made rarely have provision for this. The usual time for the making of the order relating to expert evidence is at the summons for directions. Interestingly it is open to the parties under the present rules to agree that there shall not be disclosure of expert evidence before the trial,[20] in which case it seems that the court has no power to exclude the evidence.

---

13. RSC 1965, Ord. 38, r. 24(1).
14. For a detailed examination of the nature and content of expert evidence see section 9.9 below. Here only the rules of court are examined.
15. Except personal injury actions where there are automatic provisions under RSC 1965, Ord. 25, r. 8.
16. RSC 1965, Ord. 38, r. 36.
17. RSC 1965, Ord. 38, r. 38(1).
18. RSC 1965, Ord. 38, r. 38(2).
19. RSC 1965, Ord. 38, r. 38(3).
20. RSC 1965, Ord. 38, r. 36(1).

These rules, if operated properly, enable the real issues in a technological dispute to be narrowed down very considerably. Unfortunately, in an adversarial system it is often to the advantage of one of the parties to extend or complicate the dispute, and the rules as presently formulated provide little or no disincentive to such conduct. The cost and duration of many actions could be reduced by rules which resulted in punitive orders for costs being made against parties who engage in such conduct, and it is regrettable that simple measures of this type seem to appeal neither to the Lord Chancellor nor to the judiciary.

9.6 ADMISSIONS

Admissions are a valuable aspect of the evidential side of a case although they are not strictly speaking evidence. Anything which is admitted need not be proved at the trial. Admissions are of two types, formal and informal. Formal admissions are those made within the context of the proceedings in court or in the pleadings. Informal admissions are those made outside the proceedings by a party or by someone who represents him or stands in his place. Formal admissions are binding in the action in which they are made upon the party by whom they are made unless withdrawn, which can only be done with the leave of the court.[21] Informal admissions may be contradicted or explained by evidence unless they amount to an estoppel against the party by or on whose behalf they are made.

Formal admissions are extremely powerful weapons in litigation. There is a simple scheme under the rules of court for the service of notices to admit facts during the course of an action.[22] Judgment for the whole or part of a claim may be given on such admissions.[23] Once made, admissions in response to a notice to admit form part of the pleadings in an action. Perhaps the most important aspect of the scheme relating to formal admissions is the provision as to the costs of proving any facts of which admission has been sought but not given. Provided that the notice to admit is served in due time,[24] the cost of proving any fact not admitted in response to it is paid by the party upon whom it was served.[25] This is a highly valuable tool in litigation, for a carefully structured notice to admit requires a party to examine carefully what facts he really disputes, and therefore what his case really is. The penalty for failing to do so is payment of the costs of proving facts which should have been admitted.

A further important and little-considered aspect of admissions is that resulting from the implied admissions which are made in relation to any document listed by a party in his list of documents on discovery. Any document described in such a list as an original document is deemed to be admitted by the party upon whom the list is served to be original and to have been printed,

---

21. RSC 1965, Ord. 27, r. 2(2).
22. RSC 1965, Ord. 27.
23. RSC 1965, Ord. 27, r. 3.
24. Not later than 21 days after the action is set down for trial (RSC 1965, Ord. 27, r. 2(1)).
25. RSC 1965, Ord. 62, r. 6(7).

written or executed as it purports to have been,[26] and any document described as a copy is deemed to be admitted to be a true copy. These rules apply to all documents save those whose authenticity is specifically denied in a pleading. The rules further provide that a notice may be served stating that the authenticity of a listed document is not admitted,[27] so as to avoid the implied admission.

These provisions are of great importance on two grounds. First, they highlight the advisability of ensuring that a list of discovery documents is properly prepared and that it accurately and completely describes all the documents listed, so as to obtain the fullest advantage of the implied admission. Second, it is essential in considering any list of documents to assess whether the nature, date or content of any document which is listed may need to be challenged. In such a case it is necessary to serve a notice specifying that the authenticity of the document is to be challenged. This can be of particular importance in computer cases where the dating and content of software records may be the subject of considerable dispute.

9.7 BURDEN AND STANDARD OF PROOF

The rules relating to the burden and standard of proof create some of the most intractable conceptual problems in the law of evidence. Most of these problems arise from a failure to appreciate the nature of the obligation imposed upon a party in adducing evidence, and upon which party that obligation is imposed. The first important distinction is between the burden of proof and the standard of proof. The burden of proof is used to describe the party upon which the obligation to establish something is placed. The standard of proof describes the degree of certainty with which the thing must be established.

The standard of proof in civil cases is always on the balance of probabilities. That means that the tribunal must be satisfied on the evidence that what is alleged is more likely to be correct than not. If it cannot determine whether this is so, then the burden of proving the fact has not been discharged by the party upon whom it is placed. This is in contrast to the standard of proof in criminal case which, on the prosecution, is to establish a fact beyond reasonable doubt, and where there is a burden placed on the defence, merely to establish such a doubt.

The burden of proof is used, usually without clear distinction, in relation to two entirely different things: the legal burden and the evidential burden. It is the failure to distinguish between these which leads to many failures of understanding as to the meaning of the term. The legal burden is the burden placed on a party of proving that which he asserts. It is a fixed burden, and rests on him from the beginning to the end of the case. It is only discharged if, at the end of the trial, on the balance of the evidence the fact has been established to the required standard.

26. RSC 1965, Ord. 27, r. 4(1).
27. This may be done at any time up to 21 days after inspection or after the time for inspection has passed (RSC 1965, Ord. 27, r. 4(2)).

In parallel with the legal burden is an evidential burden to adduce evidence to support the assertion. This is discharged initially by adducing evidence which supports the assertion. The result of adducing such evidence is to place upon the opposite party an evidential burden to displace that evidence by evidence of his own. If he succeeds in doing so, there is a further evidential burden placed upon the first party to displace this evidence and so meet the legal burden. This is often referred to as the shifting evidential burden, and this may move between the parties a number of times during the course of a trial. It has no effect on the legal burden, which rests throughout on the party seeking to prove the particular fact.

A practical example of the operation of these rules is when the plaintiff alleges that his software has been copied. The legal burden of doing so rests on him throughout the trial. He may seek to establish this fact by pointing to similarities between the expression of his program and the alleged copy. From this the court will infer that copying has occurred, and the plaintiff has at that point shifted the evidential burden on to the defendant, who must adduce evidence to explain how the similarities arose other than by copying the plaintiff's program. He may, for example, adduce evidence that the form of the particular code is governed by other programs or files with which it has to interact, or that the parts of the code said to be copied are common to a number of programs from different sources. The effect of this evidence will be to discharge the evidential burden on the defendant arising from the inference of copying. The evidential burden then shifts back to the plaintiff, who can discharge it by establishing in cross-examination of the defendant's witnesses that there are parts of the code which contain mistakes unique to the plaintiff's and defendant's program. If accepted, that will discharge the evidential burden placed upon the plaintiff and result in him discharging the legal burden which has rested on him throughout.

9.8   DOCUMENTARY EVIDENCE

9.8.1   Discovery generally

Underlying the whole modern approach to adversarial litigation in the English system is the process of discovery and the resultant availability to each party of the opposite party's documents. These are, as noted above, probably the most telling evidence in civil proceedings. Discovery is therefore probably the most important single facet of the litigation process.

Modern discovery has its origins in the process by which the courts of equity compelled the production of documents and verification of facts. The common law courts had a much more technical and limited approach to the disclosure of documents,[28] with the result that before the fusion of the two systems a party to a common law suit who, in order to pursue that suit, required disclosure of documents he could not obtain under the common law rules, had to file a bill in equity for discovery pending which the common law action was adjourned. With the fusion of the courts of law and equity the two systems became one,

---

28. For example, production of documents referred to in a pleading could be required. That rule is now found in RSC 1965, Ord. 24, r. 10.

with the result that unless one is aware of the origins of each particular form of discovery, the relationship between its various aspects may appear somewhat chaotic. In addition, following the decision of the House of Lords in *Norwich Pharmacal Co.* v *Commissioners of Customs & Excise* [1974] AC 133, an action for discovery alone is now available against persons who are not themselves wrongdoers and could therefore not properly be made parties to litigation claiming relief for that wrong, provided they can be shown to have become embroiled in some way in the wrong's commission. This jurisdiction is also the basis for the grant of the disclosure relief normally given in association with *Anton Piller* orders and *Mareva* injunctions.

Nowadays the term 'discovery' is generally used to refer only to the disclosure of documents, either in an action for discovery or in proceedings generally. In this context the term 'document' is not limited to what would colloquially be described as such but extends to tape recordings,[29] microfilm, computer disks and all other forms of recording information which can be extracted, whether by direct inspection or with the aid of 'the appropriate equipment'.[30]

9.8.2 The obligation to give discovery in the course of proceedings
There is an obligation on parties to litigation to give discovery of all documents which are or have been in their possession 'relating to any matter in question between them in the action'.[31] Since the decision in *Compagnie Financiere et Commerciale du Pacifique* v *Peruvian Guano Co.* (1882) 11 QBD 55 it has been clear that this obligation is not limited to documents admissible in evidence, but extends to any document it would be reasonable to think 'contains information which may enable the party applying for discovery either to advance his own case or to damage that of his adversary'. A document falls into this class 'if it is a document which may fairly lead him to a train of enquiry which may lead him to either of these two consequences'.[32]

This obligation is extremely wide ranging and gives a party very considerable opportunity to examine his opponent's case from the inside. An important consequence is that it gives outsiders a great deal of information they would not otherwise have, and it is accordingly balanced by the implied obligation not to disclose or make use of discovered documents other than for the purposes of the action.[33] Breach of this obligation is a contempt of court, although it no longer applies to documents which have been read in open court.[34]

It is important to appreciate that there is no right to hold documents back from discovery on the ground that they are confidential. To balance the fears

---

29. *Grant* v *Southwestern & County Properties Ltd* [1975] Ch 185.
30. See also the very broad definition of 'document' in s. 10(1) of the Civil Evidence Act 1968, which extends the meaning of 'document' to cover anything on which information is recorded in a manner in which it can be recovered.
31. RSC 1965, Ord. 24, r. 2(1).
32. *Compagnie Financiere et Commerciale du Pacifique* v *Peruvian Guano Co.* (1882) 11 QBD 55 at p. 63.
33. *Alterskye* v *Scott* [1948] 1 All ER 489.
34. Since the addition of RSC 1965, Ord. 24, r. 14A reversing *Home Office* v *Harman* [1983] 1 AC 280. The rule does not apply retrospectively.

of a party that his confidential material will be abused, the court will, if necessary, limit the extent of disclosure by making orders for commercially sensitive documents to be inspected only by independent experts or named individuals, upon undertakings to keep them confidential.[35]

This can be particularly important in computer litigation where the contents of a party's source code will almost certainly be highly confidential and commercially sensitive. In cases involving claims of software piracy it is common for orders to be made limiting the disclosure and use of the source code.[36] For example, orders that the material may only be inspected at the offices of the disclosing party's solicitor and that no copies may be made are common, although the courts have so far shown reluctance to insist on the use of independent experts in such cases because of the cost and time involved in educating them in the intricacies of the software in question. As with many other aspects of the development of computers, things are changing rapidly here. With the advent of wider, industry-standard operating methods and systems, the number of experts who are able to deal much more readily with the software of others is growing, and it may well be that the courts will be more willing to insist on their use where serious wrongdoing is alleged.

9.8.3 Orders for discovery in proceedings

The court may order further discovery either generally or in relation to specific documents which the party applying for discovery is able to show are or have been in the other's possession.[37] Under these rules the court can also require a party to swear an affidavit explaining what has become of documents no longer in his possession or to verify that there are no such documents. This is one of the most important aspects of the evidential process in technological litigation. Using these rules a party can force his opponent to disclose his working papers or materials or explain what has happened to them. Fault logs and rectification records can be forced out of a party. This can reveal precisely the information that a dissatisfied user needs to make good his claim that a particular aspect of his system is defective. It can also force a party's hand because it is difficult to explain the production of documents whose existence has previously been denied in an affidavit.

For these reasons proper use of the wide-ranging powers of the court to order discovery is vital to the successful prosecution of computer-related litigation.

9.8.4 The action for discovery

This was recreated in modern jurisprudence by *Norwich Pharmacal Co.* v *Commissioners of Customs & Excise* [1974] AC 133 and is a powerful, if costly,[38] weapon which enables a potential litigant to extract information about the

---

35. See, e.g., *Format Communications Mfg Ltd* v *ITT (United Kingdom) Ltd* [1983] FSR 473.
36. Ibid., and see also *Warner-Lambert Co.* v *Glaxo Laboratories Ltd* [1975] RPC 354.
37. RSC 1965, Ord. 24, rr. 3 and 7.
38. In an action for discovery against a person who is not himself a wrongdoer, the plaintiff will normally have to pay all the costs of those proceedings, although they may be recoverable as damages in subsequent proceedings against the wrongdoer revealed by the action for discovery; see *Morton-Norwich Products Inc.* v *Intercen Ltd (No. 2)* [1981] FSR 337.

identity of the wrongdoer and the extent of the wrongdoing from someone who has merely become involved in the commission of that wrong.

Although this action is now routinely used to ground applications for interlocutory discovery of the identities of other infringers in intellectual property actions, it has limitations. It cannot be used to obtain the names of customers to whom goods have been supplied in infringement of copyright because, without knowledge of the claim, they are not themselves wrongdoers, so to order their disclosure would be to enable the plaintiff to make good his claim against them.[39]

9.8.5 Documents protected by privilege

As has been seen, it is not a ground for non-production of documents that they are confidential. However, documents are not required to be disclosed if they are protected by privilege. The most important categories of privileged documents are those protected by legal professional privilege and the privilege against self-incrimination.[40] A full discussion is beyond the present chapter,[41] but a basic understanding of legal professional privilege is essential to an appreciation of the limitations on discovery.

Documents protected by legal professional privilege fall into two broad classes; those protected only when litigation was contemplated or pending, and those protected in any event. In essence, communications between a party and his legal advisers by which advice is sought or given are in the latter class unless the nature of the advice, or whether it was given, are themselves in issue. Other communications between lawyers and third parties, and some documents passing between a party and others in the course of gathering evidence, are in the former class. The law on this is not entirely clear, and a document which has more than one purpose may well fall to be disclosed even though one of those purposes was actual or potential proceedings. There are now special rules relating to privilege for communications with patent and trade mark agents.[42]

An important and often overlooked aspect of the protection of privilege is that it is an evidential and not a substantive rule. Thus, if secondary evidence of the contents of a privileged document is available, it is admissible in evidence[43] provided the evidence has not been obtained improperly,[44] and a

---

39. *Roberts v Jump Knitwear* [1981] FSR 527. That case was decided under the previous copyright law, and it will be interesting to see how the courts approach the same problem under the more relaxed requirement of the Copyright, Designs and Patents Act 1988 that, to be a secondary infringer, one only has to have 'reason to believe' that the goods are infringing – see 4.4.3.

40. Which is not available in claims relating to intellectual property following the passing of the Supreme Court Act 1981, s. 72, statutorily reversing *Rank Film Distributors Ltd* v *Video Information Centre* [1982] AC 380.

41. For further information see C. Style and C. Hollander, *Documentary Evidence* (London: Longman, 1991) and the extensive and informative notes to RSC 1965, Ord. 24 in the *Supreme Court Practice* (the White Book).

42. Copyright, Designs and Patents Act 1988, ss. 280 and 284. The protection for communications with patent agents has existed since the Civil Evidence Act 1968, but that for communications with trade mark agents is new and reverses the previous law.

43. *Calcraft v Guest* [1898] 1 QB 759.

44. *ITC Film Distributors Ltd* v *Video Exchange Ltd* [1982] Ch 431.

claim that a person intends to use a copy of a document in litigation is no answer to an order for its delivery up by the person in whom the privilege in the original is vested.[45]

9.9 EXPERT EVIDENCE

9.9.1 The nature and role of expert evidence
Expert evidence is nearly always essential in actions involving technical issues. The role and purpose of experts is to educate the court and explain to it the technical matters which arise in the action, so that the court thus educated can properly adjudicate upon the matters in issue. Thus experts can explain the meanings of words used in documents as terms of scientific art, but they cannot construe the document in the light of the meaning so attributed to the words. That is a matter solely for the court. Experts may give evidence on any matters in which there is recognised skill and learning. For example, accountants now commonly give evidence on assessment of damages in commercial cases, and market researchers on the ascertainment of public opinion.[46] However, for present purposes the discussion will be confined to technical expert evidence, which is the most important kind. The usual rule that there is no property in a witness applies equally to expert witnesses as to witnesses of fact.[47]

Expert evidence usually consists of both fact and opinion. Experts are often able to recognise particular facts (such as the function and structure of a computer program written in a language with which they are familiar) which are not evident to those without their skill and training. In addition experts can also draw inferences from those and other facts which require the use of their surrounding knowledge. However, experts can only give their opinion based upon material which has itself been proved in evidence. Thus, the primary facts upon which the expert's views are based must, unless they are matters on which the expert is able to give direct evidence or are admitted or agreed, be separately proved by witnesses of fact who are able to give admissible evidence of them.

9.9.2 Technical issues on which expert evidence is appropriate
In most technological cases there will be issues which can only be resolved if the court understands something about the technological background to the case. Take one of the simplest examples: where infringement of copyright in a computer program is alleged. The plaintiff's evidence is that there is a series of similarities between his and the defendant's program code which indicate that there has been derivation. The defendant's answer is that the areas of alleged

---

45. *Goddard* v *Nationwide Building Society* [1987] QB 670.
46. Although the use of such evidence has a highly chequered career in the English courts, often having been roundly condemned by judges unwilling to step outside areas of which they have a personal, intuitive understanding.
47. An expert witness who has given an opinion to one side can also do so for the other side in the same proceedings and can be subpoenaed by the other side, although it is highly undesirable that this should happen (*Harmony Shipping Co. SA* v *Saudi Europe Line Ltd* [1979] 1 WLR 81).

similarity are mere commonplace routines used by many programmers in such circumstances. The plaintiff relies in particular upon the fact that particular arrays of data have the same dimensions and structure in both programs. The court will be unable to resolve this dispute unless it understands the nature of the routines and code in question, and how they are derived by programmers. For example, the material complained of may be part of the input and output routines for particular configurations of hardware and operating system, so that the way in which the data are packaged and moved is dictated to the programmer. The setting up of identical arrays to hold that data would then be innocuous. But the court can only judge this in the light of an explanation of the limitations placed on a programmer by the system within which he is working. Nothing but evidence from an appropriately qualified expert can assist the court in these circumstances.

This does not necessarily mean that an independent expert must be instructed to prepare and give such evidence. The programmers themselves are perfectly qualified, and may well be the ideal witnesses to explain to the court how the task is defined and carried out.

Expert evidence is generally most useful for educating the court in the workings and limitations of the particular hardware and software in issue in the action. Much impenetrable jargon is used by those in the computer world, and a concise and comprehensible explanation of what it means is indispensable in the proper presentation of technological cases to the court.

9.9.3   Practice

The use of expert evidence is now closely controlled by rules of court.[48] The effect of these rules is to limit the number of expert witnesses who can be called, and to require preparation and exchange of reports setting out the substance of the evidence the experts will give. In practice such reports are treated as the experts' evidence in chief. A practice[49] is growing up of requiring experts to meet and draw up a joint report of the matters on which they are agreed. Such matters then cease to be the subject of contention at the trial; agreed reports can be highly valuable in saving time during the trial.

9.9.4   Some practical considerations in using experts

The courts have issued cautions against expert reports being settled by lawyers and as a result turning into pieces of advocacy of their clients' case. As Lord Denning MR said of a report he found guilty of this, 'it wears the colour of special pleading rather than an impartial report'.[50] Reports cast in this vein usually do more harm than good. It is therefore important to ensure that the expert's views are not coloured by the result he knows his client is seeking. In

---

48. The general High Court rules are to be found in RSC 1965, Ord. 38, rr. 35 to 44. The substantive rules, rr. 37 to 44, are applied in the county court by CCR 1981, Ord, 20, rr. 27 and 28. For patent actions the rules are slightly different and are found in RSC 1965, Ord. 104, rr. 13 and 14. For an explanation of their operation see 9.5.
49. Taken from the procedure usually adopted before the official referees.
50. *Whitehouse* v *Jordan* [1980] 1 All ER 650 at p. 655.

any event, if he does not think his client's case is sound, it is better to discover this at an early stage so that the prospects can be reassessed before substantial costs are incurred.

A good expert can, and often does, turn a case. The value of an expert and the effect of his evidence depend entirely upon his being fully involved in consideration of all matters which bear on his testimony. It is nearly always cheaper and better in the long run to bring in any necessary expert witnesses at the earliest opportunity to deal with the technical issues.

An expert's report should be much more than just a summary of what he will say. It is the document to which the judge should be turning at every opportunity to understand the nature of the case. It is crucial that it is drafted so as to set out clearly in language which will be understood by the court the matters of fact which are important and upon which the expert's views are based. It must then set out fully and precisely the reasoning by which those views are derived from the base material. For example, where there is an issue as to the functioning of a particular piece of software and it is sought to demonstrate by an operational test of that software what results, it is essential that the report sets out clearly the precise sequence of operations performed, identifies the output resulting from each operation, and explains what the contents of the output mean both directly and in relation to the point being made.

These matters ought to be obvious from first principles. In practice one comes across numerous expert reports which are masses of technical detail with no clear conclusions or, worse, baldly stated conclusions with no explanation of how or from what they are derived. Such reports are not only unhelpful in the subsequent preparation for and presentation in court but can be positively destructive, because they make the judge feel that the expert's views are not to be relied upon even when they are in fact sound. Unfortunately the production of a good expert report is not easy. It demands considerable time – and hence cost – and the involvement of both lawyers and experts working closely together.

9.10   ASSEMBLING EVIDENCE AND PRESENTING IT TO THE COURT

9.10.1   What evidence?

The principal types of action in which the functioning of a computer is likely to be at issue are those in which it is said that a computer system does not perform properly, and those in which it is said that it contains software or parts copied from something else in infringement of intellectual property rights.

Each of these types of actions presents its own particular problems of establishing the facts and proving them in evidence. This has to be done in at least two stages. The first is when the information is gathered at the outset to determine whether there is the basis for a claim or defence, and the second when the cases on either side have been pleaded so that it has (or should have) become apparent what are the issues which are in truth in dispute. With these points in mind, what to look for in each case and how to present it to the court will now be considered.

9.10.2 Claims for poor system performance

The principal problems for lawyers dealing with claims of this type fall into three main categories:

(a) Establishing the nature and terms of the contract and any associated representations.

(b) Finding out what each of the parties to the transaction thought the computer system was supposed to do.

(c) Finding out what the system will actually do.

If you deal successfully with each of these, you are well on the way to resolving a dispute. There is an additional problem of a rather different kind; determining the nature of the contract under discussion. Was it a contract for the supply of a complete system from one supplier who was obtaining the parts of it from other suppliers, or was it a contract for the supply of a number of 'boxes' to be put together by the user. In each case the nature of the obligations undertaken by the supplier, express or implied, is likely to be rather different. The legal consequences of a failure of one or more parts of the system to perform properly, or to perform properly together, will also obviously be rather different.

Evidentially the nature and terms of the contract will be found or elucidated by the documents (if any) which appear to constitute the contract, the temporally surrounding documents both before and after the contractual documents, and the contents of any conversations in which these documents and the nature of the computer system were discussed between the parties. It is an unfortunate fact that in many cases major purchases of computer equipment are made without great thought being devoted to what the system is to do. This problem is increasing as multi-user microcomputers with large quantities of package software flood the market at ever lower prices. It is therefore more than possible that there will be very little in the way of formal documentation other than an invoice with some standard terms which may be utterly inappropriate for the transaction in which they are used.

Perhaps the first document to look for is the system specification. If there is one at all, and there often is not, it should cast considerable light on what the parties thought they were talking about. But beware of the pitfalls contained in such documents. There is no definition of what a system specification should contain. Nor is there even agreement within the industry about how such documents should be prepared. With off-the-shelf packages, there may be no more than a user manual with additional 'help' files on the disks containing the program, to deal with problems which have come to light in using the software or, more usually, the manual itself.

Many modern microcomputer-based systems are a hotchpotch of hardware, operating system software and application software. The number of cases in which the supplying dealer has simply failed to establish that all the elements of the system are wholly compatible with each other is legion. With such systems it is essential to establish precisely the make and model or version of each part of the system. For example, some versions of some operating systems are incompatible with particular models of microcomputer although they work perfectly on previous and subsequent models. The reason for this is that the designer of either the hardware or software has made a change to some aspect of its operation without any specific reference or explanation. This is fine so long as the changes do not result in unforeseen consequences elsewhere in the system. The complexity of most operating systems and the hardware on which they run, coupled with the propensity of programmers to take short cuts if they possibly can, means that this is not always so. The result not infrequently is that the use of an illegal instruction in the microchip instruction set, or the use of an instruction in circumstances in which the chip designer did not intend it to be used, causes serious operating problems. The reason that they disappear in subsequent versions is simply that they have been reported and corrected. Only someone with a close and detailed knowledge of the number and type of version and model changes to the equipment in question will be aware of the rise and fall of many of these problems. In order to define the nature and extent of the failure it is necessary to use the services of such a person as an expert for guidance. Accordingly it is vital to establish at the outset exactly what hardware and software are being talked about before going on to consider the problems themselves. If this not done, the expert adviser will not be able to assist effectively.

If there is no system specification, then it will be necessary to find the exchange of correspondence or meeting notes which were used in substitution for it. Only in the last resort should mere recollection be relied upon, even at the earliest stages of investigating the problem. The human memory is notoriously fallible when it comes to trying to recall details of discussions and arrangements entered into some time before, and precision in such detail is essential in dealing with these claims. If it is necessary to rely solely upon recollection, it is essential that it is checked against any contemporary documents which do exist. For example, if it is suggested that a payroll facility was ordered but there is none on the system and no sign of any software links which would enable a payroll system to be coupled to the other ledgers to produce management accounts, the discrepancy must be investigated so that it becomes clear why, if there was intended to be a payroll facility, it was to stand apart from the rest of the system.

Having found the system specification (or such documents as there are in substitution) and established a proper description of the hardware and software, the next step is to determine with these and other surrounding documents what the parties thought the system was supposed to do. It is necessary to reconstruct the negotiations and discussions which led to the contract for the system being entered into. Using this technique, it should be possible to discover what numbers and types of transactions were contemplated, what functional operations the system was to perform on the data, how many terminals the system was to have and what they were to be used for, and so on. Properly carried out this task will be well rewarded, for it will enable a much more accurate assessment of the merit of the claim being made.

9.10.3   Claims for infringement of intellectual property rights

For the purpose of examining the evidential issues, it is easiest to include in this category claims relating to breach of confidence and other related claims which might be thought not to constitute intellectual property as this term is generally used, as well as contractual terms limiting the use which may be made of a computer system or software. They raise substantially similar factual and evidential problems. In each case the task is to establish whether anything has been copied, and if so, what.

For a full trial it is necessary to take copies of the programs and assess them against each other for evidence of similarity. This has to be done on source code material which is intelligible to human beings and is a task best performed by experts in the case. The results of that examination can be presented in joint or separate experts' reports. In assembling the evidence for this to be done it is important to ensure that all stages of the development process, from the overall program design down to the coding and updating of the individual modules, are looked at. If they are from your own side, it is essential to search them all out or to establish where they have gone. If from the other side, it is important to pursue discovery until you are as certain as possible that everything has been dug out and disclosed. From these and the surrounding documents it should be possible to determine, with the assistance of a good expert, whether or not there has been copying.

Interlocutory injunctions present special problems of proof of infringement, for there will often be scant evidence available of the source code of an allegedly infringing program. All the plaintiff will have access to at best is the defendant's object code. *Thrustcode Ltd* v *WW Computing Ltd* [1983] FSR 502 is a powerful demonstration of the problems a plaintiff can face. Megarry V-C rejected a claim for an interlocutory injunction, the plaintiff having produced little of its own source code and none of the defendant's. He observed that in such cases it might often be impossible for the plaintiff at that stage of the litigation to demonstrate directly that there had been copying. He rejected the plaintiff's attempt, by producing evidence that the functions performed by its program had been copied, to raise an inference that the source code had been copied.

However, there are other ways of dealing with this problem, at least in principle. Where there has been slavish copying of the object code and the plaintiff can obtain a copy of the defendant's program, comparison of the hexadecimal or binary printout should show this. Where the plaintiff's case is more complex, for example, that the source code has been translated into another language, the plaintiff's task in evidence is to assemble sufficient circumstantial evidence such as access, copying of parts of manuals, displayed technology and suchlike, to shift the evidential burden of proof on to the defendant to displace the inference of copying. Of course, if the defendant can do this, the claim fails.

9.10.4   The nature and role of systems tests and simulations

The systems test or simulation is often a vital part of the evidence in claims for poor system performance or infringement of copyright. By conducting a systems test it is possible to demonstrate exactly how a computer system performs under set conditions. The test is usually set up by one of the parties' experts and attended by representatives of both, although there is obviously no objection to the form of the tests being agreed between the experts, possibly as a result of their preliminary meeting.

In a claim concerned with system performance the object of the test is to establish how the system functions under particular conditions. The test should be designed to create the circumstances under which each alleged fault condition manifests itself in order to determine whether or not the fault is present. It is surprising how often a fault which has been complained of cannot be demonstrated when this is done. Sometimes this is because the fault arises from incorrect use of the system which is not properly recorded. This is usually revealed when the expert is seeking his instructions to set up the test. Sometimes, however, it is because the faulty operation has been disguised by temporary or partial 'bug fixes', the nature and operation of which have not been properly documented. It is faults of this kind which demonstrate the value of discovery most clearly: the description of similar faults on other systems disclosed in the discovery will greatly assist in determining how the fault is caused and thus how to recreate it.

In copyright infringement cases a test or simulation can be used to demonstrate whether or not the functions and routines of the allegedly copied program operate in exactly the same way in both programs. If so, the inference of copying is almost irresistible, even if the tell-tale markers of copying have otherwise been removed.[51] A program which does not show such similarity to the program it is copied from is very unlikely to be sufficiently similar to infringe unless areas of code have simply been copied directly.

9.10.5   Presenting the evidence to the court

Courts are traditional creatures and, until relatively recently, have preferred to receive evidence in the traditional form of oral evidence from live witnesses. Explanation in this way of what is in the technical documents has been thought to be the most comprehensible form of material to a judge. Oral evidence is led from a witness duly sworn. This is, however, a slow and generally laborious way of receiving information, particularly about technical facts. As has been noted in 9.4 and 9.5 above, expert and hearsay evidence have to be disclosed in advance of the trial. This practice has now been extended to direct witnesses of fact as well.[52]

Under this procedure the court may order disclosure in the form of written witness statements of the oral evidence the party intends to adduce at the trial. The court may direct that the statement stands as the witness's evidence in chief and, where a statement is served under an order for disclosure of witness statements, no further evidence may be led from the witness save by consent or with the leave of the court except in relation to new matters which have arisen in the course of the trial. Whilst use of this practice remains optional, in

---

51. See, e.g., *M.S. Associates Ltd* v *Power* [1988] FSR 242 and 4.5.6.
52. RSC 1965, Ord. 38, r. 2A.

the Chancery Division and the Commercial Court the approach is now that such orders will be made on the summons for directions unless one of the parties objects, when he must raise the point specifically for decision.[53] It is normal, in the interests of fairness, that the orders made under this procedure provide for mutual exchange of witness statements (as is also done with expert reports) in order to prevent one party from obtaining the advantage of seeing the other's evidence before preparing his own.

This practice has the potential greatly to reduce the length of trials, particularly if used in conjunction with the scheme now operating in the Patents Court, the Patents County Court and the Commercial Court where the judge will read large parts of the documents before the commencement of the trial so that he begins the hearing with an understanding of the areas of dispute and the parties' respective positions in relation to them. There is, however, some anecdotal evidence that the costs of trial preparation are being significantly increased by the requirement for witness statements. As these have to be disclosed to the opposition, it is essential that they are carefully honed. The quality of the proofs of witnesses' evidence which were previously prepared only for internal circulation often left a lot to be desired. Nevertheless, full disclosure before the trial of the evidence to be adduced is generally thought to be beneficial to the parties, not least by removing unfairness created by the element of surprise arising from new matters only coming out during the trial. From the advocate's point of view there is no doubt that the new approach greatly assists in the preparation of a case for trial. Overall, experience so far of the use of witness statements has generally been that they are extremely valuable. It is likely that they will be used in almost all cases in time.

Evidence may now also be given by witnesses not present at a trial by a video conference link if the trial judge so directs. This was so held at first instance in *Garcin* v *Amerindo Investment Advisors Ltd* [1991] 1 WLR 1140 and the decision has since been approved by the Court of Appeal in *Henderson* v *SBS Realisations* (13 April 1992 unreported). The court will, it appears, make such an order where witnesses are abroad and it is cheaper and easier to take evidence by video link than to have the evidence taken on commission abroad before the trial.

Preparation of witnesses to give evidence is a difficult matter, particularly now that they will not in general be giving evidence in chief before they are cross-examined. It is not thought proper in the English litigation system to prepare witnesses in the manner commonly done in the US, where important witnesses will be taken through their evidence and cross-examined by attorneys pretending to represent the opposition. However, some preparation is clearly necessary, if only to ensure that a full and accurate witness statement is obtained. In addition, someone who is unfamiliar with the court-room atmosphere and the nature of an adversarial hearing may well not give his evidence as completely and convincingly as it deserves, merely because of that. It is necessary too for witnesses to be taken carefully through all important documents which concern them, with particular reference to documents

---

53. *Practice Direction (Chancery: Summons for Directions)* [1989] 1 WLR 133.

created or modified by the witness, and asked to explain what is in the document. This is not a task which can be safely left to the witnesses themselves. They do not know what they are looking for. Only a lawyer who has been through the evidence as described above will be able properly to direct their attention to the critical parts of the documents.

Other ways in which evidence can be presented helpfully in technical cases include models or demonstrations of the operation of a computer system or particular aspects of a program and agreed written descriptions of the operation of the equipment in dispute. Agreed descriptions have become considerably more popular in the courts as they have had to struggle with ever more complex technical matters; that which the parties agree the judge does not have to decide. As a result the court will often direct that one of the parties prepares such a description and that the parties endeavour to agree it. This at least enables the areas in which the parties disagree to be pinpointed so that time is not wasted at the trial.

At present relatively little use is made of video recordings, slides or other visual aids in technical cases. There is no reason in principle why such materials should not be used. For example, computer simulations of various kinds have been used in criminal fraud trials to demonstrate points which would be extremely difficult to explain by traditional methods, particularly to a jury. It is certainly the writer's impression that, since the first edition of this book appeared, the courts are generally demonstrating a much greater willingness to receive evidence in less conventional ways if the justice of the case requires them to do so.

9.11   A NOTE ON CRIMINAL EVIDENCE
Chris Reed

The application of the hearsay rule to criminal cases has always been particularly strict, in recognition of the danger of depriving a person of his liberty on evidence whose truth cannot be tested in cross-examination. However, modern business practices mean that in many cases the only record of some fact is contained in documents, often stored on a computer. If such records were never admissible, either the person who compiled the record would have to give oral evidence (stating, probably inaccurately, that the document had recalled the matter to his mind) or criminal conduct would go unpunished. The clearest illustration of this problem came in *Myers* v *Director of Public Prosecutions* [1965] AC 1001. In that case the defendant was accused of the theft of motor vehicles, and an essential part of the evidence was the serial numbers of the various vehicle parts, which had been noted down by workers as the vehicles were assembled and then transferred to microfilm. The House of Lords held that these records were inadmissible because they were hearsay, and that the only admissible evidence would have been that of the workers who recorded the numbers (who clearly could not be identified, or even if identified, could not swear truthfully that they recalled the serial numbers).

This case led to the Criminal Evidence Act 1965, now replaced by the Police and Criminal Evidence Act 1984 and the Criminal Justice Act 1988. The purpose of these statutes is to set out the circumstances in which documentary evidence will be admitted as an exception to the hearsay rule, and to make provision to ensure that such documents, when stored on computer, are sufficiently accurate to be used in evidence. The Court of Appeal has held in *R v Minors* [1989] 1 WLR 441 that computer records have to satisfy *both* these hurdles, and the mere fact that a record satisfies the accuracy requirements of the Police and Criminal Evidence Act 1984, s. 69, does not exempt it from the admissibility requirements of the Criminal Justice Act 1988, s. 24.

9.11.1   The distinction between 'real' and hearsay evidence

As explained earlier, a record stored on a computer will only be hearsay if it is a record of some observation made by a human being, in which case the human is prima facie the best source of evidence. If the information is collected directly by the computer itself it is not hearsay, and there are no barriers to its admissibility as evidence. The failure to understand this distinction led to the erroneous decision in *R v Pettigrew* (1980) 71 Cr App R 39. In that case the defendant was accused of the theft of some banknotes, and a Bank of England computer printout was used to show that the notes in his possession had previously been in the possession of the person from whom they were stolen. The procedure used for collecting the serial numbers of the notes was as follows: a bundle of notes with consecutive numbers was placed in an automatic sorting machine, the employee who did so recording the first and last numbers on a computer, and then the machine ran through the notes rejecting those which were defective and recording their numbers directly on the computer. Thus, except for the start and finish numbers, the record was produced by the computer with no human intervention. However, the Court of Appeal held that the printout was not admissible under the exceptions to the hearsay rule contained in the Criminal Evidence Act 1965 as no human being ever had knowledge of the numbers of the rejected notes. This decision is clearly incorrect – the evidence was not hearsay but real evidence of what the sorting machine did, and should thus have been admitted.[54]

In the later case of *R v Wood* [1982] Crim LR 667, however, the Court of Appeal took the opportunity to distinguish *R v Pettigrew* as a case on its own facts, and held that a computer analysis of spectrometer readings was not hearsay but real evidence and thus admissible. It should thus be clear that, wherever a computer record is a direct recording of external facts (e.g., the bar-code readings at a supermarket till) or a record of the operation of the computer itself and the results it produced, there will be no need to bring it within one of the exceptions to the hearsay rule for it to be admissible. This point has been confirmed by the Court of Appeal decision in *R v Spiby* (1990) 91 Cr App R 186, where it was held that an automatically recorded list of telephone calls made by the defendant from his hotel room did not have to satisfy the requirements of ss. 68 and 69 of the Police and Criminal Evidence Act 1984 as it was real evidence, not hearsay. However, the court will still need to be convinced that it is an accurate and authentic record, and expert evidence

---

54. See J. C. Smith, 'The Admissibility of Statements by Computer' [1981] Crim LR 387.

on this point may be required. Interestingly, in *R* v *Spiby* the court was satisfied on this point by evidence from the hotel manager that the computer had, so far as he knew, always produced accurate records. Indeed, the court was prepared to assume that a machine is working properly in the absence of evidence to the contrary. However, the defence did not contest the accuracy of the computer, merely the admissibility of its records. If the accuracy of the records were put in question it is likely that more detailed evidence would be required.

9.11.2   Exceptions to the hearsay rule

So far as computer records are concerned, the Criminal Justice Act 1988, s. 24, replacing the Police and Criminal Evidence Act 1984, s. 68, provides that documents arising from trade, business, professional, occupational or official activities which record information supplied by a person who has personal knowledge of the matters recorded is admissible in criminal proceedings provided the requirements of s. 23(2) or s. 24(4)(iii) are satisfied. Under s. 23(2), the document is admissible if the person who would otherwise give oral evidence is dead or unfit to testify, if he is abroad and it is not practicable for him to testify, or if he cannot be found although reasonable steps have been taken to find him. Perhaps more importantly, s. 24(4)(iii) permits the document to be given in evidence if the maker of the statement cannot reasonably be expected to remember the matters contained in the record.

Sections 25 to 28 of the 1988 Act give the court further powers to exclude the evidence if, for example, its exclusion is in the interest of justice or its admission would be prejudicial to the accused out of proportion to its probative value. It is important to note that, where a document is sought to be admitted under s. 24, oral evidence must be given that the requirements of the section have been complied with.[55] This is in contrast to the accuracy requirements of the Police and Criminal Evidence Act 1984, s. 69, which can be proved by certificate.

9.11.3   The accuracy of hearsay statements held on computer

Even where a computer-stored statement fulfils the requirements of s. 24 of the Criminal Justice Act 1988, it will not be admissible unless it also meets the provisions of the Police and Criminal Evidence Act 1984, s. 69(1). These are:

(a)   that there are no reasonable grounds to believe that improper operation of the computer renders the statement inaccurate;

(b)   that at all material times the computer was operating properly, or if not, that this does not affect the statement's accuracy; and

(c)   that any rules of court are satisfied. So far, no rules of court have been made under s. 69(2).

These provisions are designed to overcome any doubts about the accuracy of the statement, either because it was not stored correctly in the first instance or has become corrupt over time. This is not likely to be a problem with, say,

---

55. *R* v *Minors* [1989] 1 WLR 441.

a record of serial numbers which are input once and then stored until needed. However, if the computer is programmed to collate a number of separately input records (e.g., the various serial numbers of the component parts of a car) to make the record sought to be admitted, the court will need to be convinced that no inaccuracy has crept in during the processing of the data.

These matters may be evidenced by a certificate under para. 8 of sch. 3. The certificate must identify the document and describe the manner of its production, give particulars of the equipment used in its production, deal with the requirements of s. 69(1) and purport to be signed by a person 'occupying a responsible position in relation to the operation of the computer'. It is sufficient for the certificate to be signed to the best of the knowledge and belief of that person. Paragraph 9 gives the court power to require oral evidence of any of these matters, but it is unlikely to do so in practice unless the accuracy of the certificate is disputed.

Although the provisions of s. 69 only apply to hearsay evidence held on computer, the court will, as already stated, require some evidence of the accuracy of any real evidence which is sought to be adduced. Oral evidence will be needed on this matter, but the requirements of s. 69 provide a useful guide to what that oral evidence should contain.

CHAPTER TEN

Electronic data interchange

Chris Reed

10.1   WHAT IS EDI?

Electronic data interchange (EDI) is, at the simplest level, nothing more than a technology for exchanging information. One computer is linked to another and a stream of data is sent across the link. At this level, the only distinction from, say, a fax message is that the recipient can easily edit his copy.

Where EDI becomes interesting, both commercially and legally, is if the messages are structured in such a way that they can be processed automatically. The most common use of such messages is to carry out trade, particularly international trade, and it is in this sense that the term EDI is most commonly used. This also gives rise to the alternative term 'paperless trading', which is particularly common in the United States[1].

Structured EDI messages offer their users two potential benefits, which can be of immense commercial value:

(a)   The abolition (or near abolition) of the physical, paper documents which previously effected the transaction. Estimates of the costs involved in producing and processing this paper range as high as 10 per cent of the value of the goods.

(b)   The complete automation of the ordering/delivery/payment cycle.

10.1.1   Replacing paper
To take an example, suppose a motor manufacturer has a need to purchase parts from a supplier. In a paper-based system a human being examines the stock inventory, decides which parts are needed, and informs the purchasing

---

1. See, e.g., Wright, *The Law of Electronic Commerce* (Boston Mass: Little, Brown & Co., 1991).

department. The purchasing department issues an order to the supplier. Payment may need to be effected through a documentary credit, necessitating further communications between the manufacturer, one or more banks, and the supplier. Once the supplier has the parts ready to ship he must engage a carrier, thus generating further documentation which must be processed by all the parties involved in the transaction.

The EDI ideal is quite different. Here the manufacturer's stock control system automatically generates the order when stocks of any part are low. The order is sent without any human intervention to the supplier's computer, which accepts the order and commences manufacture. The payment mechanism is set up in a similar way, again with little or no human intervention, as is the contract of carriage. To perform the contract the only physical movement is that of the goods from the supplier's premises to those of the manufacturer. All the messages which would have been placed on paper and circulated along the chain of banks to the manufacturer are replaced by structured EDI messages which are processed automatically, the relevant portions being copied to accounting and other computer systems.

This technology exists and is in use, though not in quite such a perfect form as the example above. The benefits it brings are increasing the pressure for its adoption, as large customers force their suppliers to adopt EDI. The time saved in the ordering process makes 'just in time' ordering possible, cutting stocks held to the bare minimum. It also offers the flexibility of production seen in the Japanese motor industry where a production line can be switched from one model to another in a very short space of time. The manpower savings are also potentially large, as EDI prevents the redundant manual processing of information in stock control, purchasing and accounts departments.

10.1.2   EDI and networks

Whilst it is possible to set up dedicated EDI links with each of one's trading partners, this rarely makes sense in practice. The volume of communications is likely to be too small to be economical. For this reason most EDI users communicate via a Value Added Network Service (VAN) such as INS or AT&T Istel.

In this model the user's computer system generates the messages to the network, rather than directly to the intended recipient – see figure 10.1 on p. 256. The network's computer systems ensure, using the address information which is part of the message structure,[2] that the message is delivered to the addressee's computer. The delivery may be near-instantaneous or may take several hours, depending on the number of time zones which separate the parties and the level of service contracted for. In most cases there will be an element of 'store and forward' which, as we shall see, raises potential problems when forming contracts using EDI.

Additionally, the VAN may not be the only network involved. Although it is not common practice at present, the technology exists for a sender using one

---

2. See Walden (ed.), *EDI and the Law* (London: Blenheim OnLine, 1989), app. E for examples of message structures.

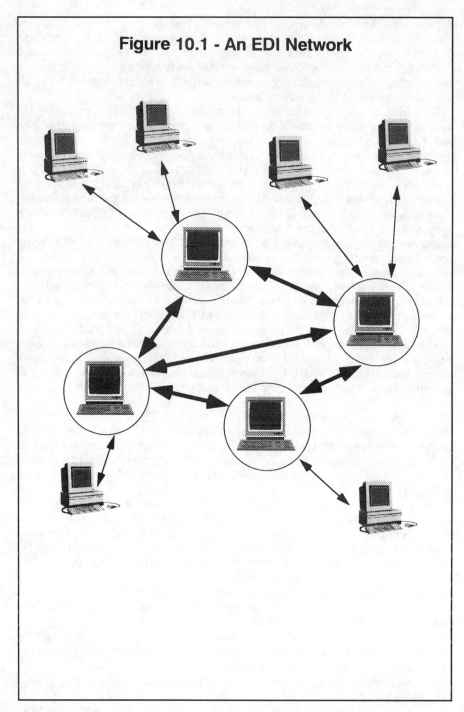

Figure 10.1 - An EDI Network

VAN to communicate with an addressee using another via a 'gateway' between the two VANs. The address segment of the message contains the information required to route the message to the gateway, and thence to the addressee across his own VAN. Linking VANs in this way raises interesting liability questions, as the nature of the legal relationship between the sender and the addressee's VAN is unclear.

10.2   LEGAL ISSUES[3]

The legal issues raised by EDI fall into two basic categories; those that arise between the user and the network provider(s) and those that arise between users themselves.

10.2.1   Issues between user and network provider

The relationship between a user and the VAN to which he connects is primarily contractual. Sa'id Mosteshar identifies four main responsibilities of the network provider:[4]

(a)   Conveyance of the message in the correct format and protocol.
(b)   Safeguarding against corruption of the message.
(c)   Securing that the message is conveyed to the recipient.
(d)   Preserving the confidentiality and security of the message.

The method by which these responsibilities are to be carried out will largely be covered by the user handbook, the technical manual for connecting to the VAN. It is most likely that the contract between user and network provider will contain an obligation that the user's communications with other users of the network should comply with the technical and operational requirements of the user handbook, but even if this is not expressly stated it is likely that the users will be contractually bound to each other under the principle in *Clarke* v *Dunraven* [1897] AC 59. The effect of the agreement will be to create a contract between each user and all the other users, either because entering into the agreement amounts to a standing offer to future users to be bound which is accepted by joining the system, or perhaps more logically, by impliedly giving the system provider authority to contract as agent on behalf of the user.

The contract may also make express provision for the level and quality of service to be provided, though in most cases VAN operators will seek to exclude much, if not all, of their liability for breach of these obligations.[5] These

---

3. These problems have been examined on an international scale in TEDIS, *The Legal Position of the Member States with respect to Electronic Data Interchange* (Brussels: EC Commission, 1991).

4. Mosteshar, *Liability issues of EDI* in Walden (ed.), *EDI and the Law* (London: Blenheim OnLine, 1989), p. 50.

5. One of the few exceptions to this practice is Swift, the Society for Worldwide Interbank Financial Telecommunications. Swift is a closed network for electronic funds transfer, used only by the banks which own it or organisations sponsored by a member. Swift limits its liability to 3,000 million Belgian francs per loss or series of losses caused by Swift's negligence, error or omission – see B. Petre, 'Network Providers' (1990) 7 CL&P 8, n. 18.

exclusions will be subject to the Unfair Contract Terms Act 1977, and may also be limited in scope by the terms of the network operator's telecommunications licence.[6]

The VAN operator's contractual liability to the user will primarily be based on the Supply of Goods and Services Act 1982, s. 13, which will imply into the contract an obligation to take reasonable care in supplying the service contracted for. This obligation may be breached in a number of ways:

(a) if the system goes down;
(b) if a message is not transmitted;
(c) if it is sent to the wrong person;
(d) if it is intercepted or copied by an unauthorised person; or
(e) if it is garbled in transmission.

In each case, however, the system provider will only be liable for breach of the implied term if the problem was caused by a lack of care. Such negligence might take one of two forms: a failure to be sufficiently careful in selecting the hardware and software which comprise the system, or a failure to take sufficient care in operating the system. Provided the hardware and software are from reputable sources, then unless the system provider is also the designer of the hardware or software a defect in either will not normally render him in breach.

Although there is no doubt that this term will be implied into the contract between the system provider and each user, it is less clear that the users are providing services to each other. It is probable that their contractual liability to other users, in the absence of a formal interchange agreement, is limited to observing the terms of their agreement with the VAN operator.

10.2.2 Issues between users

10.2.2.1 Contract formation Not all EDI transactions result in the formation of a contract. Although a number of attempts have been made to classify EDI messages according to the different legal problems raised,[7] for our purposes it is sufficient to note three broad categories:

The transmission of mere information Generally, the sender does not intend a message of this type to have legal consequences. Examples might range from the trivial

---

6. E.g., condition 7.1 of the Value Added Data Services Licence issued under the Telecommunications Act 1984 requires the operator to take reasonable steps to safeguard the privacy and confidentiality of messages.
7. For example, Goode and Bergsten identify five types of communication:
     (a) Communications having no legal significance.
     (b) Communications having legal significance.
     (c) Communications operative to transfer ownership, control or contract rights.
     (d) Communications required by law.
     (e) Communications requiring legal authority or licence.
   Thomsen and Wheble, *Trading with EDI: the Legal Issues* (London: IBC, 1989), pp. 131–3.

Our Chairman will arrive on the 15.20 flight

to the vital

Maximum safe operating pressure = 130 p.s.i.

The only legal problem arising from this type of message is the potential liability where the sender owes a duty to the recipient to take care to ensure that the information is correct, and as a result of his carelessness the recipient suffers loss.[8]

The transmission of unilateral notices　This type of communication will be intended to have a legal effect and will in most cases be made in performing an existing contract. Typical examples of this category might be invoices, which are often a prerequisite for payment, or a notice under a charterparty that a ship is ready to load, thus fixing the laytime and demurrage periods.

This type of communication may raise three sorts of legal questions:

(a)　Is it effective as a notice? This will often depend on whether the notice is required to be in writing, or if a signature is required.

(b)　When (and possibly where) does it take effect, i.e., is the sending or receipt the legally significant point?

(c)　If its sending or contents are disputed, can these facts be proved?

One important unilateral notice is the customs declaration. The penalties for false or non-declaration are severe, so the legal effect of such a notice is easily apparent. The required form and contents of customs declarations are set out in national legislation, which will thus answer the question of whether it is possible to replace the paper documents with an EDI transmission. The main problem with customs declarations at present appears to be a general insistence on a handwritten signature, and although the technology to replace written signatures exists its adoption requires amending legislation. A further obstacle to paperless trading is the wide variety of data formats used by different national customs authorities – the work of the Customs Cooperation Council on both these points may eventually lead to a solution.[9]

Contract formation　Where, for example, goods are ordered using an EDI message, the intended result will be the formation of a contract. In most cases such messages are part of a series including negotiation, ordering and acceptance. This type of communication raises the largest number of legal questions, in particular:

(a)　Can this particular type of contract be formed using EDI? There may be requirements such as writing or signature, depending on the national

---

8. *Hedley Byrne & Co. Ltd v Heller & Partners Ltd* [1964] AC 465.
9. See generally J. Morrin, 'The Effect of EDI on Administrative Procedures' in H. Thomsen and B. Wheble, *Trading with EDI: the Legal Issues* (London: IBC, 1989).

legislation. For example, in the UK a contract of marine insurance must be embodied in a marine insurance policy signed by the insurer,[10] and in the United States a contract for the sale of goods for a price of $500 or more must be evidenced in writing and signed by the party against whom it is enforced.[11]

(b) When, and more important where, was the agreement made? This may decide which national law is to apply to the contract if there is no effective choice of law clause.

(c) If the terms of the contract are later disputed, will it be possible to prove what was agreed?

Unless particular formalities such as writing are specifically required (see 10.2.2.4), the general rule of English law and of most other jurisdictions is that a contract is formed when the parties reach an agreement on its terms – this can be done orally, as our everyday experience in shops demonstrates. There is thus no theoretical objection to using EDI for this purpose. In English law, the process of formation is analysed into two stages: the offer, when one party sets out the terms on which he is prepared to contract, either in one document or by express or implied reference to a preceding course of negotiations; and the acceptance, when the other party agrees to these terms without attempting to amend them in any way. If both parties satisfactorily perform their side of the bargain there is no need to involve the law. However, there are three types of dispute which might arise, and which can be resolved by examining the formation process:

(a) One party believes a contract to have been concluded, but the other disputes it.

(b) Both agree that a contract has been formed, but disagree about its terms.

(c) The parties disagree about when and where the contract was formed.

In order to understand how English law will deal with these disputes, a number of basic principles of contract law must be borne in mind:

(a) Unless otherwise stated, an offer remains open for a reasonable time or until it is accepted or rejected by the other party.

(b) An offer may be withdrawn (unless there has been some payment to keep it open, i.e., an option) at any time before it is accepted, but this withdrawal is only effective when it reaches the other party.[12]

(c) A counter-offer, i.e., the suggestion of different terms, brings the original offer to an end, and no contract is formed until the new offer is accepted.[13] If the parties engage in a so-called 'battle of the forms' where each

---

10. Marine Insurance Act 1906, ss. 22 to 24.
11. Uniform Commercial Code, s. 201(1).
12. *Byrne* v *Van Tienhoven* (1880) 5 CPD 344.
13. *Hyde* v *Wrench* (1840) 3 Beav 334.

purports to contract on its own terms, the set of terms that applies will be those contained in the last offer made before acceptance.[14]

(d)   The contract is formed when, and where, acceptance takes place.

In applying these principles to EDI communications, it must also be noted that whilst offers and withdrawals of offers must actually be communicated to the other party[15] the rules governing acceptances are quite different. Where acceptance is made by some instantaneous means such as face-to-face communication or telephone, it too must actually reach the offeror. It has been held that telex communications are instantaneous, and thus contracts made by telex are made where the telex is received.[16] This rule is certain to apply to EDI communications where there is a direct link between the parties.

The position may, however, be different if the VAN across which the transmission is made stores the acceptance message for an appreciable period before it is delivered to the offeror. As common law lawyers learn at an early stage, if an acceptance is made in written form the 'postal rule' applies. This provides that the acceptance takes place *when the letter is posted*, whether or not it ever arrives.[17] Might the postal rule apply to such an EDI message of acceptance?

There are two justifications suggested for the postal rule. The first is that it is an *ad hoc* method for solving what is inevitably a difficult question (if the rule were that the letter had to be received, would it be relevant that it arrived but was never read, or not read before withdrawal of the offer?). Even if this justification is the correct one, the dictum of Lord Brandon of Oakbrook in *Brinkibon Ltd* v *Stahag Stahl und Stahlwarenhandelgesellschaft mbH* [1983] 2 AC 34 suggests that the postal rule might apply to EDI acceptances:[18]

> The cases on acceptance by letter and telegram constitute an exception to the general principle of the law of contract [on grounds of commercial expediency]. That reason of commercial expediency applies to cases where there is bound to be a substantial interval between the time when the acceptance is sent and the time when it is received. In such cases the exception to the general rule is more convenient, and makes on the whole for greater fairness, than the general rule itself would do.

The second justification is that the offeror has impliedly agreed that the accepting party may entrust the transmission of his acceptance to an independent third party, the postal authorities, and that therefore the offeree has done all that the offeror requires for acceptance when he posts his letter. This too would suggest that acceptance takes place when the message is received by the system provider's computer. The clearest analogy to using a

---

14. *Butler Machine Tool Co. Ltd* v *Ex-Cell-O Corporation (England) Ltd* [1979] 1 WLR 401.
15. *Byrne* v *Van Tienhoven* (1880) 5 CPD 344.
16. *Entores Ltd* v *Miles Far East Corporation* [1955] 2 QB 327.
17. *Adams* v *Lindsell* (1818) 1 B & Ald 681; *Household Fire Insurance Co.* v *Grant* (1879) 4 ExD 216.
18. [1983] 2 AC 34 at p. 48.

store and forward EDI system is with acceptance by telegram; it is necessary for the message actually to be communicated to the telegram service, normally by telephone (an instantaneous method of communication), but once it has been received by the service acceptance is complete.[19]

The result will be that the time of acceptance is the time the EDI message was received, and the place of acceptance will therefore be that node of the network which received the message. In most cases this is likely to be in the same jurisdiction as the acceptor, but not inevitably – it is easy to conceive a Scottish company accepting an offer from a US company using an EDI system, where the message of acceptance is sent to a computer in England. The contract would be formed in England, and subject to agreement to the contrary might therefore be subject to English law, at least in respect of its formation. Fortunately, the courts have accepted that it is permissible for the parties to stipulate what acts will constitute acceptance,[20] and it would seem essential that the interchange agreement should provide exactly when a message will be taken to have effect and which law is to govern the performance of the contract. There appears to be general agreement that an EDI message should not have operative effect until it is received.[21]

10.2.2.2 Interchange agreements The purpose of an interchange agreement is to set out the terms on which the communicating parties agree to use EDI. It is important to make a distinction between the interchange agreement, which deals only with the details of the communication process, and the underlying commercial transaction such as a sale of goods, which is entered into and performed using that communication process. Although in the US it is not uncommon for both to be dealt with in the same agreement, this practice arose from the way EDI has developed there, through large customers forcing their suppliers to trade with them via EDI. In Europe the practice has been rather different. Industry groupings such as ODETTE[22] or CEFIC[23] have developed protocols for EDI, and this has focused attention on the communications aspect of EDI rather than the underlying transaction. This separation makes theoretical and practical sense, as EDI can be used for many different types of underlying transactions without changing the agreement on interchange.

As the purpose of the interchange agreement is to bind the parties to a particular, structured form of communication, there are a number of issues which it must address. Because different industry sectors will inevitably have different specific requirements, no universal standard is achievable. However, a number of organisations have produced model interchange agreements which provide a useful starting-point for negotiations,[24] and on an international level the International Chamber of Commerce has produced the Uniform Rules of

---

19. *Re London & Northern Bank* [1900] 1 Ch 200.
20. *Holwell Securities Ltd* v *Hughes* [1974] 1 WLR 155.
21. UNCID Rules, art. 7(a); UK EDI Association, Electronic Data Interchange Agreement, arts 4.1 and 5.3.
22. The motor industry.
23. The chemicals industry.
24. See, e.g., the UK EDI Association's Electronic Data Interchange Agreement.

Conduct for Interchange of Trade Data by Teletransmission (the UNCID Rules). Within the EC, DG XIII has initiated the TEDIS[25] project which is examining the technical and legal issues involved in EDI. As part of its work, TEDIS will consider the production of a model interchange agreement.[26]

Although there is insufficient space in this chapter for a detailed examination of interchange agreements[27] it is useful to set out the main areas which such an agreement should cover:

(a) A requirement to adhere to the technical procedures of the chosen communication link. This is normally done by reference to the VAN user handbook.

(b) Agreement on a particular protocol for the message format, e.g., an EDIFACT message.

(c) Agreement on acknowledgements of messages and any confirmations of their content that are required.

(d) Agreement on which of the parties takes responsibility for the completeness and accuracy of the communication. As we have already seen, it is likely that the parties will wish the received version of a message to be operative, rather than that transmitted. For this reason it will be important that the technical safeguards in (a) to (c) above are incorporated to ensure that transmission takes place and that errors are immediately detected. Whilst message corruption is almost certain not to produce an apparently sensible message with an entirely different meaning, it is quite conceivable that a £ symbol could be replaced by a $ symbol, or that an entire block could be lost. As in general it is the received version which is operative, the onus to ensure correct transmission must be on the sender.

(e) Agreement on security and confidentiality.

(f) Agreement on data logs and the storage of messages.

10.2.2.3 Evidential problems[28] Computer-related evidence falls into two clear categories. Each consists of information output by a computer, either as a result of some operation it has performed or as a hard copy of data stored in some permanent form (e.g., on magnetic disk). The first category is where the computer is used as a compact filing cabinet in which are stored records of information provided to it by human beings. These records might be almost anything – observations of the weather, the amount for which a cheque is drawn, notes of a meeting – but their essential characteristic for the purposes of admissibility is that they originate in an observation by a human. The second category consists of records generated directly by a computer, e.g., an EDI

---

25. Trade Electronic Data Interchange Systems (OJ No. L 285, 8 October 1987).
26. See generally Troye, 'The European Community and EDI' in Walden (ed.), *EDI and the Law* (London: Blenheim OnLine, 1989), p. 90.
27. For more detail see Walden (ed.), *EDI and the Law* (London: Blenheim OnLine, 1989), chs. 5 and 6.
28. A detailed examination of the evidential problems of computer records can be found in chapter 9.

purchase order produced automatically by a stock control system and transmitted to the supplier. Here the record is of an observation made directly by the machine without human intervention.

There are three reasons why a record produced by a computer might be inadmissible as evidence:

(a) Because it is not an original. This does not appear to present any real problem in relation to computer records, as the original will in almost every case be a magnetically stored version of the record which cannot be examined directly. Where the original is not available, the courts are prepared to admit properly authenticated copies.[29]

(b) Because it is hearsay. A document is hearsay if it is a record of a statement made by a human being of some fact which that human being has observed, or some action in which that human being has been involved. However, a document that does not contain a record of such a statement is not in fact hearsay. If the EDI record is a record of observations made directly by the computer, then it will not be hearsay but *direct* or *real* evidence. In general, direct evidence is admissible *per se*, though there is some debate whether this applies to computer records. This matter is dealt with in detail in chapter 9.

(c) Because some rule of law prevents the evidence from being adduced. Some commentators have argued[30] that *all* computer records fall within the definition of a statement in the Civil Evidence Act 1968, s. 10(1), which provides that a statement includes 'any representation of fact, whether made in words or otherwise'. Computer records are clearly statements of fact and, so the argument goes, are therefore subject to the requirements of s. 5[31] which prevent the statement from being admitted unless the conditions laid down in that section are fulfilled. However, it should be noted that the courts have held that direct evidence produced by a computer is not subject to the hearsay rule,[32] and it seems probable that the Civil Evidence Act 1968, s. 5 applies only to hearsay statements.[33]

So far as EDI records are concerned, therefore, it seems probable that there will be little difficulty in persuading the courts that these records are admissible. Nonetheless, there is a substantial degree of uncertainty amongst computer users about whether the admissibility of their computer records will be attacked under the Civil Evidence Act 1968, s. 5.[34] This uncertainty is one of the factors delaying the widespread use of EDI. In the long term, a more

---

29. See Chris Reed, 'Authenticating Electronic Mail Messages – Some Evidential Problems' (1989) MLR 649 at pp. 652–3.

30. See R. Bradgate, 'The Evidential Status of Computer Output and Communications' (1990) 6 CL&P 142.

31. In addition to the discussion in chapter 9 see also Tapper, *Computer Law*, (4th ed. London: Longman, 1989), ch. 9; Law Commission, *The Hearsay Rule in Civil Proceedings* (Consultation Paper No. 117) (London: HMSO 1991), 3.61–3.69.

32. *R v Wood* (1982) 76 Cr App R 23; *Castle v Cross* [1984] 1 WLR 1372; *The Statue of Liberty* [1968] 1 WLR 739; *R v Spiby* (1990) 91 Cr App R 25.

33. Chapter 9; N. J. Reville, 'The Admissibility of Computer Statements in Criminal Trials' (1989) 6 CL&P 19 at p. 20.

34. Castell, *VERDICT report* (1987).

serious problem is that of authenticating the records if there is a dispute between parties about their receipt or contents.

Authentication means satisfying the court:

(a)   that the contents of the record have remained unchanged,
(b)   that the information in the record does in fact originate from its purported source, whether human or machine, and
(c)   that extraneous information such as the apparent date of the record is accurate.

As with paper records, the necessary degree of authentication may be proved through oral and circumstantial evidence, if available, or via technological features of the system or the record. Non-technical evidence will include a wide variety of matters:[35]

> In an ideal world, the attorney would recommend that the client obtain and record countless bits of evidence for each message so that it could later be authenticated in court – autographs, fingerprints, photographic identification cards, attestations from witnesses, acknowledgements before notaries, letters of introduction, signature guarantees from banks, postmarks on envelopes, records of the return of acknowledgments and so forth. . . . [These] observations on conventional messages should apply equally to electronic messages.

Technical evidence might come from system logs, particularly if they are specifically designed with this end in mind, or through embedded features of the record itself such as digital signatures. I have argued elsewhere that these techniques will be acceptable to the courts as evidence of a record's authenticity,[36] and indeed some US courts have taken a relaxed approach to the authentication of computer records, refusing to exclude computer-related evidence merely because corruption or alteration is theoretically undetectable.[37]

Where such records are kept in physical form, i.e., on paper, there is normally little difficulty in convincing the court that the document produced as evidence is the same document as was originally stored. If the document is signed, it can be produced to prove the fact of sending and the contents of the message. The sender's physical signature will prove that he sent it, and any alteration to its contents should be apparent on its face. The problem with electronically stored messages is that alteration is simple and leaves no traces. Unless these messages can be as well-authenticated as physically signed documents, their value as evidence of the communication is somewhat problematical.

---

35. B. Wright, 'Authenticating EDI: the Location of a Trusted Recordkeeper' (1990) 6 CL&P 80.
36. Chris Reed, 'Authenticating Electronic Mail Messages – Some Evidential Problems' (1989) 52 MLR 649.
37. *United States* v *Vela* (1982) 673 F 2d 86; *United States* v *Sanders* (1984) 749 F 2d 195.

This is because electronic records consist of a stream of numbers (normally in ASCII or some proprietary code[38]) representing the letters of the message (plus, possibly, control characters that define format, emphasis etc.). When a record is edited, the new version is saved to disk and replaces the old version. The change in the stream of numbers cannot normally be discovered by examining the record itself.

The problems occur when the apparent sender of the message denies that he was responsible for it or where he alleges that his own record of the message differs from the recipient's record. There is nothing in the record itself that authenticates it, and so the court will be forced to assess its authenticity solely by reference to any oral and circumstantial evidence that may be available. It must also be remembered that most of the records will be copies, and there is thus a need to prove that each is an *authentic* copy of the message. The obvious way of so doing is to give oral evidence to that effect, and it is clear that failure to do so will render the copy inadmissible.[39]

Rowbotham has suggested that the parties might provide by contract for authentication and admissibility.[40] Whilst at first sight it seems attractive to include a provision in the interchange agreement that there shall be a rebuttable presumption that the parties' records are accurate, there appears to be no precedent deciding that such a clause can override the basic principles of the laws of evidence. In cases where an authentication dispute might arise, some further form of authentication is clearly desirable.

If communications are monitored by the VAN operator, the log of this monitoring could provide a useful level of authentication. The monitoring system should record (a) the identity of sender and recipient of the message, and (b) the message contents. So far as (b) is concerned, it might not be necessary to record the entire text of the message, so long as sufficient information is retained to enable the detection of alterations. The strongest authentication evidence would come from monitoring by an independent third party.

A good example of such a system was the SEADOCS project developed at Chase Manhattan Bank,[41] now unfortunately abandoned. This system was intended to overcome the problem of the multiple sale of cargoes at sea, when the shipping documents often fail to reach the ultimate purchaser until some time after the goods themselves. The written documents were deposited with the SEADOCS registry and all subsequent transfers made electronically. These transfers were authenticated by three tests:[42]

---

38. The American Standard Code for Information Interchange is used for most microcomputer communication. Each 8-bit binary word represents a letter of the alphabet or some control or graphics character. For example, in ASCII code A = decimal 65, a = decimal 97, carriage return = decimal 13 etc. EBCDIC (extended binary coded decimal interchange code) is the proprietary format used in IBM mainframes and minicomputers. See H. Cornwall, *Hacker's Handbook III* (London 1988), pp. 10–14 and app. IV.

39. *R v Collins* (1960) 44 Cr App R 170.

40. 'EDI: the practitioner's view', *International Financial Law Review*, Aug. 1988, p. 32.

41. See A. Urbach, 'The Electronic Presentation and Transfer of Shipping Documents' in R. Goode (ed.), *Electronic Banking – the Legal Implications* (London: Institute of Bankers & Centre for Commercial Law Studies, 1985), p. 111.

42. Ibid., p. 121.

(i) each party's message must be confirmed by at least one or more other messages, (ii) messages are re-filed to the presumed sender and must be re-acknowledged, and (iii) each message has a header code which is unique to sender and message as it must contain an element from the prior sender and from the computer acknowledgement message.

If there was any dispute about whether a message was sent or about its contents, the SEADOCS registry records would be available as evidence of what actually occurred.[43]

It is quite feasible to set up such a system on a less specialised intermediary system such as Telecom Gold. As that system currently operates it would be possible (though costly) to produce the Telecom Gold command log,[44] but in any event it would not be useful as evidence as it contains no record of the message's contents; it could only prove that *some* message was sent by one party and received by the other, and where there have been a series of messages it will not be much help in proving that the one in question was sent and received. The technology which would enable providers of communications networks to retain this information already exists, however, and the facility will no doubt be introduced as soon as there is sufficient demand to make it economically viable.

Where the VAN operator is unable to provide authentication evidence, that evidence should be found in the document itself. This already happens to some extent with telex and fax communications, as in each case the transmitting and receiving machines send messages identifying themselves. It could be argued that, so far as the transmitting machine is concerned, these messages amount to a signature. In *Clipper Maritime Ltd v Shirlstar Container Transport Ltd* [1987] 1 Lloyd's Rep 546, Staughton J, considering whether a telex might constitute a guarantee in writing and signed for the purpose of the Statute of Frauds 1677, said *obiter*:[45]

I reached a provisional conclusion in the course of the argument that the answerback of the sender of a telex would constitute a signature, whilst that of the receiver would not since it only authenticates the document and does not convey approval of the contents.

However, the point was in the end not relevant and he did not pursue the matter further. If he had, three points should have been recognised:

---

43. Other systems fulfilling the same function are found in the field of electronic banking – see A. Arora, *Electronic Banking and the Law* (London: IBC, 1988), ch. 7; Reed, *Electronic Finance Law* (Cambridge: Woodhead Faulkner, 1991).
44. This command log, unlike the SEADOCS system, was not designed so as to be easily producible. It is possible to compel the production of information in the hands of a third party by serving a *subpoena duces tecum*, but this can only be done on notice and the court has jurisdiction to refuse the order if it would be unreasonable, oppressive or otherwise not proper. In any event it will ensure that the third party is properly reimbursed by the parties for his expenses, which in such a case would be substantial – see *Senior v Holdsworth, ex parte Independent Television News Ltd* [1976] QB 23.
45. [1987] 1 Lloyd's Rep 546 at p. 554.

(a)   The identification messages of telex and fax machines only identify the *machine*, not the sender.

(b)   It is quite possible to program a telex or fax card to send a false identification message.

(c)   If the message is stored on disk it is possible to edit the contents and amend the identification message to take account of the alteration.

In the case in question there was no dispute that the telex had been sent nor about its contents, so only the first point would be relevant to the question of signature. If in another case there were to be such a dispute, all three points would weigh strongly against any suggestion that the telex could be treated as signed.[46]

What is really required, therefore, is some method of authenticating the message while permitting the sender and recipient to store it on their own computers. This might be achieved through some form of digital signature.

A digital signature gets its name from the fact that electronic messages are transmitted as a stream of digital information. Such a signature is a mathematical function of the message content, or part of it, which gives the identity of the sender and authenticates the contents. To be an effective signature, it must be producible by the sender alone, and any attempt to change the content of the message must be seen to be incompatible with the signature. Digital signatures have been made possible by the advances in cryptography since 1945.

The two main cryptographic candidates for producing digital signatures are the Data Encryption Standard (DES)[47] and the RSA[48] cipher. DES is normally effected in hardware, and requires a 64-bit key which is common to sender and recipient and kept secret from all others, which is used to scramble the message to such a degree that it is computationally infeasible[49] to unscramble it without knowing the key. The fact that a message is DES encrypted is therefore extremely strong evidence that it could have emanated only from one or other of the keyholders. This, however, does not authenticate it fully as both parties have the key. Either could alter the contents of the message and then re-encrypt it. The alteration would be undetectable, and the court would still be left with two messages, each claimed to be authentic.

In order for a digital signature to be effective it must be a 'one-way function', i.e., for a message from A to B, A must be able to encrypt and B to decrypt, but

---

46. On this point in relation to direct E-mail see B. Amory and Y. Poullet, 'Computers in the Law of Evidence – a Comparative Approach in Civil and Common Law Systems' (1987) 3 CL&P 114 at p. 118.

47. National Bureau of Standards FIPS Publication 64 (1977), ANSI X3.92–1981.

48. Named after its inventors – see R. L. Rivest, A. Shamir and L. Adleman, 'A method of obtaining digital signatures and public key cryptosystems' (1978) 21 Communications of the ACM 120.

49. Computational infeasibility means that although the message can in theory be decoded, the amount of time this would take is so large that for practical purposes the encryption can be regarded as secure. For DES the time required to break the code using a computer that checks one potential key per microsecond, operating 24 hours a day, is on average over 1,000 years – see B. Beckett, *Introduction to Cryptology* (Oxford: Blackwell, 1988), p. 277.

B must be unable to re-encrypt the message. This is possible within DES using complicated techniques such as the Lamport-Diffie signature[50] or the Rabin signature.[51] All these techniques suffer from two drawbacks: (a) they are difficult to implement and require complicated validation procedures, and more importantly (b) each message requires a unique key to effect the signature. Although they are theoretically capable of producing an acceptable signature, the practical difficulties of administration and of devising and recording a number of unique keys every time a signature is required make DES inappropriate for regular use.

Probably the best candidates for digital signatures are 'public key' crypto-systems such as RSA. These cryptosystems were devised so as to enable secret communications without the two parties having to agree on an encryption method and exchange keys. This cypher requires three numbers: N, K_p (the public key, used for encryption) and K_s (the secret key, used for decryption). The numbers N and K_p are published to form the recipient's public key, but K_s is kept secret. The sender of a message encrypts it by raising the digital form of the message to the power K_p and then calculating the residue modulus N (i.e., the remainder when (message) ^{Kp} is successively divided by N until it will no longer divide). The recipient decrypts the message using the formula:

$$(\text{message}) = (\text{encrypted message})^{K_s} (\text{mod}) \, N$$

Because of the way K_p, K_s and N are derived it is computationally infeasible to calculate K_s knowing only K_p and N – see figure 10.2 on p. 270.

Because the encryption formula is symmetrical it is possible to encrypt a message using the sender's private key K_s and decrypt it with K_p, and thus effect a digital signature. The sender encrypts his message using K_s. When it is received, the recipient decrypts the message using the sender's public key, K_p and N. As only the sender could have encrypted the message, if both encrypted and plain-text versions are produced in court the judge can check the identity of the sender by decrypting the message and checking it against the plain-text version. This also authenticates the contents of the message, as if the recipient alters the contents he will not be able to re-encrypt the message so that it decrypts with K_p and N. In the present state of cryptological knowledge, provided N is sufficiently large it is harder to forge an RSA digital signature than a written one. In civil cases the burden of proof is merely the balance of probabilities, and the mathematical basis of the RSA cipher is clearly strong enough to discharge that burden.[52]

10.2.2.4 Formalities in the underlying transaction It has already been pointed out (see 10.2.2.1) that certain types of contract require particular

50. D. Longley and M. Shain, *Data and Computer Security – Dictionary of Standard Concepts and Terms* (New York 1987), p. 193.
51. Ibid., p. 281.
52. If N has more than 200 digits it is calculated that, using a computer which eliminated one potential factor of N every microsecond, the task would on average take longer than the expected lifetime of the universe – see Beckett, *Introduction to Cryptology* (Oxford: Blackwell 1988), ch. 9.

Figure 10.2 - RSA Encryption as a Digital Signature

Public Key Encryption Using RSA

| Cyphertext | = | Plaintext | ^{K_p} mod N | *[encryption]* |

| Plaintext | = | Cyphertext | ^{K_s} mod N | *[decryption]* |

Inverse Process for Digital Signature

| Cyphertext | = | Plaintext | ^{K_s} mod N | *[digital signature]* |

| Plaintext | = | Cyphertext | ^{K_p} mod N | *[authentication]* |

N.B. The encrypted signature *must* be preserved. The *act of decryption* is what authenticates the signature, and this must therefore be performed for the court.

formalities to be observed if they are to be enforceable. The most common of these are that the contract must be made or evidenced in writing or in a document, and that it must be signed.

Unless there is legislation which specifically provides to the contrary,[53] 'writing' under English law requires the communication to be in some visible form.[54] However, if all that is required is a 'document'[55] then, unless this is also defined in the legislation or case law governing the transaction to require visible form, there seems no reason why it might not be produced electronically.[56]

A requirement for a signature is more problematic. Given that in many cases English law permits signatures to be typewritten or made via a stamp,[57] there seems no reason to insist on a handwritten signature. Attention should instead be focused on the purpose of the signature: to authenticate the message as originating from the purported sender. If this is correct (and it must be recognised that there are no clear authorities on the matter), cryptography offers the possibility of producing digital signatures (see 10.2.2.3 above) that are more difficult to forge than handwriting.

10.2.2.5 Data protection[58] Although the vast majority of EDI transactions are purely commercial in nature, this does not mean that the law on data protection is entirely irrelevant. The Data Protection Act 1984, s. 1(3), defines personal data as: 'information which relates to a living individual who can be identified from that information (or from that and other information in the possession of the data user)'. It is therefore likely that an appreciable proportion of EDI messages will contain personal data. As a result, EDI users should register under the Act and take the appropriate measures to comply with its provisions.

The position is further complicated by the fact that many EDI messages cross national boundaries. This means that the power of data protection authorities to issue transfer prohibition notices must be borne in mind when advising on EDI usage. The EC Draft Directive Concerning the Protection of Individuals in Relation to the Processing of Personal Data[59] proposes a change to a 'white list' plus individual exemptions regime, which will have a major impact on EDI if implemented in its current form.[60]

---

53. E.g., art. 1(4)(b) of the Unidroit Convention on International Factoring 1988 defines notice in writing to include 'any other telecommunication capable of being reproduced in tangible form'.
54. See, e.g., Interpretation Act 1978, sch. 1.
55. In civil proceedings this includes 'any disc, tape, soundtrack or other device in which . . . data (not being visual images) are embodied so as to be capable (with or without the aid of some other equipment) of being reproduced therefrom.' (Civil Evidence Act 1968, s. 10(1)).
56. See Bergsten and Goode, 'Legal questions and problems to be overcome' in Thomsen and Wheble, *Trading with EDI: the Legal Issues* (London: IBC, 1989), pp. 136–8.
57. See, e.g., *Chapman* v *Smethurst* [1909] 1 KB 927.
58. See further chapter 11.
59. COM(90) 314 final – SYN 287, 13 September 1990.
60. For a full examination of the Data Protection Act 1984 and the draft Directive see chapter 11.

10.2.2.6 EDI and payment systems[61] There are no theoretical difficulties, and comparatively trivial technical problems, in linking EDI with the existing international EFT (electronic funds transfer) systems. However, major problems do arise where payment for the underlying transaction is to be made using document-based payment methods such as documentary credits and bills of exchange. There is no space in this chapter to examine these problems,[62] but it is important to recognise that the substantial body of law which exists for both of these payment systems predicates the existence of physical paper documents. It is therefore not possible simply to replace them by EDI messages which have the same data content; additionally, the EDI payment messages must offer the advantages of negotiability and security currently exhibited by the paper documents.

10.3 CONCLUSIONS

The law governing EDI is very much in its infancy, as the degree of speculative comment in this chapter demonstrates. Nonetheless, one comforting conclusion that can be drawn from the state of the law is that many of the potential problems, once they are properly identified, can be overcome quite simply through the mechanism of properly drafted contracts. This is a task for which the commercial lawyer is ideally suited, and lawyers will play a crucial role in facilitating the inevitable spread of EDI in the trading community.

---

61. Recommendations for legislation at an international level can be found in the *UNCITRAL Legal Guide to Electronic Funds Transfers* (New York 1987) and the *Draft UNCITRAL Model Law on International Credit Transfers* (Vienna 1991).
62. A detailed examination of the problems and techniques for dematerialising payment systems of this type can be found in Reed, *Electronic Finance Law* (Cambridge: Woodhead Faulkner, 1991), ch. 8.

CHAPTER ELEVEN

Data protection

Ian Walden

Throughout this chapter the reader will be introduced to elements which go towards an understanding of data protection legislation. The first part will give consideration to the nature of the subject itself from a West European perspective, as well as the initiatives of international organisations in this field. The second part will focus more specifically on the UK Data Protection Act 1984 and its component elements.

11.1 DEFINITIONS

Data protection legislation currently exists in 17 West European countries,[1] as well as other industrialised nations such as Japan and Canada. Nearly all other West European countries have put forward proposals for legislation, while of the 17 countries which have already acted a number have already revised or amended their original legislation.

Such widespread acceptance of data protection legislation does not necessarily indicate a common perception of the scope of such legislation. One of the most straightforward definitions of data protection is given in the British government's explanatory report, appended to the draft of the Council of Europe Convention on Data Protection:[2]

---

1. Austria, Denmark, Finland, France, Germany, Guernsey, Iceland, Ireland, Isle of Man, Israel, Jersey, Luxembourg, the Netherlands, Norway, Portugal, Sweden and the UK.
2. *Convention for the Protection of Individuals with regard to Automatic Processing of Personal Data*, Strasbourg, 28 January 1981 (Cmnd 8341) (London: HMSO, 1981), Explanatory Report, p. 5.

the legal protection of individuals with regard to automatic processing of personal information relating to them.

An expanded definition of data protection has been put forward by a number of Third World countries. They have concluded that data protection is a legal regime that should also be applied to information pertaining to States. Resolutions at Latin American and African conferences proposed that 'information and knowledge affecting national sovereignty, security, economic well-being and socio-cultural interests should be brought within the ambit of data protection'.[3]

Indeed, our initial definition is not even sufficient to cover the variations of data protection legislation between industrialised nations, or even within Western Europe. Some countries such as Denmark and Austria extend protection to legal persons, such as companies and trade unions. Other countries, including France and the Netherlands, have legislation that extends to manual records as well as computer data. Data protection legislation in countries such as the United States and New Zealand is primarily limited to public-sector data processing.

It is also necessary to distinguish data protection from the related, but distinct, areas of 'privacy' and data security. A simple distinction between data protection and 'privacy' is made in the Lindop Report,[4] which gives an example that the use of inaccurate or incomplete information when decision-making, although within the proper scope of data protection, is not necessarily a privacy issue. Data security is more closely linked with data protection, being a part of the requirements of adequate data protection, but it also covers issues of computer crime as well as ensuring that computer systems are protected from physical disasters.

Data protection legislation can be seen to be primarily concerned with the problems related to information communication, rather than information possession. Legislation is generally concerned that individuals upon whom data is held are able to discover the existence of the information, as well as the motives behind such possession. However, legislation does not always give individuals the right to stop an organisation from holding their personal data. The legislative focus in countries such as the UK is less on the type of data held than on the conditions under which it is held.

An alternative definition of data protection legislation has been suggested by the Office of the Data Protection Registrar. At a 1988 conference, the Deputy Registrar defined data protection as 'fairness legislation', not requiring a balance between data users and data subjects but simply being fair to an individual.[5]

Within Western Europe the 1981 Council of Europe Convention on Data Protection forms the basis of all national legislation. Two distinct motives exist

---

3. Intergovernmental Bureau for Informatics, TDF 270, p. 55.
4. *Report of the Committee on Data Protection* (Chairman: Sir Norman Lindop) (Cmnd 7341) (London: HMSO, 1978), para. 2.03.
5. CBI Conference, London, 4 March 1988.

for the Convention: the threat to individual privacy posed by computerisation; and the need to maintain a free flow of information in an international market. The Convention therefore attempts to reconcile art. 8 of the European Human Rights Convention, concerning an individual's right to privacy, with the principle of free flow of information enshrined in art. 10 of the Human Rights Convention.

Indeed, in the course of the Parliamentary debates on the United Kingdom Data Protection Act 1984 the Under-Secretary of State at the Home Office clearly put forward these two objectives:[6]

> . . . the Bill is drafted to fulfil two purposes. The first is to protect private individuals from the threat of the use of erroneous information about them – or indeed, the misuse of correct information about them – held on computers. The second is to provide that protection in a form that will enable us to satisfy the Council of Europe Convention on Data Processing so as to enable our own data processing industry to participate freely in the European market.

11.2 DATA PROTECTION AND PRIVACY

Since the Warren and Brandeis definition of privacy as the 'right to be let alone', a great amount of time has been devoted to defining an exhaustive list of the constituent components of the term 'privacy', a problem we have considered above with respect to data protection. For example, the United Nations Declaration of Human Rights, art. 12, states that every individual has a right to privacy, yet fails to define the term. However, what does seem to be agreed upon is the extent to which the meaning of 'privacy' is dependent on a nation's culture.

The classic contrast to the British attitude to privacy is Sweden. On the one hand, Sweden has had 'freedom of information' legislation since 1776, but it also has a social system based on the existence of a mandatory, unique personal identifier for each citizen, something which would not be acceptable in this country at the present time.

What is the difference between the principles upon which data protection legislation is based and justified and those that lie behind the 'right to privacy'? The 1978 Lindop Report on data protection acknowledged the following distinction:[7]

> . . . the function of a data protection law should be different from that of a law on privacy: rather than establishing rights, it should provide a framework for finding a balance between the interests of the individual, the data user and the community at large.

Such a balancing act can be easily recognised in the two motives behind the Council of Europe Convention.

---

6. Parliamentary Debates (Hansard), Lords, 5th ser., vol. 443, col. 509 (statement of Lord Eton).
7. Lindop Report (see note 4), p. xix.

Despite this difference between the concept of data protection and privacy, developing data protection case law can extend the scope of the legislation to wider questions regarding an individual's 'right to privacy'. In Germany, a Constitutional Court decision declared unconstitutional an Act which had authorised the government to undertake a comprehensive population census. The court declared that each data subject has a right to 'determine in general the release and use of his or her personal data'; therefore establishing a constitutional right of individual 'informational self-determination'.[8] The decision also led to a fundamental review of the German Data Protection Act. It has also been noted that some judicial opinion within the European Court of Human Rights has begun to use the Council of Europe Convention on Data Protection to enliven and strengthen art. 8 of the European Convention on Human Rights.[9]

A related question concerns the issue of freedom of information: How does the right to 'freedom of information' relate to data protection? A committee of the Council of Europe is currently considering the potentially conflicting interests of data protection and 'freedom of information'. The committee is looking into problems concerning access rights, often into public archives, that may lead to an infringement of an individual's privacy. However, in the UK, it has been claimed that the Data Protection Act 1984 has been used as an excuse by some government authorities to refuse the disclosure of legitimate public documents, and therefore maintain greater secrecy![10]

Data protection can also be seen to function as a supplement to freedom of information legislation, by increasing the transparency of an authority's decision-making processes. For instance, individuals are able to ascertain, through use of their 'data protection' access rights, the extent of personal information that public authorities hold and can therefore be presumed to use in decision-making. In Quebec, Canada, legislation has been adopted covering both access to documents held by public bodies and the protection of personal information in the same statute.

11.3   INTERNATIONAL ACTIVITY

The data processing industry has an international character. Large amounts of data cross national borders every day, either electronically via cables or satellites or through the manual transfer of media such as magnetic tapes. The former will usually be transferred without control or supervision by any form of governmental authority. Such transfers thus pose a threat to individual privacy, since national laws can be circumvented by transferring data to a so-called 'data haven' which lacks such legislation.

---

8. Judgment of 15 December 1983, Bundesverfassungsgericht [BVerfG], 65 Entscheidungen des Bundesverfassungsgericht [BVerfGE] 1, at p. 43.

9. P. Hustinx, 'The role of the Council of Europe', Privacy, Laws and Business Conference on Data Protection in Ireland, the Netherlands and Switzerland, 19 October 1988.

10. Duncan Campbell and Steve Connor, *On the Record: Surveillance, Computers and Privacy* (London: Michael Joseph, 1986), p. 35.

In order to prevent organisations from avoiding data protection controls, and therefore guaranteeing a free flow of information, international governmental organisations have become involved in attempting to obtain international harmonisation for data protection legislation. These include the Council of Europe, the OECD, the United Nations and the European Community.

11.3.1 The Council of Europe

The Council of Europe has been the major international force in the field of data protection since the 1981 Convention for the Protection of Individuals with regard to Automatic Processing of Personal Data was agreed upon.[11] Currently 19 of the 26 Council of Europe members have signed the Convention, and have therefore accepted an obligation to incorporate certain data protection principles into national law. The Convention came into force on 1 October 1985 when five countries had ratified it: Sweden, Norway, France, Federal Republic of Germany and Spain.

The Council of Europe has been involved in this area since 1968, when the Parliamentary Assembly passed recommendation 509 (68) asking the Council of Ministers to look at the European Human Rights Convention to see if domestic laws gave adequate protection for personal privacy in the light of modern scientific and technical developments. The Council of Ministers asked the Committee of Experts on Human Rights to study the issue and they reported that insufficient protection existed.

A specialist Committee of Experts on the Protection of Privacy was subsequently asked to draft appropriate resolutions for the Committee of Ministers to adopt. Resolution 22 (1973) covered the 'ground rules' for data protection in the private sector while resolution 29 (1974) focused on the public sector.

In 1976 the Committee of Experts on Data Protection was established. Its primary task was to prepare a Convention on the protection of privacy in relation to data processing abroad and transfrontier data processing. The text of this Convention was finalised in April 1980, and opened for signature on 28 January 1981.

The Convention is based on a number of basic principles of data protection, upon which each country is expected to draft appropriate legislation. Such legislative provisions will provide for a minimum degree of harmonisation between signatories, and should therefore prevent restrictions on transborder data flows for reasons of 'privacy' protection.

Since 1981 the Committee of Experts on Data Protection has been primarily involved in the drafting of sectoral rules on data protection. These form part of an ongoing series of recommendations issued by the Committee of Ministers designed to supplement the provisions of the Convention.[12] There are

11. See note 2.
12. Recommendations have already been produced to cover the areas of personal data in 'medical data banks' (81); 'scientific research and statistics' (R(83) 10); 'direct marketing' (R(85) 20); Soccial security records' (R(86) 1); 'the police sector' (R(87) 15); 'employment records' (R(89) 2) and 'the communication to third parties of personal data held by public bodies' (R(91) 10).

currently Council of Europe working parties looking into the particular sectoral issues raised within the telecommunications, banking and media sectors; and the data protection issues created by the use of personal identification numbers and genetic data.

The major weakness of the Convention is its lack of enforceability against countries that fail to uphold the basic principles. No enforcement machinery was created under the Convention, and therefore any disputes have to be resolved at the diplomatic level.

11.3.2 OECD

The Organisation for Economic Co-operation and Development was established in 1961 and currently comprises 24 of the leading industrial nations. The nature of the organisation has meant that interest in data protection has centred primarily on the promotion of trade and economic advancement of member States rather than 'privacy' concerns.

In 1963 a Computer Utilisation Group was set up by the 3rd Ministerial Meeting. Aspects of the Group's work concerned with privacy went to a subgroup, the Data Bank Panel. This body issued a set of principles in 1977. In the same year the Working Party on Information Computers and Communications Policy (ICCP) was created out of the Computer Utilisation and Scientific and Technical Policy Groups. Within this body the Data Bank Panel became the Group of Government Experts on Transborder Data Barriers and the Protection of Privacy. Its remit was:

> to develop guidelines on basic rules governing the transborder flow and the protection of personal data and privacy, in order to facilitate the harmonisation of national legislation.

The OECD guidelines were drafted by 1979, adopted September 1980, and endorsed by the UK government in 1981.[13]

The guidelines are based, as is the Council of Europe Convention, upon eight, self-explanatory principles of good data protection practice. The Republic of Ireland became the last country to sign the guidelines in January 1987.

The guidelines are simply a recommendation to countries to adopt good data protection practices in order to prevent unnecessary restrictions on transborder data flows and have no formal authority. However, some companies and trade associations, particularly in the United States and Canada, have formally supported the guidelines.

11.3.3 The United Nations

The United Nations has only focused on the human rights aspects of the use of computer technology comparatively recently. In 1989 the General Assembly

---

13. Organisation for Economic Co-operation and Development, *Guidelines on the Protection of Privacy and Transborder Flows of Personal Data* (Paris: OECD, 1980).

of the Commission on Human Rights adopted a set of draft 'guidelines for the regulation of computerised personal data files'.

These draft guidelines were subsequently referred to the Commission on Human Rights' special rapporteur, Mr Louis Joinet for redrafting, based on the comments and suggestions received from the Member governments and other interested international organisations. A revised version of the guidelines was presented in February 1990.[14] Since then, however, no significant further action has taken place.

The guidelines are divided into two sections. The first section covers principles concerning the minimum guarantees that should be provided in national legislations. These 'principles' echo those put forward by both the Council of Europe Convention and the OECD guidelines, except for three additional terms:

(a) Principle of non-discrimination – sensitive data, such as racial or ethnic origin, should not be compiled at all.

(b) Power to make exceptions – justified only for reasons of national security, public order, public health or morality.

(c) Supervision and sanctions – the data protection authority 'shall offer guarantees of impartiality, independence *vis-à-vis* persons or agencies responsible for processing . . . and technical competence'.

The second section considers the application of the guidelines to personal data files kept by governmental international organisations. This requires that international organisations designate a particular supervisory authority to oversee their compliance. In addition, it includes a 'humanitarian clause' which states that:

a derogation from these principles may be specifically provided for when the purpose of the file is the protection of human rights and fundamental freedoms of the individual concerned or humanitarian assistance.

Such a clause is intended to cover such organisations as Amnesty International, which holds large amounts of personal data but would be wary of sending information out to a data subject on the basis of an access request made while the person was still imprisoned.

11.3.4 The European Community

Despite interest and involvement in data protection and privacy issues for nearly two decades from both the European Parliament and the Commission, the emergence of a Directive concerning this area only appeared in July 1990. The Directive, if adopted, would oblige Member States to undertake appropriate legislative measures to fulfil the objectives of the Directive.

---

14. UN General Assembly, 44th session, Resolution 44/132, on 15 December, 1989 (original guidelines). UN Economic and Social Council, 'Human Rights and Scientific and Technological Developments', E/CN.4/1990/72, 20 February 1990 (revised draft).

The European Parliament's involvement in data protection issues has primarily been through its Legal Affairs Committee, though the issue has been subject to Parliamentary questions and debates for the past 10 years. In 1976, the European Parliament adopted a resolution calling for a Directive to ensure that 'Community citizens enjoy maximum protection against abuses or failures of data processing' as well as 'to avoid the development of conflicting legislation'.[15]

In 1977 the Legal Affairs Committee established the Subcommittee on Data Processing and the Rights of the Individual. The Subcommittee produced the 'Bayerl Report' in May 1979.[16] The resultant debate in the European Parliament led to recommendations being made to the Commission and the Council of Ministers concerning the principles that should form the basis of the Community's attitude to data protection.[17] These recommendations called on the European Commission to draft a Directive to complement a common communications system; to harmonise the data protection laws and to secure the privacy of information on individuals in computer files.

In July 1981 the European Commission recommended that all members sign the Council of Europe Convention and seek to ratify it by the end of 1982.[18] However, as yet only eight out of the 12 Member States have passed data protection legislation.

A second Parliamentary report, the 'Sieglerschidt' Report, was published in 1982.[19] The report noted 'that data transmission in general should be placed on a legal footing and not be determined merely by technical reasons'.[20] It recommended the establishment of a 'European Zone' of members in the EEC and Council of Europe, within which authorisation prior to the export of data would not be needed. It also indicated that initiatives such as a Directive were still necessary. Following the report, a resolution was adopted by the European Parliament on 9 March 1982, calling for a Directive if the Convention proved inadequate.[21]

In July 1990 the European Commission finally published a proposed Directive on data protection. The Directive, when adopted, is likely to require significant changes in the UK's Data Protection Act 1984 and impose new burdens on businesses with regard to the processing of personal data.

The Commission's data protection Directive was part of a package of six proposals:

---

15. Resolution on the protection of the rights of individuals in connection with data processing; OJ No. C. 100, 3 May 1976, p. 27.
16. Named after the rapporteur. Report on the Protection of the Individual in the Face of the Technical Developments in Data Processing, 1979–1980 Eur.Parl.Doc. (No. 100) 13 (1979).
17. OJ No. C 140, 5 June 1979, p. 34.
18. Commission Recommendation of 29 July 1981, relating to the Council of Europe Convention for the protection of individuals with regard to automatic processing of personal data, OJ No. L 246, 29 August 1979, p. 31, 81/679/EEC.
19. Second Report on the Protection of the Rights of the Individual in the Face of Technical Developments in Data Processing, E.P.Doc.1-548/81, 12 October 1981.
20. Ibid., p. 7.
21. OJ No. C 87, 5 April 1982, p. 39.

(a)   A draft framework Directive on data protection, based upon a number of principles.[22]

(b)   A recommendation that the European Community adheres to the Council of Europe Convention on Data Protection. It is within the framework of this international agreement that the EC intends to ensure the protection of personal data transferred to third countries, in particular Eastern Europe.

(c)   A resolution to extend the protection offered by the Directive to all personal data held in the public sector, that do not fall under the scope of European Community law (e.g., crime and defence).

(d)   A declaration extending the data protection principles to all the personal data held by Community institutions and bodies.

(e)   A draft Directive for the telecommunications sector, especially integrated services digital networks (ISDNs).[23]

(f)   A draft Council Decision to adopt a two-year plan in the area of security for information systems.

These proposals arose from the work of DG-III (Internal Market) and DG-XIII (Telecommunications, Information Industries and Innovation) of the Commission.

The Commission put forward a number of reasons to justify the need for data protection activity. The primary purpose is to ensure the free flow of data as part of the programme to establish the 'Single Market' under art. 100a of the EEC Treaty. Since 1981 only eight of the 12 Member States have passed data protection legislation: the UK, the Republic of Ireland, France, Germany, the Netherlands, Denmark, Portugal and Luxembourg. Even between these eight member States 'remarkable divergences' exist in the legislation, and in particular the Commission noted six key differences:

(a)   Coverage of manual data.

(b)   Protection for legal persons (e.g., companies).

(c)   The extent of a data user's duty to inform the data protection authority of what personal data is held (e.g., the registration requirement).

(d)   The giving of information to the data subject at the point of data collection.

(e)   Additional protection for categories of 'sensitive' data.

(f)   Restrictions on the export of personal data.

---

22. Draft proposal for a Council Directive Approximating Certain Laws, Regulations and Administrative Provisions of the Member States Concerning the Protection of Individuals in Relation to the Processing of Personal Data, COM(90) 314 final – SYN 287, 13.8.1990; OJ No. C 277, 5 November 1990.

23. Proposal for a Council Directive Concerning the Protection of Personal Data and Privacy in the Context of Public Digital Telecommunications Networks, in Particular the Integrated Services Digital Network (ISDN) and Public Digital Mobile Networks, SYN 288. The telecoms Directive has been greeted with a significant amount of opposition from the industry, and there is a strong move to limit the scope of the Directive to voice telephony. Substantive discussions on amending the text are being delayed until the future structure of the framework Directive has been clarified.

The Commission also asserted the need to protect an individual's right to privacy.

The different levels of data protection in the Community are seen as a potential obstacle to the development of the Community's data processing and telecommunications industries. The existence of 'data havens', countries with no data protection, is also seen as potentially distorting competition within the Community, since businesses might move to such countries to avoid the processing restrictions that exist in other Member States. Overall, the intention of the Directive is to establish 'a high level of protection throughout the Community'.

The draft Directive is ambitious in seeking to cover 'every situation in which the processing of personal data involves the risk to the data subject'. The text therefore covers both manual and automated files and both public and private sectors. The movement of data from the public to the private sector is seen as posing the greatest threat to individuals. The Directive does not extend protection to legal persons.

It is intended that the Commission will issue further sectoral data protection Directives (the first covering the telecommunications sector) as appropriate; or alternatively will encourage the use of codes of conduct.

It was originally intended that the Directive be in force by 1 January 1993, in line with the establishment of the Single Market. Once passed, countries will have two years in which to implement the Directive in national legislation. Considerable lobbying from interest groups is currently taking place before the final text is agreed.

The primary aim of the draft Directives is to enhance harmonisation, removing restrictions on the flow of data between Member States. However, current developments could also result in the creation of a 'fortress Europe' with respect to data protection.

11.3.5 Transborder data flows

Despite the international initiatives outlined above, a number of the major trading nations still lack significant legislative data protection, e.g., the United States. Where countries do not have legislation, or indeed where the level of protection is of a different nature (e.g., extended to manual data), there is the problem of equivalency: Does the country to which the data is to be sent have 'equivalent' protection?

This question can be answered in two ways, legally or functionally:

(a) Does the recipient country have substantive data protection legislation?
(b) Can data protection be guaranteed through other means?

The requirement for 'legislative equivalence' can be a significant obstacle for a company wishing to transfer data to a country without legislation. The lesser requirement of 'functional equivalence', on the other hand, could allow data transfers to countries without legislation where it can be shown that 'equivalent' data protection exists in the recipient country and/or that the real risk to personal data is low due to one or a combination of alternative forms of control, for example:

(a)   constitutional provisions,
(b)   State, provincial, territorial, or local legislation,
(c)   sectoral law,
(d)   industry self-regulatory codes,
(e)   corporate data protection and security procedures and codes of conduct,
(f)   consumer protection measures,
(g)   judicial decisions,
(h)   consensual arrangements,
(i)   adherence to international instruments.[24]

In particular, interest has recently been shown in the use of contractual terms between the sender and recipient of the data to achieve 'equivalent' protection. A drafting group within the Council of Europe's Committee of Experts on data protection has recently circulated six draft clauses for inclusion in 'a model contract designed to ensure equivalent data protection in the context of transborder data flows'.[25]

The clauses are primarily intended for situations where a 'contracting party' to the Council of Europe Convention receives a request to export personal data to a State which has not legislated for data protection. The clauses are not, however, intended to replace the need for legislation.

A second contractual method for ensuring international data protection 'equivalence' is through incorporation, either directly or by reference, of the provisions included in either (a) the national data protection legislation of the exporting country, or (b) one of the international legal instruments. The problem with the latter is that both the Council of Europe Convention and the OECD Guidelines are primarily principle-based, and therefore do not provide any clearly applicable actions or standards.

The major question with contractual safeguards is whether such provisions can be sufficiently enforceable. The data user exporting the data is unlikely to suffer damage from any breach of such contractual terms, and will therefore have little incentive either to police the agreement or to sue for any breach. However, the primary legal obstacle to any third party such as a data subject acting against the importing data user is the rule of privity of contract, whereby only the parties to a contract can enforce its obligations.

The use of contractual terms to achieve international equivalency is certainly a solution being promoted by industry at the current time. It is recognised that the legislative process is slow, and it could be many years, if ever, before certain major trading nations introduce appropriate legislation. Companies therefore perceive contractual terms as a practical means of providing for data protection. The widespread adoption of such terms will, however, depend on the attitude of the appropriate national data protection authorities.

---

24. ICC, *Protection of Personal Data: An International Business View*, Doc. No. 373/128, 4 October 1991, p. 7.
25. Council of Europe, *Revised Version of Proposed Clauses for Inclusion in a Model Contract Designed to Ensure Equivalent Data Protection in the Context of Transborder Data Flows*, T-PD (91) 8.

11.4   THE UNITED KINGDOM DATA PROTECTION ACT 1984

11.4.1   A history of legislative activity

In 1961 Lord Mancroft introduced a Right of Privacy Bill. This can be seen to mark the beginning of a 13-year history which finally led to the successful passage of the Data Protection Act 1984. This first private member's Bill was followed by four others, from both the House of Commons and the Lords, until the government decided to establish a formal committee of inquiry into this area, precipitated by a Parliamentary debate on a private member's Bill.

In May 1970 a Committee on Privacy was appointed under the chairmanship of Kenneth Younger. Its terms of reference were:

To consider whether legislation is needed to give further protection to the individual citizen and to commercial and industrial interests against intrusions into privacy by private persons and organisations, or by companies, and to make recommendations.

The committee's purview was limited to the private sector despite the committee's request that it be reviewed. The final report was completed and presented to Parliament in July 1972.[26]

During its establishment the committee set up a special working party on computers. Its terms of reference were:

To examine the alternative means of controlling the handling of information by computers and to recommend those which seem most appropriate, having regard to practicability and cost, and also to survey the present scale of computer use and likely evolution, with special reference to the implications for controls.

The working party concluded that: 'Put quite simply, the computer problem as it affects privacy in Great Britain is one of apprehensions and fears and not so far one of facts and figures'.[27] Indeed, the report went on to note that the most credible anxieties were those held about computers in the *public* sector, an area outside the committee's scope. The committee noted that the main areas of public concern were with universities, bank records and credit agencies. It recommended that an independent body (standing commission), composed of computer experts and lay persons, should be established to monitor growth in the processing of personal information by computer, as well as the use of new technologies and practices.

In response to the Younger Report a White Paper was promised. However, the government's response actually took three years to appear!

The White Paper, *Computers and Privacy* (Cmnd 6353), was presented to Parliament by the Home Secretary, Roy Jenkins, in December 1975. In it the government accepted the need for legislation to protect computer-based

---

26. *Report of the Committee on Privacy* (Cmnd 5012) (London: HMSO, 1972).
27. Ibid., p. 179, para. 580.

information. Despite the concerns expressed in the Younger Report with regard to manual records, the government felt that computers posed a special threat to individual privacy:

> The speed of computers, their capacity to store, combine, retrieve and transfer data, their flexibility, and the low unit cost of the work which they can do have the following practical implications for privacy:
> (1) they facilitate the maintenance of extensive record systems and the retention of data on those systems;
> (2) they can make data easily and quickly accessible from many distant points;
> (3) they make it possible for data to be transferred quickly from one information system to another;
> (4) they make it possible for data to be combined in ways which might not otherwise be practicable;
> (5) because the data are stored, processed and often transmitted in a form which is not directly intelligible, few people may know what is in the records, or what is happening to them.

The government also issued a second White Paper, entitled *Computers: Safeguards for Privacy* (Cmnd 6354), which agreed with the comments made by the Younger Report with regard to the concerns generated by public-sector information. The paper considered the extent, nature and proper safeguarding of personal data held on computers in the public sector.

Rather than establish a standing commission to monitor the use of personal data, the White Paper proposed legislation to cover both public and private-sector information systems. The creation of a Data Protection Authority was also proposed, to supervise the legislation and ensure that appropriate safeguards for individual privacy were implemented.

In order to provide a detailed structure for the proposed Data Protection Authority the government established a Data Protection Committee. The 12-person committee, under the chairmanship of Sir Norman Lindop, reported in 1978.[28]

The Lindop Report proposed that a number of data protection principles should form the core of the legislation, with the Data Protection Authority being responsible for ensuring compliance with those principles. In particular, the Authority would be required to draft codes of practice for various sectors based on consultations with interested parties and associations, which would then become law as statutory instruments. Failure to comply with a code would lead to criminal sanctions.

Overall, the Lindop Report was concerned to produce a flexible solution which would not act so as to hold back the growing use of computers within both the public and private sector:

> [A] single set of rules to govern the handling of personal data by computers simply will not do. The legislation must provide a means of finding

---

28. See note 4.

appropriate balances between all legitimate interests. The scheme of regulation must therefore be a flexible one: flexible as between different cases, different times and different interests. (Lindop Report, p. 7.)

After the fall of the government in 1979, legislation on data protection was further delayed. Finally, in 1982, the government issued a White Paper, *Data Protection: the Government's Proposals for Legislation* (Cmnd 8539). The approach put forward in the White Paper was much less thorough than that proposed in the Lindop Report. The idea of a Data Protection Authority was replaced by an individual Registrar of Data Protection. The Registrar's primary duty would be to establish and maintain a register of data users. For this task, the government estimated that the Registrar 'may need a staff of about 20'!

The White Paper also rejected the idea of statutory codes of practice. Although they saw the value of such codes, the government felt that the length of time necessary to create an adequate range of statutory codes of practice would be unacceptable.

The Data Protection Act 1984 received the royal assent on 12 July 1984. The provisions of the Act were phased in over a three-year period, with the Act becoming fully operational on 11 November 1987.

11.4.2   Terms

The Data Protection Act 1984 is concerned with personal data. 'Data' is defined as: 'information recorded in a form in which it can be processed by equipment operating automatically in response to instructions given for that purpose' (s. 1(2)) while 'personal data' consists of: 'information which relates to a living individual who can be identified from that information (or from that and other information in the possession of the data user)' (s. 1(3)).

The Act was limited to computer data because the government felt that computers posed a unique threat to individual privacy through their ability to store, link and manipulate large amounts of data. The Lindop Committee's terms of reference had also been restricted to 'computerised information systems', although it did consider the arguments in favour of inclusion of all forms of personal data. The primary reasons for limiting protection to computer systems were practical; the cost and size of such regulation.

Protection is also restricted to 'living individuals', therefore excluding the data protection claims of legal persons such as companies and trade unions. Arguments in favour of the inclusion of legal persons are that information on organisations may ultimately be information about individuals; and secondly, that collective interests also need protection against the threats posed by data processing.

The Data Protection Act 1984 is primarily based upon three categories of persons:

(a)   'Data subjects' (s. 1(4)): any living individuals.

(b)   'Data users' (s. 1(5)): those individuals or organisations that control the use of automatically processed personal data. The need for control over the contents and use of the data is distinguished from mere physical possession.

(c) 'Computer bureaux' (s. 1(6)): third parties that simply maintain and process the data on behalf of a data user without controlling the contents or use of the data.

11.4.3 The Registrar

The Data Protection Act 1984 establishes the position of Data Protection Registrar (s. 3) to supervise the implementation of the legislation. The Registrar is provided with a number of powers and duties under the Act (ss. 36 and 37). The Registrar's major duty is to ensure that data users abide by the data protection principles. Fulfilling this task involves promotion of the Act through the provision of advice to data users, and in particular by encouraging the drafting of sectoral codes of practice (s. 36(4)). These codes apply the vague provisions of the Act to the specific data processing activities of data users in various sectors. These codes are then approved by the Registrar and become a base level of good practice. The first such codes were drawn up within the Advertising Association, the Association of British Travel Agents and the Association of Chief Police Officers.

The Registrar is also under a duty to consider complaints from data subjects concerning breaches of the data protection principles, provided they are of a substantial nature. If such a complaint seems justified then the Registrar has a number of powers to act against offenders. The Registrar can obtain a warrant in order to access, search and seize material held by an individual or organisation (s. 16). The Registrar can then instigate a prosecution against the offender, on behalf of the data subject. However, the Registrar cannot prosecute an offender in situations where a data subject's statutory rights have been breached.

The Act also provides the Registrar with the ability to serve various notices against data users. An 'enforcement notice' (s. 10) can be issued against a data user that has failed to observe the principles. The notice specifies the nature of the breach that has occurred and outlines the measures that will need to be taken in order to correct the breach. If the data user fails to comply with the notice then an offence is committed, leading to the possibility of a 'deregistration notice' (s. 11) being issued by the Registrar. This notice orders a data user to stop processing personal data immediately.

The Registrar also has the power to issue a 'transfer prohibition notice' (s. 12) against a data user. This would prevent a data user from sending personal data out of the United Kingdom to a place where there is a likelihood that the data protection principles will be breached.

Where the transfer of data is to a country that is a signatory to the Council of Europe Convention, the Registrar only has the power to restrict the transfer of data if he is satisfied that either of two conditions exist:

(a) There is likely to be a *further* transfer to a country, not a signatory to the Convention, and the result of this transfer is likely to be a contravention of the data protection principles; or

(b) Where the data are considered sensitive (under s. 2(3)), with additional safeguards under the Act (s. 12(3)).

The second body created under the Act is the Data Protection Tribunal (s. 3(2)). This body hears appeals by data users in respect of decisions and actions taken by the Registrar. It was established to counter the power of the Registrar to prevent an organisation from continuing its activities with respect to data processing. If an appeal is lodged against the Registrar's decision then the data user may be able to continue interim processing arrangements until the Tribunal's decision. A data subject has no such right to appeal against the Registrar's decision.

11.4.4   The Register
The Registrar's initial and major task under the Data Protection Act 1984 has been the establishment of a public register of all data users and computer bureaux. In Western Europe, a consistent feature of national data protection legislation is the requirement that all relevant organisations must register personal data systems, the Federal Republic of Germany being the notable exception. Registration involves essential information about a databank being placed on a record that can be referenced by both the authorities and the public. The principal function of registration is simply to identify systems and facilitate supervision and compliance with standards.

The method chosen by the government to regulate data processing was through the creation of a register under the supervision of the Registrar. This was much less rigorous than the 'licensing approach' adopted in the Swedish Data Act 1973 and considered by the Lindop Committee. Licensing had been rejected in the Lindop Report because it would require the inspection of all computer systems prior to use. Such a system would inevitably be very expensive, extend bureaucracy and could lead to delays in the introduction of new computer systems.

Registration, the committee noted, would avoid the problems of licensing. Users would not have to be inspected or examined before processing personal data, and the 'negative control' would be that of deregistration. It would also be a source of public information that might help in reducing the 'Big Brother' image of public authorities and large corporations. The Lindop Committee also saw registration as a means of making the proposed Data Protection Authority self-financing, thus placing the burden of paying for the Authority on the public and private-sector users who create the risk as well as giving the Authority independence from the government.

The creation of a register of personal data users was also seen as necessary to meet the obligation imposed by art. 8(a) of the 1981 Council of Europe Convention on Data Protection, that:

Any person shall be enabled to establish the existence of an automated personal data file, its main purposes, as well as the identity and habitual residence or principal place of business of the controller of the file.

Formal registration of data users began on 11 November 1985, after a three-phase consultation process leading up to the final format for registration.

The Office of the Data Protection Registrar initially estimated the number of registrations to be around 300,000, but only about half that number have since been received.[29]

The overall aim of the Registrar when constructing the register was to achieve 'the maximum openness consistent with simplicity of application for the data user'. However, much inevitable criticism has been levelled at the process from both data users and subjects, and the whole system is currently under review. Indeed, a shortened version of the registration form, specifically designed to aid small businesses in complying with the Act, has been available for some time.

11.4.5   The principles

The Data Protection Act 1984 is based around eight general principles (sch. 1). These principles are intended to be good practices that users should comply with in order to protect the data they hold, in both their own interests and those of their data subjects. These principles are fundamental to an understanding of the basis of data protection legislation in Western Europe.

The principles were originally developed in the 1972 Younger Report, which argued that the government should ensure that private-sector data users comply with 10 principles of good data processing. These principles, reduced down to eight, were considered central to the recommendations of the 1978 Lindop Report.

Internationally, the data protection principles were adopted as the basis for the 1980 OECD Guidelines. Indeed, the general concern over transborder data flow restrictions within the OECD led to the drafting of separate principles to safeguard the flow of non-technical data, although they were never adopted. The principles contained within the 1984 Act are designed to comply with the principles as stated in the Council of Europe Convention on Data Protection.

The first principle states that the 'information to be contained in personal data shall be obtained, and personal data shall be processed, fairly and lawfully'. Within this definition, the Registrar distinguishes two separate concerns: the concepts of 'fair obtaining' and 'fair processing'.

With regard to 'fair obtaining', the Registrar believes that this means that when information is collected the data user needs to inform the data subject of certain matters that will enable the individual to decide whether to provide the information or not. This includes information about who the data user is, what are the intended uses for the data (unless obvious) and to whom the data will be disclosed.

At the next stage the Registrar believes that 'fair processing' requires, for example, that if an individual subsequently decides that he does not want further unsolicited mailings, once the data user has been informed either directly in writing or via an intermediary (such as the Mailing Preference Service), then the data subject's name must be suppressed. Further unsolicited mailing would then be viewed by the Registrar as unfair processing. Overall, the Registrar believes that 'fair' obtaining and processing must be assessed in

---

29. Seventh Report of the Data Protection Registrar, June 1991, p. 36.

relation to each individual, rather than to the general procedures of the data user.[30]

The second data protection principle specifies that 'Personal data shall be held for one or more specified and lawful purposes'. For example, it would be a contravention of this principle for an organisation to register the holding of personal data for purposes of personnel management and use it additionally for marketing purposes. The principle does not limit the processing of data, but merely requires such activities to be properly registered.

The third principle states that 'personal data held for any purpose or purposes shall not be used or disclosed in any manner incompatible with that purpose or purposes'. Disclosure is therefore not restricted as long as details are made public within the register. This principle would be breached if an organisation sold information to a third party after collecting the information for the purpose of internal use.

Principle four relates to the requirement to hold only personal data that is 'adequate, relevant and not excessive in relation to that purpose or those purposes'. This principle is also concerned with the collection of data, an operation outside the computer process. In this respect the Registrar believes the data user 'should not record personal data merely because there is a slight possibility that this will become one of the special cases where the extra information might be useful'.[31]

The fifth principle requires that all personal data 'shall be accurate and, where necessary, kept up to date'. If, for example, an organisation purports to keep a list of undischarged bankrupts, but makes no effort to seek information on persons discharging themselves from bankruptcy, it will be contravening this principle.

Opinions that do not claim to be a statement of fact are therefore not covered by this principle. The fact that information has been obtained from a third party has to be recorded, as well as any challenge to the accuracy of the information by the data subject to whom it refers – see 11.4.6. If these conditions are met then the inaccurate data do not breach this principle.

The Registrar has put forward the issues that he may consider when dealing with a potential breach of the fifth principle, including: the significance of the inaccuracy, whether reasonable steps were taken by the data user to check the accuracy of information held and what procedures were followed by the data user once the inaccuracy was brought to light.

Data users should also focus particular attention on the accuracy of the 'identifying data element' – the data element which relates the stored data to a certain individual. This component can be viewed as the means of authenticating the data. The need for accuracy and degree of protection attached to this element should therefore reflect its unique nature. For example, if indentification of an individual is made via an address then it is crucial that this data

---

30. Data Protection Registrar, *The Data Protection Principles* (Guideline Series, Guideline 4), p. 11. The Guideline Series is available free from the Office of the Data Protection Registrar, Wilmslow. See further 11.4.9 below.

31. Ibid., at p. 16 and Guidance Note GN25-RPJ-10/91.

element is detailed enough to reflect the fact that the location at that address may be divided into separate units.

With regard to keeping information up to date, the nature of the information and its purpose will be relevant to compliance. Therefore, for information acting as a historical record it may not be necessary to carry out periodic examinations to determine if the data require updating.

Principle six states that personal data 'shall not be kept for longer than is necessary for that purpose or those purposes'. This principle implies that data should be destroyed when the specified purpose or purposes for which they were collected has been achieved. Such a process will require the same form of periodic review mentioned with regard to principle five.

The seventh principle relates to a data subject's right to know 'at reasonable intervals' if personal data is held on him or her and to have access to such data. The data subject is also given the right to have such data corrected or erased 'where appropriate'.

A data subject has an 'appropriate' right to correction or erasure of personal data only where it is necessary to comply with the other data protection principles, such as when data is irrelevant or inaccurate. However, a data subject does not have a right to get personal data removed simply because he does not want particular data users to have data about him.

An individual's 'access rights' are central to West European data protection legislation. The first necessary stage in the exercise of the 'right of access' is to discover the existence of the files, since 'access' is not a meaningful term unless combined with a knowledge of where the files are.

Two main procedures have been adopted to achieve the objective of discovering the existence of a file:

(a)   a public register, or
(b)   a notification procedure.

The former is the one adopted by the UK Data Protection Act 1984, and seems to involve a lot of effort for very little effect. The register is a record of the range of files held by the data user, but does not tell an individual if he or she is included. On the other hand, 'notification' usually involves the data user informing the subject when a file is created on him or her. This is very bureaucratic in terms of the data user's administration, but does establish the positive 'right to be informed' which is more meaningful than mere 'access' rights.

The last principle concerns data security, and requires that 'appropriate security measures' are installed by data users against 'unauthorised access to, or alteration, disclosure or destruction of, personal data and against accidental loss or destruction of personal data'.

11.4.6   Rights of data subjects

The Data Protection Act 1984 was passed to provide protection for individuals against abuses of their personal data, and therefore creates a number of rights for data subjects (Part III). The principal right is the right of subject access (s. 21).

The 'subject access' provisions of the Act came into force on 11 November 1987 as part of the final stage in the implementation of the 1984 Act. The Home Secretary announced in early summer 1987 that the maximum fee which data users may charge for subject access is £10, a figure considerably higher than that sought by the Registrar.[32]

Overall, organisations have received far fewer access requests than might have been expected, although this echoes the experience of other European countries. Public-sector data users have generally had considerably more requests than the private sector, which conforms with evidence put forward at the committee stages of the Data Protection Bill that the public sector is viewed as offering the greatest threat to individual liberties.

If a data subject suffers as a result of an abuse of personal data then the individual is able to claim compensation from the data user. Compensation can be awarded in situations of inaccuracy, loss, destruction and unauthorised disclosure or access. Any potential claim must be pursued through the courts by the individual, not the Registrar. Compensation will only be awarded if the individual can prove that actual loss or damage has been suffered. 'Damage' covers financial or physical loss, but would not include distress caused to the individual.

Data users are able to avoid liability for damage if they can prove that reasonable care was taken to ensure that such a loss does not arise (s. 23(3)). In the case of an inaccuracy, compensation is not payable if the inaccurate information was provided either by the data subject or a third party, although this fact would have to have been appropriately recorded. These rights of compensation do not apply if the personal data is exempt from the provisions of the Act.

11.4.7 Exemptions

The Data Protection Act 1984 provides for three categories of exemption:

(a)   from the whole Act (e.g., s. 33 – domestic data);
(b)   from the disclosure provisions (e.g., s. 34(8) – in an emergency);
(c)   from the subject access provisions (e.g., s. 31(1) – judicial appointments).

In general the exemptions have been granted because they are perceived not to pose a threat to the privacy of data subjects, and their inclusion in the Act's provisions would be an unnecessary burden on data users. In addition, the interests of the State necessitate certain exemptions on the grounds of national security, or during the investigation of a crime.

Payroll, pensions and accounting data (s. 31(1)) were exempted from the Act's provisions because it was felt that this was a category of information of which the data subject was well aware, and for whom it had a direct benefit. The exemption is very narrowly drafted to avoid it being exploited. For example, a record of employee sick days for the purposes of calculating

---

32. Third Report of the Data Protection Registrar, June 1987, p. 24.

remuneration would fall under the exemption. However, if those data were also kept over a period of time in order to monitor employee behaviour then they would be subject to the Act.

Membership details and name and address files (s. 33(2)) are exempt provided that the data subject has been asked if data about him or her may be held and he or she does not object. The first part is intended to exclude clubs and societies from the need to register. 'Name and address' data are exempt if 'held by a data user only for the purpose of distributing, or recording the distribution of, articles or information to the data subjects and consisting only of their names, addresses or other particulars necessary for effecting distribution' (s. 33(2)). Therefore, this exemption will not generally apply to commercial mail order firms, since they usually record more information than simply name and address.

Statistical and research data (s. 33(6)) are exempt from the subject access provisions, but not registration, provided that the data are not disclosed for any other purpose. The results of such work, when made available, must also be presented in such a form that the data subject cannot be identified.

Under the Act the Secretary of State was empowered to alter the subject access provisions relating to health and social work data (s. 29(1)) in situations where it was felt that the confidential nature of the information ought to prevail over the subject access provisions. Subsequent to the Act, three statutory instruments were issued which came into force on 11 November 1987. Generally, access can be refused to data subjects if it is felt by a relevant qualified professional that knowledge of the information could be detrimental to the subject.

Data can be certified by a Minister of the Crown as exempt from the whole Act in order to safeguard national security (s. 27); alternatively, the exemption may only extend to the non-disclosure provisions. This provision has been criticised as too wide. It has been suggested that all national security information should come under the Act, with a member of the Office of the Data Protection Registrar 'having sufficient security clearance to investigate complaints and make reports'.[33] Such a system has been employed under the Swedish and French data protection legislation.

The other exemptions contained in the Act apply to areas where the need for an exemption is self-explanatory. Data relating to the investigation of a crime or a person's tax affairs are exempt from the subject access provisions provided such knowledge would prejudice these tasks. Domestic data and publicly available data are excluded from the Act altogether.

In his second annual report, the Data Protection Registrar noted that the exemptions had caused considerable confusion among data users, while undue reliance on them has been suggested as a contributory factor behind the lower than estimated registration levels. The exemptions for 'payroll, accounts' and 'name and address' data have caused particular uncertainty, and the Registrar has suggested they be removed.[34]

---

33. *What are your views? – Monitoring and Assessment of the Data Protection Act 1984 – A Consultation Document from the Data Protection Registrar*, May 1988, p. 63.
34. Ibid., p. 32.

11.4.8 Data security

A crucial element of effective data protection is the need for data security. The eighth principle of the Data Protection Act 1984 directs that data users should ensure that they have 'appropriate security measures' against possible loss, destruction, unauthorised disclosure or alteration. Therefore, data users are required to maintain the confidentiality and accuracy of the data and be able to satisfy the subject's right to access the data and correct them if necessary. Although a failure to comply with the principle is not directly an offence, it could result in an enforcement notice being issued by the Registrar.

The Act quite clearly outlines the range of issues that should be considered when implementing 'appropriate' data security. Schedule 1, Part II, para. 6 states:

Regard shall be had—
    (a)   to the nature of the personal data and the harm that would result from such access, alteration, disclosure, loss or destruction as are mentioned in this principle; and
    (b)   to the place where the personal data are stored, to security measures programmed into the relevant equipment and to measures taken for ensuring the reliability of staff having access to the data.

Data users are therefore expected to consider the sensitivity of the personal data they hold and implement suitable security procedures. Such measures involve different aspects: physical security, such as the security of disk storage facilities, from such dangers as fire and flood as well as unauthorised access; software security, such as maintaining a log of all failed access requests; and operational security, for example, with regard to work data being taken home by employees and periodic data protection audits of computer systems.

The Registrar has also commented that the mere fact that a breach of security has occurred will not be proof that the data user has been negligent provided the data user has 'done everything which could reasonably be expected' (Guideline 4).

Article 6 of the Council of Europe Convention mentions that 'special categories of data' may need to be given additional safeguards. Indeed, most European data protection legislation including that of France, Norway and Sweden has provisions which explicitly address the question of 'sensitive' data. However, different national traditions make it impossible to offer general rules to categorise 'sensitive' data. For example, under Norwegian law data concerning a person's sexual life is considered 'sensitive', while it is not mentioned in French law. However, under French law trade union affiliation is considered 'sensitive' but not in Norway. Under s. 2(3) of the UK Act the Secretary of State has the power to provide additional safeguards for information relating to:

    (a)   the racial origin of the data subject;
    (b)   his political opinions or religious or other beliefs;
    (c)   his physical or mental health or his sexual life; or
    (d)   his criminal convictions.

To date, no such supplementary provisions have been made.

The Data Protection Act 1984 has encouraged more data users to focus their attention on the importance of adequate data security and therefore devote greater resources to it. Most of the security measures implemented under the Act will generally tie in closely with the needs of the data users themselves.

There has recently been an attempt to extend the impact of the security provisions of the Act. In 1990 a private member's Bill was presented to the House of Commons which was designed to: 'provide entitlement to compensation, in certain circumstances, to an individual who suffers damage . . . by reason of the unreliability or lack of security, of a computer, data or program'.[35] Although the Bill failed to get Parliamentary support, it does illustrate the possible nature of future legislation under a government of a different political persuasion.

11.4.9 Enforcement

The Data Protection Act 1984 creates or gives rise to the possibility of criminal prosecution under six different categories of offence:

(a) Non-registration (e.g., s. 5(1), holding personal data when not registered).

(b) Registration information (e.g., s. 6(6), furnishing false or misleading registration details).

(c) Acting outside register entry (e.g., s. 5(2)(a), holding personal data other than that registered).

(d) Failure to comply with notice (e.g., s. 12(10), contravention of transfer prohibition notice).

(e) Warrant offences (e.g., sch. 4, para. 12, obstructing a person executing a warrant); and

(f) Bureaux disclosure (s. 15, disclosure of personal data without authority of data user).[36]

These offences can be further divided into offences of strict or absolute liability and those which require the data user to have acted 'knowingly or recklessly'. Criminal proceedings can only be begun by the Data Protection Registrar with the consent of the Director of Public Prosecutions.

Under s. 20 of the Act, in addition to the company being prosecuted for an offence a 'director, manager, secretary or similar officer' can also be found *personally liable*, where the offence was committed with 'the consent or connivance of or [was] attributable to any neglect on the part of' any such individual.

---

35. H. Rowe, 'The UK Computers (Compensation for Damage) Bill', (1990) 7(8) Applied Computer and Communications Law 6.
36. Under s. 19, the penalties for the offences are: (a) for offences of registration under s. 6 and obstructing the execution of a warrant, a fine not exceeding the fifth level on the standard scale (as defined by s. 75 of the Criminal Justice Act 1982 – current maximum £2,000); (b) for all other offences, either (i) a fine on conviction on indictment; or (ii) a fine for summary conviction up to the statutory maximum under s. 74 of the Criminal Justice Act 1982 – current maximum £2,000.

To date the Registrar has only prosecuted some 70 data users, and many of these were brought for non-registration offences (s. 5(1)). However, as part of his increasing activity in the area of enforcement the Registrar has begun to focus increasingly on particular sectors, such as professional advisers, and in specific geographical areas such as Cambridge.

The Data Protection Tribunal has completed six full hearings and one in which the decision was made with the consent of the parties. These Tribunal hearings covered three different issues: community charge registration officers (CCROs), credit reference agencies and the Halifax Building Society.

The Registrar issued 'enforcement notices' against a number of CCROs who were accused of intending to collect and hold excessive amounts of data in breach of the fourth principle. The Tribunal upheld the Registrar's viewpoint. Additionally, one CCRO was successfully prosecuted for failing to comply with the notice.

The Registrar has been in a long-running dispute with the four UK credit reference agencies concerning the definition of what information it is 'fair' for the agencies to consider when assessing a person's eligibility for credit. In particular, the Registrar has been concerned over the use of information relating to past residents of a person's accommodation. In *CCN Systems Ltd* v *Data Protection Registrar* (1991)[37] the Registrar had issued an enforcement notice to the appellants, requiring them to cease to provide information relating to applicants for credit that was based purely on their address. The practice of CCN and other credit reference agencies is to provide not only details of the applicant's credit record, but also details of others (whether they bear the same name or not) who formerly or subsequently resided at the applicant's current or previous address. CCN appealed against this notice on the ground that the processing they undertook was not unfair.

The Data Protection Tribunal held that:[38]

The case was concerned entirely with that part of the principle that can be reduced to: 'Personal data shall be processed fairly.'

The relevant aspect of 'processing' taken from the definition in s. 1(7) of the Data Protection Act 1984 is the extraction of the data, and the question was refined to whether the processing undertaken by the appellants extracted data which were *relevant* to the decision whether to grant credit. CCN argued that such data were relevant to the credit decision because, on the statistical evidence presented, adverse information against third parties at the same address increased the likelihood *in the aggregate* that applicants in that category would default on the loan. On the other hand, the Registrar argued that the proper test was whether the information was relevant *to the particular applicant*, and it was clear that for any individual case such third-party information did not generally increase the risk of default. In coming to its judgment on this point, the tribunal held:[39]

---

37. Unreported. All page references are to the transcript.
38. Transcript, p. 3.
39. Transcript, p. 16.

In our view, in deciding whether the processing . . . is fair we must give first and paramount consideration to the interests of the applicant for credit – the 'data subject' in the Act's terms. We are not ignoring the consequences for the credit industry of a finding of unfairness, and we sympathise with their problems, but we believe that they will accept that they must carry on their activities in accordance with the principles laid down in the Act of Parliament.

The tribunal therefore held that CCN's processing was unfair in this respect, and disallowed the appeal on that point. It was particularly influenced by the fact that in some cases the inquirer never saw the raw data, and thus had no opportunity to make a separate assessment of their relevance, because CCN offered a number of credit scoring systems which gave the inquirer only a credit score, based in part on this third-party information.

However, the Tribunal did hold that the enforcement notice had been too wide, as certain types of third-party information would be relevant and thus fairly extracted if there was a clear connection with the applicant for credit. The enforcement notice was therefore amended so as to permit the extraction of the following types of third-party information:[40]

[Information about individuals]:

(a) who have the same surname and forenames or initials as the subject or, where the forename and initials are not known, the same surname or, where the precise surname is not known, a similar name, or

(b) who have the same surname as the subject or, where the precise surname is not known, a similar name, and who are reasonably believed to live as members of the family of the subject in a single household, or

(c) who do not have the same surname as the subject but, on the basis of information obtained before such processing, are reasonably believed to live as members of the family of the subject in a single household.

The most important principle to be extracted from this judgment is that 'fairness' must always be assessed in relation to the data subject. The mere fact that such processing is to the advantage of the data user is not a relevant consideration.

The Halifax Building Society case was in two parts; a criminal conviction and a Tribunal hearing. In the former the Registrar failed to prove that the Halifax was 'knowingly or recklessly holding personal data for the purposes of crime prevention when not properly registered under the Act'. In the second, some form of mutual settlement was arrived at between the parties.

The central issue of these cases involved the definition of 'personal data' under the Act. The issue arose following a subject access request to the Halifax. Although certain data were provided to the data subject, other items of data such as the times of transactions made through ATMs were not released. The argument revolves around whether a distinction can be made between

---

40. Transcript, p. 20.

'personal data' and 'system data', which is not directly related to an individual. As the Registrar notes with respect to the definition of 'personal data', 'inevitably, there are some borderline situations where the position is not immediately apparent' (Guideline 2, p. 20). Unfortunately, due to the mutual agreement reached between the parties at the Tribunal, this issue has still yet to be clearly resolved.

Since the Act was passed there has only been one instance where the Registrar has issued a transfer prohibition notice. The case involved the sending of personal data to the US for direct mailings back to the UK. The US operation was, at the time of the request, involved in a legal action with the US Postal Service, which was attempting to restrict the company's actions on the grounds of fraud and misleading promotions. The Registrar felt in the circumstances that such a transfer would be likely to lead to a breach of three of the data protection principles which form the basis of the Act.[41]

11.4.10   Revision

A process of reviewing the Data Protection Act 1984 was carried out in 1988–9. The Home Office established an interdepartmental review committee to carry out the review procedure. In this respect, the Home Secretary stated:[42]

> It has always been our intention to review the Act once it was fully in force and experience gained of its practical operation. . . . The committee has been asked to review the implementation of the Act, particularly with regard to the impact on data users of the registration requirements.

In conjunction with this review, the Data Protection Registrar also carried out an assessment of the Act based on the invited submissions of all interested groups.[43]

Arising from this review procedure, it appeared that the most likely area to be significantly amended would be the registration procedure. This requirement has prompted most criticism from data users and subjects. Overall, the Registrar considers that there are two major alternatives to the present system:

(a)   The removal of all small, non-sensitive data users from the register, allowing more resources for investigation and individual case work.

(b)   A 'near-universal' registration system, with little detail except for holders of sensitive data.

The other major area of complaint concerned subject access rights. Research by the Office of the Registrar has supported the conclusion that the access fee deters individuals from exercising their rights. Indeed, other research has found that most private-sector data users that charge do so as a deterrent rather than to cover costs.

---

41. Seventh Report of the Data Protection Registrar, p. 33–4, June 1981, HMSO.
42. Reported in *Computer Law and Security Report* (September–October 1988), p. 35.
43. See note 33.

By the time the review process was completed the European Commission had embarked on drafting a Directive, and therefore all decisions on reform have been shelved pending the outcome of the final Directive.

11.5 DEVELOPMENTS IN DATA PROTECTION LEGISLATION

11.5.1 Technological developments

When the first national data protection legislation was passed in Sweden in 1973, the major privacy fears were generated through the use of large mainframe computers. However, the rapid growth of microcomputers has altered the focus of concern. The ability of smaller machines to process larger amounts of information is a trend which seems set to continue in the foreseeable future.

Such rapid technological change makes legal regulation in this field potentially obsolete, and inevitably leads to criticism from both data users and data subjects. The former fear that regulation may serve to curb the development and use of new technologies. The latter warn that the new technologies create threats to personal privacy not covered by legislation. One solution to the problem of legislation becoming technologically obsolescent has been to include within the corpus of the statute a time-limit for revision of the Act. Such an approach has been adopted within the data protection legislation of Canada and Iceland.

The Council of Europe Committee of Experts on Data Protection has published a document that considers the challenges that new technologies present for the protection of personal data, and in particular whether the principles laid down in the Convention remain adequate as a basis for protection.[44]

'Electronic tracing' is an example of a concern that has originated in the development and increased use of telematic services. In this situation, 'confidential' or 'sensitive' personal data arise not from the level of detail of information which is stored in a database but from the personal data that arise through the use of a service, such as monitoring a person's use of ATMs to determine spending patterns. Such large databases allow the possibility of constructing a 'profile' of every user, or group of users, of a particular service.

The fear of 'electronic tracing' has not sprung simply from the possibilities inherent in the technology but also the developments within the European Community to remove border controls, which, it has been suggested by Jon Bing, will 'be compensated by increased use of surveillance based on electronic traces'.

Changing technologies would also seem to make it necessary to distinguish the idea of data files from that of the processing location. The growth of the computer network has given rise to the need for a reconsideration of legislative terminology; for example, possibly moving from the traditional data protection concept of the 'controller of the file', which is now considered an obsolete

---

44. *New Technologies: a Challenge to Privacy Protection?* (Strasbourg: Council of Europe, 1989); see also *Computer Law and Security Report*, vol. 5, No. 3 (1989), pp. 19–20.

concept, to that of 'controller of the network'. The role of the latter person would be to take responsibility for all the personal data held on a data subject throughout the network. Also, with regard to the growth of international networks, the aim of achieving 'transparency' for data subjects can become significantly more difficult as increasing numbers of persons have access to the data.

Such a change would require that a clear legal distinction be made between the obligations and responsibilities of the 'network controller' and other relevant parties such as the network provider.

11.5.2 Differentiation and self-regulation

Over the past two years, there has emerged a 'second generation' of data protection legislation within Western Europe. This legislation, in the Netherlands, Switzerland and Ireland, exhibits a number of characteristics that differentiate it from the legislation passed in the 1970s, such as that of Sweden, France and Austria, although even these countries are amending their legislation in the same direction. There is a trend towards simplification, the increased use of informal and civil sanctions as a means of enforcing data protection, a greater amount of regulatory differentiation for different sectors of data users and a trend in favour of self-regulation. The need for simplification has arisen in the face of the bureaucracy that implementation of data protection legislation has created, and the corresponding costs involved both for data users and the regulatory authorities themselves.

Few cases of criminal prosecutions under data protection legislation have occurred in Western Europe, and it would seem that data protection authorities tend to rely on informal and civil sanctions against offending data users. Informal sanctions generally involve an investigation by the authority, with the threat of publicity as the incentive for data users to remedy the identified problem areas.

The trend toward differentiation of data protection rules (the sectoral approach) has been a result of the ageing and experience of existing legislation. Such a process of differentiation enables an increased level of protection for data subjects as well as tailoring the legislation to fit in more suitably with the conditions within particular industries, and thus prevents the creation of unnecessary and unsuitable bureaucratic requirements. Division into sectors has occurred along such lines as the sensitivity of the data and the purpose of the data. The Council of Europe has set up a number of sectoral working parties to draw up regulations for different categories of data users, while the European Commission has proposed a similar sectoral approach.

Also related to the greater differentiation of data protection rules is the trend towards self-regulation. Sectors of data users are drafting quasi-legal, enforceable codes of practice on data protection. Indeed, in some countries such as Japan, voluntary codes of practice are the only form of private-sector data protection regulation. Under the Netherlands Act the private sector is strongly encouraged to establish codes of conduct. Indeed, if after a certain period of time no satisfactory code has been produced then there is a power to issue general administrative orders statutorily imposing codes of conduct.

11.6   CONCLUSION

Data protection legislation gained a significant profile during the late 1970s and early 1980s, as companies voiced their fears that the spread of data protection laws would act as an obstacle to the use of international data communication technologies. In the UK, for example, much was written about how the potential restrictions could deter the adoption of IT altogether! The literature and results of various studies would suggest that such fears were generally unfounded.

Recently, however, the draft European data protection Directive has given new life to the debate. The need for any such European Community initiative is itself controversial. However, data users need to take account of data protection requirements when trading within Europe, both with regard to their internal procedures and in any contractual agreements.

The data security provisions, contained in all European national legislation, are of a vague enough nature not to be unnecessarily restrictive upon companies. Rather, data security managers need to use the existence of such provisions to encourage a greater priority and increased resources for general data security issues at board level.

One current significant issue in the field of data protection concerns how companies, particularly those based in, or trading with, countries such as the United States, can achieve an international functional equivalency of protection in the absence of national legislation. If such equivalency is not possible unless in statutory form, then potential problems will continue to exist for international data flows in the foreseeable future.

CHAPTER TWELVE

EC computer law

Tim Cowen and Thomas Hoeren

12.1 INTRODUCTION: 1992

A great deal has been written on the national aspects of computer law, but comparatively little is available on the European aspects of procuring, selling and distributing computers and computing equipment. Nonetheless, these aspects have become more and more important, particularly in the context of the EC's aim of establishing a Single Market by the end of 1992.

From the beginning of the 1980s, standardised rules were created for software protection, product liability and computer contracts, thereby eliminating the differences between the Member States' laws. These efforts seem to culminate in uniform EC computer law which will be able to fulfil the major aims of the EEC Treaty:

(a)   To abolish the proliferation of differences between national computer laws and nationalistic purchasing practices which act as disguised barriers to free trade (arts 30, 59–66 and 100).

(b)   Once the barriers to trade have been abolished to ensure free and open competition through the application of EC competition law (arts 85–94).

(c)   To support the development of a single internal market (art. 100(a)).

(d)   To promote a common commercial policy in the relations of the EEC to non-member States (art. 113).

These objectives were to be realised step by step following the publication of the Commission's White Paper in 1985.[1] In that paper, the EC Commission

---

1. For a more detailed discussion of this development see Corinna M. Wissels, 'European Community Law' in A. P. Meijboom and C. Prins (eds), *The Law of Information Technology in Europe 1992* (Deventer 1991), p. 3 et seq.

presented an extensive programme for the completion of the single internal market by 31 December 1992. The intention was that by that date, all restrictions on the free movement of goods, persons, services and capital within the European Community should be eliminated.[2]

This ambitious programme could only be realised with the aid of the Single European Act (SEA) which came into force on 1 July 1987.[3] The SEA amended the EEC Treaty. One of the major changes was to clear the log-jam of legislation on which agreement had not been reached in the Council of Ministers. The SEA achieved this by changing the voting rules so that more legislation could be enacted by a majority of Member States rather than by unanimity.[4]

As part of its 1992 initiative the EC authorities took a number of initiatives to harmonise computer law within Europe. Among the most important were:

(a)   The Council Directive on the Approximation of the Laws, Regulations and Administrative Provisions of the Member States Concerning Liability for Defective Products issued on 25 July 1985.[5]

(b)   The Council Directive on the Protection of Semiconductor Product Designs issued on 16 December 1986.[6]

(c)   The Council Directive on Approximation of Trade Mark Laws.[7]

(d)   The Council Directive on the Legal Protection of Computer Programs adopted by the Council of Ministers on 14 May 1991.[8]

(e)   The proposal for a Council Directive Concerning the Protection of Individuals in Relation to the Processing of Personal Data submitted by the Commission on 27 July 1990.[9]

(f)   The proposal for a Council Directive on the Legal Protection of Databases announced on 29 January 1992.[10]

The 1992 programme is not only important for the EC Member States. It will also change the whole legal structure within the EFTA States, because on 2 May 1992 the EFTA States agreed with the EC to create a European Economic Area (EEA). On the basis of that agreement the EFTA States will

---

2. It is doubtful whether all parts of the Single Market programme will be implemented by 1 January 1993. As at 30 November 1991, 188 of the 282 Single Market measures had entered into force; only 108 of these measures had been implemented by all member States. See *The Single Market: Progress on Commission White Paper* (London: DTI, 1991).

3. Single European Act, OJ No. L 169, 1987.

4. See P. Pescatore, 'Some Critical Remarks on the Single European Act' 24 CML Rev 19; J. Lodge, 'The Single European Act: towards a New Euro-dynamism?' (1986) 24 Journal of Common Market Studies 203.

5. 83/374/EEC OJ No. L 210, 1985.

6. 87/54/EEC, OJ No. L 24, 27 January 1987, p. 36.

7. 89/104/EEC OJ No. L 40, 11 February 1989, p. 1.

8. 91/250/EEC. OJ No. L 122, 17 May 1991, p. 42.

9. COM(90) 314 final – SYN 287, 90/C 277/03. OJ No. C 277, 5 November 1990, p. 12. This proposal has been published together with some other regulations on data protection especially with regard to the telecommunications sector.

10. COM(92) 24 final – SYN 393, OJ No. C 156, 23 June 1992, p. 4.

implement EC regulations into national law in the same way as EC Member States.

Before the 1992 programme of legislation, whether by design or for other reasons, Member States did not comply with their fundamental Treaty obligations. The basic rules contained in the Treaty therefore needed to be supplemented by regulations applying those rules in individual market sectors. The 1992 programme of legislation was created to achieve this aim. The fundamental Treaty rules are addressed briefly below. Where relevant the specific regulations are referred to, and other chapters of this book provide greater detail on the specific regulations. This chapter is primarily concerned with the following areas:

(a)   The free trade provisions of the EC Treaty and the obligations on governments and government bodies to purchase from any EC supplier.

(b)   The competition rules which apply to ensure that barriers to free trade are not re-erected by agreements between businesses, and which impose obligations on all concerned in the sale and distribution of computer products throughout the Community.

12.2   THE FREEDOM TO TRADE THROUGHOUT THE EUROPEAN COMMUNITY

Perhaps the most important amendments to national laws which govern the information technology industry, and which lead to a degree of harmonisation of those laws, derive from the EEC Treaty itself. As indicated above, arts 30 and 59 to 66 of the EEC Treaty abolished disguised barriers to free trade within the European Community.

The EEC Treaty established a customs union in which duties were eliminated between Member States and a common customs tariff was adopted in trade relations with non-EEC Member States. As a customs union, the free-movement provisions concerning both goods and services apply not only to goods originating within the Community, but also to products which have entered the Community from non-Member countries, once those products are in 'free circulation' within a single Member State. A substantial percentage of computer products or components are manufactured outside the Community. Once those products have lawfully[11] entered the Community, in their subsequent trade between Member States it is possible to rely on the free-movement provisions to the same extent as if those goods had originated within the Community.[12]

The origin of products may, however, be of significance if a Member State invokes art. 115 which may entitle it to prevent the free circulation of goods from another Member State. Substantial investment into the EEC from Far

11. EEC Treaty, art. 10, which requires import formalities to have been complied with and customs duties or charges having equivalent effect to have been levied without reimbursement of such duties or charges.
12. Regulation 802/68, OJ English Sp. Ed. 1968 (I), p. 15.

Eastern companies occurred during the 1980s and some of their products may be affected by these rules. The basic rule which defines the origin of goods is contained in Regulation 802/68. This provides that a product which is wholly obtained or produced in one country originates there. Goods produced in two or more countries are regarded as originating in the country where the last substantial process or operation that is economically justified was performed, having been carried out in an undertaking equipped for the purpose, and resulting in the manufacture of a new product or representing an important stage in manufacture. (Particular legislation has been adopted under Regulation 802/68 for specific types of information technology products.)

In practice, a Community transit system has been introduced to facilitate internal Community transit and external Community transit (an exporter must make a 'T1' declaration for exports, whereas a 'T2' declaration is used for internal Community transit where the goods are in free circulation).

12.2.1 Measures which restrict the free movement of goods

Lifting the barriers to free trade may prompt a Member State to protect its national (domestic) industry. One mechanism for restricting the extent to which overseas competition may compete with domestic industry is to impose disguised restrictions on non-domestic goods. Such restrictions are abolished under art. 30 of the EEC Treaty. Article 30 has been interpreted very widely and any measure which affects trade in goods between Member States may fall within its prohibition. Measures such as labelling or origin-marking, differing product standards, import licences or 'buy national campaigns' can fall within art. 30. Directive 70/50/EEC[13] provides guidance on those measures which can be regarded as infringing art. 30. The European Court of Justice has widened the scope of art. 30 to encompass 'all trading rules enacted by Member States which are capable of injuring directly or indirectly, actually or potentially, intra-Community trade'.[14] It is of no consequence that the trading rules in question are applicable to both imports and products which have been produced domestically if the *effect* is to discriminate against imports.

Products which can be valued in money and which are capable of forming the subject of commercial transactions will be regarded as 'goods' under art. 30. This is a wide definition and may encompass products which in other areas of law would be regarded as services.[15] It is likely, although undecided, that computer software would be regarded as 'goods' if transported around the Community on disk or some other form of hardware (including firmware). However, if the software is used for providing a service between Member States such as an E-mail service or a remote data-processing service, it may be more appropriate to seek to rely on the equivalent rules concerned with the freedom to provide services under arts 59 to 66 of the EEC Treaty (see 12.2.3 for further discussion).

---

13. OJ Sp. Ed. 1970 (I), p. 17 (technically only applies to measures in force at the end of the transitional period, which has now ended). Recently referred to by the European Court of Justice in *Torfaen Borough Council* v *B & Q plc* (case 145/88) [1990] 2 QB 19.
14. *Procureur du Roi* v *Dassonville* (case 8/74) [1974] ECR 837 at p. 852.
15. *Commission* v *Italy* (case 7/68) [1968] ECR 423.

12.2.2 Exceptions and limitations

Under art. 36 of the EEC Treaty, it is possible for a government or government authority to justify its restrictions on trade on the grounds of:

(a)   morality;
(b)   public policy or public security;
(c)   protection of health and life of humans, animals or plants;
(d)   protection of national treasures possessing artistic, historic or archaelological value; or
(e)   protection of industrial and commercial property.

In addition, there is an obligation imposed on the government bodies concerned that any exemptions to the principles of free movement should not constitute a means of arbitrary discrimination or a disguised restriction on trade. Exemptions to the free movement rules are to be restrictively interpreted and measures taken should not be disproportionate to their objective. Once the Community authorities have issued harmonising measures, it becomes impossible for a government body to rely on an equivalent national law to justify restrictive conduct. However, the European Court of Justice has recognised certain further grounds for excluding goods from particular territories. In particular, it has recognised the following as potential justifications for restrictions on the free movement of goods:

(a)   fiscal supervision;
(b)   public health;
(c)   fairness of commercial transactions;
(d)   protection of the consumer.

12.2.3 Freedom to provide services: article 59

Article 59 of the EEC Treaty guarantees, as a general rule, the freedom to provide cross-border services. In its *Sacchi* decision[16] the European Court of Justice held that a television signal should be regarded as a provision of services. It is likely that transborder computer services or telecommunications services would be regarded as services falling within the definition of art. 60. Such services must be provided for remuneration and must not fall within the rules concerning the free movement of goods, capital or persons.

In order to rely on the free movement of services provisions contained in the Treaty a national must be 'established' in one of the EC Member States. This may normally be accomplished by setting up a company.

Article 59 is subject to limitations which may be invoked by Member States or government bodies on the grounds of:

(a)   activities concerned with the exercise of official authority (art. 55);
(b)   public policy, public security or public health (art. 56);
(c)   non-economic public interest exceptions, e.g., where copyright owners have 'performance' rights in the services concerned.

---

16. *Italy* v *Sacchi* (Case 155/73) [1974] ECR 409.

12.2.4 Public procurement

Public bodies are the biggest purchasers of information technology in most parts of Europe. It has for instance been estimated that in the UK 45 per cent of all computers are bought through public procurement.[17]

The prohibitions contained in arts 30 and 59 of the EEC Treaty are the bases for the specific public procurement rules. In its 1985 White Paper, the Commission identified concerns about the purchasing practices of Government bodies.[18] In summary, these concerns were:

(a)   The authorities concerned purchased on a national basis which led to the continued partitioning of national markets contrary to the single market objective.

(b)   The EEC Treaty as a whole, and arts 30 and 59 in particular, lays down basic rules which mean that discrimination by governments and government bodies in favour of national suppliers is illegal. However, these rules were ignored in practice.

A particular example of such discrimination occurred when the Dundalk Urban District Council required all tenders for the construction of a water main to comply with Irish standards. Only one company had obtained such approval and, perhaps unsurprisingly, that was an Irish company. A Spanish manufacturer tendering pipes which met an equivalent international standard complained to the Commission which took Ireland to the European Court of Justice.[19] The European Court held Ireland to have breached art. 30. This case demonstrates the application of the underlying Treaty rules. However, specific rules which supplement but do not override the Treaty have now been created so that the rules are more widely observed.[20] The following have now been adopted:

(a)   The Council Directive of 17 December 1969 on the Supply of Goods to the State and Other Authorities.[21]

(b)   The Council Directive of 21 December 1976 on the Coordination of Procedures for the Award of Public Supply Contracts.[22]

(c)   The Council Directive of 22 July 1980 on the Adaptation and Supplementation of Directive 77/62/EEC on the Coordination of Procedures for the Award of Public Supply Contracts.[23]

---

17. Clifford Chance, *Information Technology 1992* (London: Clifford Chance 1990), p. 31.
18. See International Institute for Legal and Administrative Technology, *Public Procurement* (Cologne 1990), p. 14 et seq.; Brechon and Moulenes, *Les Marchés Publics Européens* (Droit Communautaire, droit comparé), Dossiers et documents de la Revue française de Droit administrative (Paris 1989), pp. 37–69.
19. *Commission* v *Ireland* (case 45/87) [1988] ECR 4929.
20. See Elke Schmitz, *Das Recht der öffentlichen Aufträge im Gemeinsamen Markt* (Baden-Baden 1972), p. 128 et seq.
21. Directive 70/32/EEC, OJ No. L 13, 19 January 1970, p. 1.
22. Directive 77/62/EEC, OJ No. L 13 of 15 January 1977, p. 1.
23. Directive 80/767/EEC, OJ No. L 215 of 18 August 1980, p. 1.

(d)   The Council Directive of 22 March 1988 on the Coordination of Procedures on the Award of Public Supply Contracts.[24]

(e)   The Council Directive of 21 December 1989 on the Coordination of the Laws, Regulations and Administrative Provisions Relating to the Application of Review Procedures to the Award of Public Supply and Public Works Contracts.[25]

12.2.4.1   Applicability of the Directives   All the rules mentioned above apply through implementing national laws to written contracts for the supply of goods. The Directive of 22 March 1988 has extended their applicability to leasing agreements and contracts for hire.

The Directives do not, however, refer to services or works.[26] This restriction leads to unforeseeable consequences with regard to information technology contracts, as the rules are not applicable where public authorities are awarding contracts on:[27]

(a)   project management services and consultancy;
(b)   training;
(c)   maintenance;
(d)   services of a bureau; or
(e)   bespoke software.

In March 1991, the Commission published a proposal for a Directive on services which will close this dangerous gap in the future.[28]

Additionally, the regulations only deal with contracts for the supply of 'goods'. This terminology leads to the problem whether standard software may be regarded as a 'good' within these EC Directives. This issue has been the subject of controversial discussion for some time with regard to the applicability of the Sale of Goods Act 1979. The New South Wales Supreme Court[29] has held that the sale and installation of hardware and software constitutes a sale of goods and the judgment has been used to support the general classification of software itself as a 'good'.[30] This view has, however, been rejected by some voices in the literature stating that standard software has to be regarded as intangible.[31] (Further discussion of this issue can be found in 2.1.4.)

Even the EC authorities appear to have given divergent views on this issue. On the one hand, the EC Commission took the view that software is a product

---

24. Directive 88/295/EEC, OJ No. L 127 of 20 May 1988, p. 1.
25. Directive 89/665/EEC, OJ No. L 395 of 30 December 1989, p. 33.
26. See art. 1(b) of Council Directive 77/62/EEC.
27. Stephen Saxby (ed.), *Encyclopedia of Information Technology Law* (London: Sweet & Maxwell, 1992), paras 6.118 to 6.293.
28. COM(90) 372 final – SYN 293, 91/C 23/01, OJ No. C 23, 31 January 1991, p. 1. Cf. the first (unofficial) proposal of the Commission submitted in April 1990 (Doc. CCO/90/28).
29. *Toby Constructions Products Ltd* v *Computa Bar (Sales) Pty Ltd* [1983] 2 NSWLR 48.
30. See also Reed (1988) 4 CL&P 149.
31. See S. W. Cavanagh, 'The Supply of Computer Software – Goods or Services?' (1984) 12 ABLR 195.

for the purposes of the EC Directive on product liability.[32] On the other hand, the regulations on the public procurement of telecommunications services (see 12.2.4.3) make a distinction between software and goods.[33]

The Public Supply Directives apply to all public supply contracts of a value of at least 200,000 ECUs. The sectors of telecommunications, energy, transport and water were expressly excluded. A separate Directive, concerned with both supplies and works, will apply the EC procurement rules to the telecommunications, energy, transport and water sectors from 1 January 1993 at the earliest.

12.2.4.2 Main elements The Directives state that public bodies have generally to award their supply contracts by open tendering, i.e., tendering which is open to all interested suppliers. Selective tendering or negotiations with chosen suppliers are only lawful in some special circumstances described in the Directives; the use of these procedures must be justified by the public body in a report. This choice of open tendering is contrary to past practice in the UK which has been to award the bulk of contracts by selective tendering.[34]

The Directives have additionally stressed the importance of transparency in the public procurement sector. Public bodies are required to publish announcements of an award in the Official Journal of the EC. Furthermore, they have to announce their award decisions and the total sum of expected purchases for the year.

12.2.4.3 Public telecommunications contracts As mentioned above, the Directives on public supply contracts do not apply to telecommunications. This exemption proved to be unsatisfactory so the EC authorities created a separate Directive to deal with public telecommunications contracts. On 17 September 1990 these considerations led to the announcement of the Council Directive on Public Procurement in the Sectors of Water, Energy, Transport and Telecommunications.[35]

This Directive applies to all public bodies' contracts for telecommunication products (including software) and services; the relevant threshold is 600,000 ECUs. Contracting entities have to define technical specifications by reference to European standards; they are free to choose open, selective or negotiated tendering procedures. In addition, they have to publish a list of their total anticipated procurement during the next 12 months. The Directive allows the bodies to which it applies, which are known as 'contracting entities', to maintain approved lists of contractors competent to carry out particular work. The contract has to be awarded to the tenderer who submitted the lowest assessed tender, i.e., the tenderer whose tender offers the best overall value for

---

32. Answer to written question No. 706/88, OJ No. C 114, 8 May 1989, p. 42.
33. See art. 1(3)(a) of Council Directive 90/351/EEC referring to supply contracts on 'goods or software'. See also art. 29(2) of that Directive stating that software has to be regarded as a 'good' for the purpose of the article.
34. International Institute for Legal and Administrative Technology, *Public Procurement* (Cologne 1990), p. 81 et seq.
35. Directive 90/351/EEC, OJ No. L 297, 25 October 1990, p. 1.

money. According to the Directive, the contracting entities may refuse to award a tender on the grounds of non-EEC origin under certain circumstances.

The EC Commission is preparing a second Directive on the coordination of public procurement regulations with regard to these four sectors[36] which has recently been approved by the European Parliament.[37]

12.2.4.4 Council Decision 87/95/EEC On 22 December 1986, the Council announced its Decision on standardisation in the field of information technology and telecommunications.[38] This Decision calls for the mandatory use of European and international standards by public-sector authorities. Contracts for information systems of value above 100,000 ECUs must refer to these standards. This obligation is not binding upon orders concerning 'innovative' systems or if an adherence to the standards would lead to an 'uneconomic solution'.

The Decision is binding upon the EC Member States, which have to transform it into national law. In March 1988 a number of functional standards were published by the UK Central Computer and Telecommunications Agency (CCTA) which are now used as mandatory standards under Decision 87/95/EEC.

12.2.5 EC law remedies

According to the Remedies Directive (89/665/EEC) of 21 December 1989, the Member States have to set up a judicial or administrative authority which examines alleged infringements against the EC public procurement regulations. This authority must be able:

(a) to suspend the award procedure;
(b) to cancel unlawful decisions;
(c) to order the removal of discriminatory specifications; and
(d) to grant damages to injured parties.

In addition to the Remedies Directive (89/665/EEC), arts 30 and 59 of the EEC Treaty may be relied upon in national courts and it is possible to complain to the European Commission to ensure that the national authority complies with the Member State's treaty obligations. This may provide an effective practical remedy where, for example, a supplier considers he has been discriminated against as a result of the nationalistic purchasing practices of the government authority or where a supplier suffers from some other form of discrimination by government authorities.

In the *Francovich* case,[39] the European Court of Justice held that directly effective provisions (such as arts 30 and 59) may be relied upon by individuals

---

36. Second proposal of the EC Commission, OJ No. C 179, 19 July 1991, p. 18. For the first proposal see OJ No. L 297, 29 October 1990, p. 1.
37. EP Doc A3-339/91.
38. Decision 87/95/EEC, OJ No. 36, 7 February 1987, p. 31.
39. *Francovich Bonifaci v Italy* (cases C60/90 and C9/90). *The Times*, 20 November 1991.

against the State. It also reviewed the issue of State liability and held that the principle of Member State liability for damage resulting from infringements of Community law was inherent in the EEC Treaty. Uncertainty remains over the full extent of a Member State's liability, but in principle it is possible to claim damages against a Member State for its failure to observe art. 30 or art. 59. This might be of considerable importance in the context of the public procurement regime as an additional weapon against a Member State body such as a local authority.

12.3   EC COMPETITION LAW

The objects of EC competition law can be regarded as twofold. Article 3 of the EEC Treaty provides that:

> For the purposes set out in art. 2, the activities of the Community shall include, as provided in this Treaty and in accordance with the timetable set out therein:
>   (a)   the elimination, as between Member States, of customs duties and of quantitative restrictions on the import and export of goods, and of all other measures having equivalent effect; . . .
>   (f)   the institution of a system ensuring that competition in the common market is not distorted.

The European Court of Justice has held that the competition rules should be construed in the light of the aims and intentions expressed in these provisions.

The first aim is to preserve and create unrestricted competition between businesses as a stimulant to economic activities in the Community. The Treaty recognises, and there is a presumption in favour of, a 'free market' economic policy.[40]

The second intention is that the economic benefits of the market should be available to all, and that the market should truly be regarded as a 'common' market, or to adopt more recent terminology, a 'single' market. The second intention is that competition policy should be used as a method of prohibiting agreements which create obstacles to trade between Member States. The aim of provisions such as arts 30 and 59 of the EEC Treaty was to abolish government restrictions on the movement of goods and services across Community borders. The competition rules strike down agreements which attempt to divide markets or re-erect such barriers to trade.

---

40. As the Commission stated in its First Report on Competition Policy: 'An active competition policy pursued in accordance with the provisions of the Treaties establishing the Communities makes it easier for the supply and demand structure continuously to adjust to technological development. Through the interplay of decentralised decision-making machinery, competition enables enterprises continuously to improve their efficiency, which is the *sine qua non* for a steady improvement in living standards and employment prospects within the countries of the Community.'

12.3.1 EC Treaty competition rules

Articles 85 to 94 of the EEC Treaty are the principal Treaty provisions which contain the competition rules. The broad scheme of these provisions is as follows:

Article 85 prohibits all agreements and restrictive practices, decisions by associations of undertakings and concerted practices which may affect trade and which have as their object or effect the prevention, restriction or distortion of competition within the Community.

Article 86 prohibits all abuses of 'dominant' or 'monopoly' power in the Community.

Articles 87 to 89 provide the basis for the EC Council of Ministers, acting by qualified majority and after consulting the European Parliament, to adopt implementing Regulations and Directives. This machinery has been used to grant the Commission its powers of monitoring and enforcement.

Articles 88 and 89 provide for transitional rules. These presently apply in relation to air and sea transport.

Article 91 provides the basis (along with art. 113) for the rules which prohibit the 'dumping' of goods from outside the Community on to the Community market. Dumping essentially consists of an anticompetitive practice by which goods are sold in the Community at less than the price they are sold in a non-EC market.

Articles 92 to 94 provide the Commission with supervisory responsibilities and powers in relation to government grants and aids to industry throughout the Community. These are the so-called 'State aid' rules. The Commission can only allow aids to be permitted where certain economic and social objectives are fulfilled. One intention is to prevent governments providing incentives to inefficient national champions or industries.

12.3.2 Article 85(1)

Article 85 deals with collusion or cooperative behaviour between independent businesses. The scheme of the article is to prohibit all such arrangements or practices and provide for an exemption for particular types of beneficial arrangements (art. 85(3)). In order to take advantage of the exemption, the economic benefits must outweigh the anticompetitive effects.

Infringement of art. 85(1) will arise where the following are fulfilled:

(a) some form of cooperation occurs between undertakings, being either an agreement, decision or concerted practice; and

(b) that cooperation has as its object or effect the restriction of competition within the Common Market; and

(c) that cooperation has some effect on trade between Member States; and

(d) that cooperation is not '*de minimis*'.

Infringement of art. 85 has the consequence that the restrictive provisions are void and the Commission is entitled to impose fines of up to 10 per cent of the combined group worldwide turnovers of the businesses concerned.

However, as indicated above, exemptions are available from art. 85(1). These exemptions are only available on limited grounds and may be granted to an individual agreement following a notification or where the agreement corresponds to an exemption for a particular category of agreements (known as a 'block exemption') (see 12.3.2.13).

12.3.2.1   Cooperation between undertakings   'Undertakings' means all legal or natural persons carrying on economic or commercial activities.[41] The definition of 'undertakings' is important in considering agreements between members of the same economic group, e.g., between parent and subsidiary or between two companies having the same parent. Provided such arrangements can be regarded as the allocation of internal functions within one and the same unit, they will not be regarded as infringing art. 85(1). Whether or not one company is to be regarded as part of a single 'undertaking' depends on whether these companies are economically independent. The factors to take into account will be the level of shareholding, and the extent to which the business plans and policies of the subsidiary are controlled by the parent and whether the subsidiary's decision-making responsibilities are truly independent.

An 'agreement' will usually be easy to identify. It will include a contract or other form of written arrangement such as 'heads of agreement' or memoranda of understanding. There is no requirement that the agreement should be legally binding. Oral and written arrangements and gentlemen's agreements may amount to an agreement within the meaning of art. 85(1). Where an agreement has been ended but the parties to that agreement continue to abide by its terms, it can be viewed as a concerted practice. Evidence of a concerted practice may be found by the Commission from a number of sources. Parallel behaviour may not, by itself, amount to a concerted practice, but where such parallel behaviour occurs in circumstances where the perpetrators meet together, follow each other's prices and there is limited circumstantial evidence of collusion, the Commission has found a concerted practice.[42] The European Court of Justice has defined a concerted practice as:

A form of coordination between undertakings which, without having reached the stage when an agreement properly so-called has been concluded, knowingly substitutes practical cooperation between them for the risks of competition.

In practice, a company must be extremely careful to ensure that direct or indirect contact with competitors does not lead to any limitation of competition.

A decision of an association of undertakings would typically include trade association resolutions and recommendations. Such activities, if they fulfil the other criteria of art. 85(1), will be regarded either as an agreement (in consequence of the general internal regulations or constitution of the trade

41. *Polypropylene*, OJ No. L230, 18 August 1986, p. 1.
42. *Imperial Chemical Industries Ltd* v *Commission* (case 48/69) [1972] ECR 619.

association) or as a concerted practice between the members of the association. The Commission, in an appropriate case, may find in addition to the members that the association itself has committed an infringement of the rules. As with agreements, there is no requirement that a decision should be legally binding.

12.3.2.2 Object or effect There is, strictly, no need for an agreement to have an anticompetitive effect to infringe art. 85(1), it need only have that 'object'.[43] Typically, the Commission could regard an 'exclusivity' clause providing a dealer or licensee with an exclusive territory and preventing the supplier from appointing another dealer or licensee as having the 'object' of restricting competition contrary to art. 85(1). However, an exemption may be available under art. 85(3) for such an exclusivity clause.

To establish whether an agreement has an anticompetitive effect a market analysis is required. It is necessary to take into account the nature and quality of the products covered by the agreement, the agreement in question as part of a series of agreements, the severity of the clauses intended to protect a supplier or distributor, the opportunities available for other commercial operators to supply the same products etc. Market research and analysis would be necessary in justifying an agreement before the Commission for exemption under art. 85(3).

12.3.2.3 Effect on trade The requirement for an 'effect on trade between Member States' provides a limited jurisdictional test. The intention of this part of art. 85 was to define the boundary between Community and national law. However, in practice the Commission has been unwilling to deny itself jurisdiction. The goal of market integration, which is the essential aim of the EEC Treaty, can be prevented even where an agreement is confined to one Member State. It is sufficient that an agreement is capable of having an effect on trade between Member States. The basic test is that an agreement must foreseeably affect the pattern of trade between Member States.

12.3.2.4 De minimis The effect of an agreement on both inter-State trade and on competition within the Common Market must be appreciable. As has been described above, restrictions on competition must be judged in relation to the market in question, e.g., restrictive clauses in a software licence would need to be looked at in the context of the software market as a whole.[44] The Commission has clarified this issue by an advisory notice.[45] An agreement will not normally be regarded as appreciable and hence will not infringe art. 85(1) if it is between undertakings belonging to groups which:

(a)   have a combined turnover which does not exceed 200 million ECUs; and

---

43. *Société Technique Minière* v *Maschinenbau Ulm* (case 56/65) [1966] ECR 235. See also *Etablissements Consten SA* v *Commission* (cases 56 and 58/64) [1966] ECR 299.
44. *Völk* v *Établissements Vervaecke Sprl* (case 5/69) [1969] ECR 295.
45. OJ No. C 231, 1986, p. 2.

(b)   together enjoy not more than 5 per cent of the total market for the relevant goods or services in the area of the Common Market affected by the agreement.

Members of large corporate groups are excluded but small firms may not be able to rely on the notice since it does not apply where competition in the market in question is restricted by the cumulative effects of 'parallel networks of similar agreements established by several manufacturers or dealers'. This may occur where the market in question is characterised by parallel networks of similar distribution or franchise agreements. It may thus be difficult for the computer industry to rely on the Commission's notice.

12.3.2.5   Typical agreements caught by article 85(1)   Article 85(1) lists examples of types of agreement which it prohibits. These are agreements which:

(a)   '. . . directly or indirectly fix purchase or selling prices or any other trading conditions'. This includes price-fixing agreements between competitors about the prices at which goods or services are to be supplied to customers. Direct influences on pricing policies are also prohibited. Information exchanges between competitors which disclose prices, discounts or other business secrets, will be viewed as reducing the normal risks of competition and creating cooperation in practice.

(b)   '. . . limit or control production, markets, technical development or investment', e.g., agreements between competitors about which of them is to supply particular customers or territories. Price-fixing agreements are often supported by quotas so that each party can maintain its share of demand. Such agreements are likely to be prohibited.

(c)   '. . . share markets or sources of supply'. Market-sharing has been referred to above. Joint purchasing agreements by which competitors agree to combine their buying power are, equally, prohibited. Collective aggregate discounts are also likely to be condemned.

Export bans, i.e., clauses in agreements that prevent parties from exporting goods from one Member State to another are also regarded as a serious violation of art. 85. Care should be taken in computer agreements that clauses intended to ensure compliance with national security law obligations, e.g. to prevent the sale of high-tech products to the former Eastern bloc countries, do not go further than is necessary, and restrict resale within the Community.

In addition, although the Commission does not necessarily object to all of them, agreements for the creation of joint ventures, long-term purchase, supply or distribution agreements, subcontracting agreements, agency agreements, industrial property licences and agreements for joint purchase and joint sale agreements may all infringe art. 85(1).

12.3.2.6   Common clauses   A number of clauses may be regarded as having the object or effect of restricting competition contrary to art. 85(1):

Exclusivity. An exclusivity obligation would usually restrict the seller or licensor from competing with the reseller or licensee. It may also restrict the seller or licensor from selling to firms other than the reseller or licensee, either within or outside a particular territory. A licensee or reseller may be restricted from competing with other licensees or resellers in other territories.

Exclusivity obligations in contracts for the resale of goods (as opposed to agreements which involve the licensing and sublicensing of intellectual property rights) may benefit from the exclusive distribution or exclusive purchasing block exemptions. Where the licensee of intellectual property rights is concerned, there are at present two block exemptions which may exempt the exclusivity clauses:

(a)   A block exemption is available for patent licensing agreements which contain exclusivity obligations.

(b)   Exclusive agreements for the transfer of technology which are substantially comprised as know-how will benefit from the know-how licence block exemption. Know-how which is combined with other forms of intellectual property is covered by the know-how licence block exemption and, to an extent, certain computer software licences may benefit from this block exemption, provided the software is 'of assistance in achieving the object of the know-how licence'.

Non-compete. Non-compete provisions may well infringe art. 85(1). However, it may be economically efficient for a reseller to be forced to concentrate his sales on the goods in question. In consequence, non-compete provisions are exempted under the exclusive distribution, purchasing, patent and know-how block exemptions.

No-challenge clauses. Clauses where the licensee is prohibited from challenging the validity of the licensed intellectual property right.

Post-term use provisions. Provisions where the duration of the licensing agreement is automatically prolonged beyond the expiry of intellectual property rights existing at the time the agreement was entered into.

Royalty calculation clauses. Agreements under which the licensee is charged royalties on products which are not entirely or partially produced by means of the intellectual-property-based process in question (specifically in relation to patents and know-how) or where the licensee is charged royalties on the use of know-how or confidential information which has entered into the public domain otherwise than by the fault of the licensee.

Quantity restrictions. Where the quantity of licensed products one party may manufacture or sell is restricted or where other quantitative restrictions on the exploitation of the intellectual property rights in question are imposed.

Price and discount restrictions.

Customer restrictions. Where one party is restricted as to the type or class of customer he may serve.

Grant-back arrangements. Where the licensee is obliged to assign or grant back all the improvements to intellectual property rights which are created independently from the licensed intellectual property rights and are not part of the licensed intellectual property rights.

Tying restrictions. Where the licensee is required to accept goods or services which he does not want as a condition of entering into an intellectual property right licence, e.g., a requirement to obtain maintenance or support for licensed software. However, such a restriction may be acceptable when it can be shown that it is necessary for the technically satisfactory exploitation of the product concerned.

Export restraints. Where one or other of the parties is required to refuse (without objective reason) to meet demand from users or resellers in other Member States of the Community.

12.3.2.7 Acceptable cooperation The Commission issued in 1968 a 'notice on cooperation agreements' which sets out categories of agreement it considered did not fall within art. 85(1). This notice may provide useful guidance but its terms are narrowly construed by the Commission. There are eight categories of acceptable cooperative activity:

Information exchanges, e.g., exchanges of market research, comparative studies of enterprises or industries and the preparation of statistics and calculation models, provided that this information does not lead to coordination of market behaviour. The line may be difficult to draw and extreme caution should be exercised where an information exchange is proposed.

Financial cooperation, e.g., accountancy cooperation, the provision of credit guarantees, debt collection and consultancy facilities on business and tax matters.

Research and development. See also block exemption Regulation 418/85[46] at 12.3.3.5.

Sharing of production, storage and transport facilities.

Tendering on cooperation in the execution of orders, where either the parties are not in competition with each other or, where they are competitors, they would not be able individually to execute a given order.

Joint selling or joint provision of after-sales services, but only where the partners are not actual or potential competitors.

Joint advertising, provided that there is no restriction on individual advertising.

Common quality symbols or labels, where the label is available to all competitors on the same conditions.

12.3.2.8 Agreements outside the scope of article 85(1) Apart from the Commission's notice on cooperation agreements, it has issued notices on agency[47] and subcontracting.[48] In its agency notice the Commission stated that agreements between principal and agent do not infringe art. 85(1). In several cases since, both the Commission and Court have made it clear that it is difficult to rely on this exception. In order to come within the exception the agent must take instructions in detail from the principal and not be a firm capable of acting

---

46. OJ No. L 53, 1985, L p. 5.
47. 24 December 1962.
48. OJ No. C 1, 3 January 1979, p. 2.

in its own name and on its own behalf. The test is difficult to apply and will not apply to dealers which are independent firms. Subcontracting arrangements are those arrangements by which the contractor sets out in detail the products he wishes a subcontractor to manufacture. The subcontracting notice may be valuable in the context of software development agreements since it may entitle firms commissioning software to obtain exclusive rights over the software once it has been developed.

12.3.2.9   Selective distribution   Selective distribution is widely used in the computer industry for the distribution of both hardware and software. A system of selective distribution, i.e., the appointment of distributors which are 'selected' on objective criteria relating to the quality of the distributor, will be compatible with art. 85(1) provided that:

(a)   The products concerned are sophisticated, e.g., computer products which require a high level of expertise or back-up services.

(b)   The qualitative criteria for the appointment of distributors relate to the technical capability to supply the goods or services in question and the suitability of their premises.

(c)   The qualitative criteria must be applied in a nondiscriminatory way – any qualified reseller who wishes to join the system must be admitted.[49]

(d)   No 'quantitative' restrictions may be included, i.e., no restrictions may be included on the number of resellers admitted to the system and restrictions on the geographic location of dealers cannot be included. If such restrictions are included, the system may be suitable for individual exemption under art. 85(3) or the franchise block exemption should be considered.

Selective distribution systems are likely to create higher prices to the consumer and to restrict, to an extent, the outlets for a particular product. An obligation can be imposed on authorised resellers to sell only to other authorised resellers or end-users and the supplier may refuse to admit insufficiently-qualified dealers to the network.[50]

In the context of distribution of computers, the Commission accepted that no infringement of art. 85(1) occurred for IBM's selective distribution system for personal computers (PCs).[51] The following were important to the Commission's decision:

(a)   IBM PCs were sophisticated products and customers were unsophisticated (although this may change over time).

(b)   The capabilities and price of the IBM PC meant that it was likely to be sold to business and professional users who required information on:
    (i)   the type of services a computer may offer;

---

49. *AEG* v *Commission* (case 107/82) [1983] ECR 3151. A fine of 1 million ECUs was imposed where a qualified reseller was refused admission.
50. *Metro* v *Commission (No. 1)* [1970] ECR 1875.
51. OJ No. L 118, 1984, p. 24.

(ii)   how computers work and the capabilities of the software; and

(iii)   the costs, benefits, advantages and disadvantages of alternative systems.

The Commission accepted certain criteria for the appointment of dealers:

(a)   Dealers needed to have appropriate space for demonstration purposes and were required to keep at least one PC available for demonstration purposes.

(b)   Dealers were required to show ability to provide customers with technical support and training.

(c)   Dealers had to employ sales staff experienced in the use of PCs or willing to be trained (one week) in IBM's PCs.

(d)   Dealers were to provide service facilities and experienced staff trained in servicing IBM's PCs.

(e)   Dealers had to show an ability to run a PC-sales business.

12.3.2.10   Intellectual property   It is possible to argue that certain contractual restrictions, relating to the 'essential subject-matter of intellectual property rights' do not restrict competition. This approach identifies the essence of an intellectual property right and then regards any clause which relates to that right as being outside the scope of art. 85(1). For example, copyright protection entitles the copyright owner to restrict the reproduction of the copyright work. An agreement between a supplier and a distributor which involves a copyright licence, such as a software licence, would usually restrict the distributor from copying, except for back-up purposes, and may also impose restrictions on end-users from making copies other than back-up copies. Since the copyright owner is legitimately entitled to impose such a requirement as it relates to copyright in the software being licensed, those 'restrictions' which relate to 'copying' cannot be regarded as infringements of art. 85(1). Obligations are often imposed in software licences preventing a licensee from modifying the software, reverse engineering the object code, or sublicensing or assigning without the permission of the licensor. Such obligations could in the past be regarded as not infringing art. 85(1) since they could be viewed as relating to the essential subject-matter of the copyright which was being licensed.

Following the Commission's directive (91/250/EEC) on scope of copyright protection given to software, the 'essential subject-matter' of the software has been defined. Restrictions on modification or reverse engineering which go beyond the Directive may now be regarded as restrictions of competition.

Any restrictions which relate to the exercise of the copyright which is being licensed may be struck down if they appreciably restrict competition and trade between Member States and hence infringe art. 85(1).

12.3.2.11   Nungesser   In a number of cases, the European Court of Justice has held that contractual provisions giving a degree of protection against competition do not fall within art. 85(1) if they are necessary to establish competition in the first place. This is a 'but for' test; but for a restrictive clause, no competition would exist since no agreement would be entered into.[52] In its judgment in *L. C. Nungesser KG* v *Commission* (case 258/78) [1982] ECR 2015, the European Court of Justice considered an exclusive licensing agreement which had appointed a licensor for a particular territory but prevented the licensor from competing with the licensee or granting further licences in the territory in question. The European Court of Justice held that no restriction within art. 85(1) arose and stated that its reasoning could apply to agreements involving intellectual property rights but only where the subject-matter of the contract involved the introduction of something 'new' into the territory in which it was being marketed, and in the circumstances the products in question involved significant research and development. Without the restrictions the licensor would not have entered into the agreement – the restrictions were vital to secure the risk of launching the new product.

It is possible to develop this argument by analogy and regard source code to be similar, in economic terms, to basic maize seed which was at issue in *L. C. Nungesser KG* v *Commission*, since they both involve considerable research and development. On this basis a licensor could restrict the reseller from sublicensing source code.[53]

12.3.2.12 *Coditel* In its judgments concerning *Coditel*,[54] the European Court of Justice considered that exclusivity and prohibition on resale outside an exclusive territory did not infringe art. 85(1). The particular characteristics of the market and the intellectual property right concerned were taken into account. It is possible to regard this case as a case concerned with performance rights which are subject to copyright protection in many Member States. Without relying on his performance right the licensor would be unable to predict actual or probable royalty levels for films which have been licensed.

This characteristic of films, that they can be shown a number of different times to different sizes of audience, influenced the European Court of Justice to hold that in the circumstances:[55]

The right of the copyright owner . . . to require fees for any showing of a film is part of the essential function of the copyright in this type of literary or artistic work.

Many types of information technology products may benefit from this approach.

Protection may be available for different parts of a computer system. A restriction may be imposed on the distribution of computer software as part of the right to prevent copying. In addition, provided the performance-right type

---

52. *Société Technique Miniére* v *Maschinenbau Ulm* (case 56/65) [1966] ECR 235 (otherwise known as the indispensable inducement rationale).
53. See also *SPRL Louis Erauw-Jacquery* v *SC La Hesbignonne* (case 27/87) [1988] 4 CMLR 576.
54. *Coditel SA* v *Ciné Vog Films (No. 1)* (case 62/79) [1980] ECR 881, *Coditel SA* v *Ciné Vog Films (No. 2)* (case 262/81) [1982] ECR 3381.
55. See also cases concerning copyright protection such as *Basset* v *Sacem* (case 402/85) [1987] ECR 1747 and *Ministère Public* v *Tournier* (case 395/87) [1991] 4 CMLR 248.

of copyright protection is available (and this is usually only the case where the work is shown or broadcast to the public), performance of that software may be regarded in a similar way to the performance of a film. In such cases, restrictions on licensees which limit the place of performance (site restrictions), the number of performances (e.g., limitation on the use of software to a particular computer system) and the performance of that software via remote terminals or via a number of remote terminals may be regarded as falling outside art. 85(1).

The *Coditel* and *Nungesser* cases may be regarded as examples of a 'rule of reason' approach which is being applied in the computer/communications industry. Such an approach may find wider application in future cases. The Court of Justice has adopted this approach in other industries in a number of cases. (As a recent example, see *Stergios Delimitis* v *Henninger Brau* (case 234/89), judgment 28 February 1991.)

12.3.3   Exemption: Article 85(3)

Article 85(3) provides for exemptions from art. 85(1). As mentioned above, an exemption may be available for an individual agreement on notification or for an agreement satisfying the terms of a block exemption Regulation. Article 85(3) provides that two positive and two negative conditions must be satisfied. An exemption will be available if:

(a)   the agreement contributes to improving the production or distribution of goods or to promoting technical or economic progress; and

(b)   consumers are allowed a fair share of the resulting benefit; and

(c)   only those restrictions in the agreement which are 'indispensable' to the attainment of the objectives of the agreement are imposed on the undertakings concerned; and

(d)   the undertakings concerned are not afforded the possibility of eliminating competition in respect of a substantial part of the products in question.

Exemptions are available either on an individual basis or may be published in the form of Regulations by the Commission exempting categories of agreements which fall within the terms of the regulation. Such exemptions are known as 'block exemptions'. The following points should be noted about block exemptions:

(a)   Unless expressly permitted, any restriction contained in an agreement which falls outside the terms of the block exemptions may mean that the entire agreement falls outside the block exemption.

(b)   The Commission specifies permitted and non-permitted clauses – the block exemption may not be sufficiently flexible for many types of commercial agreements.

The most important block exemptions are briefly described below.

12.3.3.1 Exclusive distribution[56] Agreements for the resale of goods under which a supplier agrees with the distributor to supply goods only to that distributor may benefit from this block exemption. Software licensing agreements will probably not be regarded as relating to goods. Shrink-wrap software will thus probably not be covered. However, where software is part of a hardware product and a low-value part, the product should benefit from the block exemption. This block exemption would probably not apply to 'value-added reseller agreements' which would probably not be regarded as agreements for resale. The block exemption will probably also be inapplicable to OEM agreements (i.e., where a supplier's products are sold only under the distributor's trademarks).[57] Under the block exemption, in addition to exclusivity obligations, the supplier, at his option, may agree not to supply contract goods to users in the contract territory. Often the computer equipment supplier will want to retain the ability to supply large users direct. A distributor may be required to refrain 'from seeking customers, from establishing any branch and from retaining any distribution depot' for the contract goods outside the contract territory. The block exemption will not apply if certain blacklisted clauses are included.

12.3.3.2 Exclusive purchasing agreements[58] Where goods are supplied to a reseller which undertakes to obtain its requirements only from one supplier, the agreement may benefit from the exclusive purchasing block exemption. By contrast with exclusive distribution, the exclusive purchasing block exemption does not allow any restriction on the supplier to refrain from delivering the products concerned to other resellers in the same territory. The only obligation which may be imposed on a supplier without loss of the exemption is the obligation not to compete directly with the reseller in his principal sales area: a supplier cannot be prevented from appointing other resellers in that area. The reseller may be required not to manufacture or sell goods competing with the contract goods and he may accept marketing obligations similar to those provided under the exclusive distribution block exemption.

12.3.3.3 Franchising[59] This block exemption is only available for obligations relating to the use of a common name or shop sign, the communication of know-how by the franchisor to the franchisee and the continuing provision of commercial or technical assistance during the life of the agreement. The know-how in question must be 'secret, substantial and identified'. The franchisor may grant an exclusive territory and agree not to grant a franchise or himself exploit the franchise in that territory. The franchisor may also agree not to supply goods to third parties. The franchisee may be required to limit the exploitation of his franchise only to the contract premises and not to seek customers outside his territory, and to buy the franchisor's goods only from

---

56. Regulation 1983/83 OJ No. L 171, 1983, p. 1.
57. *ICL/Fujitsu* OJ No. C 120, 21 August 1986, p. 5.
58. Regulation 1984/83, OJ No. L 173, 1983, p. 5.
59. Regulation 407/88, OJ No. L 359, 1988, p. 46.

nominated sources and not to buy competing goods. Like the exclusive distribution and purchasing block exemptions, this block exemption contains blacklists of prohibited clauses.[60]

12.3.3.4 Specialisation agreements[61]   A block exemption is granted to agreements under which the parties accept 'reciprocal obligations':

(a)   to specialise in the manufacture of one product and to leave to the other party the manufacture of another product; or
(b)   to manufacture certain products or to have them manufactured only jointly.

A non-reciprocal obligation to cease production is not within the Regulation. Care needs to be taken to decide whether an agreement is a specialisation agreement and not a market-sharing agreement. This block exemption is subject to a threshold – the undertaking concerned must not represent more than 20 per cent of the market for such products in a substantial part of the Common Market and there is also a turnover threshold.

12.3.3.5 Research and development agreements[62]   Three types of agreement may be exempted under the research and development (R & D) block exemption:

(a)   Joint R & D products or processes and joint exploitation of the results.
(b)   Joint exploitation of the results of R & D jointly carried out under a prior agreement or plan between the parties.
(c)   Joint R & D without subsequent exploitation.

Exploitation includes manufacture, and licensing of intellectual property rights, but not distribution or selling.

12.3.3.6 Patent licensing[63]   Exclusive and other patent licences are exempted under this block exemption. The licence may include know-how where it permits a better exploitation of the licensed patent. The licensor may agree not to license anyone else in the licensee's territory and not to exploit the licensed technology there himself. The licensee may also be restricted from exploiting the licensed invention in the territory of the licensor. Competition between licensees may also be restricted to a limited degree. Provisions that restrict competition and are not specifically exempted may benefit from the 'opposition procedure'.

---

60. By contrast to the Commission's approach, the European Court of Justice indicated in *Pronuptia de Paris GmbH* v *Pronuptia de Paris Irmgard Schillgallis* (case 161/84) [1986] ECR 353 that many clauses in a franchise agreement fell outside the scope of art. 85(1) in any event.
61. Regulation 417/85, OJ No. L 53, 1985, p. 1.
62. Regulation 418/85, OJ No. L 53, 1985, p. 5.
63. Regulation 2349/84, OJ No. L 219, 1984, p. 15.

12.3.3.7   Know-how licensing agreements[64]   Provided know-how is substantial and secret, it may benefit from the know-how licensing block exemption for exclusive know-how licences. Combined know-how and trade-mark or other intellectual-property-type licences may be governed by the Regulation, but only where restrictions relating to the other intellectual property are ancillary to the know-how. The Regulation is very similar to the patent licence block exemption but the periods for territorial protection are different. A period of protection for patent licensing is for five years from the first time the contract products were first put into the market within the EC – the know-how licence block exemption applies for 10 years from the first licence in the territory. In other respects the know-how licence block exemption is similar to the patent licence block exemption.

12.3.3.8   Intellectual property licensing generally   As indicated above at 12.3.2.6, a number of common clauses in intellectual property licences are likely to infringe art. 85(1). These clauses do not benefit from exemptions in relation to either patent or know-how licensing and they are likely to be prohibited in the context of copyright (software) and trade-mark licensing. The existing block exemption regulations may provide arguments for the individual exemption of information technology agreements containing software. However, such arguments will only be appropriate when applying for individual exemption in the context of an agreement with similar economic benefits to a patent or a know-how licence.

12.3.4   Article 86
Article 86 of the EEC Treaty is concerned with unilateral activity by one party. It provides that:

> Any abuse by one or more undertakings of a dominant position within the common market or in a substantial part of it shall be prohibited as incompatible with the common market insofar as it may affect trade between Member States.

A dominant position is defined in qualitative terms:[65]

> A position of economic strength enjoyed by an undertaking which enables it to hinder the maintenance of effective competition in the relevant market by allowing it to behave to an appreciable extent independently of its competitors and customers and ultimately of consumers.

A number of factors are to be taken into account in order to establish whether a particular undertaking is in a dominant position:

(a)   the market share of the undertaking and of its competitors;

---

64. Regulation 556/89, OJ No. L 61, 1989, p. 1.
65. *Michelin* v *Commission* (case 322/81) [1983] ECR 3461.

(b) the undertaking's supply and/or purchasing power;
(c) technical knowledge and expertise of the undertaking;
(d) availability of raw materials and supplies;
(e) the scale of the undertaking's activities – its capital and resources;
(f) exclusionary effect of any sales or distribution networks;
(g) intellectual property right protection;
(h) customer dependence;
(i) the exclusionary effect of government licences (such as telecommunications licences limiting the number of competitors in a particular market).

Dominance is assessed in relation to a relevant market which comprises the products which may be regarded as substitutable by users (demand substitutability) and in relation to the ability of suppliers or manufacturers to switch from one product to another (supply substitutability). A product market can only exist in relation to a particular geographic area where the conditions for competition are sufficiently similar.

As a practical guide, a dominant position is not normally found unless the market share of the business concerned is above 35 per cent. However, in relation to the computer industry, the relevant market may be narrowly defined, or even defined in terms of a single computer supplier's products, services or software. The more narrowly defined the market, the higher a particular supplier's market share. Also, a supplier may find himself dominant in the spare parts or maintenance services for its own products.

12.3.4.1 Types of abuse   A number of types of abusive conduct are listed in art. 86: directly or indirectly imposing unfair purchase or selling prices or other unfair trading conditions, limiting production, markets or technical development, discrimination by applying dissimilar conditions to equivalent transactions, or similar conditions to dissimilar transactions, tying practices by which unrelated products are only supplied together.

Practical examples of abuses in the computer industry would include:

(a) Predatory pricing, where a computer manufacturer lowers its price below its average variable cost of production, or sets its prices between average variable and average total cost, with an intent to eliminate a competitor.

(b) Monopoly pricing, where a company prices its products with no relation to costs or the likely reaction of competitors and obtains 'excessive' profits.

(c) Discriminatory prices – charging different prices to different customers without any cost justification for the difference, e.g. a pricing structure under which ex-factory sale prices of products vary depending on the Member State to which they are ultimately sold.

(d) Unfair, anticompetitive or discriminatory terms or conditions such as arrangements whereby a purchaser of a product (hardware) is obliged to purchase from the dominant supplier unrelated products (other add-on hardware, or software, or maintenance services, or a complete range of other products).

(e)   Restrictions on resale.

(f)   Refusal to deal, e.g., refusal by a dominant supplier to continue to deal with a long-standing customer for no objective reason.

12.3.4.2 British Telecommunications   The European Court of Justice had occasion to consider the position of British Telecommunications at the time when it was a statutory corporation. A complaint was lodged with the European Commission by Telespeed,[66] which wished to take advantage of lower tariffs in the UK than in other parts of Europe. Before the formation of BT, the Post Office had incorporated in its standard terms of service certain restrictions on re-forwarding messages in this way. The Commission held that BT held a statutory monopoly at the time, and was therefore in a dominant position. In addition, the refusal to permit message re-forwarding services was considered to be an abuse.[67]

12.3.4.3 IBM   Although it was never finally decided, the Commission has alleged that IBM was in a dominant position under art. 86. The allegation related to the market for IBM's System/370 central processing units and operating system. The allegation was made that the dominant position in relation to those two products allowed IBM to control the market for the supply of compatible products. The allegations of abuse involved:

(a)   Failure to supply other manufacturers with interface information.

(b)   Not offering System/370 central processing units without a capacity of main memory included in the price (memory tying or memory bundling).

(c)   Not offering System/370 central processing units without basic software included in the price (software tying or software bundling).

(d)   Discriminating between different users of IBM software, i.e., refusing to supply certain software installation services to users of non-IBM central processing units.

The Commission eventually accepted IBM's undertakings in relation to these issues, and in particular in relation to interface information and memory bundling.

The IBM proceedings[68] are an illustration of the Commission's general approach to defining markets in very narrow terms. From this approach, it is possible that:

(a)   a relevant market may be very narrowly defined in terms of a manufacturer's own products; and

(b)   a hardware manufacturer may find itself in a dominant position over the supply of interrelated software, e.g., interface information.

---

66. *Italy v Commission* (case 41/83) [1985] ECR 873.
67. OJ No. L 360, 21 December 1982, p. 36.
68. *International Business Machines Corporation v Commission* (case 60/81) [1981] 3 CMLR 635, [1984] 3 CMLR 147.

Particular care will need to be taken in marketing and pricing policies which might be regarded as abusive.[69]

12.3.4.4   Magill   The motive behind the particular method chosen to enforce intellectual property rights is important, as can be seen from the Commission's decision in *Magill TV Guide/ITP, BBC and RTE*.[70] Here the defendant television companies used copyright in their programme listings to prevent Magill from publishing a weekly programme guide for Ireland. Copyright in these listings had already been established, and the defendants were granted an injunction against Magill. The Commission also found a history of taking similar action against other intending publishers of weekly guides.

The Commission held that the companies were in a dominant position with regard to their programme listings (a very narrow market definition), and that by enforcing their copyright in this manner they were abusing that position. The defendants argued that their current policies of licensing only same-day publication was necessary to ensure that all their programmes were adequately listed, but the Commission rejected this submission, noting that the same effect could be produced by conditions in any licences to publish weekly listings, and that in practice none of the defendants were willing to grant such licences.

> [The] Commission concludes that the current policies and practices of ITP, BBC and RTE in relation to their respective advance weekly listings are *intended* to protect and have the effect of protecting the position of their individual TV guides, which do not compete with one another or with any other guides. . . . By limiting the scope of their licensing policies so as to prevent the production and sale of comprehensive TV guides . . . they restrict competition to the prejudice of consumers.

The case has been affirmed by the Court of First Instance of the EC on substantially the same grounds,[71] and that judgment has reiterated the principle that EC competition law prevails over the national rights to exploit intellectual property:[72]

> . . . while it is plain that the exercise of the exclusive right to reproduce a protected work is not in itself an abuse, that does not apply when, in the light of the details of each individual case, it is apparent that such right is exercised in such ways and circumstances as in fact *to pursue an aim manifestly contrary to the objectives of article 86*. In that event the copyright is no longer exercised in a manner which corresponds to its essential function, within the meaning of article 36 of the Treaty, *which is to protect the moral rights in the work and*

---

69. A legitimate business objective such as the leveraging of software sales via a strong presence in hardware may amount to an abuse. Also, arbitrary refusals to license intellectual property rights may constitute an abuse (*Volvo AB* v *Erik Veng (UK) Ltd* [1989] 4 CMLR 122).
70. OJ No. L 78, 21 March 1989, p. 43.
71. *Independent Television Publications Ltd* v *Commission* (case T-76/89) [1991] 4 CMLR 745.
72. [1991] 4 CMLR 745, at pp. 767–8 (emphasis added).

ensure a reward for the creative effort, while respecting the aims of, in particular, article 86. In that case, the primacy of Community law, particularly as regards principles as fundamental as those of the free movement of goods and freedom of competition, prevails over any use of national intellectual property law in a manner contrary to those principles.

This case is an example of the relationship between competition law and copyright. If a software house were to claim copyright in data formats and exercise it to retain a *de facto* monopoly position, art. 86 would provide competitors with a possible line of defence. The case is presently on appeal to the European Court of Justice. Although the basic principles are well-established and are unlikely to be overturned, the Commission's application of the law is likely to be clarified by the European Court of Justice.

12.3.4.5 Recent Developments A series of recent cases on the application of art. 86 confirm an underlying trend; the Commission will narrowly define markets to create more open markets and foster the increase of competition. In *Porto di Genova* (case C-179/90 unreported), a dominant position was found to exist over harbour operations in the port of Genoa. Failure to provide adequate unloading services was then characterised as an abuse of a dominant position. (See also *Tetra Pak*; OJ 1992 L72/1 for a recent example of narrow market definition.) A narrow market definition will probably be adopted where the Commission perceives that a business holds an essential resource which is necessary for the development of new entrant competition. This is known as the concept of an 'essential facility'. The Commission took such an approach to market definition in its recent application for interim measures in the *B & I* case (Press Release IP(92)478; 11.6.92) and is understood to be taking a similar approach to slot allocation in the airline industry. The *Magill* case may also be an example of this approach. By defining markets in terms of essential facilities, the Commission could characterise interface information as the market, as it did in *IBM*, and require interconnection. Any arbitrary or discriminatory refusal to interconnect could otherwise be regarded as an abuse. This could lead to more open markets but is likely to cause considerable difficulties for the major computer and communication companies.

12.4 SANCTIONS AND REMEDIES

If an agreement infringes art. 85(1) or conduct is an abuse under art. 86, the agreement will be void and the Commission is entitled to impose fines of up to 10 per cent of the combined group worldwide turnovers of the companies concerned.

The scope of invalidity is a matter for national law. Under English law, the doctrine of severance would apply to cut out or 'blue-pencil' the restrictive provisions in the agreement. The court would then be required to decide whether the resulting agreement is one the parties should be held to perform or whether the restrictions are fundamental and strike the heart of the agreement. It is likely that clauses which are of considerable commercial importance, such as exclusivity, would, if found to infringe art. 85(1), be struck out and the resulting agreement may be rendered unenforceable. In a technology transfer, this risk of unenforceability is probably of more serious commercial concern than the risk of fines.[73]

There is limited precedent[74] to support an action for damages for breach of EC law. A third party which has lost business as a consequence of a restrictive agreement might wish to take such action.

Recently, the Commission has encouraged individuals affected by anti-competitive practices or abuses of dominant positions to take actions in national courts. However, an effective and perhaps cheaper remedy is to lodge a complaint with the Commission where infringement of the rules is suspected. The Commission has very wide search and seizure powers which may be used to establish the truth of the complaint.

Breaches of Member State obligations may entitle an individual to damages where that breach has resulted in loss. A Member State's failure to comply with art. 30 or art. 59 or even its failure properly to implement a Directive, may also form the basis for a damages action in a national court.[75]

---

73. See also *Irish Aerospace (Belgium)* v *Euro Control* (10 June 1991 unreported).
74. *Garden Cottage Foods Ltd* v *Milk Marketing Board* [1984] AC 1390.
75. *Francovich, Bonifaci* v *Italy* (cases C60/90 and C9/90), *The Times*, 20 November 1991.

Index